FRENCH

In the same series

FRENCH

Eugene Jackson and
Antonio Rubio, Ph.D.

Advisory editor
Jacqueline Janvier,
L. ès. L., Dip. d'Et. Sup. (Sorbonne)

MADE SIMPLE
B O O K S

Made Simple
An imprint of Butterworth–Heinemann Ltd
Linacre House, Jordan Hill, Oxford OX2 8DP

 PART OF REED INTERNATIONAL BOOKS

OXFORD   LONDON   BOSTON
MUNICH   NEW DELHI   SINGAPORE   SYDNEY
TOKYO   TORONTO   WELLINGTON

First published 1967
Reprinted 1967, 1969, 1970, 1973, 1974, 1975
Second edition 1977
Reprinted 1979, 1980, 1981, 1983, 1984, 1986, 1987, 1991, 1992

© Butterworth–Heinemann Ltd 1981

British Library Cataloguing in Publication Data
Jackson, Eugene
  French made simple.—2nd ed.
  (Made simple books)
  1. French language—Grammar—1950—
  I. Title   II. Rubio, Antonio
  III. Janvier, Jacqueline   IV. Series
  448.2′421   PC2112

ISBN 0 7506 0254 6

Printed in England by Clays Ltd, St Ives plc

Preface

French Made Simple is a pleasant, practical course designed especially for the student who wants to gain a working knowledge of the language in the shortest possible time. Bilingual texts and dialogues make it very easy for the reader to learn phrases and colloquial expressions, while also acquiring some information about France and French customs.

Although the book is ideal for self-study, it is equally recommended for use by teachers in evening institutes or in secondary schools. Students working for GCSE will also find the book invaluable as an introductory course.

The best way of acquiring a good pronunciation in any language is, of course, to hear it spoken by natives of the country; but this is not always possible, and the student should take every opportunity of listening to French films, television, radio broadcasts, tapes and records.

In *French Made Simple* the best form of pronunciation guide employed in present-day language teaching is used: the International Phonetic Alphabet. All the signs are fully explained in Chapter 2, and once they have been learned, the student will not only be able to master the accurate pronunciation of the French language; he will also be able to apply his knowledge to any other language he chooses to study.

JACQUELINE JANVIER

Contents

CHAPTER 6

CHAPTER 7

CHAPTER 8

CHAPTER 9

REVISION 2

CHAPTER 10

CHAPTER 11

NUMBERS, ALWAYS NUMBERS
Les nombres, toujours les nombres

Present tense of the verbs **vouloir** to wish, want, **pouvoir** to be able—Numbers 1 to 69—Arithmetical terms.

CHAPTER 12

THE MONETARY SYSTEM OF FRANCE
Le système monétaire de la France

Present tense of **faire** to make, to do; **croire** to believe, to think—Numbers 70 to 100—Table for converting sterling to **francs** and vice versa.

CHAPTER 13

PROBLEMS IN ARITHMETIC IN THE RESTAURANT, AT THE STATION, IN A SHOP
Les problèmes d'arithmétique, au restaurant, à la gare, dans une boutique

Weights and measures—Present tense of **savoir** to know (how); **connaître** to know, to be acquainted with—Possessive adjectives.

CHAPTER 14

WHAT TIME IS IT?
Quelle heure est-il?

Words of approval and praise—Words dealing with railway travel—Present tense of **partir** to leave, and **sortir** to go out—Expressions of time of day.

REVISION 3

REVISION OF CHAPTERS 10–14

Vocabulary revision—Vocabulary and Grammar Exercises—Dialogue: **Un touriste prend des renseignements sur la poterie française**—Reading Selections: **La famille Davis rend une petite visite à papa** . . . **Le percheron et l'automobile (Une fable moderne)**—Present Tense of **boire,** to drink.

CHAPTER 15

THE CINEMA
Le cinéma

Words dealing with films—Present tense **venir** to come—Direct object pronouns—Use of **y** (there).

CHAPTER 16

CHAPTER 17

CHAPTER 18

CHAPTER 19

REVISION 4

CHAPTER 20

CHAPTER 21

FRENCH MADE SIMPLE

LANGUAGE CASSETTE RECORDINGS
BASED ON THIS BOOK
FRENCH MADE SIMPLE

Two excellent cassette recordings have been produced, based on all the conversation and dialogue passages which appear at the beginning of each chapter in this book. They are highly recommended for all who want to hear everyday spoken French at its best.

These Made Simple recordings, by experienced French linguists, bring all the conversation passages to life, providing not only an enjoyable listening experience but an invaluable expert guide to help *you* speak French with self-confidence and conviction.

Whilst you listen you learn, naturally and in your own time, at your own pace—and remember you can replay the sections you want over and over again until you feel confident to progress to the next passage.

The French Made Simple cassettes (Reference WH/1 & WH/2)
cost £18 for the set of two, fully inclusive, in the UK.
Europe £20 per set of two inclusive of postage.
Overseas £25 per set of two inclusive of airmail postage.

Please send your order and remittance direct to:

SR World Languages,
PO Box 8,
Newent
Gloucestershire GL18 1PJ
England

CHAPITRE 1 (UN)—CHAPTER 1

MEET THE FRENCH LANGUAGE

1 *French is no Stranger*

In beginning your study of the French language you will be surprised to learn that you already know, or can make a good guess at, the meaning of thousands of French words. For there are some 4,000 words which are of the same spelling and meaning in French and English, and thousands more of the same meaning which differ only slightly in spelling. Of course the pronunciation of the French words differs greatly from that of the corresponding English words.

There are also many words borrowed directly from the French without any change in spelling and with little or no change at all in pronunciation.

Here are a few examples of words alike or very similar in French and English:

(*a*) Words spelt alike and having the same meaning but different in pronunciation:

vain	fruit	danger	nation
page	image	humble	nature
train	table	public	voyage
place	index	bureau	client

absent	station	excellent
avenue	question	important
action	original	patient
cousin	accident	intelligent

(*b*) Words of the same meaning, slightly different in spelling and different in pronunciation:

riche	oncle	balle	objet
rich	*uncle*	*ball*	*object*
salade	madame	touriste	sévère
salad	*madam*	*tourist*	*severe*
difficile	famille	qualité	liberté
difficult	*family*	*quality*	*liberty*
visiter	excuser	arriver	entrer
to visit	*to excuse*	*to arrive*	*to enter*
scène	hôtel	brun	bleu
scene	*hotel*	*brown*	*blue*
rivière	parfum	mètre	poste
river	*perfume*	*metre*	*post*
docteur	acteur	enveloppe	signe
doctor	*actor*	*envelope*	*sign*
désirer	commencer	dîner	inviter
to desire	*to commence*	*to dine*	*to invite*

1

(c) Words borrowed directly from the French with no changes in spelling and only minor changes in pronunciation. These words contain some good clues to French pronunciation:

café	garage	ennui	lingerie
route	chauffeur	encore	ensemble
rôle	liqueur	chemise	consommé
rouge	à propos	routine	à la carte
château	coquette	nouveau riche
bouquet	rendez-vous	laisser-faire
matinée	coup d'état	savoir-faire
entrée	sabotage	table d'hôte

There are some French words whose appearance is deceiving. Thus: **demander** means to *ask* or *ask for*, not to *demand*. You must be on the watch for such deceivers.

2 French and English Pronunciation Differ Greatly

The similarities between French and English in vocabulary will be of great help to you in learning French. However, French and English pronunciations are very different, so that you must learn not only to pronounce the French words correctly but also to understand them when you hear them. As in English, there are many silent letters, and some sounds, particularly the vowel sounds, are spelt in various ways. You will have little difficulty with the spelling if you practise writing as well as saying new words and exercises. The most important words appear many times in this book, which will also aid you greatly in remembering pronunciation, meaning and spelling.

In Chapter 2 the pronunciation of the French sounds and their spelling is explained in detail. The description of the sounds and the pronunciation key should enable you to pronounce them quite well, but the assistance of a French person is of great value, for it is of paramount importance to hear the sounds correctly spoken and to have your own pronunciation checked.

You can improve your pronunciation and understanding of the spoken word by listening to French recordings and radio broadcasting. At first a few minutes of listening each day will suffice. As you progress in your study of French you should increase the amount.

3 French is Spoken by Many People

French is spoken not only by the 53,000,000 people of France. The language of about one half of the population of Belgium and about one fifth of that of Switzerland is French. In Morocco and Algeria French is spoken by large groups of people. In the Western Hemisphere French is the language of the inhabitants of Quebec in Canada and of the people of French Guiana and Haiti.

For many years French was the sole language of diplomacy and the favourite foreign language among educated people in European countries. It is today the most useful single language for tourists and for the Common Market and business people who are flocking to the Continent in increasing numbers.

A knowledge of French is not only of great practical value. In addition, it opens the door to a better and deeper understanding of the great French people, their culture, art, literature, science, and way of life.

CHAPITRE 2 (DEUX)
FRENCH PRONUNCIATION

In Part 1 of this chapter you will learn the elements of French pronunciation. The words used to illustrate the French sounds need no translation, for they have the same or almost the same spelling as corresponding English words of like meaning, such as you have met in Chapter 1. As you learn the correct French pronunciation of these words, you are, without further effort, gradually adding to your French vocabulary.

The description of each French sound is accompanied by a pronunciation key, which indicates the nearest English equivalent of that sound. This key will be used freely throughout the book to ease your way in the pronunciation of new words, phrases and sentences.

In Part 2 and Part 3 of this chapter you will practise correct French pronunciation in words and expressions useful for the traveller, and in short easy dialogues.

PREMIÈRE PARTIE (FIRST PART)

FRENCH SOUNDS ILLUSTRATED IN FAMILIAR WORDS

Pronounce each sound and the words which illustrate it three times. Stress (emphasize) lightly the syllable in heavy type in the pronunciation key of each word. Note well:

In French words the last syllable or sometimes the last but one is stressed. The stressed syllable is indicated by heavy type in the pronunciation key.

The sign : indicates that the preceding vowel is slightly lengthened.

a (a)   **madame** (ma-**dam**). French **a** is generally like *a* in *cat*. Key symbol a. Occasionally French **a** is like *a* in *father*. Key symbol ɑ. Classe (klɑːs). Practise:
balle (bal) **place** (plas) **salade** (sa-**lad**) **table** (tabl) **garage** (ga-ra:ʒ) **classe** (klɑːs).
>*Note:* French g before e or i equals s as in *measure*. Key symbol ʒ.

i (i)   **difficile** (di-fi-**sil**). French **i** equals *ee* in *feet*. Key symbol i. Practise by drawing lips towards ears as in a smile:
riche (riʃ) **image** (i-**ma:ʒ**) **famille** (fa-**mi:j**) **Paris** (pa-**ri**).
>*Note:* French **ch** equals *sh* in *short*. Key symbol ʃ. French **ll** is usually pronounced like *y* in *yes*. Key symbol j.

é (e)   **café** (ka-**fe**). French **é** is like *a* in *hate*. Key symbol e. The mark over this letter (′) is called the acute accent. Draw lips towards ears, but less so than for **i**. Practise:
matinée (ma-ti-**ne**) **qualité** (ka-li-**te**) **papier** (pa-**pje**) **désirer** (de-zi-**re**).

3

Note: French -er at the end of a word often equals é (e). The r is silent. French qu always equals k. French c equals s before i or e; French c is like k before any other letter except ch as above in riche.

è (ε) scène (sεːn). French è is like *e* in *there*. Key symbol ε. The mark over this letter (`) is called the grave accent. Other spellings of this sound are ai and ê. The mark (^) is called the circumflex accent. Practise by opening mouth with lower lip showing teeth and with tongue placed against lower teeth. Practise:
mètre (mεtr)   crème (krεm)   fête (fεːt)   laisser-faire (lε-se-fεːr).

e (ə) Chemise (ʃə-miz). French e without any accent mark is pronounced like *e* in *father* when it ends the first syllable of a word. Key symbol ə. Practise:
menace (mə-nas)   regard (rə-gaːr).
At the end of a word, e without accent mark is silent except in words of one syllable. Practise:
le (lə)   je (ʒə)   me (mə)   ne (nə)   ce (sə)   de (də)   que (kə)
e without accent mark is often pronounced like é (e) or è (ε) when followed by one or two consonants. Practise:
et (e) assez (a-se)   pied (pje)   effet (e-fε)   dessert (de-sεːr)   est (ε) elle (ε-l).

o (ɔ) poste (pɔst) French o is like *o* in *hot*. Key symbol ɔ. Practise an open pout:
objet (ɔb-ʒε)   poème (pɔ-εːm)   effort (e-fɔːr)   original (ɔ-ri-ʒi-nal).

o (o) rôle (roːl). French o is like *o* in *rôle*. Key symbol o. Other spellings of this sound are ô, au, and eau. Practise:
hôtel (o-tεl)   rose (roːz)   chapeau (ʃa-po).
Note: French oi equals wa. French h is always silent.

ou (u) route (rut). French ou is like *oo* in *boot*. Key symbol u. Practise a round, narrow pout:
rouge (ruːʒ)   routine (ru-tin)   touriste (tu-rist)   coup d'état (ku-de-ta).
Note: Final consonants (except c, f, l, r) in French are usually silent: bouquet (bu-kε)   Paris (pa-ri)   regard (rə-gaːr) but chef (ʃεf)   hôtel (o-tεl).

u (y) bureau (by-ro). French u has no equivalent in English. Practise: rounding lips tightly:
nature (na-tyːr)   public (py-blik)   avenue (av-ny)   excuser (εks-ky-ze).

eu (œ) liqueur (li-kœːr). French eu is like *u* in *urge*. Practise by pouting lower lip well forward:
docteur (dɔk-tœːr)   acteur (ak-tœːr)   professeur (pro-fε-sœːr).

eu (ø) fameux (fa-mø). This is a shorter sound than the previous one, and the lips are placed farther forward but less open: monsieur (mə-sjø).

French Nasal Vowel Sounds

In syllables ending in n and m the n and m are not pronounced. Instead, the preceding vowel sound is nasalized as described below. There are four nasal sounds in French. As you will note, each has a number of spellings. In the pronunciation key, ~ over the symbo' indicates that the preceding vowel sound is nazalized.

an (ã) **piquant** (pi-kã). Say the English syllable *an* as in *want* in one sound. Mouth wide open. Hold the tongue down with a pencil so that it cannot rise for the **n** and try to say *an*. A French nasal **an**, key symbol ã, will result. Now practise the sound without using the pencil. Be sure to keep the tongue down. Other spellings of the nasal sound **an** (ã) are **am, en, em**. Practise:
France (frã:s) danger (dã-ʒe) encore (ã-kɔ:r) absent (ap-sã) ensemble (ã-sã:bl) rendez-vous (rã-de-vu) enveloppe (ã-vlɔp).

on (ɔ̃) **consommé** (kɔ̃-sɔ-me). Say the English sound *awn* as in *dawn*. Hold the tongue down with a pencil, so that it cannot rise for the *n* and try to say *awn*. A French nasal **on**, key symbol ɔ̃ results. Practise the sound without using a pencil. Another spelling of the nasal **on** is **om**. Practise:
oncle (ɔ̃:kl) nation (na-sjɔ̃) station (sta-sjɔ̃) question (kɛs-tjɔ̃).

in (ɛ̃) **lingerie** (lɛ̃ʒ-ri). Draw back the corners of the lips as in a smile. Hold tongue so that it cannot rise for the *n* and try to say *in*. The French nasal **in**, key symbol ɛ̃, results. Practise the sound without using the pencil. Other spellings of the nasal **in** are **im, ain, aim, ein, oin**. Practise:
index (ɛ̃-dɛks) vain (vɛ̃) train (trɛ̃) important (ɛ̃-pɔr-tã) intelligent (ɛ̃-tɛ-li-ʒã) américain (a-me-ri-kɛ̃) meringue (mrɛ̃:g).

un (œ̃) **brun** (brœ̃). Pronounce the nasal sound *in* (ɛ̃). For the nasal sound *in* (ɛ̃) the corners of the lips are drawn back as in a smile. Round the lips as if pouting, at the same time thrust the lower lip forward and try to say *in* (ɛ̃). The result is a French nasal **un**, key symbol œ̃. Another spelling of the nasal **un** (œ̃) is **um** (œ̃). Practise:
un (œ̃) brun (brœ̃) parfum (par-fœ̃) humble (œ̃:bl) Verdun (vɛr-dœ̃).

French Diphthong Sounds

These are represented by the following phonetic symbols:
j as in **yacht, papier**
w as in **oui, ouest**
y as in **lui, huit, muet**

Summary of French Vowel Sounds

Letters:	a	é	è	e	i	o	ou	u	eu	au(eau)	oi
Key Symbols:	a ɑ	e	ɛ	ə	i	ɔ	u	y	œ ø	o	wa

Summary of French Nasals

Letters:	an (am, en, em)	in (im, ain, aim, ein, eim)	on (om)	un (um)
Key Symbols:	ã	ɛ̃	ɔ̃	œ̃

Summary of French Consonants

Most French consonant sounds are like the corresponding English consonant sounds. The following, however, need special attention:

c   before **e** or **i** is like *s* in *see*, key symbol *s*. **difficile** (di-fi-sil)
c   before any other letter (except **ch**) is like *k*, key symbol k. **café** (ka-fe)
ç   with cedilla is always like hissing *s*, key symbol s. **français** (frã-sɛ)
ch is like English *sh*, key symbol ʃ. **riche** (ri:ʃ)
g   before **e** or **i** is like *s* in *measure*, key symbol ʒ. **rouge** (ru:ʒ)
g   before any other letter is like *g* in *goat*, key symbol g. **Garage** (ga-ra:ʒ)
h   is always silent: **hôtel** (o-tɛl)
j   is like *s* in *measure*, key symbol ʒ: **je** (ʒə)
ll is usually like *y* in *yes*, key symbol j: **famille** (fa-mi:j)
r   is produced at the back of the throat by letting the air vibrate over the glottis. Practise by holding the tongue down with a pencil, so that it cannot rise and touch the palate. Practise the following syllables: **ra** (ra) **re** (rə) **ri** (ri) **ro** (ro) **ru** (ry).
qu is always like **k**, key symbol k. **bouquet** (bu-kɛ)
gn is like *ny* in *canyon*, key symbol ɲ. **espagnol** (ɛs-pa-ɲɔl)

DEUXIÈME PARTIE (dø-zjɛm par-ti) SECOND PART

The second and third parts of this chapter contain important words and expressions of common usage. If you follow carefully the instructions for pronunciation practice you will acquire many of these without difficulty. *Do not try to memorize all of them at this point, as they will appear again in later chapters when you will have the opportunity to learn them thoroughly.*

Some Useful Words and Expressions for the Traveller

A. Practise the French aloud. Stress slightly the key syllables in heavy type.

1 **Pardon** (par-dɔ̃)	1 I beg your pardon.
2 **S'il vous plaît** (sil-vu-plɛ)	2 Please; if you please.
3 **Monsieur** (mə-sjø); **Madame** (ma-dam) **Mademoiselle** (mad-mwa-zɛl)	3 Mr., sir; Mrs., madam Miss, young lady
4 **Où est l'hôtel . . . ?** (u ɛ lo-tɛl)	4 Where is the hotel . . . ?
5 **Combien coûte le livre, etc.?** (kɔ̃-bjɛ̃ kut lə li:vr)	5 How much does the book, etc., cost?
6 **Je voudrais . . .** (ʒə vu-drɛ)	6 I should like . . .
7 **Merci beaucoup** (mɛr-si bo-ku)	7 Many thanks
8 **Il n'y pas de quoi** (il nja pɑd kwa)	8 Don't mention it, *or* You are welcome
9 **C'est trop cher** (sɛ tro ʃɛr). **Très cher** (trɛ ʃɛr)	9 It's too dear. Very dear.
10 **bon marché** (bɔ̃ mar-ʃe) **meilleur marché** (mɛ-jœr mar-ʃe)	10 cheap cheaper

Combien coûte . . . ? (kɔ̃-bjɛ̃ kut . . . ?)

B. Read each heading aloud, completing it with the words listed under it. Thus:

Combien coûte le chapeau? Combien coûte la chemise? etc.

1 **le chapeau** (lə ʃa-po), the hat	6 **le parapluie** (lə pa-ra-plyi), umbrella
2 **la chemise** (la ʃmiz), the shirt	7 **le parfum** (lə par-fœ̃), the perfume
3 **la blouse** (la bluz), the blouse	8 **la cravate** (la kra-vat), the tie
4 **la robe** (la rɔb), dress	9 **une auto** (y-no-to), **la voiture** (la vwa-ty:r), car
5 **la montre** (la mɔ̃:tr), the watch	

Pardon, monsieur. Où est . . . , s'il vous plaît?
(par-dɔ̃ mə-sjø), (u ɛ . . . , sil vu plɛ?)

1 **la rue Drouot** (la ry dru-o), Drouot Street
2 **l'avenue de la République** (lav-ny dla re-py-**blik**), The Avenue of the Republic
3 **la place de la Concorde** (la plas də la kɔ̃-**kɔrd**), the Place of the Concord
4 **la gare du Nord** (la gar dy nɔːr), The Nord Station
5 **L'Hôtel Albert** (lo-tɛl al-bɛːr), The Albert Hotel
6 **le boulevard Saint-Michel** (le bul-vaːr sɛ̃ mi-ʃel), The Saint Michael boulevard
7 **le bureau de poste** (lə by-rod-**pɔst**), the post office
8 **la salle d'attente** (la sal da-**tãt**), the waiting room
9 **la toilette** (la twa-lɛt), the toilet

Je voudrais. . . . (ʒə vu-drɛ)

1 **une chambre avec bain** (yn ʃãːbr avɛk bɛ̃), a room with bath
2 **de l'eau chaude** (də lo ʃoːd), some hot water
3 **des serviettes de toilette** (dɛ sɛr-vjɛt də twa-lɛt), some bath towels
4 **la carte** (la kart), the menu
5 **une addition** (y-na-di-sjɔ̃), a bill
6 **la revue** (la rvy), the magazine
7 **le journal** (lə ʒur-nal), the newspaper
8 **du savon** (dy sa-võ), some soap
9 **téléphoner** (te-le-fɔ-ne), to telephone
10 **changer de l'argent** (ʃã-ʒe dlar-ʒã) to change money

C. Practise aloud many times the numbers 1 to 21.

1 **un** (œ̃), **une** (yn)	8 **huit** (ɥit)	15 **quinze** (kɛ̃z)
2 **deux** (dø)	9 **neuf** (nœf)	16 **seize** (sɛz)
3 **trois** (trwɑ)	10 **dix** (dis)	17 **dix-sept** (di-sɛt)
4 **quatre** (katr)	11 **onze** (ɔ̃z)	18 **dix-huit** (di-zɥit)
5 **cinq** (sɛ̃k)	12 **douze** (duz)	19 **dix-neuf** (diz-nœf)
6 **six** (sis)	13 **treize** (trɛz)	20 **vingt** (vɛ̃)
7 **sept** (sɛt)	14 **quatorze** (ka-tɔrz)	21 **vingt et un** (vɛ̃-te-œ̃)

TROISIÈME PARTIE (trwɑ-zjɛm par-ti) THIRD PART

Liaison (lje-zɔ̃) Linking

The final consonant of a French word is generally silent. However, when the next word begins with a vowel or **h** the final consonant is usually pronounced and linked to the next word unless there is a natural pause.

Final **s** and **x**, when linked, are pronounced like **z**; final **f** like **v**; and final **d** like **t**.

Comment allez-vous?
(kɔ-mã-ta-le-**vu**)
How are you?

trois arts
(trwɑ zar)
three arts

dix ans
(di zã)
ten years

neuf ans
(nœ vã)
nine years

le grand homme
(lə grã tɔm)
the great man

Élision (e-li-zjɔ̃) Elision

The letters e and a of the words **le, la, je, me, te, se, de, ne, que** are dropped before words beginning with a vowel or an **h** (usually) and are replaced by an apostrophe. This process is called elision. Thus:

le + **oncle** becomes **l'oncle** (lɔ̃:kl) the uncle
le + **hôtel** becomes **l'hôtel** (lo-tɛl) the hotel
la + **école** becomes **l'école** (le-kɔl) the school
je + **ai** becomes **j'ai** (ʒe) I have
que + **avez-vous?** becomes **qu'avez-vous?** (ka-ve-vu) What have you?

The Stress in French Words and Sentences

1 In French all the syllables of a word are spoken with equal force except the last or the last but one which is stressed slightly.
général (ʒe-ne-ral) **madame** (ma-dam) **chauffeur** (ʃo-fœːr) **répéter** (re-pe-te)
2 In short sentences, only the last syllable or the last but one of the final word is stressed.
La leçon est difficile (la lsɔ̃ ɛ di-fi-sil). The lesson is difficult.
3 In longer sentences, the above syllables are stressed at the end of clauses and of other groups of words which make sense together.

Dialogue 1 (dja-lɔg)

Directions for Study.

1 Read the French text silently, sentence by sentence, using the English translation to get the meaning.
2 Read the whole French text aloud three or more times, using the pronunciation key as an aid. Stress lightly the key syllables in heavy type.

Comment allez-vous (kɔ-mã-ta-le-vu)? How are you?

1 — Bonjour, monsieur Picard. Comment allez-vous? (Bɔ̃-ʒur, mə-sjø pi-kaːr. Kɔ-mã ta-le-vu?)
2 — Très bien, merci. Et vous? (Trɛ bjɛ̃, mɛr-si. E vu?)
3 — Très bien, merci. (Trɛ bjɛ̃, mɛr-si)
4 — Au revoir, monsieur Picard. (ɔ rvwaːr, mə-sjø pi kaːr)
5 — Au revoir, Philippe. (ɔ rvwaːr, fi-lip)

1 Good day, Mr. Picard. How are you?
2 Very well, thank you. And you?
3 Very well, thank you.
4 Goodbye, Mr. Picard.
5 Goodbye, Philip.

Dialogue 2

French people address each other frequently as 'monsieur', 'madame', 'mademoiselle' (for unmarried women) in conversation thus:

bonjour, monsieur
au revoir, madame
merci, mademoiselle

oui, monsieur
non, madame

English people do not use 'Sir', 'Madam' and 'Miss' as frequently in conversation, or in the same way, therefore the French forms of address will often remain untranslated in the English equivalent.

Parlez-vous français? (par-le-vu frã-sɛ) Do you speak French?

1 — Parlez-vous français, Jeanne? (Par-le-vu frã-sɛ, ӡaːn?)
2 — Oui, monsieur, je parle français. (Wi mǝ-sjø, ӡǝ parl frã-sɛ)
3 — Est-ce que François parle français? (ɛs-kǝ frã-swa parl frã-sɛ?)
4 — Oui, madame, il parle bien le français. (Wi, ma-dam, il parl bjɛ̃ lǝ frã-sɛ)
5 — Est-ce que Louise parle français? (ɛs-kǝ lwiːz parl frã-sɛ?)
6 — Non, madame, elle parle anglais. (Nɔ̃, ma-dam, ɛl parl ã-glɛ)

1 Do you speak French, Jane?
2 Yes, I speak French.
3 Does Frank speak French? (*Lit.*[1] Is it that Frank speaks French?)
4 Yes, he speaks French well.
5 Does Louise speak French? (*Lit.* Is it that Louise speaks French?)
6 No, she speaks English.

NOTE 1. *Lit.* is an abbreviation of *literally*, that is: *word for word.*

Dialogue 3

Les jours de la semaine[1] (le ӡur dǝ la smɛn) The Days of the Week

1 — Écoutez, Jacques! Combien de jours y a-t-il dans une semaine? (E-ku-te, ӡaːk! kɔ̃-bjɛ̃d ӡur i ja-til dã zyn smɛn?)
2 — Il y a sept jours dans une semaine. (Il ja sɛt ӡur dã zyn smɛn)
3 — Bien. Donnez-moi le nom[2] des sept jours, s'il vous plaît? (Bjɛ̃. Dɔ-ne-mwa lǝ nɔ̃ dɛ sɛt ӡur, sil vu plɛ?)
4 — Dimanche, lundi, mardi, mercredi, jeudi, vendredi et samedi. (Di-mãʃ, lœ̃-di, mar-di, mɛr-krǝ-di, ӡø-di, vã-drǝ-di e sam-di)
5 — Très bien. Écoutez, Georges! Quel jour de la semaine sommes-nous? (Trɛ bjɛ̃. E-ku-te ӡɔrӡ! Kɛl ӡur dǝ la smɛn sɔm-nu?)
6 — C'est aujourd'hui lundi. (Sɛ to-ӡur-dɥi lœ̃-di)
7 — Très bien, Georges. (Trɛ bjɛ̃, ӡɔrӡ)

1 Listen James! How many days are there in a week?
2 There are seven days in a week.
3 Good. Give me the names of the seven days of the week, please. (*Lit.* if it pleases you.)
4 Sunday, Monday, Tuesday, Wednesday, Thursday, Friday, and Saturday.
5 Very good. Listen, George! What day of the week is today? (*Lit.* What day of the week are we?)
6 Today is Monday.
7 Very good, George.

NOTE 1. All days are masculine.
NOTE 2. In French one says *the name* of the days, of things etc., not *the names*, as in English, because each has one name only.

CHAPITRE 3 (TROIS)

QUI EST MONSIEUR DAVIS?

You now have a good working knowledge of French pronunciation and are ready for a more intimate study of the language. Practise the pronunciation aids after each conversational text and follow all directions for reading aloud and speaking. Remember: the only way you can learn to speak a language is by speaking it.

This chapter will introduce you to Mr. Davis, a London businessman who is as eager as you are to learn French. You will also meet his congenial teacher, monsieur Picard, a Frenchman living in London. As he teaches Mr. Davis he will also teach you in a pleasant and interesting way.

So **Bonne chance** (*Good Luck*) and **Bon voyage** (*Happy Journey*) as you accompany Mr. Davis on the road which leads to a practical knowledge of the French language.

Comment étudier le texte. How to study the text.

Read the French text silently, referring to the English only when necessary to get the meaning.

Cover up the English text and read the French text silently.

Study the 'Pronunciation and Spelling Aids' and the sections 'Building Vocabulary' and 'Locutions françaises' which follow the text.

Then read the French text aloud, pronouncing carefully.

Do the exercise 'Completion of Text'.

Proceed to 'Grammar Notes', etc.

Follow these instructions with the conventional texts in succeeding chapters.

Qui est monsieur Davis?

1 Monsieur Davis est un commerçant anglais.

2 Il habite dans une petite ville dans les environs de Londres.

3 Il y a six personnes dans la famille Davis: le père, monsieur Davis; la mère, madame Davis; deux fils, et deux filles. Monsieur Davis est un homme de quarante ans. Madame Davis est une femme de trente-cinq ans.

4 Les fils s'appellent[1] Philippe et Henri. Les filles s'appellent Rosette et Annette.

5 Monsieur Davis habite dans une villa.

6 Dans la maison il y a cinq pièces: le salon, la salle à manger, et trois chambres à coucher. Il y a aussi la cuisine et la salle de bain.

7 Le bureau de monsieur Davis est dans Oxford Street.

8 Il est au dernier étage d'un grand immeuble.

9 Le lundi, le mardi, le mercredi, le jeudi, et le vendredi, monsieur Davis prend le train pour arriver à son bureau en ville.

10 Toute la journée il travaille assidûment dans son bureau.

Who is Mr. Davis?

1 Mr. Davis is an English businessman.

2 He lives in a small town on the outskirts of London.

3 There are six persons in the Davis family: the father, Mr. Davis; the mother, Mrs. Davis; two sons, and two daughters. Mr. Davis is a man of forty years of age. Mrs. Davis is a woman of thirty-five.

4 The sons are called[1] Philip and Henry. The daughters are called Rosie and Annie.

5 Mr. Davis lives in a detached house.

6 In the house there are five rooms: the living-room, the dining-room, and three bedrooms. There is also the kitchen and the bathroom.

7 The office of Mr. Davis is in Oxford Street.

8 It is on the top floor of a big block of offices.

9 On Mondays, Tuesdays, Wednesdays, Thursdays and Fridays Mr. Davis takes the train in order to reach his office in town.

10 All day he works diligently in his office.

NOTE 1. s'appellent (sa-pɛl). *Lit.* call themselves.

Pronunciation and Spelling Aids

A. Practise Aloud:

1 un commerçant anglais
(œ̃ kɔ-mɛr-sɑ̃ ɑ̃-glɛ)
2 dans les environs
(dɑ̃ lɛ zɑ̃-vi-rɔ̃)
3 dans une petite ville
(dɑ̃ zyn ptit vil)
4 trois chambres à coucher
(trwɑ ʃɑ̃:br a ku-ʃe)
5 il est au dernier étage
(il ɛ to dɛr-nje re-taʒ)
6 assidûment
(a-si-dy-mɑ̃)

B. Remember: s, when linked, becomes z. les environs (lɛ zɑ̃-vi-rɔ̃)

Building Vocabulary

A. La famille (la fa-mi:j)   The Family

le père (pɛr), the father
la mère (mɛr), the mother
le fils (fis), the son
la fille (fi:j), the daughter
le frère (frɛːr), the brother
la sœur (sœːr), the sister
un oncle (œ̃-nɔ̃:kl), an uncle
la tante (tɑ̃:t), the aunt
le cousin (ku-zɛ̃), the cousin (*m*)
la cousine (ku-zin), the cousin (*f*)

un, une enfant (œ̃ yn ɑ̃-fɑ̃), a child (*m* or *f*)
le garçon (gar-sɔ̃), the boy, the waiter
la jeune fille (ʒœn fi:j), the girl
le monsieur (mə-sjø), the gentleman
monsieur, Mr., Sir
messieurs (mɛ-sjø), gentlemen
la dame (dam), the lady
madame (ma-dam), Mrs., madam
l'homme (lɔm), the man
la femme (fam), the woman, the wife
les parents (lɛ-pa-rɑ̃), the parents

B. Les pièces de la maison (lɛ pjɛs də la mɛ-zɔ̃), The Rooms of the House.

le salon (sa-lɔ̃), living-room
la chambre à coucher (ʃɑ̃:bra ku-ʃe), bedroom
la cuisine (kɥi-zin), kitchen

la salle à manger (sa-la mɑ̃-ʒe), dining-room
la salle de bain (sal də bɛ̃), bathroom

Locutions françaises (lɔ-ky-sjɔ̃ frɑ̃-sɛz)   French Expressions

1 il y a (il ja), there is, there are
2 y a-t-il? (ja-til), is there? are there?
3 par cœur (par kœr), by heart
4 toute la journée (tut la ʒur-ne), all day

Exercise No. 1—Completion of Text

For maximum benefit follow these instructions carefully in all 'Completion of Text' exercises.

Complete each sentence by putting the English words into French. Where you can, do this from memory.

If you do not remember the words refer to the French text. There you will find the words in the order of their appearance. You have only to re-read the text to find them easily.

When you have completed each sentence with the needed words, read the complete sentence aloud in French.

It will be a great help to your memory if you write each completed sentence. This is true for all exercises.

The correct French words for the 'Completion of Text' exercises are in the 'Answers' section of this book, along with the answers to all other exercises. Check all your answers.

Exemple (ɛg-zã:pl) Example: 1. Qui est monsieur Davis?

1 (Who) **est monsieur Davis?**
2 **Il est un** (business man) **anglais**
3 **Il habite** (in) **une petite ville.**
4 (There are) **six personnes dans la famille.**
5 **Monsieur Davis est le** (father).
6 **Madame Davis est la** (mother).
7 **Les** (sons) **s'appellent Philippe** (and) **Henri.**
8 **Les filles** (are named) **Rosette** (and) **Annette.**
9 **Il y a** (five rooms) **dans la maison.**
10 **Il y a une** (kitchen) **et une** (bathroom).
11 **Le** (office) **est dans Oxford Street.**
12 (It is) **dans un grand immeuble.**
13 **Il est au** (top) **étage.**
14 **Monsieur Davis travaille** (all day).

Grammar Notes

1 The Definite Article.
  Note the four ways in which the definite article *the* is expressed in French.

With Singular Nouns

Masculine: **le père**	**le fils**	**le frère**	**l'oncle**	**l'homme**	**l'enfant**
Feminine: **la mère**	**la fille**	**la sœur**	**la tante**	**la femme**	**l'enfant**

With Plural Nouns

Masculine: **les pères**	**les fils**	**les frères**	**les oncles**	**les hommes**	**les enfants**
Feminine: **les mères**	**les filles**	**les sœurs**	**les tantes**	**les femmes**	**les enfants**

The definite article in French is **le** (lə), **la** (la), **l'**, **les** (lɛ).

le is used with a masculine singular noun. **la** is used with a feminine singular noun. **l'** is used with any noun that begins with a vowel or **h** (usually). **les** is used with any plural noun, masculine or feminine.

When the **s** of **les** is linked with the following noun it is pronounced like *z*.

Thus:

les enfants (lɛ-zɑ̃-fɑ̃), **les hommes** (lɛ-zɔm)

2. The Gender of Nouns.
Nouns are either masculine or feminine. This is true for thing-nouns as well as for person-nouns.

Masculine: **le salon**   **le train**   **l'immeuble**   **l'étage**   **le père**
Feminine: **la chambre**   **la maison**   **la cuisine**   **la ville**   **la mère**

Always learn the gender of thing-nouns as they occur.

3. The Plural of Nouns.
Note the singular and plural of the following nouns:

le salon   **la chambre**   **le fils**   **l'enfant**   **le bureau**
les salons   **les chambres**   **les fils**   **les enfants**   **les bureaux**

The plural of nouns is usually formed by adding **s** to the singular. The added **s** is not pronounced. If a noun already ends in **s** in the singular it remains unchanged in the plural. Learn exceptions as you meet them. Thus:

le bureau   les bureaux.   Nouns ending in **eau** add **x** to form their plural.

4. The Indefinite Article.
Note how the indefinite article *a (one)* is expressed in French.

Masculine: **un père**   **un fils**   **un salon**   **un train**   **un homme**
Feminine: **une mère**   **une fille**   **une ville**   **une rue**   **une femme**
un (œ̃) *a, one* is used with a masculine noun.
une (yn) *a, one* is used with a feminine noun.

Exercise No. 2   Replace the English words *the* and *a (one)* by **le, la, l', les, un** or **une** as required.

Exemple: 1 La famille Davis habite à Londres.

1 (The) **famille Davis habite à Londres.**
2 **Londres est** (a) **grande ville.**
3 (The) **immeuble est dans Oxford Street.**
4 (The) **père est monsieur Davis.**
5 (The) **mère est madame Davis.**
6 **Annette est** (a) **fille.**
7 **Philippe est** (a) **fils.**
8 (The) **chambre à coucher est grande.**
9 (The) **maison est** (a) **villa.**
10 (The) **homme est dans** (the) **salon.**
11 (The) **enfant est dans** (the) **bureau.**
12 **Il y a** (one) **sœur et** (one) **frère.**

Exercise No. 3   Change the following nouns to the plural.

Exemple: la salle   les salles

1 la chambre
2 la mère
3 la pièce
4 le fils
5 l'homme
6 le salon
7 l'Anglais
8 l'étage
9 le bureau
10 la personne
11 l'oncle
12 l'enfant
13 le commerçant
14 la rue
15 l'avenue

5. Some Common Verbs.

il est (il ɛ), he is
est-il? (ɛ-til), is he?
il habite[1] (a-biːt), he lives
habite-t-il? (a-biːt-til), does he live?

il prend (prᾶ), he takes
prend-il? (prᾶ-til), does he take?
il travaille (tra-vaj), he works
travaille-t-il? (tra-vaj-til), does he work?

NOTE 1. habiter, to live, to inhabit; sometimes demeurer, to dwell, is used.

Exercise No. 4 Translate into French

1 Mr. Davis is an English businessman.
2 He lives in (à) London.
3 There are six persons in the family.
4 He lives in a private house.
5 There are five rooms in the house.
6 Mr. Davis is the father.
7 Mrs. Davis is the mother.
8 The office is in Oxford Street.
9 Mr. Davis takes the train.
10 He works in the office.

Exercise No. 5—Questionnaire

Read silently each French question and answer, noting the English meaning. Read aloud each French question and answer twice, without referring to the English.

Questions (kɛs-tjɔ̃) Questions

1 Qui est monsieur Davis?
Il est commerçant à Londres.
2 Est-il anglais?
Oui, monsieur, il est anglais.
3 Où demeure monsieur Davis?
Il demeure dans les environs de Londres.
4 Combien de personnes y a-t-il dans sa famille?
Il y a six personnes dans sa famille.
5 Comment les fils s'appellent-ils?[1]
Ils s'appellent[1] Philippe et Henri.
6 Comment les filles s'appellent-elles?
Elles[2] s'appellent Rosette et Annette.
7 Combien de pièces y a-t-il dans la maison de monsieur Davis?
Il y a cinq pièces.
8 Y a-t-il aussi une cuisine et une salle de bain?
Oui, monsieur, il y a aussi une cuisine et une salle de bain.
9 Dans quelle rue est le bureau de monsieur Davis?
Il est dans Oxford Street.

Réponses (re-põs) Answers

1 Who is Mr. Davis?
He is a businessman in London.
2 Is he English?
Yes, he is an Englishman.
3 Where does Mr. Davis live?
He lives in the suburbs of London.
4 How many people are there in his family?
There are six people in his family.
5 What are the names of the sons?[1]
They are named Philip and Henry.[1]
6 What are the names of the daughters?[1]
They are named Rosie and Annie.[1]
7 How many rooms are there in Mr. Davis' house?
There are five rooms.
8 Is there also a kitchen and a bathroom?
Yes, there is also a kitchen and a bathroom.
9 In what street is the office of Mr. Davis?
It is in Oxford Street.

10 **Comment travaille-t-il?**   10 How does he work?
    Il travaille assidûment.   He works diligently.

NOTE 1. *Lit.* How do the sons (daughters) call themselves? They call
    themselves, etc.

NOTE 2. ils, they (*masculine*)   elles, they (*feminine*)

Learn these question words:

    qui (ki), who?   **comment** (kɔ-mã), how?
    où (u), where?   **combien (de)** (kɔ̃-bjɛ̃ də), how many?

CHAPITRE 4 (QUATRE)

POURQUOI EST-CE QUE M. DAVIS ÉTUDIE LE FRANÇAIS?

Why is Mr. Davis studying French?

1 M. Davis est importateur.

2 Il importe des objets d'art et des articles divers de la France et du Maroc.

3 Au printemps, M. Davis va faire un voyage en France. Il désire rendre visite à son représentant à Paris. Il désire parler français avec lui.

4 Il désire aussi visiter des endroits intéressants en France. Il compte aussi aller au Maroc et peut-être en Corse.

5 M. Davis sait lire un peu le français. Mais il ne parle pas français. C'est pourquoi il étudie la langue française.

6 M. Picard est le professeur de M. Davis.

7 M. Picard, un ami de M. Davis, est français. C'est[1] un homme de quarante-cinq ans.

8 Tous les mardis et tous les jeudis les deux messieurs ont rendez-vous, presque toujours chez M. Davis. Là, ils parlent français.

9 M. Picard est un bon professeur.

10 M. Davis est très intelligent et il apprend rapidement.

11 Pendant la première leçon il apprend par cœur ce dialogue:

12 — Bonjour, M. Picard. Comment allez-vous? — Très bien, merci. Et vous? — Très bien, merci.

13 M. Davis apprend aussi des salutations et des adieux.

14 Bonjour.

15 Bonsoir.

16 Adieu. Au revoir. À bientôt. À tantôt. À demain.

1 Mr. Davis is an importer.

2 He imports art objects and various articles from France and from Morocco.

3 In the spring Mr. Davis is going to make a trip to France. He wants to visit his representative in Paris. He wants to speak French with him.

4 He also wants to visit some interesting places in France. He also expects to go to Morocco and perhaps to Corsica.

5 Mr. Davis knows how to read French a little. But he does not speak French. That is why he is studying the French language.

6 Mr. Picard is Mr. Davis' teacher.

7 Mr. Picard, a friend of Mr. Davis, is a Frenchman. He is a man of forty-five.

8 Every Tuesday and every Thursday the two gentlemen have an appointment, almost always at Mr. Davis' house. There they speak French.

9 Mr. Picard is a good teacher.

10 Mr. Davis is very intelligent and he learns rapidly.

11 During the first lesson he learns this dialogue by heart:

12 Good day, Mr. Picard. How are you? Very well, thank you. And you? Very well, thank you.

13 Mr. Davis also learns some greetings and some farewells.

14 Good day. (*Also* good morning, good afternoon)

15 Good evening. (*Also* good night.)

16 Goodbye, goodbye. See you soon. So long. Until tomorrow.

NOTE 1. **C'est** is used instead of **il (elle) est** *he* (*she*) *is*, when a modified noun follows. You will learn more later about the use of **c'est**.

Pronunciation and Spelling Aids

A. Practise Aloud:

1 un importateur (œ̃ nɛ̃-pɔr-ta-tœr)
2 le représentant (rə-pre-zã-tã)
3 des salutations (dɛ sa-ly-ta-sjɔ̃)
4 messieurs (mɛ-sjø)
5 la France (frãs)

6 le Maroc (ma-rɔk)
7 des adieux (dɛ za-djø)
8 des objets d'art (dɛ zɔb-ʒɛ dar)
9 des endroits intéressants (dɛ zã-drwa-ɛ̃-te-re-sã)

B. Remember: The cedilla under **ç** indicates that the **ç** is pronounced like *s* **français** (frã-sɛ).

Start names of countries, cities and people with capital letters. Adjectives of nationality, languages, days of the week, and months are written with small letters.

la = the **là** = there **ou** = or **où** = where

Building Vocabulary

A. Synonyms (Words of Like Meaning)

le professeur, professor, teacher in a secondary school.

le maître (mɛːtr), **la maîtresse** (mɛ-trɛs) teacher in an elementary school.

B. Antonyms (Words of Opposite Meaning)

1 **grand**, big; **petit**, small
2 **bon**, good; **mauvais**, bad
3 **ici**, here; **là**, there
4 **l'homme**, man; **la femme**, woman

5 **rapidement**, rapidly; **vite**, quickly **lentement**, slowly
6 **un importateur**, importer; **un exportateur**, exporter

C. Quelques langues d'Europe (dø-rɔ̃p) Some Languages of Europe.

1 **le français** (frã-sɛ), French
2 **l'anglais** (ã-glɛ), English
3 **l'espagnol** (ɛs-pa-ɲɔl), Spanish

4 **l'italien** (i-ta-ljɛ̃), Italian
5 **l'allemand** (al-mã), German
6 **le russe** (rys), Russian

Locutions françaises

1 **bonjour** (bɔ̃-ʒur), good morning (day)
2 **bonsoir** (bɔ̃-swar), good evening (night)
3 **au revoir** (ɔ-rvwar), goodbye
4 **à bientôt** (a bjɛ̃-to), see you soon
5 **à tantôt** (a tã-to), so long
6 **adieu** (a-djø), goodbye, farewell

7 **à demain** (a dmɛ̃), until tomorrow
8 **au printemps** (o prɛ̃-tã), in the spring
9 **peut-être** (pø-tɛːtr), perhaps
10 **par cœur** (par kœːr), by heart
11 **c'est pourquoi** (sɛ pur-kwa), that's why
12 **chez** (ʃe) **M. Davis,** at the house of Mr. Davis
13 **comment allez-vous?** how are you?
14 **très bien, merci.** very well, thank you

Exercise No. 6—Completion of Text

Follow carefully the instructions given in Exercise No. 1.

1 (Who) **est M. Davis?**
2 **Il est** (an importer).
3 **Il importe des** (art objects).
4 (In the spring) **il va faire un voyage.**
5 (He wants) **rendre visite à son représentant.**
6 **Il désire** (to speak) **français avec lui.**
7 **Il compte** (also) **aller au Maroc.**
8 (But) **il ne parle pas français.**
9 (That is why) **il étudie la langue.**
10 **M. Picard est** (the teacher) **de M. Davis.**
11 **C'est** (a friend of Mr. Davis).
12 **Les deux messieurs ont** (an appointment).
13 (They speak) **français.**
14 **M. Davis apprend** (rapidly).
15 **Il est** (very intelligent).
16 **M. Picard est** (a good teacher).

Grammar Notes

1. Use of **des** (dɛ)   some

des objets d'art (dɛ zɔb-ʒɛ-dar), some art objects
des maisons (dɛ mɛ-zɔ̃), some houses
des endroits (dɛ zã-drwa), some places

The word *some*, before a plural noun, may be expressed by **des.**
The word *some* may be omitted in English, but **des** is never omitted in French. Thus:
des objets d'art, some art objects *or* art objects

Quelques (kɛlk) is also used for *some*, in the sense of *several* or *a few*: quelques langues, some (several) languages.

2. Some Common Verbs

il est (il ɛ), he is
est-il? (ɛ-til), is he?
il n'est pas (il nɛ pɑ), he is not
il va, he goes, is going
va-t-il? does he go, is he going?
il parle (il parl), he speaks
parle-t-il? (parl-til), does he speak?

il compte (il kɔ̃t), he expects
il apprend (il a-prã), he learns
il sait (il sɛ), he knows, *or* he knows how
ils ont (il zɔ̃), they have
ont-ils? (ɔ̃ til), have they?
aller (a-le), to go

il ne parle pas (il nə parl pɑ), he does not speak   **parler** (par-le), to speak
il désire (il de-ziːr), he wants   **visiter** (vi-zi-te), **rendre visite à** (rãːdr vi-ʒiːt a); to visit (someone)
il étudie (il e-ty-di), he studies   **lire** (liːr), to read
   faire (fɛːr), to make

A hyphen is required in the question form. Thus:

> **Est-il?** Is he?   **Ont-ils?** Have they?   **Sait-il?** Does he know?

If the verb ends in **e** or **a** the letter **t** must be inserted between the verb and the subject pronoun. Thus:

> **Parle-t-il?** Does he speak?   **Étudie-t-il?** Does he study?   **Va-t-il?** Does he go?

Another way of forming a question is by placing **Est-ce que** (Is it that . . . ?) before the subject:

> **Est-ce qu'il apprend?** = **Apprend-il?**   **Est-ce qu'ils ont?** = **Ont-ils?**

To form the negative of a verb, place **ne** directly before the verb and **pas** directly after the verb:

> **il *ne* parle *pas*,** he does not speak   **il *ne* sait *pas*,** he does not know
> **ne** becomes **n'** before a verb that begins with a vowel or **h** (usually).
> **il n'étudie** (ne-ty-di) **pas**   **il n'apprend** (na-prã) **pas**

3. Omission of the Indefinite Article.

The indefinite article (**un, une**) is omitted with nouns for professions or nationalities after the verb *to be*: **il est professeur.** However, one can also say: **c'est un professeur,** but if the noun is modified, **c'est** must be used: **c'est un bon professeur.**

Exercise No. 7 Complete the following sentences with the correct verb form

Exemple 1. Qui est M. Davis?

1 **Qui** (is) **M. Davis?**
2 (Is he) **importateur?**
3 (He does not speak) **français.**
4 (Does he speak) **anglais?**
5 (He learns) **rapidement.**
6 (He wants) **faire un voyage.**
7 (He is not studying) **l'espagnol.**
8 (He knows how) **lire un peu.**
9 (Have they) **rendez-vous?**
10 (He expects) **visiter Paris.**
11 **Il va** (to make) **un voyage.**
12 **Il ne sait pas** (to speak) **français.**

Exercise No. 8 Select from Column II the word groups that best complete the sentences begun in Column I.

Exemple: 1 (d) M. Davis désire parler français avec son représentant à Paris.

I	II
1 M. Davis désire parler français	(a) des salutations et des adieux.
2 Il sait lire	(b) de la France et du Maroc.
3 Il est très intelligent. C'est pourquoi	(c) chez M. Davis.

4 Il importe des objets d'art   (d) avec son représentant à Paris.
5 Les deux messieurs ont rendez-vous   (e) de quarante ans.
6 M. Picard est un homme   (f) un peu le français.
7 M. Davis apprend aussi   (g) il apprend rapidement.
8 Le bureau de M. Davis n'est pas   (h) dans la famille de M. Davis.
9 Il y a cinq personnes   (i) Philippe, Henri, Rosette et Annette.
10 Les enfants de M. Davis s'appellent   (j) dans Leadenhall Street.

Exercise No. 9 Find the corresponding French words in the Reading Text or 'Building Vocabulary'. Write them. Say them aloud.

1 French (lang.)	6 the office	11 a little	16 but	21 some articles
2 the Frenchman	7 almost	12 there	17 where	22 some places
3 thank you	8 always	13 from, of	18 good	23 that is why
4 also	9 very well	14 here	19 bad	24 How are you?
5 perhaps	10 rapidly	15 big	20 with	

Exercise No. 10—Questionnaire

Follow the instructions given in Exercise No. 5.

Questions et Réponses

1 Qui est le professeur?
M. Picard est le professeur.
2 Parle-t-il français?
Oui, monsieur, il parle français.
3 Qui est le commerçant?
M. Davis est le commerçant.
4 Parle-t-il français?
Non, monsieur, il ne parle pas français.
5 Où est le bureau de M. Davis?
Il est dans Oxford Street.
6 Est-il importateur d'automobiles?
Non, monsieur, il n'est pas importateur d'automobiles.
7 Apprend-il vite ou lentement?
Il apprend vite.
8 Quand ces messieurs ont-ils rendez-vous?
Ils ont rendez-vous tous les mardis et tous les jeudis.
9 M. Davis est-il intelligent?
Il est très intelligent.
10 Pourquoi étudie-t-il le français?
Parce qu'il désire faire un voyage en France.

1 Who is the teacher?
Mr. Picard is the teacher.
2 Does he speak French?
Yes, he speaks French.
3 Who is the businessman?
Mr. Davis is the businessman.
4 Does he speak French?
No, he does not speak French.

5 Where is Mr. Davis' office?
  It is in Oxford Street.
6 Is he an importer of motor cars?
  No, he is not an importer of motor cars.
7 Does he learn quickly or slowly?
  He learns quickly.
8 When do these gentleman have an appointment?
  They have an appointment every Tuesday and every Thursday.
9 Is Mr. Davis intelligent?
  He is very intelligent.
10 Why is he studying French?
  Because he wants to make a trip to France.

Learn: **quand** (kã)? when?   **pourquoi** (pur-kwa)? why?
                                     parce que (pars-kə), because

CHAPITRE 5 (CINQ)

DANS LE SALON DE MONSIEUR DAVIS

1 C'est jeudi le 5 (cinq) janvier, 1985.

2 Il est 8 (huit) heures du soir.

3 M. Davis est assis dans le salon de sa maison. M. Picard est assis près de lui.

4 M. Picard dit à M. Davis:—Autour de nous il y a beaucoup de choses; à la maison, dans la rue, dans le bureau, dans le parc, dans la ville, et à la campagne.

5 En Angleterre il faut savoir le nom des choses en anglais. En France il faut savoir le nom des choses en français.

6 Nous sommes dans le salon de votre maison. Dites-moi, s'il vous plaît, qu'est-ce que c'est que ça?

7 — C'est un piano. Ma femme joue bien du piano. Elle chante bien aussi.

8 — Très bien. Et qu'est-ce qui est[1] sur le piano?

9 — Une lampe et un cahier de musique.

10 — Et qu'est-ce qui est au mur au-dessus du piano?

11 — C'est le portrait de ma femme.

12 — Excellent. Dites-moi, s'il vous plaît, le nom d'autres objets dans le salon, et dites-moi où ils sont.

13 — Avec plaisir.

14 — La bibliothèque est devant une fenêtre. Le miroir est entre les fenêtres. Le bureau est près de la porte. Une chaise est près du bureau. Sur le bureau il y a un crayon, un stylo, des papiers et des lettres. Il y a des livres sur la petite table.

15 — Très bien. C'est assez pour aujourd'hui. Au revoir, M. Davis.

16 — À mardi, M. Picard.

1 It is Thursday, 5 January 1985.

2 It is eight o'clock in the evening.

3 Mr. Davis is sitting in the living-room of his house. Mr. Picard is sitting near him.

4 Mr. Picard says to Mr. Davis: Around us there are many things: in the house, in the street, in the office, in the park, in the city, and in the country.

5 In England it is necessary to know the names of things in English. In France it is necessary to know the names of things in French.

6 We are in the living-room of your house. Tell me, please, what is that?

7 It is a piano. My wife plays the piano well. She also sings well.

8 Very good. And what is on the piano?

9 A lamp and a music book.

10 And what is on the wall over the piano?

11 It is the portrait of my wife.

12 Excellent. Tell me, please, the names of other objects in the living-room and tell me where they are.

13 With pleasure.

22

14 The bookcase is in front of a window. The mirror is between the windows. The desk is near the door. A chair is near the desk. On the desk there is a pencil, a fountain-pen, some papers and some letters. There are some books on the little table.

15 Very good. That's enough for today. Goodbye, Mr. Davis.

16 Till Tuesday, Mr. Picard.

NOTE 1. qu'est-ce qui est? or qu'est-ce qui se trouve? (*Lit.* What finds itself ?)

Pronunciation and Spelling Aids

Practise Aloud:

1 **Monsieur Davis est assis dans le salon de sa maison**
(mə-sjø davis ε ta-si dãl sa-lɔ̃ də sa mε-zɔ̃)
Monsieur Picard est assis près de lui
(məsjø pi-ka:r ε ta-si prε dlyi)

2 **dans la ville** (dã la vil)

3 **en France** (ã frãs)

4 **en Angleterre** (ã nã-glə-tεr)

5 **autour de nous** (o-tur də nu)

Building Vocabulary

A. **Dans le salon** (dãl sa-lɔ̃), In the Living-room.

1 **le bureau** (by-ro), desk, office
2 **la chaise** (ʃεz), chair
3 **le cahier de musique** (ka-je dmy-zik), music book
4 **le crayon** (krε-jɔ̃), pencil
5 **la fenêtre** (fnε:-tr), window
6 **la lampe** (lã:p), lamp
7 **la lettre** (lεtr), letter
8 **le miroir** (mi-rwa:r), mirror
9 **le papier** (pa-pje), paper
10 **le piano** (pja-no), piano
11 **la porte** (pɔrt), door
12 **le portrait** (pɔr-trε), portrait
13 **le stylo** (sti-lo), fountain-pen
14 **la table** (tabl), table
15 **la bibliothèque** (bi-bliɔ-tεk), bookcase

B. Some Common Prepositions

1 **à**, to, at, in, on
2 **en**, in, into
3 **de** (də), of, from
4 **autour (de)** (o-tur də), around
5 **avec** (a-vεk), with
6 **au-dessus (de)** (od-sy də), above, over
7 **près (de)** (prε də), near
8 **chez** (ʃe), at the house of
9 **entre** (ãtr), between
10 **dans** (dã), in, inside of
11 **devant** (dvã), before, in front of
12 **derrière** (dε-rjε:r), behind
13 **sous** (su), under
14 **sur** (syr), on, upon

Locutions françaises

1 **le cinq janvier** (lə sε̃ ʒã-vje), 5 January
2 **il est huit heures** (il ε ɥi tœ:r), it is eight o'clock
3 **beaucoup de choses** (bo-kud-ʃoz), many things
4 **il faut** (il fo), it is necessary
5 **dites-moi** (dit-mwa), tell me
6 **qu'est-ce que c'est que ça?** (kεs kə sεk sa), what is that?
7 **qu'est-ce qui?** (kεs ki), what?

8 **elle joue du piano** (ɛl ju dy pja-**no**), she plays the piano
9 **c'est assez** (sɛ ta-**se**), it's enough
10 **pour aujourd'hui** (pur o-ʒur-**dųi**), for today

Exercise No. 11—Completion of Text

1 **Le monsieur** (is sitting) **dans le salon.**
2 **Il y a** (many things) **dans la rue.**
3 (It is necessary to know) **le nom des choses.**
4 **Dites-moi** (what is that?).
5 **Ma femme** (plays) **bien du piano et** (sings) **bien.**
6 **Le portrait est** (over the piano).
7 **Un miroir est** (between) **les fenêtres.**
8 **Sur le bureau il y a** (some letters).
9 (That's enough) **pour aujourd'hui.**
10 (Till Tuesday), M. **Picard.**

Grammar Notes

1. The Contractions **du, des, au, aux**

> **de** (of, from) plus **le** (the) becomes **du** (of, from the)
> **de** (of, from) plus **les** (the) becomes **des** (of, from the)
> **à** (to, at, in, on) plus **le** (the) becomes **au** (to, at, in, on the)
> **à** (to, at, in, on) plus **les** (the) becomes **aux** (to, at, in, on the)

Où est le bureau *du* commerçant?　Where is the office *of the* businessman?
Mme Picard est une amie *des* enfants.　Mrs. Picard is a friend *of the* children.
M. Picard parle *au* commerçant.　Mr. Picard is speaking *to the* merchant.
Le maître parle *aux* garçons.　The teacher is speaking *to the* boys.

de la, de l', à la and **à l'** never contract. Thus:

Le salon *de la* maison est grand.　The living-room *of the* house is large.
Il sait le nom *de* l'hôtel.　He knows the name *of the* hotel.
Charles va *à la* fenêtre.　Charles is going *to the* window.
La mère parle *à* l'enfant.　The mother is speaking *to the* child.

2. Possession.

In French possession is indicated by a phrase with **de**, never by an apostrophe:

la maison du professeur, the teacher's house, the house of the teacher
l'oncle de Marie, Mary's uncle, the uncle of Mary.

Possession is also expressed by a phrase with the preposition **à**:

À qui est ce bureau?　Whose office is this? (*Lit.* To whom is this office?)
Ce bureau est au docteur.　It is the doctor's office. (*Lit.* This office is to the doctor.)

Exercise No. 12　Use **du, de l', de la, des; au, à l', à la, aux**, as required.

Exemple: Le salon du professeur est grand.

1 **Le salon** (of the) **professeur est grand.**
2 **M. Davis parle** (to the) **professeur.**

3 M. Picard est le maître (of the) garçons.
4 C'est un ami (of the) commerçant.
5 Charles va (to the) oncle.
6 L'enfant va (to the) fenêtre.
7 La mère parle (to the) enfants.
8 Le portrait est (on the) mur.
9 Il ne parle pas (to the) homme.
10 Où est la maison (of the) tante?

Exercise No. 13   Complete in French. First revision 'Building Vocabulary B'.

Exemple: 1. Au-dessus du piano il y a un portrait.

1 (Above the) piano il y a un portrait.
2 L'automobile est (near the) maison.
3 (On the) bureau il y a beaucoup de lettres.
4 Le miroir est (above the desk).
5 Une petite table est (between the) fenêtres.
6 Il y a des chaises (around the) table.
7 Qu'est-ce qui[1] est (behind the) porte?
8 Qu'est-ce qui est (in front of the) piano?
9 Qu'est-ce qui est (in the) cuisine?
10 M. Davis est (with) M. Picard (in the) salon.

NOTE: 1. Qu'est-ce qui (kɛs ki) = what? (*subject of a verb*)

Exercise No. 14—Questionnaire

1 Qui est assis dans le salon?
2 Qui est assis près de lui?
3 Y a-t-il beaucoup de choses autour de nous?
4 Est-ce que madame Davis chante bien?
5 Qui joue bien du piano?
6 Où est le cahier de musique?
7 Où est le portrait de madame Davis?
8 Qu'est-ce qui est devant une fenêtre?
9 Où est le miroir?
10 Où est le bureau?
11 Qu'est-ce qui est près du bureau?
12 Où y a-t-il des livres?

RÉVISION (REVISION) 1

CHAPITRES 1–5 PREMIÈRE PARTIE

Each Revision Chapter will begin with a summary of the most important words and expressions that have occurred in the chapters revised. Check yourself as follows:

1 Cover up the English words on the bottom of the page with a piece of paper or blotter. Read one French word at a time aloud and give the English meaning. Uncover the English word of the same number in order to check.

2 Cover up the French words. Say aloud, one at a time, the French for each English word. Uncover the French word to check.

3 Write the words you have difficulty in remembering, three or four times.

Révision de mots (Revision of Words)
NOUNS

1 un ami	16 la fille	31 le miroir
2 une amie	17 la jeune fille	32 un oncle
3 le bureau	18 le garçon	33 le papier
4 les bureaux[1]	19 un homme	34 le père
5 la campagne	20 le jour	35 la personne
6 la chaise	21 la lampe	36 la porte
7 la chambre à coucher	22 la langue	37 la rue
8 la chose	23 la leçon	38 la salle à manger
9 le commerçant	24 la lettre	39 la salle de bain
10 le crayon	25 le livre	40 le salon
11 la cuisine	26 la dame, madame	41 la sœur
12 un, une enfant	27 le monsieur, monsieur	42 le stylo
13 la famille	28 les messieurs	43 la tante
14 la femme	29 mademoiselle	44 le voyage
15 la fenêtre	30 la mère	45 la ville

1 friend (m)	16 daughter, girl	31 mirror
2 friend (f)	17 girl	32 uncle
3 office, desk	18 boy, waiter	33 paper
4 offices, desks	19 man	34 father
5 country	20 day, daylight	35 person
6 chair	21 lamp	36 door
7 bedroom	22 language, tongue	37 street
8 thing	23 lesson	38 dining-room
9 businessman, tradesman	24 letter	39 bathroom
10 pencil	25 book	40 living-room
11 kitchen	26 lady, madam, Mrs.	41 sister
12 child (m or f)	27 gentleman, sir, Mr.	42 fountain-pen
13 family	28 gentlemen	43 aunt
14 wife, woman	29 Miss	44 journey
15 window	30 mother	45 city, town

NOTE. When the noun has an irregular plural, the plural is given.

VERBS

1 aller	11 il demeure	22 il va
2 apprendre	12 il désire	23 va-t-il?
3 faire	13 il étudie	24 il y a
4 lire	14 il habite	25 y a-t-il?
5 parler	15 elle joue	26 il faut
6 visiter, rendre visite (à)	16 il parle	27 il est
7 savoir	17 parle-t-il?	28 est-il?
8 il apprend	18 il ne parle pas	29 il n'est pas
9 elle chante	19 il prend	30 ils ont
10 il compte	20 il sait	31 dites-moi
	21 il travaille	

1 to go	11 he lives, dwells	22 he goes
2 to learn	12 he wants	23 does he go?
3 to do, make	13 he studies	24 there is (are)
4 to read	14 he lives, dwells	25 is (are) there?
5 to speak	15 she plays	26 it is necessary
6 to visit, to pay a visit to	16 he speaks	27 he, it is
7 to know (how)	17 does he speak?	28 is he, is it?
8 he learns	18 he does not speak	29 he, it is not
9 she sings	19 he takes	30 they have
10 he intends, he counts, expects	20 he knows	31 tell me
	21 he works	

ADJECTIVES

1 assis	5 grand	9 premier
2 autre	6 intéressant	10 tous
3 bon	7 mauvais	11 assidu
4 divers	8 petit	

1 sitting	5 big, large	9 first
2 other	6 interesting	10 all
3 good	7 bad	11 diligent
4 various	8 little, small	

ADVERBS

1 aujourd'hui	6 ici	11 presque
2 assez (de)	7 là	12 rapidement, vite
3 beaucoup (de)	8 lentement	13 très
4 bien	9 peu (de)	14 toujours
5 assidûment	10 peut-être	

1 today	6 here	11 almost
2 enough	7 there	12 rapidly, quickly
3 much, many	8 slowly	13 very
4 well	9 little, few	14 always
5 diligently	10 perhaps	

PREPOSITIONS

1 à	6 dans	11 entre
2 au-dessus (de)	7 de	12 pour
3 autour (de)	8 derrière	13 près (de)
4 avec	9 devant	14 sous
5 chez	10 en	15 sur

1 to, at, on	6 in, inside	11 between
2 over, above	7 of, from	12 for
3 around	8 behind	13 near
4 with	9 in front of	14 under
5 at the house of	10 in, on	15 on, upon

QUESTION WORDS

1 qui?	4 combien (de)	7 pourquoi?
2 qui est-ce qui?	5 comment?	8 quand
3 qu'est-ce qui?	6 où?	9 qu'est-ce que c'est que ça?

1 who (*subject*)?	4 how much?	7 why?
2 who (*subject*)?	how many?	8 when?
3 what (*subject*)?	5 how?	9 what is that?
	6 where?	

CONJUNCTIONS

1 et	2 ou	3 mais	4 parce que
1 and	2 or	3 but	4 because

FRENCH EXPRESSIONS

1 à demain	9 au printemps
2 à bientôt	10 en Angleterre
3 à tantôt	11 c'est assez
4 au revoir	12 c'est pourquoi
5 bonjour	13 Comment allez-vous?
6 bonsoir	14 par cœur
7 à la campagne	15 s'il vous plaît
8 en ville	16 toute la journée

1 till tomorrow, goodbye	9 in the spring
2 see you soon, goodbye	10 in England
3 so long, goodbye	11 that's enough
4 goodbye	12 that's why
5 Good morning (afternoon)	13 How are you?
6 Good evening (night)	14 by heart
7 in the country	15 please
8 in (to) the city	16 all day

DEUXIÈME PARTIE

Exercise 15 From Group II select the antonym (opposite) for each word in Group I.

I

1 bon	5 sur	9 bonjour
2 oui	6 beaucoup (de)	10 le garçon
3 ici	7 le père	11 la ville
4 petit	8 derrière	12 la femme

II

(a) devant	(e) non	(i) là
(b) la campagne	(f) l'homme	(j) sous
(c) la jeune fille	(g) mauvais	(k) peu (de)
(d) bonsoir	(h) grand	(l) la mère

Exercise 16   Complete the following sentences in French:

1 M. Davis travaille (all day).	7 How are you?
2 Dites-moi (please).	8 (Where) **demeure-t-il?**
3 Il est (perhaps) **au bureau.**	9 What is this?
4 (Good evening) **monsieur.**	10 (Who) **est commerçant?**
5 M. Davis va (to the city).	11 (What) **est au mur?**
6 (That is why) **il étudie le français.**	12 (When) **va-t-il en ville?**

Exercise 17   Select the group of words in Column II which best completes each sentence begun in Column I.

Exemple: **1 (d) Dans la famille Davis il y a six personnes.**

I

1 Dans la famille Davis
2 La maison de M. Davis
3 M. Davis prend le train
4 Il étudie le français
5 Il travaille toute la journée
6 Il sait lire un peu le français
7 Il apprend rapidement
8 Pendant la première leçon
9 Tous les mardis et tous les jeudis
10 La femme de M. Davis chante bien
11 M. Davis va faire un voyage

II

(a) il apprend les salutations et les adieux.
(b) et joue bien du piano.
(c) parce qu'il est très intelligent.
(d) il y a six personnes.
(e) en France et peut-être au Maroc.
(f) est dans les environs de Londres.
(g) mais il ne parle pas le français.
(h) dans son bureau.
(i) pour arriver à son bureau en ville.
(j) les deux messieurs ont rendez-vous.
(k) parce qu'il désire voyager en France.

Exercise 18   Complete these sentences in French:

1 L'auto est (in front of the house).
2 Les chaises sont (around the table).
3 La bibliothèque est (near the door).
4 M. Davis est assis (behind the desk).
5 La lampe est (on the piano).
6 (The boy's books) **sont sur la petite table.**
7 (The girl's mother) **est en ville.**
8 (The children's teacher) **est français.**
9 Le portrait de madame Davis est (on the wall).
10 (To whom) **est l'auto?**

Exercise 19 Translate into French:

1 Who is Mr. Davis?
2 He is an English businessman.
3 Where does he live?
4 He lives in the suburbs of London.
5 Why is he learning French?
6 He wants to make a trip to France.
7 Who is his (son) teacher?
8 His teacher is Mr. Picard.
9 Why does he learn quickly?
10 He learns quickly because he is intelligent.
11 How many children are there in Mr. Davis' family?
12 There are four children.
13 How many rooms are there in Mr. Davis' house?
14 There are five rooms, a bathroom and a kitchen.

Dialogue 1

Read each dialogue silently several times, using the French translation to make certain of the meaning. Practise the French text aloud many times. Follow this procedure with all dialogues.

Où est la rue Scribe?

1 Pardon, monsieur, où est la rue Scribe?	1 Excuse me, where is rue Scribe?
2 Continuez tout droit, mademoiselle.	2 Continue straight ahead, Miss.
3 Est-ce que c'est loin?	3 Is it far?
4 Non, mademoiselle, c'est à trois rues d'ici.	4 No, it's the third street from here.
5 Merci beaucoup, monsieur.	5 Thank you very much.
6 De rien, mademoiselle.	6 Don't mention it.

Dialogue 2

Où s'arrête l'autobus?

1 S'il vous plaît, monsieur, où s'arrête l'autobus?	1 Please, where does the bus stop?
2 Il s'arrête au coin là-bas, mademoiselle.	2 It stops at the corner over there.
3 Merci beaucoup, monsieur.	3 Thank you so much.
4 Il n'y a pas de quoi.	4 Don't mention it. (You're welcome.)

LECTURE (READING SELECTION)

Exercise No. 20—How to Read the Passages

1 Read the passage silently from beginning to end to get the meaning as a whole.

2 Re-read the passage, looking up any words you may have forgotten, in the French–English vocabulary at the end of this book. There are a few new words in the 'Lectures' of the Revision Chapters and the meaning of these is given in footnotes.

3 Read the passage silently a third time. Then translate it and check your translation with that given in the answers section of the appendix.
4 Follow this procedure in all succeeding 'Lectures'.

Monsieur Davis apprend le français

Monsieur Davis est un commerçant anglais qui importe des objets d'art de France. C'est pourquoi il désire faire un voyage en France au printemps. Il désire parler avec son représentant. Il désire aussi visiter des endroits intéressants en France. Mais il ne sait pas parler français.

Monsieur Davis a un bon professeur. C'est un Français qui habite Londres et qui s'appelle monsieur Picard. Tous les mardis et tous les jeudis le professeur prend le train pour aller chez son élève.[1] Là, les deux messieurs parlent un peu en français. Monsieur Davis est très intelligent et il apprend rapidement. Pendant la première leçon, par exemple, il apprend par cœur les salutations et les adieux. Il sait déjà[2] dire: Bonjour. Comment allez-vous? À bientôt, et à demain. Il sait déjà dire en français le nom de beaucoup de choses qui[3] sont dans son salon, et il sait répondre correctement aux questions: Qu'est-ce que c'est que ça? et où est . . . ? Monsieur Picard est très content des progrès[4] de son élève et il dit: Très bien. C'est assez pour aujourd'hui. À tantôt.

NOTE 1. **chez son élève,** to the home of his pupil
2. **déjà,** already
3. **qui,** which, *relative pronoun*
4. **très . . . progrès,** very satisfied with the progress

CHAPITRE 6 (SIX)

LES VERBES SONT IMPORTANTS, MONSIEUR

1 M. Davis et M. Picard sont assis dans le salon chez M. Davis. M. Picard commence à parler. M. Davis[1] l'écoute avec attention.

2 — Vous savez déjà que le nom des choses et des personnes est important. Mais les verbes sont importants aussi. Il n'est pas possible de former une phrase sans verbes. Il n'est pas possible non plus de causer sans verbes.

3 — Nous allons étudier des verbes d'usage courant. Je vais vous[1] poser des questions. Vous allez répondre[2] aux questions.

4 Si vous ne savez pas la réponse, dites, s'il vous plaît: 'Je ne sais pas.'

5 — Très bien, dit M. Davis. Je vais dire: 'Je ne sais pas,' si je ne sais pas la réponse.

6 — Est-ce que vous êtes commerçant?

7 — Oui, monsieur, je suis commerçant; je suis importateur d'objets d'art et d'autres articles variés de la France et du Maroc.

8 — Et pourquoi est-ce que vous étudiez le français?

9 — J'étudie le français parce que je désire faire un voyage en France pour rendre visite à mon représentant à Paris. Je désire parler en français avec lui. Il ne parle pas anglais.

10 — Comptez-vous visiter d'autres pays?

11 — Je compte visiter aussi le Maroc et peut-être la Corse.

12 — Quand est-ce que vous partez en voyage?

13 — Je pars le 31 (trente et un) mai.

14 — Est-ce que vous allez prendre le bateau ou l'avion?[3]

15 — Je vais prendre l'avion parce que c'est le plus rapide.

16 — Combien coûte le trajet?

17 — Je ne sais pas. Je vais prendre des renseignements demain et je vais retenir ma place.

18 — Excellent, monsieur. Vous apprenez le français rapidement.

19 — Merci. Vous êtes trop aimable.

20 — Pas du tout. C'est la vérité. Eh bien, ça suffit pour aujourd'hui. À bientôt.

21 — A jeudi prochain.

1 Mr. Davis and Mr. Picard are sitting in the living-room in Mr. Davis' house. Mr. Picard begins to speak. Mr. Davis listens to him[1] attentively.

2 You know already that the names of things and of persons are important. But verbs are important too. It is not possible to make a sentence without verbs. It is not possible either to talk without verbs.

3 We are going to study (practise) some verbs of common usage. I am going to ask you[1] some questions. You are going to answer[2] the questions.

4 If you don't know the answer, please say: 'I don't know.'

5 Very good, says Mr. Davis. I am going to say 'I don't know' if I don't know the answer.

6 Are you a businessman?

7 Yes, I am a businessman; I am an importer of art objects and of various other articles from France and from Morocco.

8 And why are you studying French?

9 I am studying French because I want to make a trip to France in order to pay a visit to my agent in Paris. I want to speak with him in French. He does not speak English.

10 Do you expect to visit other countries?

11 I expect to visit Morocco also and perhaps Corsica.

12 When are you leaving on your trip?

13 I am leaving on 31 May.

14 Are you going to travel by boat or by plane?[3]

15 I am going to travel by plane because that is the quickest (way).

16 How much does the passage cost?

17 I don't know. I am going to get information tomorrow and I'll make a reservation. (*Lit.* I'm going to reserve my seat.)

18 Excellent. You are learning French rapidly.

19 Thank you. You are too kind.

20 Not at all. It is the truth. Well, that's enough for today. Goodbye. (*Lit.* Until soon.)

21 Till next Thursday.

NOTE 1. le(l') *him*, *it*; and vous *you*, are object pronouns. Object pronouns usually precede the verb.

2. *Lit.* to answer *to the* questions.

3. prendre l'avion, le bateau, *Lit.* to take the plane, the boat: to travel by plane, by boat.

Pronunciation and Spelling Aids

Practise Aloud:

1 attention (a-tã-sjɔ̃)
2 nous allons étudier (nu za-lɔ̃ ze-ty-dje)
3 je ne sais pas (ʒən sɛ pɑ)
4 vous êtes (vu zɛt)
5 je suis importateur (ʒə sɥi zɛ̃-pɔr-ta-tœːr)
6 d'autres articles (doːtr zar-tikl)
7 c'est le plus vite (sɛl ply vit)

Building Vocabulary

A. Quelques pays d'Europe (kɛl-kə pe-i dø-rop) et quelques pays de la Communauté Européenne Some Countries of Europe and some Countries of the European Community.

1 l'Angleterre (lã-glə-tɛːr), England
2 la Belgique (bɛl-ʒik), Belgium
3 l'Allemagne (lal-maɲ), Germany
4 la France (frãs), France
5 l'Espagne (lɛs-paɲ), Spain
6 l'Italie (li-ta-li), Italy
7 la Suisse (sɥis), Switzerland
8 la Russie (ry-si), Russia

B. Quelques pays du Commonwealth (kɛl-kə pɛ-i dy) Some countries in the Commonwealth.

1 la Grande-Bretagne (la grãːd brə-taɲ), Great Britain
2 l'Australie (lɔs-tra-li), Australia
3 la Malaisie (la ma-lɛ-zi), Malaysia

4 **en Grande-Bretagne** (ã grã:d brə-taɲ), in Great Britain
5 **en Australie** (ã nɔs-tra-li), in Australia
6 **en Malaisie** (ã ma-lɛ-zi), in Malaysia

C. **Les pays de l'Amérique du Nord** (la-me-rik dy nɔːr) The Countries of North America.

1 **Les États-Unis** (le ze-ta-zy-ni), the United States
2 **le Mexique** (mɛk-sik), Mexico
3 **le Canada** (ka-na-da), Canada
4 **aux États-Unis** (o ze-ta-zy-ni), in or to the United States
5 **au Mexique**, in or to Mexico
6 **au Canada**, in or to Canada

Locutions françaises

1 **pas . . . non plus** (nɔ̃ ply), not . . . either
2 **d'usage courant** (dy-zaʒ ku-rã), of common usage
3 **poser des questions**, to ask questions
4 **rendre visite (à)**, to pay a visit to
5 **en bateau** (ã ba-to), by boat
6 **en avion** (ã na-vjɔ̃), by aeroplane
7 **prendre des renseignements** (prãdr dɛ rã-sɛ-ɲə-mã), to get information
8 **retenir une place** (rət-nir), to reserve a seat
9 **pas du tout** (pa dy tu), not at all
10 **ça** (*or* **cela**) **suffit**, that's enough

Exercise No. 21—Completion of Text

1 **Les verbes** (are important), **monsieur.**
2 **Nous allons étudier** (some verbs).
3 (Why) **étudiez-vous le français?**
4 (Because) **je désire rendre visite à mon représentant.**
5 **Je désire parler** (with him).
6 **Je compte visiter** (other countries).
7 **Allez-vous prendre** (the boat or the plane)?
8 (How much) **coûte le trajet?**
9 **Vous apprenez** (very rapidly).
10 (That's enough for today.)

Grammar Notes

1 About Verb Endings

The infinitive is the base form of the verb. In English it is expressed by *to*. Thus: *to* speak, *to* learn, etc.

The infinitive of all French verbs ends in **-er**, **-ir**, **-re**, or **-oir**. Thus:

parler, to speak   **partir**, to leave   **apprendre**, to learn   **savoir**, to know

That part of the verb which remains after the ending is removed is called the stem. Thus: **parl-**, **part-**, **apprend-** and **sav-** are the stems of **parler**, **partir**, **apprendre** and **savoir**.

Learn the present tense of the verb **parler**, to speak. Note carefully the endings which are added to the stem **parl-**.

2 Present Tense of **parler**, to speak. Regular **-er** Verb.

je parle (parl)	I speak, am speaking	**nous parlons** (par-lɔ̃)	we speak
tu parles (parl)	you speak	**vous parlez** (par-le)	you speak
il parle (parl)	he speaks	**ils parlent** (parl)	they (*m*) speak
elle parle (parl)	she speaks	**elles parlent** (parl)	they (*f*) speak

(*a*) The endings of a regular -er verb in the present tense are:

> Singular **-e, -es, -e**   Plural **-ons, -ez, -ent**

All the endings are silent except **-ons** and **-ez**.

(*b*) The pronoun **vous** (vu), like English *you*, is used both in the singular and plural. It is the polite or usual form of address. Thus:

Parlez-vous français, monsieur?   Do you speak French, sir?
Vous parlez bien, mesdames.   You speak well, ladies.

The pronoun **tu** (ty) is used in addressing a near relative, an intimate friend, a child or an animal. It is the familiar form of address. Thus:

Tu parles trop haut, mon enfant.   You speak too loudly, child.

(*c*) The present tense may be translated in three ways:
I speak, I am speaking, I do speak. You speak, you are speaking, you do speak, etc.

3 The Imperative or Command Forms of parler.

parle, mon enfant, speak, child; **parlons,** let us speak; **parlez, monsieur (messieurs),** speak, sir (gentlemen).

The imperative forms are like the corresponding present tense forms, except that the pronouns **tu, nous** and **vous** are omitted; and the familiar singular is **parle** instead of **parles**.

4 The Interrogative.

As you have already noted there are two ways of forming the interrogative; by placing **Est-ce que?** (*Is it that?*) before the subject of the sentence; or by placing the subject after the verb (inverted form of question). The inverted form is rarely used with **je**.

There is also a third way which is used a great deal in conversation: making a statement but raising the voice at the end of the sentence instead of lowering it:

Tu travailles, mon enfant?

Question with **est-ce que**	*Inverted form of question*	
est-ce que je parle?	———	do I speak, am I speaking?
est-ce que tu parles?	parles-tu?	do you (*fam*) speak?
est-ce qu'il parle?	parle-t-il?	does he speak?
est-ce qu'elle parle?	parle-t-elle?	does she speak?
est-ce que nous parlons?	parlons-nous?	do we speak?
est-ce que vous parlez?	parlez-vous?	do you speak?
est-ce qu'ils parlent?	parlent-ils?	do they (*m*) speak?
est-ce qu'elles parlent?	parlent-elles?	do they (*f*) speak?

Note the two ways of forming a question when there is a noun subject.

Est-ce que M. Davis est commerçant?
M. Davis est-il commerçant? } Is Mr. Davis a businessman?

5 The Negative.

The negative is formed by placing **ne** before the verb and **pas** after the verb.

Il *ne* parle *pas* anglais.   He does not speak English.
Est-ce qu'il *ne* parle *pas* anglais? ⎫
Ne parle-t-il *pas* anglais?   ⎭ Does he not speak English?
Ne parlez *pas* trop haut.   Do not speak too loudly.

6 Regular -er verbs like **parler**.

The vast majority of verbs in French are regular -er verbs like **parler**. You are already familiar with the following:

causer, to chat	je cause, etc.	étudier, to study	j'étudie, etc.
compter, to expect	je compte, etc.	habiter, to live, dwell	j'habite, etc.
commencer, to begin	je commence, etc.	importer, to import	j'importe, etc.
coûter, to cost	il coûte	jouer, to play	je joue, etc.
demeurer, to live, dwell	je demeure, etc.	travailler, to work	je travaille, etc.
désirer, to want	je désire, etc.	visiter, to visit	je visite, etc.
écouter, to listen	j'écoute, etc.		

Exercise No. 22 Complete each of the following verbs with the correct ending

Exemple: j'étudie I study, I am studying

1 j'étudi......   9 nous caus......
2 ils ne parl......pas   10 vous étudi......
3 nous compt......   11 elles habit......
4 elles désir......   12 elle ne visit......pas
5 je travaill......   13 vous commenc......
6 demeur......-vous?   14 import......-t-il?
7 il écout......   15 Qui parl......?
8 il ne coût......pas   16 les enfants jou......

Exercise No. 23 Change the following sentences into the negative:

Exemple: Henri ne joue pas bien du piano.

1 Henri joue bien du piano.   6 Elle désire aller en Europe.
2 Paul étudie le français.   7 Qui étudie l'anglais?
3 Nous parlons espagnol.   8 Nous travaillons toute la journée.
4 Ils écoutent avec attention.   9 Elle compte aller au Maroc.
5 Mes enfants, jouez dans le salon. 10 Vous travaillez assidûment.

Exercise No. 24 Practise aloud the following brief dialogues:

1 — Parlez-vous français, Jean?
  — Oui monsieur, je parle français.
  — Marie parle-t-elle français?
  — Non, monsieur, elle ne parle pas français.
2 — Qui joue du piano?
  — Annette joue du piano.
  — Tu ne joues pas du piano, Rosette?
  — Non, je ne joue pas du piano.

3 — Est-ce que les garçons étudient la leçon?
   — Non, ils n'étudient pas la leçon.
   — Est-ce qu'ils jouent dans la rue?
   — Oui, ils jouent dans la rue.
4 — Qui est le professeur de M. Davis?
   — M. Picard est son professeur.
   — N'est-il pas français?
   — Si,[1] il est français.

NOTE 1. Use si in answer to a negative question instead of **oui.**

Exercise No. 25—Questionnaire

1 Où est-ce que les messieurs sont assis?
2 Qui commence à parler?
3 Qui écoute avec attention?
4 Qui pose les questions?
5 Qui est-ce qui[1] répond aux questions?
6 Est-ce que les verbes sont importants?
7 M. Davis importe-t-il des objets d'art?
8 Parle-t-il français?
9 Pourquoi étudie-t-il le français?
10 Quels pays[2] est-ce qu'il compte visiter?
11 Est-ce qu'il va prendre le bateau ou l'avion?
12 Est-ce que M. Davis apprend rapidement ou lentement?

NOTE 1. qui est-ce qui? *who?* is a longer form of **qui?** *who?*
     2. what countries.

CHAPITRE 7 (SEPT)

LA FAMILLE DE M. DAVIS

1 C'est jeudi, le 12 janvier. Il est 8 (huit) heures du soir.

2 M. Picard sonne à la porte de M. Davis. La bonne ouvre la porte et dit:
— Entrez, monsieur. Passez au salon, s'il vous plaît.

3 Dans le salon, M. Davis attend M. Picard. Quand il arrive, M. Davis dit:
— Bonsoir, monsieur. Comment allez-vous?

4 — Comme ci, comme ça. Et vous? Et la famille?

5 — Quant à moi, ça va très bien, mais ma fille Annette est malade. Elle est enrhumée.

6 — Je le[1] regrette beaucoup. Avez-vous d'autres enfants?

7 — Bien sûr. J'ai quatre enfants, deux garçons et deux filles. Nous sommes six dans notre famille.

8 — Comment vos enfants s'appellent-ils?

9 — Ils s'appellent Philippe, Henri, Rosette et Annette.

10 — Quel âge ont-ils?

11 — Philippe a dix ans. Il est l'aîné. Henri a huit ans. Rosette a six ans. Annette est la plus jeune. Elle a presque cinq ans.

12 Ils vont tous à l'école excepté Annette.

13 Les deux messieurs causent encore un peu. Ensuite M. Davis invite M. Picard à visiter son bureau lundi prochain à midi et demi. M. Picard accepte l'invitation avec plaisir.

14 À neuf heures M. Picard dit: — À tantôt.

15 M. Davis répond: — À lundi, à midi et demi.

1 It is Thursday, 12 January. It is eight o'clock in the evening.

2 Mr. Picard rings the bell (*Lit.* at the door) of Mr. Davis' house. The maid opens the door and says: Come in, sir. Please go into the living-room.

3 In the living-room Mr. Davis is waiting for Mr. Picard. When he arrives Mr. Davis says: Good evening. How are you?

4 So so. And you? And the family?

5 As for me, I'm fine. But my daughter Annie is ill. She has a cold.

6 I'm very sorry.[1] Have you any other children?

7 Yes, indeed. I have four children, two boys and two girls. We are six in our family.

8 What are the names of your children?

9 Their names are Philip, Henry, Rosie and Annie.

10 How old are they?

11 Philip is ten years old. He is the oldest. Henry is eight years old. Rosie is six years old. Annie is the youngest. She is almost five.

12 They all go to school except Annie.

13 The two gentlemen chat a while longer. Then Mr. Davis invites Mr. Picard to visit his office the following Monday at 12.30 p.m. Mr. Picard accepts the invitation with pleasure.

14 At nine o'clock Mr. Picard says: Goodbye.

15 Mr. Davis answers: Till Monday at half-past twelve.

NOTE 1. *Lit*. I regret it very much. le equals *him* or *it*. le is an object pronoun and usually precedes the verb.

Pronunciation and Spelling Aids

A. Practise Aloud:

1 passez au salon (pɑ-se o sa-lɔ̃)
2 quand il arrive (kɑ̃ til a-riv)
3 comme ci, comme ça (kɔm si kɔm sa)
4 elle est enrhumée (ɛl ɛ tɑ̃-ry-me)

5 d'autres enfants (doːtr zɑ̃-fɑ̃)
6 lundi prochain (lœ̃-di prɔ-ʃɛ̃)
7 un aîné (œ̃-nɛ-ne)
8 la plus jeune (la ply ʒœn)

B. Final **d** when linked with the next word is pronounced as **t**. Thus:

quand il (kɑ̃-til)   apprend-il (a-prɑ̃-til)

C. sur = on   sûr = sure   à = to, at, on.   a (as in il a) = has. The accent marks (ˆˋ) are used here to indicate a difference in meaning, *not* in pronunciation.

Building Vocabulary

A. Most French words ending in -tion (sjɔ̃) and sion have corresponding English words ending in *-tion* and *-sion*.

la nation (na-sjɔ̃)	une élection	la situation	une observation
la prononciation	une attention	une obligation	une invitation
la continuation	la direction	une invention	la révolution
une expression	la profession	la concession	une obsession

B. In adverbs the ending -ment (mɑ̃) is equal to the ending *-ly* in English

rapidement, rapidly	certainement, certainly	généralement, generally
assidûment, diligently	probablement, probably	facilement, easily

Locutions françaises

1 comme ci, comme ça, so so
2 quant à moi (kɑ̃ ta mwa), as for me
3 ça va très bien, I'm fine (*Lit*. it goes very well)
4 elle est enrhumée, she has a cold
5 je le regrette beaucoup, I'm sorry (*Lit*. I regret it very much)
6 bien sûr (bjɛ̃ syr), certainly; yes, indeed
7 quel âge avez-vous? how old are you? (*Lit*. what age have you?)
8 j'ai quinze ans, I am fifteen years old (*Lit*. I have fifteen years)
9 comment s'appellent-ils? what are their names? (*Lit*. what do they call themselves?)
10 ils s'appellent ... their names are ... (*Lit*. they call themselves ...)

Exercise No. 26—Completion of Text

1 La bonne (opens) la porte.
2 Elle dit:—(Come in, sir.)
3 (Go) au salon (please).
4 (My daughter) Annette est malade.
5 (Have you) d'autres enfants?
6 Bien sûr. (I have) quatre enfants.
7 (We are) six dans notre famille.
8 Philippe est (the oldest).
9 Il a (ten years).
10 Annette est (the youngest).
11 (They chat) encore un peu.
12 M. Picard (accepts) l'invitation.

Grammar Notes

1. Present Tense of avoir, to have

j'ai (ʒe)	I have	nous avons (nu za-vɔ̃)	we have
tu as (ty a)	you have	vous avez (vu za-ve)	you have
il a (il a)	he has	ils ont (il zɔ̃)	they have
elle a (ɛl a)	she has	elles ont (ɛl zɔ̃)	they have

Interrogative (have I, etc.?)   Negative (I have not, etc.)

ai-je? or

est-ce que j'ai?	avons-nous?	je n'ai pas	nous n'avons pas
as-tu?	avez-vous?	tu n'as pas	vous n'avez pas
a-t-il?	ont-ils?	il n'a pas	ils n'ont pas
a-t-elle?	ont-elles?	elle n'a pas	elles n'ont pas

Negative-Interrogative: n'a-t-il pas? has he not? n'ont-ils pas? have they not?

Exercise No. 27 Complete the following in French with the correct form of avoir.

1 Combien d'enfants (have you)?
2 (I have) six enfants.
3 Combien de filles (has she)?
4 (She has) trois filles.
5 (Do you have) les livres, Henri?
6 (We do not have) les livres.
7 Annette, (have you) le miroir?
8 (I do not have) le miroir.
9 Les jeunes filles (have they) la balle?
10 (They do not have) la balle.
11 Qui (has) quatre enfants?
12 Mme Picard (has) quatre enfants.
13 Quel âge (have) vous?
14 (I have) dix ans.
15 Quel âge (have) -elles?
16 Elles (have) vingt ans.

2. Present Tense of aller, to go

je vais (ʒə vɛ)	I go, am going	nous allons (nu za-lɔ̃)	we go
tu vas (ty va)	you go	vous allez (vu za-le)	you go
il va (il va)	he goes	ils vont (il vɔ̃)	they go
elle va (ɛl va)	she goes	elles vont (ɛl vɔ̃)	they go

Interrogative (do I go, am I going? etc.)   *Negative* (I do not go, am not going, etc.)

vais-je? or

est-ce que je vais?	allons-nous?	je ne vais pas	nous n'allons pas
vas-tu?	allez-vous?	tu ne vas pas	vous n'allez pas
va-t-il?	vont-ils?	il ne va pas	ils ne vont pas
va-t-elle?	vont-elles?	elle ne va pas	elles ne vont pas

Negative-Interrogative: ne va-t-il pas?   does he not go?
                 Ne vont-ils pas?   Do they not go?

NOTE. The verb aller is frequently used to indicate future time.

     Je vais faire un voyage en France. I am going to (I shall) take a trip to France.
     Ils vont apprendre le français. They are going to (will) learn French.

Exercise No. 28 Complete the following in French with the correct form of aller.

1 Où (is he going)?
2 (He is going) à l'hôtel.
3 (Are you going) à la campagne?
4 Non, (we are going) en Europe.

5 Les enfants (do they go) à l'école?
6 Qui (is going) **rendre visite à son représentant?**
7 Où (are you going), **mon enfant?**
8 M. Davis (is going) **faire un voyage en France.**

9 (Are you going) **visiter l'Espagne?**
10 (We are not going) **visiter l'Espagne.**
11 Où (are you going), **mes enfants?**
12 (We are going) **au parc.**
   How are you? (*Lit.* How go you?)
14 I am fine. (*Lit.* It goes well.)

3. Present Tense of **être**, to be

je suis (ʒə sɥi)	I am	nous sommes (nu sɔm)	we are
tu es (ty ɛ)	you are	vous êtes (vu zɛt)	you are
il est (il ɛ)	he is	ils sont (il sɔ̃)	they are
elle est (ɛl ɛ)	she is	elles sont (ɛl sɔ̃)	they are

Interrogative (am I, etc.?)   *Negative* (I am not, etc.)

suis-je? *or*
est-ce que je suis?	sommes-nous?	je ne suis pas	nous ne sommes pas
es-tu?	êtes-vous?	tu n'es pas	vous n'êtes pas
est-il?	sont-ils?	il n'est pas	ils ne sont pas
est-elle?	sont-elles?	elle n'est pas	elles ne sont pas

Negative-Interrogative: **n'est-il pas?** is he not?
                    ne sommes-nous pas? are we not?

Exercise No. 29 Complete the following in French with the correct form of **être**.

1 Qui (is) **dans le bureau?**
2 M. Davis (is) **dans le bureau.**
3 Où (is) **Mme Davis?**
4 Elle (is) **dans le salon.**
5 M. Picard, (is he) **américain?**
6 Non, il (is not) **américain.**
7 (Are you) **français?**
8 Non, (I am) **anglais.**

9 Où (are) **les enfants?**
10 (They are) **dans la rue.**
11 Les messieurs (are they) **assis?**
12 (They are) **assis dans le salon.**
13 (Are you) **commerçants, messieurs?**
14 Non, (we are not) **commerçants.**
15 (We are) **professeurs.**
16 (Is he not) **riche?**

Exercise No. 30—Questionnaire

1 Qui[1] sonne à la porte?
2 Qui est-ce qui ouvre la porte?
3 Où est-ce que M. Davis attend M. Picard?
4 Qui est malade?
5 Est-elle enrhumée?
6 Combien d'enfants M. Davis a-t-il?
7 Combien de personnes y a-t-il dans sa famille?
8 Comment les enfants s'appellent-ils?
9 Quel âge a Philippe?
10 Les enfants vont-ils à l'école?
11 Qui est-ce que (whom) le commerçant invite à visiter son bureau?
12 Est-ce que le professeur accepte l'invitation?

NOTE 1. qui *or* qui est-ce qui? = who? (*subject of verb*)
          qui *or* qui est-ce que? = whom? (*object of verb*)

CHAPITRE 8 (HUIT)

AU BUREAU DE M. DAVIS

1 Le bureau de M. Davis est au dernier étage d'un grand immeuble. Il n'est pas grand mais il est commode. Par deux grandes fenêtres on peut voir en bas Oxford Street. Aux murs gris il y a des affiches illustrées et une grande carte de la France.

2 Sur le bureau de M. Davis il y a beaucoup de papiers. Près de la porte il y a un petit bureau avec une machine à écrire. Entre les deux fenêtres il y a une longue table. Sur la table il y a des journaux, des revues, et un joli cendrier.

3 M. Davis est assis à son bureau quand M. Picard arrive. Il va à la porte pour le[1] saluer.

4 — Bonjour, M. Picard. Je suis très content de vous[1] voir.

5 — Bonjour, M. Davis. Comment allez-vous?

6 — Très bien, merci.

7 — Votre bureau est très beau. J'aime beaucoup cette carte de la France, et ces affiches illustrées. Quelles jolies couleurs! À propos, M. Davis, qu'est-ce que vous voyez sur cette affiche-là?

8 — Je vois le ciel et le soleil, un château blanc sur une colline, avec un toit rouge et beaucoup de cheminées.

9 — De quelle couleur est le soleil?

10 — Il est jaune et il est immense.

11 — De quelles couleurs sont le ciel, les cheminées et la colline?

12 — Le ciel est bleu. Les cheminées sont noires. La colline est verte. Mon Dieu, il est déjà une heure! C'est assez de couleurs! Je commence à avoir faim. Et vous? Vous n'avez pas faim?

13 — Eh bien, moi aussi, j'ai faim.

14 — Bon. Pas loin d'ici il y a un bon restaurant.

15 — Tant mieux! Allons-y![2]

1 The office of Mr. Davis is on the top floor of a big block. It is not large, but it is convenient. Through two large windows one can see Oxford Street below. On the grey walls there are some posters and a large map of France.

2 On the desk of Mr. Davis there are many papers. Near the door there is a small desk with a typewriter. Between the two windows there is a long table. On the table there are some newspapers, magazines and a pretty ash-tray.

3 Mr. Davis is sitting at his desk when Mr. Picard arrives. He goes to the door to greet him.[1]

4 Good afternoon, Mr. Picard. I am very glad to see you.[1]

5 Good afternoon, Mr. Davis. How are you?

6 Very well, thank you.

7 Your office is very beautiful. I like this map of France very much and these illustrated posters. What pretty colours! By the way, Mr. Davis, what do you see on that poster?

8 I see the sky and the sun, a white castle on a hill, with a red roof and many chimney-tops.

9 What colour is the sun?

10 It is yellow and it is huge.

11 What colours are the sky, the chimney-tops and the hill?

12 The sky is blue. The chimney-tops are black. The hill is green. My goodness! It's already one o'clock. That's enough of colours! I'm beginning to be hungry. How about you? Aren't you hungry?

13 Well, I am hungry, too.

14 Good. Not far from here there is a good restaurant.

15 Good! Let's go there!²

NOTE 1. **Le**, *him*, and **vous**, *you*, are object pronouns. Object pronouns usually precede the verb.

2. **y**, *there*. It is used to refer to a place already mentioned; in this case, *to a good restaurant*.

Pronunciation and Spelling Aids

1. Practise Aloud:

1 **deux grandes fenêtres**
(dø grã:d fə-nɛːtr)

2 **des affiches illustrées**
(dɛ za-fiʃ i-lys-tre)

3 **une machine à écrire**
(yn ma-ʃin a e-kriːr)

4 **quelles jolies couleurs**
(kɛl ʒɔ-li ku lœːr)

5 **beaucoup de cheminées**
(bo-kud ʃmi-ne)

6 **pas loin d'ici**
(pɑ lwɛ̃ di-si)

Building Vocabulary

Some Common Adjectives

blanc (blɑ̃), white
noir (nwaːr), black
bleu (blø), blue
gris (gri), grey
jaune (ʒoːn), yellow
rouge (ruːʒ), red
vert (vɛːr), green
bon (bɔ̃), good
mauvais (mɔ-vɛ), bad

beau (bo), beautiful
joli (ʒɔ-li), pretty
grand (grɑ̃), big
petit (pti), small
long (lɔ̃), long
court (kuːr), short
riche (riʃ), rich
haut (o), high
bas (bɑ), low

pauvre (poːvr), poor
facile (fa-sil), easy
jeune (ʒœn), young
vieux (vjø), old
difficile (di-fi-sil), difficult
malade (ma-lad), sick
important (ɛ̃ pɔr-tɑ̃), important
intéressant (ɛ̃-te-rɛ-sɑ̃), interesting
assis (a-si), seated

Locutions françaises

1 **on peut voir** (ɔ̃ pø vwaːr), one can see

2 **à propos** (a prɔ-po), by the way

3 **j'aime bien** (ʒɛm bjɛ̃), I quite like; **j'aime beaucoup**, I like very much

4 **de quelle couleur** (də kɛl ku-lœːr), (of) what colour

5 **il est une heure** (il ɛ ty-nœːr), it is one o'clock

6 **tant mieux** (tɑ̃ mjø), good; so much the better

7 **avoir faim** (a-vwaːr fɛ̃), to be hungry (*Lit.* to have hunger)

8 **j'ai faim** (ʒe fɛ̃), I am hungry (*Lit.* I have hunger)

9 **mon Dieu!** (mɔ̃ djø), goodness!

10 **moi aussi** (mwa o-si), I too

Exercise No. 31—Completion of Text

1 Il y a deux (large) fenêtres.
2 (One can) voir la rue.
3 Sur la table il y a des (newspapers).
4 M. Davis (is sitting) à son bureau.
5 Je suis content (to see you).
6 (I like) cette carte.
7 (I see) un château blanc.
8 (What colour) est le ciel?
9 Le ciel est (blue).
10 (Goodness!) Il est une heure.
11 (Not far from here) il y a un restaurant.
12 (Good! Let's go there.)

Grammar Notes

1 Agreement of Adjectives

Adjectives have masculine, feminine and plural forms, and agree in number and gender with the nouns they accompany. Study the following examples, which illustrate this agreement, noting especially the feminine and plural forms of adjectives.

le père intelligent	le crayon noir	le stylo bleu
la mère intelligente	la table noire	la carte bleue
les pères intelligents	les crayons noirs	les stylos bleus
les mères intelligentes	les tables noires	les cartes bleues
un exemple facile	l'homme riche	le mur gris
une question facile	la femme riche	la carte grise
les exemples faciles	les hommes riches	les murs gris
les questions faciles	les femmes riches	les cartes grises

(a) To make an adjective feminine, add a silent e to the masculine, unless the masculine already ends in e (riche, facile, rouge, jaune).

(b) To make an adjective plural, add -s to the singular, unless the singular adjective already ends in -s (gris, assis).

2 Position of Adjectives

In general, adjectives come *after their nouns*. However, here are some common adjectives which usually precede the noun:

bon, good	grand, big, tall	jeune, young	long, long
meilleur, better	petit, small	vieux, old	haut, high, loud
mauvais, bad	beau, beautiful	joli, pretty	gros, big, thick

un bon livre	le mauvais garçon	les hautes collines
une jolie femme	la grande station	les petites jeunes filles

Exercise No. 32 Complete in French with the correct form of the adjective. If the adjective is used after some form of the verb être, to be, the adjective must agree with the subject of the sentence.

Exemple 1: Madame Davis est assise dans le salon.

1 Mme Davis est (sitting) dans le salon.
2 Les (little) enfants jouent dans le parc.
3 Mme Davis est une femme (intelligent).
4 J'aime bien les (pretty) couleurs.

5 **M. Davis a un bureau** (convenient).
6 **Le château est situé sur une** (high) **colline.**
7 **Les murs du bureau sont** (grey).
8 **Tous les élèves sont** (diligent).
9 **Avez-vous un** (good) **stylo?**
10 **Annette et Rosette sont très** (pretty).
11 **Il y a beaucoup de** (big) **parcs à Paris.**
12 **Où sont les affiches** (illustrated)?
13 **Il y a une** (large) **carte au mur.**
14 **Le ciel est-il** (red) **ou** (blue)?
15 **Les cheminées sont-elles** (black)?
16 **Son grand-père est très** (old).

NOTE. Some plural nouns may include both masculine and feminine persons (**les élèves**, pupils; **les étudiants**, students; **les enfants**, children). In that case the agreeing adjective is in the masculine plural.

3. Some Irregular Adjectives. Note particularly the feminine forms.

(a) le bon livre   le long crayon   le beau bureau   le papier blanc
    la *bonne* fille   la *longue* table   la *belle* maison   la chaise *blanche*
    les bons livres   les longs crayons   les beaux bureaux   les papiers blancs
    les *bonnes* filles   les *longues* tables   les *belles* maisons   les chaises *blanches*

(b) Note carefully the forms and meanings of the adjective **tout**, and of the question adjective **quel**.

tout le livre, the whole book   **quel frère?** which, what brother?
toute la salle, the whole room   **quelle sœur?** which, what sister?
tous les livres, all the books   **quels frères?** which, what brothers?
toutes les salles, all the rooms   **quelles sœurs?** which, what sisters?

Exercise No. 33 Complete in French with the correct form of the adjective.

Exemple 1: Madame Picard est une belle femme.

1 **Madame Picard est une** (beautiful) **femme.**
2 **Marie est une** (good) **fille.**
3 **Les filles de M. Davis sont très** (beautiful).
4 **Elles ont beaucoup de** (good) **amies.**
5 **Voyez-vous les maisons** (white)?
6 **Où est la** (long) **table?**
7 (Which) **homme parle français?**
8 (What) **jolies jeunes filles!**
9 **De** (what) **couleur est la colline?**
10 (Which) **cendriers avez-vous?**
11 **M. Davis travaille** (all) **la journée.**
12 **Où sont** (all) **les journaux?**

Exercise No. 34 Translate into French.

1 Mr. Davis' office is very convenient.
2 The windows of the office are large.
3 There are some illustrated posters on the walls.

4 There are some French newspapers on the table.
5 The sky on the poster is blue.
6 The sun is yellow.
7 How are you, Mr. Davis?
8 Very well, thank you.
9 I am hungry.
10 I'm also hungry.

Exercise No. 35—Questionnaire

1 Où est le bureau de M. Davis?
2 Est-ce que[1] le bureau est grand?
3 Est-ce qu'il est commode?
4 Où est-ce qu'il y a des affiches illustrées?
5 Où est-ce qu'il y a beaucoup de papiers?
6 Où est-ce qu'il y a un petit bureau?
7 Où est-ce qu'il y a une longue table?
8 Qui est assis?
9 De quelle couleur est le soleil sur l'affiche?
10 De quelle couleur sont les cheminées?
11 De quelle couleur est la colline?
12 Est-ce que le ciel est bleu?
13 De quelle couleur est le château?
14 Est-ce que le toit est rouge ou jaune?
15 Est-ce que M. Davis a faim?

NOTE 1. Remember: In any question with **est-ce que** the word order is *subject—verb*.

CHAPITRE 9 (NEUF)

M. DAVIS SALUE UN AMI À SON BUREAU

1 M. Dupont, un ami de M. Davis, demeure à Londres. Cependant il parle bien le français parce que ses parents sont canadiens. C'est un homme de trente-cinq ans.

2 Il sait que son ami M. Davis apprend le français. Il désire voir si son ami fait des progrès dans ses études. Donc, il entre un jour dans le bureau de M. Davis et le salue en français. Voici leur conversation:

3 — Comment ça va?

4 — Très bien merci. Et vous?

5 — Comme ci, comme ça. À propos, vous apprenez le français, n'est-ce pas?

6 — Bien sûr. J'apprends à[1] parler, à lire et à écrire le français.

7 — Est-ce que le français est difficile à apprendre?

8 — Eh bien, non. Le français n'est pas trop difficile à apprendre. J'aime beaucoup la langue française et je l'étudie[2] assidûment.

9 — Qui est votre professeur de français?

10 — M. Picard. C'est un très bon professeur, et de jour en jour je parle, je lis et j'écris le français de mieux en mieux. J'apprends les mots et les expressions de la vie quotidienne. Je comprends M. Picard quand il parle français, et il me comprend quand je le[2] parle. Le français me plaît beaucoup.

11 — Mon ami, vous parlez français à merveille.

12 — Merci. Vous êtes trop aimable.

13 — Pas du tout. C'est la vérité. Mes amis me disent que vous allez faire un voyage en France cet été. C'est vrai?

14 — Oui. J'espère partir au printemps, le 31 mai. Je vais prendre l'avion. Je désire arriver en France le plus tôt possible.

15 — Bon voyage! Et bonne chance! Au revoir, mon vieux.

16 — À tantôt.

1 Mr. Dupont, a friend of Mr. Davis, lives in London. However, he speaks French well because his parents are Canadian. He is a man of thirty-five.

2 He knows that his friend Mr. Davis is learning French. He wants to see if his friend is making progress in his studies. Therefore he enters the office of Mr. Davis one day and greets him in French. Here is their conversation:

3 How are you? (*Lit.* How goes it?)

4 Very well thank you. And you?

5 So so. By the way, you are learning French, aren't you?

6 Yes, indeed. I am learning to[1] speak, read and write French.

7 Is French difficult to learn?

8 Well, no. French is not too difficult to learn. I like the French language very much and I study it[2] diligently.

9 Who is your French teacher?

10 Mr. Picard. He is a very good teacher, and day by day I speak, read and

47

write better and better. I learn the words and expressions of daily life. I understand Mr. Picard when he speaks French, and he understands me when I speak it. I like French very much.

11 My friend, you speak French wonderfully.

12 Thanks. You are too kind.

13 Not at all. It is the truth. My friends tell me that you are going to make a trip to France this summer. Is that true?

14 Yes. I hope to go in the spring, on May 31. I am going to travel by plane. I want to arrive in France as soon as possible.

15 Have a good trip. And good luck! Goodbye, old chap.

16 Goodbye.

NOTE 1. The *to* of infinitives (*to* read, *to* write, etc.) is often not translated in the French. However, after some verbs, including **apprendre,** to learn, **enseigner,** to teach, **commencer,** to begin, the *to* is translated by **à**.

Sometimes *to* is translated by **de. Il est content de le faire.** He is glad *to do* it.

2. **le (l'),** *him, it* **la (l'),** *her, it,* and **me,** *me,* are object pronouns. Object pronouns usually precede the verb.

Pronunciation and Spelling Aids

Practise Aloud:

1 **cependant il parle bien le français** (sə-pã-dã il parl bjɛ̃ lə frã-sɛ)

2 **ses parents sont canadiens** (sɛ pa-rã sɔ̃ ka-na-djɛ̃)

3 **Dupont** (dy-pɔ̃)

4 **donc** (dɔ̃:k)

5 **c'est un très bon professeur** (sɛ tœ̃ trɛ bɔ̃ prɔ-fɛ-sœːr)

6 **je prends** (prã), **ils prennent** (prɛn)

Building Vocabulary

Antonyms

1 **apprendre,** to learn; **enseigner,** to teach

2 **partir,** to leave; **arriver,** to arrive

3 **beaucoup de choses,** many things; **peu de choses,** few things

4 **poser une question,** to ask a question; **répondre à une question,** to answer a question

5 **loin d'ici,** far from here; **près d'ici,** near here

6 **le professeur,** the teacher, the professor; **l'étudiant,** the student

7 **le maître, la maîtresse,** the teacher; **l'élève,** the pupil

8 **il est assis,** he is sitting; **il est debout,** he is standing

9 **voici,** here is (are); **voilà,** there is (are)

Locutions françaises

1 **faire des progrès** (fɛːr dɛ prɔ-grɛ), to make progress, to progress

2 **voici** (vwa-si), here is, are

3 **n'est-ce pas** (nɛs pɑ), is it not so? Translated in various ways: isn't he, she, it? aren't you? don't you? etc.

4 **de jour en jour** (də ʒur ã ʒur), day by day

5 **de mieux en mieux** (də mjø zã mjø), better and better
6 **à merveille** (a mɛr-vej), wonderfully
7 **pas du tout** (pɑ dy **tu**), not at all
8 **le plus tôt possible** (lə ply to pɔ-**sibl**), as soon as possible
9 **bon voyage** (bõ vwa-jaː**ӡ**), happy journey
10 **bonne chance** (bɔn **ʃãːs**), good luck
11 **mon vieux** (mõ **vjø**), old chap

Exercise No. 36—Completion of Text

1 (His parents) **sont canadiens.**
2 (His friend) **fait des progrès.**
3 (Here is) **leur conversation.**
4 **Vous apprenez le français** (aren't you)?
5 (I am learning) **à parler français.**
6 **Le français** (is not too difficult) **à apprendre.**
7 (I am studying it) **assidûment.**
8 (I like French) (*Lit.* French pleases me) **beaucoup.**
9 **Vous parlez français** (wonderfully well).
10 I understand Mr. Picard.
11 (You are) **trop aimable.**
12 (Not at all.) **C'est** (the truth).

Grammar Notes

1 Present Tense of **vendre**, to sell. Regular **-re** Verb.

je vends (vã) I sell, am selling, etc. **nous vendons** (vã-dõ) we sell, are selling, etc.
tu vends (vã)   **vous vendez** (vã-**de**)
il, elle vend (vã)   **ils, elles vendent** (vãd)

Imperative: **vends**, sell; **vendons**, let us sell; **vendez**, sell.

The endings of regular **-re** verbs are:

singular **-s, -s, —**   plural **-ons, -ez, -ent**

Other regular **-re** verbs are:

attendre, to wait for, **j'attends**, etc.
entendre, to hear, **j'entends**, etc.
descendre, to go down, **je descends**, etc.
perdre, to lose, **je perds**, etc.
rendre, to give back, **je rends**, etc.
répondre, to answer, **je réponds**, etc.

2 Present Tense of **prendre**, to take, **lire**, to read, **écrire**, to write (Irregular **-re** Verbs).

I take, I am taking, etc.   I read, I am reading, etc.

je prends	**nous prenons**	**je lis**	**nous lisons**
tu prends	**vous prenez**	**tu lis**	**vous lisez**
il prend	**ils prennent**	**il lit**	**ils lisent**
elle prend	**elles prennent**	**elle lit**	**elles lisent**

I write, I am writing, you write, you are writing, etc.

j'écris	**nous écrivons**
tu écris	**vous écrivez**
il écrit	**ils écrivent**
elle écrit	**elles écrivent**

Imperative: **prends,** take; **prenons,** let us take; **prenez,** take.

Imperative: **lis,** read; **lisons,** let us read; **lisez,** read.

Imperative: **écris,** write; **écrivons,** let us write; **écrivez,** write.

Other verbs like **prendre** are:

> **apprendre,** to learn, **j'apprends, nous apprenons, ils apprennent**
> **comprendre,** to understand, **je comprends, nous comprenons, ils comprennent**

The most common irregular verbs will appear gradually in the conversation texts and Grammar Notes. You will learn them as you meet them. A summary of common irregular verbs can be found in the Appendix.

Exercise No. 37 Translate these short dialogues. Then practise them aloud. They will help you to get a 'feeling' for the correct use of the verbs.

1 — **Apprenez-vous le français?**
— **Oui monsieur, j'apprends le français.**
— **Est-ce que Charles apprend le français?**
— **Non, il n'apprend pas le français.**
2 — **Écrivez-vous une lettre?**
— **Je n'écris pas de¹ lettre.**
— **Qu'est-ce que vous écrivez?**
— **J'écris la leçon de français.**
3 — **Que lisez-vous?**
— **Je lis un journal français.**
— **Qu'est-ce qu'Anne lit?**
— **Elle lit une revue française.**
4 — **Comprenez-vous votre professeur quand il parle vite?**
— **Non madame, mais nous le comprenons bien quand il parle lentement.**
5 — **Qu'est-ce que M. Davis vend?**
  Il vend des objets d'art.
— **Vend-il en gros (wholesale) ou au détail (retail)?**
— **Il vend seulement (only) en gros.**
6 — **Qui est-ce que M. Davis attend?**
  Il attend M. Picard.
— **Où est-ce qu'il l'attend?**
  Il l'attend dans le salon.

NOTE 1. **Pas** is usually followed by **de** rather than by **un** or **une.**

Exercise No. 38 Complete these sentences in French with the correct form of the verb indicated.

Exemple: Nous vendons notre auto.

1 (We are selling) **notre auto.**
2 (We are learning) **à parler français.**
3 (I understand) **le professeur.**
4 (They read) **les journaux français.**
5 (Are you writing) **les exercices?**
6 **Que** (are you reading)?
7 (I take) **le train en ville.**
8 (They are not taking) **le train.**
9 (We answer) **à toutes les questions.**
10 **Qui** (is learning) **l'espagnol?**
11 (Is he reading) **la revue?**
12 (They do not understand) **la leçon.**
13 **Mais** (we do not write) **bien le français.**
14 (Let us write) **les lettres.**
15 **Que** (do they sell)?
16 (Read) **cette lettre, s'il vous plaît.**
17 (We are waiting for) **nos amis.**
18 (Do you hear) **le maître?**

Exercice No. 39—Questionnaire

1 Qui demeure à Londres?
2 Est-ce que M. Dupont parle bien le français?
3 Est-ce que ses parents sont américains?
4 Qu'est-ce que M. Dupont sait?
5 Où est-ce qu'il entre un jour?
6 Qui est-ce que (whom) M. Dupont salue en français?
7 Qui apprend à parler, à lire et à écrire le français?
8 Comment M. Davis étudie-t-il?
9 Qui est son professeur de français?
10 Est-ce un bon professeur?
11 Est-ce que M. Davis comprend quand M. Picard parle français?
12 Quels mots et quelles expressions M. Davis apprend-il?
13 Qui va faire un voyage en France?
14 Quand est-ce qu'il espère partir?
15 Qui dit: 'Bon voyage et bonne chance'?

RÉVISION 2

CHAPITRES 6–9 PREMIÈRE PARTIE

Révision de mots (Revision of words)

NOUNS

1 un an	11 la couleur	21 le nom
2 un avion	12 un, une élève	22 la revue
3 le bateau	13 un endroit	23 le plaisir
4 les bateaux	14 les environs (*m*)	24 le soleil
5 la bonne	15 un étage	25 le printemps
6 la carte	16 un été	26 le toit
7 le cendrier	17 un étudiant	27 le travail
8 le château	18 le journal	28 le trajet
9 les châteaux	19 les journaux	29 la vie
10 le ciel	20 le mot	30 la vérité
1 year	11 colour	21 name
2 aeroplane	12 pupil	22 magazine
3 boat	13 place	23 pleasure
4 boats	14 outskirts	24 sun
5 maid	15 storey, floor	25 spring
6 map	16 summer	26 roof
7 ash-tray	17 student	27 work
8 castle	18 newspaper	28 passage, journey
9 castles	19 newspapers	29 life
10 sky	20 word	30 truth

VERBS

1 aimer	11 écouter	22 travailler
2 s'appeler	12 entrer (dans)	23 voyager
3 il s'appelle	13 espérer	24 répondre
4 causer	14 étudier	25 vendre
5 commencer	15 habiter	26 dire
6 coûter	16 jouer	27 écrire
7 chanter	17 poser une question	28 voir
8 demeurer	18 prendre,	29 partir
9 demander	prendre l'avion etc.	30 je sais
10 désirer	19 regretter	31 je ne sais pas
	20 saluer	32 je vais dire
	21 sonner	
1 to like, love	11 to listen	22 to work
2 to be called	12 to enter	23 to travel
3 his name is	13 to hope	24 to answer
4 to chat, talk	14 to study	25 to sell
5 to begin	15 to inhabit, to live	26 to say
6 to cost	16 to play	27 to write
7 to sing	17 to ask a question	28 to see
8 to live, dwell	18 to take, to travel	29 to leave, go away,
9 to ask	by plane etc.	depart

10 to want	19 to regret	30 I know
	20 to greet	31 I don't know
	21 to ring	32 I'm going to say

ADJECTIVES

1 blanc	11 bonne (*f*)	21 prochain
2 blanche (*f*)	12 commode	22 riche
3 bleu	13 difficile	23 quel homme
4 gris	14 facile	24 quelle femme
5 jaune	15 joli	25 quels garçons
6 rouge	16 jeune	26 quelles filles (*f*)
7 vert	17 long	27 tout le mur
8 beau (*bel*)	18 longue (*f*)	28 toute la cuisine
9 belle (*f*)	19 malade	29 tous les journaux
10 bon	20 pauvre	30 toutes les revues

1 white	11 good (*f*)	21 next
2 white (*f*)	12 convenient	22 rich
3 blue	13 difficult	23 which man
4 grey	14 easy	24 which woman
5 yellow	15 pretty	25 which boys
6 red	16 young	26 which girls
7 green	17 long	27 the whole wall
8 beautiful	18 long (*f*)	28 the whole kitchen
9 beautiful (*f*)	19 sick	29 all the newspapers
10 good	20 poor	30 all the magazines

NOTE 1. If adjectives are irregular, the masculine and feminine forms are given.
NOTE 2. **bel** is used only before a masculine noun beginning with a vowel or **h** (usually).
  un beau portrait   un bel ami   un bel hôtel   une belle amie

ADVERBS

1 déjà	3 trop	5 vite
2 ensuite	4 demain	6 le plus vite
1 already	3 too much, too	5 quickly
2 then	4 tomorrow	6 most quickly

PREPOSITIONS

1 après	2 par	3 pour	4 loin (de)
1 after	2 by, through	3 for, in order to	4 far from

CONJUNCTIONS

1 cependant	2 donc	3 si	4 que
1 however	2 therefore	3 if, whether	4 that

FRENCH EXPRESSIONS

1 à propos	14 moi aussi
2 à merveille	15 pas du tout
3 bien sûr	16 demander des renseignements
4 bon voyage	17 poser des questions
5 bonne chance	18 répondre aux questions
6 comme ci, comme ça	19 partir en voyage
7 eh bien	20 le plus tôt possible
8 mon Dieu!	21 quant à moi

9 de quelle couleur est?	22 elle est enrhumée
10 de jour en jour	23 voici
11 de mieux en mieux	24 j'ai faim
12 tant mieux	25 quel âge avez-vous?
13 en avion	26 n'est-ce pas?

1 by the way	14 I also
2 wonderfully	15 not at all
3 certainly	16 to ask for information
4 happy journey	17 to ask questions
5 good luck	18 to answer questions
6 so so	19 to leave on a trip, go on a journey
7 well	20 as soon as possible
8 goodness! (Lit. my God!)	21 as for me
9 what colour is?	22 she has a cold
10 day by day	23 here is (are)
11 better and better	24 I am hungry
12 so much the better	25 how old are you?
13 by plane	26 is it not so; isn't it? etc.

Exercise No. 40 Select the words in Column II which best complete each sentence begun in Column I.

Exemple: 1c: Je suis importateur d'objets d'art de la France et du Maroc.

I	**II**
1 Je suis importateur d'objets d'art	(a) dites: Je ne sais pas.
2 Je ne comprends pas bien	(b) nous allons faire des progrès de jour en jour.
3 Si vous ne savez pas la réponse	
4 M. Picard dit: Je le regrette beaucoup	(c) de la France et du Maroc.
	(d) pas loin d'ici.
5 Ils prennent l'avion parce que	(e) quand le professeur parle vite.
6 Si nous étudions assidûment	(f) du trajet.
7 Quand j'ai faim	(g) parce que l'enfant est enrhumée.
8 Il y a un bon restaurant	(h) Comment ça va?
9 Son ami salue M. Davis et dit:	(i) c'est le plus rapide.
10 Je ne sais pas le prix	(j) je vais au restaurant.

Exercise No. 41 Answer each of the following questions in complete sentences, using the suggested words in the answer. Make the adjectives agree with their nouns in number and gender.

Exemple: De quelle couleur sont les toits? (blanc) Ils sont blancs.

1 Quelle langue parlez-vous? (français)
2 Où demeurent-ils? (en Angleterre)
3 Qui a faim? (Nous)
4 De quelles couleurs est la revue? (blanc et noir)
5 De quelle couleur sont les maisons? (rouge)
6 Quel âge avez-vous? (quinze ans)
7 Qui pose des questions? (les professeurs)
8 Qui répond aux questions? (nous)
9 Qui est-ce que M. Davis attend? (son ami)
10 Qu'est-ce que vous écrivez? (des lettres)

Exercise No. 42 Complete each verb with the correct ending:

1 nous travaill......	7 il étudi......
2 elles apprenn......	8 vous pren......
3 vous ne sav......pas	9 elles attend......
4 tu écri......	10 vous ne répond......pas
5 ils lis......	11 lis......!
6 je ne comprend......pas	12 n'attend......pas, M. Picard.

Exercise No. 43 Answer each of the following questions in the affirmative and negative singular.

Exemple 1: Oui, monsieur, j'ai faim. Non, madame, je n'ai pas faim.

1 Avez-vous faim?	7 Lisez-vous la revue?
2 Êtes-vous enrhumé?	8 Écrivez-vous la lettre?
3 Étudiez-vous la leçon?	9 Comprenez-vous les questions?
4 Attendez-vous le professeur?	10 Acceptez-vous l'invitation?
5 Comptez-vous voyager en France?	11 Commencez-vous à lire?
6 Apprenez-vous à écrire le français?	12 Répondez-vous à la question?

Exercise No. 44 You have met the following interrogative pronouns:

1 qui *or* qui est-ce qui?	3 qu'est-ce qui?
who? (*subject of verb*)	what? (*subject of verb*)
2 qui *or* qui est-ce que?	4 que *or* qu'est-ce que?
whom? (*object of verb or with a preposition*)	what (*object of verb*)

Supply the correct question pronouns in the French sentences which follow. Remember: **que** becomes **qu'** if the next word begins with a vowel or **h** (usually).

All question pronouns containing **est-ce que** are followed by the regular word order (*subject—verb*).

1 (Who) sait parler français?
2 (Whom) voyez-vous tous les jours?
3 (Whom) M. Picard voit-il le mardi et le jeudi?
4 Avec (whom) Madame Davis parle-t-elle?
5 À (whom) parlez-vous?
6 (What) M. Davis apprend?
7 (What) apprenez-vous?
8 (Who) va faire un voyage en France?
9 (What) est sur le toit de la maison?
10 (What) lisez-vous?
11 (What) les enfants lisent?
12 (What) est au mur au-dessus du piano?

Dialogue 1

Quel autobus faut-il prendre?[1]

1 Pardon monsieur, quel autobus faut-il prendre pour l'Étoile? (pour le quai Voltaire)? (pour la place Vendôme)?
2 Prenez l'autobus AS[2], etc. Il s'arrête ici-même, au coin.
3 Merci beaucoup, monsieur.
4 De rien, monsieur.

What Bus Do I Take?

1 Excuse me, which bus do I take for the Étoile? (for the Quai Voltaire)? (for the Place Vendôme)?
2 Take the AS bus, etc. It stops just here at the corner.
3 Thank you very much.
4 Don't mention it.
   NOTE 1. *Lit.* What bus is it necessary to take?
        2. ɑ ɛs

Dialogue 2

Quel autobus va à.........?

1 **Pardon monsieur, pouvez-vous me dire quel autobus va à l'Opéra? (au jardin du Luxembourg)? (au Louvre)?**
2 **Je regrette. Je ne suis pas d'ici, monsieur. Je ne sais pas. Mais cet agent au coin va certainement vous le dire.**
3 **Merci beaucoup, monsieur. Je vais lui demander.**

Which Bus Goes to .... ?

1 Excuse me, can you tell me which bus goes to the Opera? (the Luxembourg Gardens)? (the Louvre)?
2 I'm sorry. I am a stranger here. I don't know. But that policeman at the corner will certainly tell you.
3 Thank you very much. I am going to ask him.

Exercise No. 45—Lecture 1

M. Davis sait déjà le nom de tous les objets dans sa maison. Maintenant il commence à étudier les verbes parce qu'il désire apprendre à lire, à écrire et à parler en français. Il désire aussi apprendre les nombres en français. Comme[1] il désire rendre visite à[2] son représentant à Paris qui ne parle pas anglais, il désire apprendre à parler français le plus tôt possible. Donc il lui faut[3] beaucoup de pratique avec des personnes qui parlent bien le français. Heureusement, il a deux amis français qui sont dans les affaires[4] près de son bureau dans Oxford Street.

Un jour M. Davis rend visite à ces messieurs français. Les deux messieurs écoutent avec attention pendant que[5] M. Davis cause avec eux[6] en français. Après dix minutes de conversation, les messieurs posent beaucoup de questions à leur[7] ami, et ils sont très contents de ses[8] progrès.

NOTE 1. **comme,** as.
     2. **rendre visite (à),** to pay a visit (to).
     3. Therefore he needs (*Lit.* it is necessary to him).
     4. **être dans les affaires,** to be in business.
     5. **pendant que,** while.
     6. **eux,** them.
     7. **leur,** their.
     8. **ses,** his.

Exercise No. 46—Lecture 2

Jeudi le vingt-six avril à neuf heures du soir M. Picard arrive chez[1] son élève, M. Davis. Le fils aîné,[2] un garçon, de dix ans, ouvre la porte, et salue le professeur poliment. Ils entrent dans le salon où d'habitude[3] M. Davis attend son professeur.

Mais ce soir il n'est pas là. Mme Davis n'est pas là non plus. M. Picard est très surpris, et il demande au garçon: — Où est ton papa? Le fils répond tristement[4]: — Papa est malade. Il est au lit[5] parce qu'il est très enrhumé.

Le professeur devient[6] triste et dit: — Quel dommage![7] Eh bien, la semaine prochaine nous allons étudier deux heures. A mardi prochain, alors. Au revoir, mon petit. Le garçon répond: — Au revoir, monsieur.

NOTE 1. **chez**, at the house of.
    2. **le fils aîné**, the eldest son.
    3. usually.
    4. sadly.
    5. **au lit**, in bed.
    6. **devenir**, to become; **il devient**, he becomes.
    7. **Quel dommage!** what a pity!

CHAPITRE 10 (DIX)

DANS LA SALLE À MANGER

1 M. Davis et M. Picard sont assis dans la salle à manger chez M. Davis. Sur la table il y a deux tasses et deux soucoupes, des cuillers à thé, des fourchettes, un couteau, un pot au lait, un sucrier, et un plat avec une tarte aux fruits. Les deux messieurs prennent du café avec des gâteaux.

2 M. Davis dit: — Comment trouvez-vous ces tasses et ces soucoupes? —

3 — Je les[1] trouve charmantes, répond M. Picard. Cette tasse blanche ornée de fleurs bleues est de Limoges, n'est-ce pas?

4 — Mais oui. La porcelaine fine de Limoges est célèbre. Il y a plusieurs régions en France connues pour leurs produits céramiques et chaque région a son style individuel.

5 — Et ce petit pot au lait jaune avec des dessins verts, d'où est-il?

6 — Ce pot au lait est de Vallauris, en Provence. C'est une ville célèbre pour sa poterie. La petite ville de Biot, près de Vallauris, est aussi un centre de l'industrie céramique.

7 — Il y a d'autres régions en France connues pour leurs produits céramiques, n'est-ce pas?

8 — Bien sûr. Il y a surtout la Bretagne. La poterie bretonne est très jolie. La poterie de Normandie est presque aussi jolie.

9 — Je vois que vous connaissez bien votre métier, dit M. Picard.

10 — Mais oui, il le faut, dit M. Davis.

11 — C'est vrai, répond M. Picard. En tout cas, je vois ici beaucoup de beaux échantillons de l'industrie céramique française.

12 — Naturellement. Comme vous dites, c'est mon métier. J'ai aussi des échantillons de poterie ordinaire pour la cuisine. Cette poterie est généralement très simple, de couleur unie, tout en marron, comme ce plat-là près de vous.

13 — C'est un plat simple, mais beau, dit M. Picard.

14 — Voulez-vous encore une tasse de café? Un peu de cette tarte aux fruits?

15 — Merci bien. Tout est délicieux.

1 Mr. Davis and Mr. Picard are sitting in the dining-room at Mr. Davis' house. On the table there are two cups and saucers, teaspoons, forks, a knife, a milk jug, a sugar bowl and a plate with a fruit tart. The two gentlemen are having coffee and cakes.

2 Mr. Davis says: How do you like (*Lit.* find) these cups and saucers?

3 I find them[1] charming, answers Mr. Picard. This white cup decorated with blue flowers is from Limoges, isn't it?

4 Yes, indeed. The fine porcelain of Limoges is famous. There are several districts in France known for their ceramic products and each district has its individual style.

5 And this little milk jug, yellow with green designs, where does that come from?

6 This milk jug is from Vallauris, in Provence. It is a town famous for its pottery. The little town of Biot, near Vallauris, is also a centre for the ceramic industry.

7 There are other regions in France known for their ceramic products, aren't there?

8 Certainly. There is above all Brittany. Breton pottery is very lovely. The pottery of Normandy is almost as pretty.

9 I see that you know your trade very well, says Mr. Picard.

10 Yes indeed; it is necessary, says Mr. Davis.

11 That's true, answers Mr. Picard. At any rate, I see here many fine samples of the French ceramic industry.

12 Naturally. As you say, it's my trade. I also have some samples of ordinary pottery for kitchen use. This pottery is usually very simple and all of one colour, all in brown, like this dish near you.

13 It is a simple dish, but it is handsome, says Mr. Picard.

14 Do you want another cup of coffee? A little of this fruit tart?

15 Thanks very much. Everything is delicious.

NOTE 1. **les** *them* is an object pronoun. Object pronouns usually precede the verb.

Pronunciation and Spelling Aids

Practise Aloud:

1 **Limoges** (li-mɔʒ)
2 **Vallauris** (va-lɔ-ris)
3 **la Provence** (prɔ-vãːs)
4 **la Normandie** (nɔr-mã-di)
5 **la Bretagne** (brə-taŋ)
6 **breton** (brə-tɔ̃) **bretonne** (brə-tɔn) (ʃ)
7 **l'industrie céramique** (lɛ̃-dys-tri se-ra-mik)
8 **leurs produits** (lœːr prɔ-dyi)
9 **son style individuel** (sɔ̃ stil ɛ̃-di-vi-dyɛl)
10 **tout est délicieux** (tu-tɛ de-li-sjø)

Building Vocabulary

Dans la salle à manger (sal a mã-ʒe) In the Dining-Room

1 **le plat** (pla), dish
2 **la tasse** (tɑːs), cup
3 **la soucoupe** (su-kup), saucer
4 **le couteau** (ku-to), knife
5 **la fourchette** (fur-ʃɛt), fork
6 **la cuiller** (kɥi-jɛːr), spoon
7 **la cuiller à soupe** (sup), soup spoon
8 **une assiette** (a-sjɛt), a plate
9 **la cuiller à thé** (te), teaspoon
10 **le pot au lait** (pɔ to-lɛ), milk jug
11 **le sucrier** (sy-krie), sugar bowl
12 **le verre** (vɛːr), the glass
13 **manger** (mã-ʒe), to eat; **on mange** (ɔ̃ mãʒ), one eats

Locutions françaises

1 **c'est vrai** (sɛ vrɛ), certainly
2 **comment trouvez-vous?** how do you like (*Lit.* find)?
3 **surtout** (syr-tu), above all, especially
4 **en tout cas** (ã tu kɑ), at any rate
5 **il le faut** (il lə fo), it is necessary
6 **d'ordinaire** (dɔr-di-nɛːr), usually
7 **encore une tasse** (ã-kɔːr yn tɑːs), another, i.e. one more, cup
8 **autre** (otr), another, i.e. a different one

Exercise No. 47—Completion of Text

1 (They are having) **du café avec des gâteaux.**
2 **Comment trouvez-vous** (these cups)?
3 **Cette tasse est ornée de** (blue flowers).
4 **La porcelaine fine de Limoges est** (famous).
5 (Each region) **a son style individuel.**
6 **La poterie bretonne est** (very pretty).
7 **La poterie de Normandie est** (almost as pretty).
8 (You know) **bien votre métier.**
9 — (That's true), **répond M. Picard.**
10 **Je vois** (many) **beaux échantillons.**
11 (As you say), **c'est mon métier.**
12 — (It's a simple dish), **dit M. Picard.**
13 **Voulez-vous** (another cup) **de café?**
14 **Merci bien.** (Everything) **est délicieux.**

Grammar Notes

1 The Verbs **dire,** to say; **voir,** to see

I say, I am saying, etc.   I see, I am seeing, etc.

je dis (di)	**nous disons** (di-zɔ̃)	**je vois** (vwa)	**nous voyons** (vwa-jɔ̃)
tu dis (di)	**vous dites** (diːt)	**tu vois** (vwa)	**vous voyez** (vwa-je)
il dit (di)	**ils disent** (diːz)	**il voit** (vwa)	**ils voient** (vwa)
elle dit (di)	**elles disent** (diːz)	**elle voit** (vwa)	**elles voient** (vwa)

Imperative		*Imperative*	
dis,	say;	**vois,**	see;
disons,	let us say;	**voyons,**	let us see;
dites,	say;	**voyez,**	see.

Exercise No. 48 Practise these questions and answers.

1 **Que dites-vous? Je dis: — Non.**
2 **Que dit-il? Il dit: — Oui.**
3 **Que dit-elle? Elle dit: — C'est vrai.**
4 **Que disent-elles? Elles disent: — Ce n'est pas vrai.**
5 **Dites-moi où vous demeurez. — Je demeure dans cette rue.**
6 **Qu'est-ce que vous voyez au mur? — Je vois une carte de France.**
7 **Voyez-vous le château sur une colline? — Nous le voyons.**
8 **Voit-il son ami Jean le dimanche? Non, il ne le voit pas le dimanche, il le voit le samedi.**

Exercise No. 49 Translate into French.

1 we say
2 I see
3 he does not say
4 he says
5 Does he say?
6 What do you say?
7 What do you see?
8 they see
9 Do you (**tu**) see?
10 I do not see
11 they are saying
12 What are they saying?
13 she does not see
14 let's see
15 tell me.

2 The Demonstrative (Pointing out) Adjective **ce**, this, that.

Study the following sentences. They show the various forms of the demonstrative adjective **ce**.

Ce garçon apprend le français. *This* (*that*) boy is learning French.
Cet article est de la France. *This* (*that*) article is from France.
Cet homme est professeur. *This* (*that*) man is a teacher.
Cette jeune fille est ma sœur. *This* (*that*) girl is my sister.
Ces garçons apprennent le français. *These* (*those*) boys are learning French.
Ces jeunes filles sont mes sœurs. *These* (*those*) girls are my sisters.

(*a*) **ce** (*this*, *that*) is used before masculine singular nouns.
    cet is used instead of **ce** before masculine singular nouns beginning with a vowel or **h** (usually).
    cette (*this*, *that*) is used before feminine singular nouns.
    ces (*these*, *those*) is used before all nouns in the plural.

(*b*) **-ci** (contraction of **ici** *here*) and **-là** *there*, are added to the noun to distinguish between *this* and *that*, and *these* and *those*, if the meaning is not clear without them. Thus:

ce pot-ci, this pot   **cette tasse-ci**, this cup   **ces plats-ci**, those dishes
ce pot-là, that pot   **cette tasse-là**, that cup   **ces plats-là**, those dishes

Exercise No. 50 Complete the following expressions in French.

1 (this) **soir**
2 (these) **couteaux-ci**
3 (that) **portrait-là**
4 (those) **plats-là**
5 (this) **tasse-ci**
6 (that) **étudiant-là**
7 (this) **mot-ci**
8 (that) **fleur-là**
9 (these) **échantillons-ci**
10 (that) **homme-là**
11 (these) **revues-ci**
12 (that) **ami-là**

3 Use of **c'est** *this is, it is*, instead of **il est, elle est**.

(*a*) **c'est** is used before an adjective, when this adjective refers to a thought already expressed in a sentence, and not to a single noun. Thus:

M. Davis étudie le français. C'est vrai. It's (That's) true.

(*b*) **c'est** is used for **il (elle) est** and **ce sont** for **ils (elles) sont**, when a modified noun or a proper noun follows. Thus:

C'est une ville célèbre. It is (this is) a famous town.
Ce sont des portraits de mes enfants. They are portraits of my children.
C'est M. Picard. It's Mr. Picard.

Exercise No. 51 Practise these common **c'est** expressions aloud.

1 **C'est assez.** It's enough.
2 **C'est bon.** It's good.
3 **C'est mal.** It's bad.
4 **C'est bien.** It's (that's) all right.
5 **C'est ça (cela).** That's it. That's right. O.K.
6 **C'est ceci.** This is it.
7 **Ce n'est rien.** It's nothing.
8 **C'est facile.** It's easy.
9 **C'est difficile.** It's hard.
10 **C'est ici.** It's here.
11 **C'est là.** It's there.
12 **C'est près d'ici.** It's near here.
13 **C'est loin d'ici.** It's far from here.
14 **Ce n'est pas loin.** It's not far.

Exercise No. 52—Questions

1 Où M. Picard et M. Davis sont-ils assis?
2 Qu'est-ce qu'ils prennent?
3 Que dit M. Davis?
4 D'où est la tasse blanche?
5 Quelle porcelaine est célèbre?
6 D'où est le petit pot au lait?
7 Pourquoi la ville de Vallauris est-elle célèbre?
8 Où est la ville de Vallauris?
9 Est-ce que la poterie de la Bretagne est jolie?
10 Qui connaît bien son métier?
11 Qu'est-ce que M. Davis a pour la cuisine?
12 La poterie ordinaire, est-elle simple ou ornée?
13 Est-ce que M. Picard accepte encore une tasse de café?
14 Qu'est-ce qu'il dit?

CHAPITRE 11 (ONZE)

LES NOMBRES, TOUJOURS LES NOMBRES

1 — M. Davis, vous savez déjà que le nom des choses et des personnes est important. Vous savez qu'il n'est pas possible de former une phrase sans verbes.

2 — C'est vrai, M. Picard.

3 — Eh bien, monsieur, il y a une catégorie de mots qui est tout aussi importante que les noms et les verbes. En effet, il est difficile d'imaginer notre civilisation moderne sans ces mots. Pouvez-vous deviner à quoi je pense?

4 — Je crois que oui. Vous voulez dire les nombres.

5 — Vous avez raison. Pouvez-vous expliquer comment les nombres sont indispensables à la vie moderne?

6 — Certainement, rien de plus facile. Nous avons besoin des nombres pour le commerce.

7 — Ha, Ha! Le commerçant pense tout de suite au commerce. Cependant, sans argent les nombres ne valent pas grand-chose, n'est-ce pas?

8 — Évidemment. Eh bien, nous avons besoin des nombres pour désigner les dates, l'heure, la température; pour exprimer les quantités et les mesures; pour téléphoner; pour la radio; pour la télévision; pour toutes les sciences, et pour des milliers d'autres choses.

9 — Les nombres, toujours les nombres. Oui, M. Davis, les nombres sont essentiels. Cependant, il est nécessaire non seulement de connaître les nombres mais aussi de savoir les employer correctement et rapidement dans la vie quotidienne.

10 — Vous avez raison. Je vais faire tout mon possible pour les comprendre et les employer correctement.

11 — En attendant, je veux vous dire que vous avancez rapidement dans vos études.

12 — Vous êtes trop aimable M. Picard.

13 — Pas du tout. C'est la vérité. Eh bien, c'est assez pour aujourd'hui. Au revoir.

14 — Au revoir, monsieur. À jeudi prochain.

1 You already know that the names of things and of persons are important. You know that it is not possible to make a sentence without verbs.

2 That's true, Mr. Picard.

3 Well, there is a class of words which is just as important as nouns and verbs. In fact, it is difficult to imagine our modern civilization without these words. Can you guess what I am thinking of?

4 I think so. You mean numbers.

5 You are right. Can you explain how numbers are indispensable to modern life?

6 Certainly. Nothing easier. We need numbers for business.

7 Ha, ha! The businessman thinks immediately of business. However without money, numbers are not worth much, are they?

8 Of course. Well, we need numbers to indicate dates, the time (of the day), the temperature; to express quantities; to telephone; for the radio; for television; for all the sciences, and for thousands of other things.

9 Numbers, always numbers. Yes, Mr. Davis, numbers are essential. However, it is necessary not only to know the numbers but also to know how to use them rapidly and correctly in daily life.

10 You are right. I am going to do all I can to understand and use them correctly.

11 Meanwhile, I want to tell you that you are progressing rapidly in your studies.

12 You are too kind, Mr. Picard.

13 Not at all. It's the truth. Well, enough for today. Goodbye.

14 Goodbye. Till next Thursday.

Pronunciation and Spelling Aids

Practise Aloud. Stress slightly only the key syllables in heavy type.

il y a une **caté**gorie de mots	(il ja yn ka-te-**gɔ**-ri dmo)
qui est tout aussi im**por**tante	(ki ɛ tu to-si ɛ̃-pɔr-**tɑ̃:**t)
que les **noms** et les **verbes**.	(kə lɛ nɔ̃ e lɛ vɛrb)

Building Vocabulary

Related Words

1 **vrai**, true; **la vérité**, the truth
2 **répondre**, to answer; **la réponse**, the answer
3 **étudier**, to study; **une étude**, a study
4 **savoir**, to know; **le savant**, the scientist, scholar
5 **connaître**, to know; **la connaissance**, knowledge
6 **le commerce**, the commerce; **le commerçant**, the businessman
7 **civiliser**, to civilize; **la civilisation**, the civilization
8 **le jour**, the day; **le journal**, the daily newspaper

Locutions françaises

1 **aussi bien que**, as well as
2 **en effet** (ɑ̃ ne-fɛ), in fact
3 **penser (à)**, to think of; **à quoi**[1] **pensez-vous?** of what are you thinking?
4 **je crois que oui**, I think so, **je crois que non**, I think not
5 **vous voulez dire** . . . you mean . . . (*Lit.* you wish to say)
6 **avoir raison**, to be right, (*Lit.* to have right); **vous avez raison**, you are right
7 **avoir besoin (de)** (a-vwa:r bə-zwɛ̃ də), to need (*Lit.* to have need of); **vous avez besoin d'argent**, you need money
8 **tout de suite** (tud sɥit), at once
9 **pas du tout** (pɑ dy **tu**), not at all
10 **rien de plus facile** (rjɛ̃d ply fa-**sil**), nothing easier

   NOTE 1. **quoi?** *what?* (interrogative pronoun) is used after prepositions: **à quoi? de quoi? dans quoi? avec quoi?** etc.

Exercise No. 53—Completion of Test

1 (You know) **déjà le nom des choses.**
2 **Cette catégorie de mots est tout** (as important as) **les noms et les verbes.**

3 **Pouvez-vous deviner** (of what) **je pense?**
4 (I think so.) **Vous** (mean) **les nombres.**
5 (You are right.) **Les nombres** (are indispensable).
6 (We need) **des nombres pour le commerce.**
7 (Without money) **les nombres ne valent pas** (much).
8 (In the meantime), **je veux vous dire que** (you are progressing rapidly) **dans vos études.**
9 (It is) **la vérité.**
10 Till next Thursday.

Grammar Notes

1 Present Tense of the verbs **vouloir**, to wish, want; **pouvoir**, to be able

I wish, want, you wish, want, etc.   I can (am able), you can, etc.

je veux (vø)   **je peux** (pø) or **je puis** (pɥi)
tu veux (vø)   **tu peux** (pø)
il, elle veut (vø)   **il, elle peut** (pø)
nous voulons (vu-lɔ̃)   **nous pouvons** (pu-vɔ̃)
vous voulez (vu-le)   **voux pouvez** (pu-ve)
ils, elles veulent (vœl)   **ils, elles peuvent** (pœv)

Exercise No. 54 Translate into French

1 (I want) **savoir.**   6 (We are not able) **attendre.**
2 (I am able) **deviner.**   7 (They do not want) **travailler.**
3 (Do you want) **manger?**   8 (Are you able) **travailler?**
4 (Can you) **jouer?**   9 (Does he wish) **comprendre?**
5 (We wish) **étudier.**   10 (Is she able) **apprendre?**

2 **Les nombres de 1 (un) à 69 (soixante-neuf)**

1 **un** (œ̃) **une** (yn)	15 **quinze** (kɛ̃:z)	28 **vingt-huit** (vɛ̃t-ɥit)
2 **deux** (dø)	16 **seize** (sɛ:z)	29 **vingt-neuf** (vɛ̃t-nœf)
3 **trois** (trwa)	17 **dix-sept** (di-sɛt)	30 **trente** (trɑ̃:t)
4 **quatre** (katr)	18 **dix-huit** (di-zɥit)	31 **trente et un**
5 **cinq** (sɛ̃k)	19 **dix-neuf** (diz-nœf)	32 **trente-deux**
6 **six** (sis)	20 **vingt** (vɛ̃)	40 **quarante** (ka-rɑ̃:t)
7 **sept** (sɛt)	21 **vingt et un** (vɛ̃-te œ̃)	41 **quarante et un**
8 **huit** (ɥit)	22 **vingt-deux** (vɛ̃t-dø)	50 **cinquante** (sɛ̃-kɑ:t)
9 **neuf** (nœf)	23 **vingt-trois** (vɛ̃t-trwa)	51 **cinquante et un**
10 **dix** (dis)	24 **vingt-quatre** (vɛ̃t-katr)	60 **soixante** (swa-sɑ̃:t)
11 **onze** (ɔ̃:z)	25 **vingt-cinq** (vɛ̃t-sɛ̃k)	61 **soixante et un**
12 **douze** (du:z)	26 **vingt-six** (vɛ̃t-sis)	65 **soixante-cinq**
13 **treize** (trɛ:z)	27 **vingt-sept** (vɛt-sɛt)	69 **soixante-neuf**
14 **quatorze** (ka-tɔrz)		

NOTE: The final consonants of 5, 6, 8, 10 are silent before words beginning with a consonant.

cinq livres (sɛ̃ li:vr)   **dix choses** (di ʃo:z)

Exercise No. 55 Write the numbers in French. Then read each expression aloud saying the numbers in French.

Exemple: 1. (30) trente mots français

(*a*) **30 mots français**   (*e*) **16 maisons blanches**   (*i*) **62 papiers verts**
(*b*) **10 leçons faciles**   (*f*) **38 étudiantes anglaises** (*j*) **68 hommes riches**
(*c*) **50 bonnes phrases**   (*g*) **17 belles filles**   (*k*) **24 grandes villes**
(*d*) **49 affiches françaises** (*h*) **15 longues tables**   (*l*) **13 plumes noires**

Exercise No. 56 Write each arithmetical expression in French. Then read each expression aloud.

Note: $+ = $ **et** $- = $ **moins** $\times = $ **fois** $\div = $ **divisé par** makes $= $ **fait**

Exemples: $4 + 6 = 10$ **quatre et six font dix**

$20 \div 5 = 4$ **vingt divisé par cinq fait quatre**

(*a*) $2 + 6 = 8$ (*c*) $7 \times 8 = 56$ (*e*) $19 - 8 = 11$ (*g*) $60 \div 10 = 6$
(*b*) $10 + 7 = 17$ (*d*) $9 \times 7 = 63$ (*f*) $18 - 6 = 12$ (*h*) $69 \div 3 = 23$

Exercise No. 57 Read each question aloud in French. Answer it aloud in a complete French sentence.

Exemple 1. Il y a sept jours dans une semaine.

1 **Combien de jours y a-t-il dans une semaine?**
2 **Combien de mois y a-t-il dans une année?**
3 **Combien d'heures y a-t-il dans une journée?**
4 **Combien de minutes y a-t-il dans une heure?**
5 **Combien de secondes y a-t-il dans une minute?**
6 **Combien de jours y a-t-il dans le mois de septembre?**
7 **Combien d'étudiants y a-t-il dans la classe? (36 étudiants)**
8 **Quel âge avez-vous? (17 ans)**
9 **Quel âge a Louis? (19 ans)**
10 **Combien d'autos y a-t-il dans le garage? (15 autos)**

Exercise No. 58—Questionnaire

1 **Qu'est-ce que M. Davis sait déjà?**
2 **Quelle catégorie de mots est aussi importante que les noms et les verbes?**
3 **De quoi avons-nous besoin pour le commerce?**
4 **À quoi est-ce que le commerçant pense tout de suite?**
5 **Avons-nous besoin des nombres pour téléphoner?**
6 **Qui veut comprendre et employer les nombres correctement?**
7 **Comment est-ce que M. Davis avance dans ses études?**
8 **Dites à haute voix (aloud) en français les nombres 10, 20, 30, 40, 50, 60.**

CHAPITRE 12 (DOUZE)

LE SYSTÈME MONÉTAIRE DE LA FRANCE

1 — Dans notre dernière conversation nous avons dit qu'il est difficile d'imaginer notre civilisation moderne sans nombres, c'est-à-dire, sans mathématiques. Il est difficile également d'imaginer un voyage sans mathématiques.

2 — Savez-vous combien de fois on fait usage des mathématiques en voyage?

3 — Je crois que oui. On en[1] fait usage pour changer de l'argent, pour acheter des billets, pour payer ses repas et sa note d'hôtel, pour faire peser ses bagages, pour estimer les distances, pour faire des achats dans les grands magasins, dans les boutiques et au marché.

4 — Connaissez-vous le système monétaire de la France?

5 — Par exemple! Je le connais à fond. Je suis importateur d'articles français, n'est-ce pas? Le franc est l'unité monétaire de la France. La livre sterling vaut 10 F (dix francs).

6 — Si vous voulez changer 10 (dix) livres en francs, combien de francs allez-vous recevoir?

7 — Je vais recevoir 100 F (cent francs).

8 — Si vous voulez changer 100 (cent) livres en francs, combien de francs allez-vous recevoir?

9 — Je vais recevoir 1000 F (mille francs).

10 — C'est ça. Encore: vous allez à la gare. Vous voulez prendre deux billets de chemin de fer. Chaque billet coûte 99 F et vous donnez 200 F à l'employé du guichet. Combien de francs est-ce qu'il vous rend en monnaie?

11 — Il me rend deux francs. Deux fois 99 font 198; et 200 F moins 198 F égalent deux francs.

12 — C'est ça. Dans notre prochaine conversation, continuons ce sujet important. Usage rend maître.

1 In our last conversation we said that it is difficult to imagine our modern civilization without numbers, that is to say, without mathematics. It is equally difficult to imagine a trip without mathematics.

2 Do you know how many times one makes use of mathematics on a trip?

3 I think so. One makes use of it[1] in order to change money, to buy tickets, to pay for one's meals and hotel bill, to weigh luggage, to estimate distances, to make purchases in departmental stores, in the shops and at the markets.

4 Are you familiar with the monetary system of France?

5 Well, really! I know it thoroughly. I am an importer of French articles, am I not? The franc is the monetary unit in France. The English pound is worth 10 francs.

6 If you want to change 10 pounds into francs, how many francs will you receive?

7 I shall receive 100 francs.

8 If you want to change 100 pounds into francs, how many francs will you receive?

9 I shall receive 1000 francs.

10 That's right. Again: You go to the railway station. You want to buy two railway tickets. Each ticket costs 99 francs and you give the ticket agent 200 francs. How much does he give you back in change?

11 He gives me back two francs. Twice 99 is 198; and 200 francs minus 198 francs equals two francs.

12 Right. In our next conversation let us continue this important subject. Practice makes perfect. (*Lit.* Practice makes the master.)

NOTE 1. en before a verb means *of it* or *of them*. You will learn more about this form later.

Pronunciation and Spelling Aids

1 Practise Aloud:

1 **une unité monétaire** (y-ny-ni-te mɔ-ne-tɛːr)
2 **la civilisation** (si-vi-li-za-sjɔ̃)
3 **les mathématiques** (ma-te-ma-tik)
4 **les boutiques** (bu-tik)
5 **les billets** (bi-jɛ)
6 **un million** (mi-ljɔ̃)

Building Vocabulary

A. Le système monétaire de la France (sis-tɛm mɔne-tɛːr)

The monetary unit of France is the franc. At the present time the franc is worth 10 to the pound. (See Note 1, on p. 71.)

The word **la monnaie**, money, refers in general to change, i.e. coins. **l'argent**, money, is used for any kind of money, **les billets** are notes or tickets. **en monnaie** means *in change*.

le porte-monnaie purse, is made up of the words **porte**, it carries and **monnaie**, money.

B. Antonyms

1 **vendre**, to sell; **acheter**, to buy; **je vends**, I sell; **j'achète**, I buy
2 **le vendeur**, **la vendeuse**, seller; **un acheteur**, **une acheteuse**, buyer
3 **donner**, to give; **recevoir**, to receive
4 **emprunter**, to borrow; **rendre**, to give back
5 **vrai**, true; **faux**, false
6 **vous avez raison**, you are right, **vous avez tort**, you are wrong

Locutions françaises

1 **c'est-à-dire** (sɛ ta-diːr), that is to say
2 **combien de fois** (kɔ̃-bjɛ̃ fwa), how many times
3 **changer de l'argent** (ʃɑ̃-ʒe dlar-ʒɑ̃), to change money
4 **par exemple!** (ɛg-zɑ̃ːpl), the idea! really!
5 **payer ses repas**, to pay for one's meals
6 **faire peser les bagages** (fɛːr pə-ze lɛ ba-gaːʒ), to have the baggage weighed
7 **faire des achats** (dɛ-za-ʃa), *or* **faire des emplettes** (dɛ zɑ̃-plɛt), *or* **faire des courses** (dɛ kurs), to go shopping
8 **c'est ça** (sɛ sa), that's right
9 **usage rend maître** (y-zaːʒ rɑ̃ mɛːtr), practice makes perfect (the master).
10 **à peu près** (a pø prɛ), about, nearly

Exercise No. 59—Completion of Text

1 (How many times) **fait-on usage des mathématiques** (on a trip)?
2 (One) **en fait usage** (in order to buy tickets).
3 **Nous faisons des achats** (in the department stores).
4 (Are you familiar with) **le système monétaire de la France?**
5 (I know it) **à fond.**
6 **La livre** (is worth) **10 F.**
7 **Je vais recevoir** (about) **1000 francs.**
8 (You want to purchase) **deux billets de chemin de fer.**
9 (You give) **198 francs à l'employé du guichet.**
10 (He gives me back) **deux francs en monnaie.**

Grammar Notes

1 Present Tense of **faire**, to make, to do; **croire**, to believe, to think

I make, do, am making, doing, etc.	I believe, think, am believing, etc.
je fais (fɛ)	**je crois** (krwa)
tu fais (fɛ)	**tu crois** (krwa)
il, elle fait (fɛ)	**il, elle croit** (krwa)
nous faisons (fzɔ̃)	**nous croyons** (krwa-jɔ̃)
vous faites (fɛːt)	**vous croyez** (krwa-je)
ils, elles font (fɔ̃)	**ils, elles croient** (krwa)

Imperative	*Imperative*
fais, make or do;	**crois**, believe or think;
faisons, let us make or do;	**croyons**, let us believe or think;
faites, make or do;	**croyez**, believe or think.

Exercise No. 60 Translate into English. Then practise aloud in French.

1 **Que faites–vous?**
  J'écris une lettre.
2 **Qu'est-ce que Jean fait?**
  Il joue du piano.
3 **Qu'est-ce que Marie fait?**
  Elle étudie la leçon de français.
4 **Qu'est-ce que les jeunes filles font?**
  Elles font des achats.
5 **Que fais-tu, mon enfant?**
  Je joue à la balle.
6 **Qu'est-ce que M. Martin fait?**
  Il fait peser les bagages.
7 **Croyez-vous cette histoire** (story)?
  Je ne la crois pas.
8 **Est-ce que votre ami la croit?**
  Il ne la croit pas non plus.

2 **Les nombres de 70 (soixante-dix) à 1000 (mille)**

70 soixante-dix	80 quatre-vingts (katr-vɛ̃)
71 soixante et onze	81 quatre-vingt-un
72 soixante-douze	89 quatre-vingt-neuf
73 soixante-treize	90 quatre-vingt-dix
74 soixante-quatorze	91 quatre-vingt-onze
75 soixante-quinze	92 quatre-vingt-douze
76 soixante-seize	93 quatre-vingt-treize
77 soixante-dix-sept	94 quatre-vingt-quatorze
78 soixante-dix-huit	95 quatre-vingt-quinze
79 soixante-dix-neuf	96 quatre-vingt-seize

97 **quatre-vingt-dix-sept**
98 **quatre-vingt-dix-huit**
99 **quatre-vingt-dix-neuf**
100 **cent** (sã)
101 **cent un** (sã œ̃)
102 **cent deux** (sã dø)
200 **deux cents** (dø sã)
345 **trois cent quarante-cinq**
1 000 **mille** (mil)
2 000 **deux mille**

(*a*) By combining various numbers between 1 and 1 000 (**mille**), any number up to a million, **un million** (mi-lj3) may be formed. Thus:

987 896   **neuf cent quatre-vingt-sept mille huit cent quatre-vingt-seize**

(*b*) **et** is used in 21, 31, 41, 51, 61, 71; never in 81, 91, 101.
(*c*) **quatre-vingts** drops the s when followed by another number:

quatre-vingt-deux;

cent has an s when preceded but not followed by another number:

trois cents but **trois cent un**, etc.

(*d*) **mille** never takes an s when multiplied by a preceding number.

deux mille 2 000

Exercise No. 61 Write out the numbers in French.

Exemple: 18 942   **dix-huit mille neuf cent quarante-deux**

(*a*)	400	(*c*)	753	(*e*) 95		(*g*) 86		(*i*)	670
(*b*)	1 000	(*d*)	1 974	(*f*) 77		(*h*) 71		(*j*)	14 586

Exercise No. 62 Practise the following table aloud:

5p **cinq pence valent 0,50 F (cinquante centimes)**
10p **dix pence valent 1 F (un franc)**
50p **cinquante pence valent 5 F (cinq francs)**
£1·00 **une livre vaut 10 F (dix francs)**
£2·00 **deux livres valent 20 F (vingt francs)**
£3·00 **trois livres valent 30 F (trente francs)**
£4·00 **quatre livres valent 40 F (quarante francs)**
£5·00 **cinq livres valent 50 F (cinquante francs)**
£6·00 **six livres valent 60 F (soixante francs)**
£7·00 **sept livres valent 70 F (soixante-dix francs)**
£8·00 **huit livres valent 80 F (quatre-vingts francs)**
£9·00 **neuf livres valent 90 F (quatre-vingt-dix francs)**
£10·00 **dix livres valent 1000 F (mille francs)**

Exercise No. 63—Questionnaire

1 Si quelque chose[2] coûte 40 (quarante) francs et si vous donnez un billet de 100 (cent) francs, combien recevez-vous en monnaie?

2 Si un billet coûte 75 (soixante-quinze) F, combien payez-vous deux billets?

3 Si une revue coûte 8,50 F (huit francs cinquante) combien payez-vous quatre revues?

4 Si un journal coûte 3,50 F (trois francs cinquante) et si vous donnez un billet de dix francs au vendeur, combien recevez-vous en monnaie?

5 Si vous avez une pièce[2] de cinq francs, deux billets de dix francs et trois billets de cinquante francs, combien d'argent avez-vous en poche (in your pocket)?

6 Si un homme a un million de livres, est-il millionnaire?

7 Qu'est-ce qui a plus de valeur (more value), un billet de dix francs, ou un billet de cinq livres?

8 Savez-vous combien d'argent il y a dans la banque de France?

NOTE 1. The rate of exchange mentioned in this section is quoted by way of illustration only. It is, of course, subject to constant variation.

2. Quelque chose, something.

3. Une pièce, a coin.

CHAPITRE 13 (TREIZE)

LES PROBLÈMES D'ARITHMÉTIQUE AU RESTAURANT, À LA GARE, DANS UNE BOUTIQUE

1 — Continuons notre étude de l'usage des mathématiques en voyage.

2 — Nous dînons au restaurant. Nous sommes quatre. Les quatre repas coûtent 90 F (quatre-vingt-dix francs), 95 F (quatre-vingt-quinze francs), 76 F (soixante-seize francs) et 62 F (soixante-deux francs). Combien est l'addition pour tout le monde, service compris à 15 %?

3 — L'addition pour tout le monde se monte à 371,45 F (trois cent soixante et onze francs quarante-cinq) en tout. Nous ne laissons pas de pourboire.

4 — Très bien. Continuons. Je suis à la gare et je porte deux valises assez lourdes. Je les fais peser. L'une pèse 30 kg (trente kilos) et l'autre 28,50 kg (vingt-huit kilos cinquante). Combien pèsent-elles ensemble?

5 — Ça alors, c'est facile. Elles pèsent 58,50 kg (cinquante-huit kilos cinquante).

6 — Correct. En France et dans les autres pays de l'Europe continentale on ne compte pas les distances en milles mais en kilomètres. Savez-vous changer les kilomètres en milles?

7 — Certainement. Je divise par huit et je multiplie par cinq. Ainsi, quatre-vingts kilomètres équivalent à cinquante milles. C'est facile, n'est-ce pas?

8 — Vous calculez vite et bien. Encore un problème, le dernier : vous entrez dans une boutique. Vous achetez une paire de gants pour vous-même à 100 F (cent francs), deux paires de gants pour votre femme a 130 F (cent trente francs) chacune et une ceinture de plastique pour chacun de vos quatre enfants à 37 F (trente-sept francs) chacune. Quel est le montant de tous vos achats?

9 — 508 F (cinq cent huit francs). Si je donne à la vendeuse six billets de cent francs, je vais recevoir 92 F (quatre-vingt douze francs) de monnaie.

10 — Parfait. Assez de mathématiques pour aujourd'hui. Jeudi nous allons parler des heures de la journée. C'est un sujet très important.

11 — Bien sûr. Je compte sur une conversation intéressante.

12 — À propos, M. Davis, je ne peux pas arriver avant huit heures et demie jeudi prochain.

13 — C'est bien. Mieux vaut tard que jamais.

14 — Bien dit! Au revoir, M. Davis.

15 — Au revoir. À jeudi, M. Picard.

1 Let us continue our study of the uses of mathematics on a journey.

2 We are dining at a restaurant. We are four. The four meals cost 90 francs, 95 francs, 76 francs and 62 francs. What is the bill for everybody including 15 % service charge?

3 The total bill comes to 371 francs 45. We don't leave any tip.

4 Very good. Let us continue. I am at the railway station and I am carrying two fairly heavy suitcases. I have them weighed. One weighs 30 kilos and the other 28.50 kilos. What do they weigh together?

5 Really, that is easy. They weigh 58.50 kilos.

6 Correct. In France and in the other countries of continental Europe one does not measure distance in miles but in kilometres. Do you know how to change kilometres into miles?

7 Certainly. I divide by eight and I multiply by five. Thus 80 kilometres are equal to 50 miles. It's easy, isn't it?

8 You reckon fast and well. One more problem, the last one: you go into a shop. You are buying a pair of gloves for yourself for 100 francs, two pairs of gloves for your wife at 130 francs each, and a plastic belt for each of your four children at 37 francs each. How much do your purchases come to?

9 508 francs. If I give the salesgirl six 100 franc notes, I am going to receive 92 francs change.

10 Perfect. Enough mathematics for today. On Thursday we are going to talk about the time of day. It is a very important subject.

11 Yes indeed. I am expecting an interesting conversation.

12 By the way, Mr. Davis, I cannot arrive before 8.30 next Thursday.

13 That's all right. Better late than never.

14 Well said. Goodbye, Mr. Davis.

15 Goodbye. Till Thursday, Mr. Picard.

Pronunciation and Spelling Aids

A. Practise Aloud:

1 **les problèmes d'arithmétique** (prɔ-blɛːm da rit-me-**tik**)
2 **les autres pays** (lɛ zoːtr pe-**i**)
3 **une addition** (y-na-di-sjɔ̃)
4 **le restaurant** (rɛs-tɔ-rɑ̃)
5 **la ceinture** (sɛ̃-tyːr)
6 **parfait** (par-fɛ)
7 **la virgule** (vir-gyl)
8 **je multiplie** (myl-ti-**pli**)

B. in French a comma is used instead of a full stop to set off decimals, thus: 2,2 (**deux virgule deux**) instead of 2.2.

Building Vocabulary

Some weights and measures

    le kilo = 1 000 grammes
    le demi-kilo
or **la livre = 500 grammes**
    la demi-livre = 250 grammes
    le quart = 125 grammes
    le mètre = 100 centimètres

NOTE **la livre** = pound, **le livre** = book.

Locutions françaises

1 **comme pourboire** (pur-bwaːr), as a tip
2 **tout le monde** (tul mɔ̃ːd), everybody
3 **en monnaie** (ɑ̃ mɔ-nɛ), in change
4 **mieux vaut tard que jamais** (mjø vo taːr kə ʒa-mɛ), better late than never
5 **ça alors!** really!

Grammar Notes

1 Present Tense of savoir, to know; connaître, to know, to be acquainted, (how) to be familiar with

I know (how), you know (how) etc.		I know (am acquainted with, etc.)	
je sais (sɛ)	nous savons (sa-vɔ̃)	je connais	nous connaissons
tu sais (sɛ)	vous savez (sa-ve)	tu connais	vous connaissez
il sait (sɛ)	ils savent (sav)	il connaît	ils connaissent
elle sait (sɛ)	elles savent (sav)	elle connaît	elles connaissent

(*a*) **savoir**, to know or to know how (with or without **comment**); to know facts, rules, etc. In general, this verb implies mental action, memory.

(*b*) **connaître**, means to know, in the sense of to be acquainted with, to be familiar with persons or things. In general, this verb implies knowing through the senses—hearing, seeing, etc.

Vous savez le nom des choses.   You know the names of things.
Il sait lire le français.   He knows how to read French.
Je sais où cet homme travaille.   I know where that man works.
Je connais cet homme.   I know (am acquainted with) that man.
Nous connaissons cette rue.   We know (are familiar with) this street.

Exercise No. 64 Complete these sentences with the correct form of **savoir** or **connaître** as required.

1 (Do you know) **le nom de ces choses?**
2 (We know) **cet homme.**
3 (We do not know) **où il habite.**
4 (He knows how) **écrire le français.**
5 (I know) **qui est ici.**
6 (They do not know) **cette région de la France.**
7 (I know) **les enfants de M. Picard.**
8 (Do you know how) **changer les kilomètres en milles?**
9 (Do they know) **les musées de Paris?**
10 **Que veulent-elles** (to know)?

2 The Possessive Adjectives. You are already familiar with most of the possessive adjectives. Here is a summary of the forms and meanings of all of them.

	Singular		Plural	
	Mas.	Fem.	Mas.	Fem.
my	mon frère	ma sœur	mes frères	mes sœurs
your	ton oncle	ta tante	tes oncles	tes tantes
his, her	son fils	sa fille	ses fils	ses filles
our	notre salon	notre rue	nos salons	nos rues
your	votre crayon	votre plume	vos crayons	vos plumes
their	leur bureau	leur maison	leurs bureaux	leurs maisons

(*a*) Possessive adjectives agree in number and gender with the nouns they precede.

(*b*) **ton, ta, tes,** your, like **tu,** you, are used only in addressing children, relatives, close friends, or animals.

(c) **son, sa, ses** mean either *his* or *her*, according to the sense of the sentence.

(d) **mon, ton, son** are used instead of **ma, ta, sa**, before feminine nouns, beginning with a vowel or **h** (usually)

mon amie (*f*)   **ton école** (*f*)   **son histoire** (*f*)

Exercise No. 65 Complete these sentences with the correct form of **mon, ton, son, votre, notre,** or **leur,** as required.

1 (Our) conversations sont très intéressantes.
2 Je vais payer (my) note d'hôtel.
3 Continuons (our) étude des nombres.
4 (Their) valises sont très lourdes.
5 M. Davis est un de (his) amis.
6 Où sont (your) bagages, monsieur?
7 Achetez-vous une paire de gants pour (your) femme?
8 (His) professeur est M. Picard.
9 (His) femme joue du piano.
10 (Their) enfants vont à l'école.
11 Nous sommes six dans (our) famille.
12 Qui est (her) professeur?
13 Aimes-tu (your) maître, (my) enfant?
14 Où est (his) bureau?
15 Je ne connais pas (their) professeur.

Exercise No. 66 Write out in French the numbers in the following table. Then read the table aloud.

Exemples: Seize kilomètres équivalent (e-ki-val) à dix milles.

16 kilomètres = 10 milles	64 kilomètres = 40 milles
32 kilomètres = 20 milles	80 kilomètres = 50 milles
48 kilomètres = 30 milles	160 kilomètres = 100 milles

Exercise No. 67—Questionnaire

1 Où est-ce que vous dînez?
2 Combien est l'addition pour tout le monde?
3 Qu'est-ce que vous laissez comme pourboire?
4 Où portez-vous une valise très lourde?
5 Combien de kilos pèse-t-elle?
6 Comment est-ce qu'on compte les distances en France, en milles ou en kilomètres?
7 Qui sait changer les kilomètres en milles?
8 Combien de paires de gants est-ce que M. Davis achète dans une boutique?
9 Quel est le sujet de la prochaine conversation?
10 De quel proverbe M. Davis fait-il usage?

CHAPITRE 14 (QUATORZE)

QUELLE HEURE EST-IL?

1 — Tout le monde veut savoir l'heure: — Quelle heure est-il? À quelle heure est-ce que l'avion arrive? À quelle heure est-ce que le train part? À quelle heure est-ce que les examens commencent? À quelle heure est-ce que le film commence? À quelle heure est-ce que la séance commence? et des milliers d'autres questions.

2 — M. Davis, je vais jouer le rôle de l'employé du guichet à la gare. Vous allez jouer le rôle d'un voyageur qui désire acheter[1] un billet et qui demande des renseignements. Voulez-vous commencer, s'il vous plaît?

3 — Bonjour, monsieur. Un billet pour Chartres, s'il vous plaît.

4 — Oui, monsieur. Première ou deuxième classe?

5 — Deuxième classe, s'il vous plaît. Quel est le prix de la place?

6 — Trente-sept francs pour un billet d'aller.

7 — Donnez-moi un billet d'aller et retour, s'il vous plaît. Je désire partir lundi.

8 — Voici votre billet. Ça fait soixante-quatorze francs.

9 — Merci, monsieur. À quelle heure est-ce que le train part et à quelle heure arrive-t-il à Chartres?

10 — Il y a plusieurs trains par jour pour Chartres. Vous avez un bon train à quinze heures quarante-cinq, qui arrive à seize heures cinquante-cinq.

11 — Merci beaucoup, monsieur.

12 — À votre service, monsieur.

13 — Excellent, M. Davis. Vous jouez votre rôle à merveille.

1 Everyone wants to know the time: What time is it? At what time does the plane arrive? At what time does the train leave? At what time do the examinations begin? At what time does the film begin? At what time does the performance begin? And thousands of other questions.

2 Mr. Davis, I am going to play the role of the booking clerk at the railway station. You are going to play the role of a traveller who wants to buy a ticket and is asking for information. Will you begin, please?

3 Good day. One ticket to Chartres, please.

4 Yes sir. First or second class?

5 Second class, please. How much is the fare?

6 37 francs for a single ticket.

7 Please give me a return ticket. I wish to leave on Monday.

8 Here is your ticket. That makes 74 francs.

9 Thank you. At what time does the train leave, and when does it arrive at Chartres?

10 There are several trains a day for Chartres. You have a good train at 15.45, which arrives at 16.55.

11 Thank you very much.

12 At your service.

13 Excellent Mr. Davis. You play your part wonderfully.

NOTE 1. One also says **prendre un billet.**

76

1 — Maintenant, je joue le rôle de l'employée du cinéma. Vous demandez des renseignements sur les séances. Voulez-vous commencer, s'il vous plaît?

2 — Dites-moi, s'il vous plaît, à quelle heure les séances commencent-elles?

3 — Il y a trois séances. La première commence à seize heures vingt, la deuxième à dix-huit heures cinquante, et la troisième à vingt et une heures dix.

4 — Y a-t-il des actualités?

5 — Mais non, il n' y en a plus. Vous avez les informations à la télé.

6 — Quel est le prix des billets?

7 — Les billets coûtent vingt-six francs. Si vous arrivez de bonne heure vous allez avoir de bonnes places.

8 — Donnez-moi deux billets pour la troisième séance s'il vous plaît.

9 — Les voici. Merci bien.

10 — Admirable. Je le répète: vous jouez votre rôle à merveille.

1 Now I am playing the role of the girl at the booking office at the cinema. You are asking for information about the performances. Will you begin, please?

2 Please tell me at what time the performances begin?

3 There are three performances. The first one begins at 16.20, the second at 18.50 and the third at 21.10.

4 Is there a newsreel?

5 Why, no more. You have the news on T.V.

6 What is the price of the tickets?

7 The tickets cost 26 francs. If you come early you will get good seats.

8 Please give me two tickets for the third performance.

9 Here they are. Thank you very much.

10 Admirable. I repeat: you play your part wonderfully.

Pronunciation and Spelling Aids

A. Practise Aloud:

1 tout le monde veut savoir l'heure: — quelle heure est-il?

2 vous demandez des renseignements sur les séances

3 des milliers d'autres questions

1 (tul mɔ̃ːd vø sa-vwaːr lœːr, kɛ lœːr ɛ-til)

2 (vu də-mɑ̃-de dɛ rɑ̃-sɛ-ɳə-mɑ̃ syr lɛ se-ɑ̃ːs)

3 (dɛ mi-lje doːtr kɛs-tjɔ̃)

B. Remember: ll is usually pronounced like j:

fille (fiːj)   billet (bi-jɛ)   merveille (mɛr-vɛːj)   Marseille (mar-sɛːj)

Exceptions: 1 ll is like lj in million (mi-ljɔ̃)   milliers (mi-lje)

2 ll is like *l* in mille, ville (vil)   tranquille (trɑ̃-kil)

Building Vocabulary

A. Words of Approval and Praise

1 admirable (ad-mi-**rabl**), splendid

2 excellent (ɛk-sɛ-lɑ̃), excellent

3 très bien (trɛ bjɛ̃), very good

4 c'est ça (sɛ sa), right, that's right

5 correct (kɔ-rɛkt), correct

6 parfait (par-fɛ), perfect

7 c'est bien (sɛ bjɛ̃), that's good

8 c'est exact (sɛ-tɛg-zakt), that's so

9 c'est vrai (sɛ vrɛ), that's true

10 à merveille (a mɛr-vɛːj), wonderfully

B. Words Dealing with Railway Travel

1 **la gare,** the railway station
2 **à quelle heure est-ce que le train part pour . . . ?** at what time does the train leave for . . . ?
3 **à quelle heure est-ce que le train arrive à (de) . . . ?** at what time does the train arrive at (from) . . . ?
4 **le train arrive (part) à sept heures du matin,** the train arrives (leaves) at 7 a.m.
5 **un billet de première (deuxième) classe,** a first (second) class ticket
6 **un billet d'aller (*or* billet simple),** a single ticket
7 **un billet d'aller et retour,** a return ticket
8 **quel est le prix de la place?** *or* **combien coûte la place?** what is the fare?
9 **plusieurs trains par jour,** several trains a day
10 **payer les billets,** to pay for the tickets
11 **en voiture!** all aboard!
12 **la salle des bagages,** luggage room
13 **un wagon-lit,** sleeper
14 **un wagon-restaurant,** dining-car

Locutions françaises

1 **demander des renseignements,** to ask for information
2 **jouer le rôle,** to play the role
3 **mais oui (mɛ wi),** yes indeed, of course
4 **mais non,** indeed no, of course not
5 **de bonne heure (də bɔ-nœːr),** early
6 **les voici (lɛ vwa-si),** here they are
7 **les voilà,** there they are

Exercise No. 68—Completion of Text

1 (At what time) **est-ce que le film commence?**
2 (The first performance) **commence à (16.30).**
3 **Il y a des milliers** (of other questions).
4 **Où est** (the railway station)?
5 **Vous êtes un voyageur qui** (asks for information).
6 **Donnez-moi** (a return ticket).
7 **A quelle heure** (does the train leave)?
8 (Does it arrive) **à neuf heures du matin?**
9 **Venez** (early) **si vous désirez de bonnes places.**
10 (Here they are.)
11 (Many thanks, sir.)
12 (At your service), **monsieur.**

Grammar Notes

1 Present Tense of **partir,** to leave;   **sortir,** to go out

I leave, I am leaving, you leave, you are leaving, etc.	I go out, I am going out, you go out, you are going out, etc.

je pars (par)	nous partons (par-tɔ̃)	je sors (sɔr)	nous sortons (sɔr-tɔ̃)
tu pars (par)	vous partez (par-te)	tu sors (sɔr)	vous sortez (sɔr-te)
il part (par)	ils partent (part)	il sort (sɔr)	ils sortent (sɔrt)
elle part (par)	elles partent (part)	elle sort (sɔr)	elles sortent (sɔrt)

Imperative	*Imperative*
pars, leave;	**sors**, go out;
partons, let us leave;	**sortons**, let us go out;
partez, leave;	**sortez**, go out.

Verbs like **partir** and **sortir** are:

servir, to serve: **je sers, tu sers, il sert, nous servons, vous servez, ils servent**
sentir, to feel, smell: **je sens, tu sens, il sent, nous sentons, vous sentez, ils sentent**
dormir, to sleep: **je dors, tu dors, il dort, nous dormons, vous dormez, ils dorment**

Exercise No. 69 Complete these sentences by writing the correct forms of **partir, sortir, dormir, sentir, servir.**

Read the completed sentences aloud.

1 **Le train** (leaves) **à sept heures.**
2 **À quelle heure** (do you leave)?
3 (We sleep) **jusqu'à** (until) **huit heures.**
4 **Elle** (does not sleep) **bien.**
5 **Madame Davis** (serves) **le café.**
6 (Do you smell) **le parfum?**
7 (I do not smell) **le parfum.**
8 **À quelle heure** (do they go out) **de la maison?**
9 (I go out) **du bureau à cinq heures.**
10 (Do not sleep) **jusqu'à neuf heures.**

2 Time of Day

Quelle heure est-il? What time is it?
Il est une heure. It is one o'clock.
Il est deux heures. It is two o'clock.
Il est deux heures cinq. It is five past two.
Il est trois heures dix. It is ten past three.
Il est quatre heures et quart. It is a quarter past four.
Il est cinq heures vingt. It is twenty past five.
Il est six heures vingt-cinq. It is twenty-five past six.
Il est sept heures et demie. It is half past seven.
Il est huit heures moins vingt-cinq. It is twenty-five to eight.
Il est neuf heures moins vingt. It is twenty to nine.
Il est dix heures moins le quart. It is a quarter to ten.
Il est onze heures moins dix. It is ten to eleven.
Il est midi moins cinq. It is five to twelve a.m.
midi, noon   **minuit,** midnight
midi et demi, half past twelve   **minuit et demi,** half past twelve

NOTE **et**, and, is used for time after the hour. **moins**, less *or* minus, is used for time before the hour; **minutes** is omitted; **heures** is never omitted.

Time expressions after the half hour are based on the hour which follows. Thus: **6.40 Il est sept heures moins vingt.** It is twenty minutes to seven.

However, as in English, you may say: **six heures quarante,** six forty.
     du matin, in the morning (a.m.)   **du soir,** in the evening (p.m.)
         de l'après-midi, in the afternoon (p.m.)

In French timetables, time is indicated by 24 hours beginning with midnight. The hours 24.00 until 11.59 are a.m. The hours 12.00 (noon) until 23.59 are p.m. Thus in the timetable (l'horaire):

0.20 (zéro heure vingt) = 12.20 a.m. (minuit vingt)
12.20 (douze heures vingt) = 12.20 p.m. (midi vingt)
15.20 (quinze heures vingt) = 3.20 p.m. (trois heures vingt de l'après-midi)

Exercise No. 70 Write out the time expressions. Then read the sentences aloud giving the time in French.

Exemple 1: Le train de Lyon arrive à dix-neuf heures trente

1 Le train de Lyon arrive à (19.30)
2 Le train arrive à Paris à (22.15)
3 Le train pour Marseille part à (6.30)
4 Le train pour Rouen part à (12.00)
5 La première séance commence à (16.30)
6 La deuxième séance commence à (18.40)
7 La troisième séance commence à (21.00)
8 Le film commence à (16.10)
9 M. Davis prend le train en ville à (7.45) précises.
10 Il arrive en ville à (8.40)

Exercise No. 71—Questionnaire

1 Qu'est-ce que tout le monde veut savoir?
2 Qui joue le rôle du voyageur?
3 Qui joue le rôle de l'employé du guichet?
4 Quelle classe de billet est-ce que M. Davis désire?
5 Combien coûte un billet d'aller et retour?
6 Qui joue le rôle de l'employée du cinéma?
7 Qui demande des renseignements?
8 Combien de séances y a-t-il à ce cinéma?
9 Pour quelle séance est-ce que M. Davis prend deux billets?
10 Combien paie-t-il ces billets?

RÉVISION 3

CHAPITRES 10–14 PREMIÈRE PARTIE

Révision de mots

NOUNS

1 un acheteur, une acheteuse	15 la fourchette	29 le pot au lait
2 une addition	16 le gant	30 le porte-monnaie
3 un argent	17 la gare	31 le prix
4 les bagages (*m*)	18 le gâteau	32 la radio
5 le billet	19 le guichet	33 le repas
6 la boutique	20 une heure	34 la séance
7 le chemin de fer	21 la livre	35 la soucoupe
8 le couteau	22 le magasin	36 le style
9 la cuiller	23 le maître	37 le sujet
10 un échantillon	24 le marché	38 la tarte
11 une employé	25 la note	39 la tasse
12 une employée	26 le pays	40 le verre
13 la fleur	27 le plat	41 le vendeur
14 une fois	28 la poche	42 le voyageur

1 buyer (*m* and *f*)	15 fork	29 milk jug
2 bill (restaurant)	16 glove	30 purse
3 money, silver	17 station	31 price, prize
4 luggage	18 cake	32 radio
5 ticket	19 booking-office	33 meal
6 shop	20 hour, time	34 performance
7 railway	21 pound	35 saucer
8 knife	22 store	36 style
9 spoon	23 teacher, master	37 subject
10 sample	24 market	38 tart
11 employee, clerk	25 bill (hotel, etc.)	39 cup
12 employee (*f*), clerk	26 country (nation)	40 glass
13 flower	27 dish	41 seller
14 one time, once	28 pocket	42 traveller

VERBS

1 acheter	14 trouver	27 sentir
2 avancer	15 connaître	28 sortir (de)
3 changer	16 n. connaissons	29 venir
4 continuer	17 croire	30 pouvoir
5 dîner	18 perdre	31 je peux
6 donner	19 rendre	32 recevoir
7 laisser	20 faire	33 je reçois
8 manger	21 je fais	34 savoir
9 payer	22 dire	35 je sais
10 penser (à)	23 nous disons	36 valoir
11 peser	24 dormir	37 il vaut
12 porter	25 partir	38 vouloir
13 téléphoner	26 je pars	39 je veux

1 to buy
2 to progress
3 to change
4 to continue
5 to dine
6 to give
7 to let
8 to eat
9 to pay for
10 to think of
11 to weigh
12 to carry, wear
13 to telephone

14 to find
15 to know
16 we know
17 to believe
18 to lose
19 to give back
20 to make, do
21 I make, do
22 to say
23 we say
24 to sleep
25 to leave
26 I leave

27 to feel
28 to go out (of)
29 to come
30 to be able
31 I can
32 to receive
33 I receive
34 to know (how)
35 I know (how)
36 to be worth
37 it is worth
38 to want
39 I want

ADJECTIVES

1 célèbre
2 chaque
3 charmant
4 connu
5 délicieux

6 délicieuse (*f*)
7 gai
8 lourd
9 ordinaire
10 parfait

11 plusieurs
12 précis
13 premier
14 première (*f*)
15 vrai

1 famous
2 each
3 charming
4 known
5 delicious

6 delicious (*f*)
7 gay, bright
8 heavy
9 ordinary
10 perfect

11 several
12 exact
13 first
14 first (*f*)
15 true

ADVERBS

1 à peu près
2 comme
3 correctement
4 d'ordinaire

5 encore
6 encore un
7 maintenant
8 moins

9 naturellement
10 presque
11 surtout
12 tout de suite

1 more or less
2 as, like, how
3 correctly
4 generally

5 again
6 one more
7 now
8 less

9 naturally
10 almost, nearly
11 especially
12 at once

PREPOSITIONS

1 avant
2 après

3 devant
4 derrière

5 pour
6 vers

1 before
2 after

3 in front of
4 behind

5 for, in order to
6 towards, about

FRENCH EXPRESSIONS

1 j'ai besoin (de)
2 j'ai raison
3 vous avez tort
4 c'est ça
5 c'est vrai
6 c'est-à-dire
7 changer de l'argent
8 combien de fois?
9 je crois que oui
10 je crois que non
11 en tout cas
12 en effet

13 en monnaie
14 il le faut
15 faire des emplettes *or* des achats
16 faire peser
17 mais oui (non)
18 payer ses repas
19 par exemple!
20 comme pourboire
21 merci bien
22 rien de plus facile
23 toute le monde
24 que veut dire?

25 cela veut dire	⎰27 il n'y a pas de quoi
26 les voici	⎱28 de rien
	29 ça alors!

1 I need	15 to go shopping
2 I am right	16 to have weighed
3 you are wrong	17 indeed yes (no)
4 that's correct	18 to pay for one's meals
5 that's true	19 the idea!
6 that is to say	20 as a tip
7 to change money	21 many thanks
8 how many times?	22 nothing easier
9 I think so	23 everybody
10 I think not	24 what does . . . mean?
11 in any case	25 it means . . .
12 as a matter of fact	26 here they are
13 in change	⎰27 you're welcome, *or*
14 it is necessary	⎱28 don't mention it
	29 really!

DEUXIÈME PARTIE

Exercise No. 72 Select the group of words in Column II which best completes each sentence begun in Column I.

Exemple 1: (1f) Cette région en France est connue pour ses produits céramiques.

I	II
1 Cette région en France est connue	(a) tout de suite au commerce?
2 De quelle région sont	(b) que jamais.
3 Est-ce que le commerçant pense	(c) dans les grands magasins.
4 Vous savez qu'usage	(d) le système monétaire de la France.
5 Mieux vaut tard	(e) d'aller et retour.
6 Le voyageur a besoin d'argent	(f) pour ses produits céramiques.
7 Nous faisons des achats	(g) à seize heures.
8 Ils ne connaissent pas	(h) ces tasses et ces soucoupes?
9 Donnez-moi un billet	(i) pour prendre des billets.
10 La première séance commence	(j) rend maître.

Exercise No. 73 Complete these sentences by choosing the correct expression from those listed below. Be sure to use the correct form of the verb.

Exemple 1: Le touriste demande des renseignements.

1 Le touriste (asks for information).
2 (We need) **un porte-monnaie.**
3 M. Davis (knows his trade).
4 Ils veulent (to change some money).
5 À quoi (are you thinking)?
6 (Do you like) **ce portrait?**
7 Je mange quand (I am hungry).
8 Que (do you mean)?
9 (We pay for our meals) **en francs.**
10 (You are right) **M. Davis.**
11 J'ai raison, mais (you are wrong).
12 De quoi (do you need)?

demander des renseignements	payer nos repas	changer de l'argent
avoir raison (tort)	connaître son métier	aimer bien
avoir faim	penser (à)	vouloir dire
avoir besoin (de)		

Exercise No. 74 From Group II select antonyms for each word in Group I.

I		II	
1 arriver	7 vendre	(a) moins (de)	(g) perdre
2 donner	8 apprendre	(b) acheter	(h) recevoir
3 plus (de)	9 avant	(c) partir	(i) peu (de)
4 devant	10 le vendeur	(d) derrière	(j) j'ai tort
5 trouver	11 beaucoup (de)	(e) enseigner	(k) écouter
6 parler	12 j'ai raison	(f) l'acheteur	(l) après

Exercise No. 75 Answer these questions in the affirmative in complete sentences. Use the pronoun **je** in the answers.

Exemple: 1. Oui, monsieur, je pense à mon ami.

1 Pensez-vous à votre ami?
2 Voulez-vous faire un voyage en France?
3 Pouvez-vous acheter une auto?
4 Portez-vous les bagages à la gare?
5 Partez-vous demain de la ville?
6 Comptez-vous toujours la monnaie?
7 Dites-vous les mots deux fois?
8 Connaissez-vous cet homme-là?
9 Donnez-vous un pourboire au garçon?
10 Savez-vous compter en français?

Exercise No. 76 Answer these questions in the negative in complete sentences. Use **nous** in the answers.

Exemple 1: Non, madame, nous ne posons pas beaucoup de questions.

1 Posez-vous beaucoup de questions?
2 Calculez-vous rapidement en français?
3 Trouvez-vous cette revue intéressante?
4 Lisez-vous les journaux français?
5 Écrivez-vous bien en français?
6 Dînez-vous au restaurant?
7 Connaissez-vous la ville de Biot?
8 Achetez-vous beaucoup de parfum?
9 Avez-vous besoin d'une valise?
10 Savez-vous l'adresse de M. Picard?

Dialogue

Un touriste prend des renseignements
sur la poterie française

1 — Dites-moi, s'il vous plaît, monsieur, dans quelles régions de la France peut-on trouver de la jolie poterie? Je désire acheter un service à thé: tasses, soucoupes, et assiettes.

2 — Eh bien, chaque région a son style individuel: Limoges, la Bretagne et la Provence sont toutes connues pour leurs produits céramiques.

3 — Est-ce qu'il faut aller dans ces régions pour trouver de la poterie régionale?

4 — Pas du tout. Vous pouvez acheter de la poterie de toutes les régions ici même à Paris.

5 — Est-ce que ça coûte plus cher ici?

6 — Naturellement, ça coûte plus cher. Mais vous avez un assortiment bien choisi.

7 — Voulez-vous me dire où est-ce qu'on peut acheter de la poterie à Paris?

8 — Vous allez trouver le meilleur assortiment dans les grands magasins: aux Galeries Lafayette, au Printemps, et surtout au Bazar de l'Hôtel de Ville.

9 — Merci infiniment, monsieur.
10 — De rien, mademoiselle.

1 Please tell me, sir, in which regions of France can one find beautiful pottery? I want to buy a tea-set: cups, saucers and plates.

2 Well, each region has its own individual style: Limoges, Brittany and Provence are all well known for their ceramic products.

3 Does one have to go to these districts to find regional pottery?

4 Not at all. You can buy pottery from all the regions here in Paris.

5 Does it cost more here?

6 Of course it costs more. But you have a well-chosen assortment.

7 Will you tell me please where one can buy pottery in Paris?

8 You will find the best assortment in the stores: at the Galeries Lafayette, at the Printemps and especially at the Bazar de l'Hôtel de Ville.

9 Thank you very much indeed.

10 Don't mention it.

Exercise No. 77—Lecture 1
La famille Davis rend une petite visite à papa

C'est la première fois que la famille Davis vient voir M. Davis à son bureau. Madame Davis et ses quatre enfants entrent dans un grand immeuble et ils montent par l'ascenseur jusqu'au dernier étage. Annette, la plus jeune, qui n'a que cinq ans,[1] est très curieuse. Elle pose beaucoup de questions à sa maman au sujet du bureau.

Quand ils arrivent au bureau, le père se lève[2] et dit: — Quelle bonne surprise! Que je suis content de vous voir!

Les enfants admirent tous les objets qu'ils voient dans le bureau: la machine à écrire, les articles de Paris, les échantillons de céramique française, les revues françaises et surtout les affiches illustrées aux murs. Tout le monde est très content.

Philippe, l'aîné, regarde par la grande fenêtre, et il voit le ciel bleu et le soleil qui brille. En bas il voit les autos qui passent dans la rue. Du haut du dernier étage elles paraissent[3] toutes petites.

La visite terminée, toute la famille entre dans un restaurant qui n'est pas loin du bureau. Ils mangent tous de bon appétit, surtout les garçons, parce qu'ils ont très faim.

NOTE 1. **qui . . . ans** who is *only* five years old. **ne** (verb) **que** = *only*.
  2. **gets up.**
  3. **paraître** to seem, **il, elle paraît** he, she, it seems, **ils, elles paraissent** they seem.

Exercise No. 78—Lecture 2
Le percheron[1] et l'automobile
Fable moderne

Annette, la plus jeune des enfants de M. Davis, aime beaucoup les fables anciennes[2] d'Ésope. Elle aime bien aussi cette fable moderne que M. Picard a écrite[3] pour elle. Voici la fable: 'Le percheron et l'auto.'

Une auto passe sur la route et voit un percheron. Le percheron est un cheval français, grand et fort.[4] Cependant ce percheron paraît très fatigué.[5] Il est attelé[6] à une charrette très lourde.[7]

L'auto s'arrête et dit au percheron: — Bonjour. Vous allez bien lentement. Vous ne voulez pas aller vite comme moi?

— Oh oui, madame! Mais dites-moi comment est-ce possible?

— Ce n'est pas difficile, dit l'auto. Mon réservoir à essence[8] est plein. Buvez-en[9] et vous allez voir ça.

Alors le percheron boit de l'essence. Maintenant, il ne va plus lentement. Il ne va pas vite non plus. En effet, il ne va pas du tout. Il a mal à l'estomac.[10]

Ce pauvre cheval! Il n'est pas très intelligent, n'est-ce pas? Il ne sait pas que l'essence est bonne pour les autos, mais qu'elle[11] ne vaut rien pour les chevaux.

Note 1. **le percheron**, draught horse; **le cheval**, horse: **les chevaux**, the horses.

    2. **ancien (ancienne *f*)**, old, ancient.

    3. has written.

    4. strong.

    5. tired.

    6. harnessed.

    7. a very heavy cart.

    8. petrol tank.

    9. drink some. **boire**, to drink: **je bois, tu bois, il, elle boit; nous buvons, vous buvez, ils, elles boivent.**

  10. **Il a mal à l'estomac (il a mal à la tête, il a mal aux dents).** He has a stomach ache (he has a headache, he has a toothache).

  11. **qu'elle ... rien** that it is not good.

CHAPITRE 15 (QUINZE)

LE CINÉMA

1 — M. Davis, vous savez déjà demander des renseignements sur les séances des cinémas. Mais dites-moi: êtes-vous amateur de cinéma?

2 — Eh bien, quelquefois, j'aime voir un bon film mais, pour la plupart, les films ne m'intéressent pas.

3 — Alors vous préférez le théâtre?

4 — Mais oui. Ma femme et moi nous le préférons. Nous y[1] allons souvent voir une bonne pièce ou une opérette.

5 — Et vos enfants? Est-ce qu'ils préfèrent le théâtre?

6 — Pas du tout! Ils adorent les films policiers et les opérettes en couleurs qui nous[1] ennuient à mourir.

7 — Ils connaissent toutes les vedettes de l'écran, n'est-ce pas?

8 — Naturellement. Ils les[2] connaissent bien. Ils connaissent aussi les vedettes de la télévision et de la radio.

9 — Vous habitez une petite ville dans les environs de Londres. Y a-t-il un cinéma près de chez vous?

10 — Oui monsieur, pas loin. Nous y allons à pied en un quart d'heure environ.

11 — Quelles places préférez-vous, les places aux premiers rangs, ou les places au fond?

12 — Nous préférons les places au quatorzième ou au quinzième rang. De là, on peut bien voir et bien entendre. De là, la lumière et les mouvements sur l'écran ne font pas mal aux yeux.

13 — Que faites-vous si la plupart des places sont occupées?

14 — Alors l'ouvreuse vient nous[2] aider. Nous prenons n'importe quelles places libres, devant, au fond, ou de côté. Mais nous n'aimons pas ces places. Nous n'aimons pas non plus rester debout au cinéma. Donc nous arrivons de bonne heure.

15 — Merveilleux, M. Davis! Vous avancez très rapidement.

16 — Grâce à vous, M. Picard.

1 Mr. Davis, you already know how to ask for information about the cinema performances. But tell me: are you fond of the cinema?

2 Well, I like to see a good picture sometimes, but for the most part films do not interest me.

3 Then you prefer the theatre?

4 Oh, yes. My wife and I prefer it. We go there[1] often to see a good play or a musical comedy.

5 And your children? Do they prefer the theatre?

6 Not at all! They love thrillers and musicals in colour which bore us[2] to death.

7 They know all the stars of the screen, don't they?

8 Of course. They know them well. They also know the stars of television and radio.

9 You live in a small town on the outskirts of London. Is there a cinema near your house?

10 Yes, not far away. We can go there on foot in about fifteen minutes.

11 Which seats do you prefer, the seats in the front rows or the seats at the back?

12 We prefer the seats in rows fourteen or fifteen. From there, one can see and hear well. From there, the light and the movements on the screen do not hurt (*Lit.* do no harm to) the eyes.

13 What do you do if most of the seats are occupied?

14 Then the usherette comes to help us.[2] We take any vacant seats, in front, at the back, or at the side. But we do not like those seats. Nor do we like to stand at the cinema. Therefore we come early.

15 Splendid, Mr. Davis! You are progressing very fast.

16 Thanks to you, Mr. Picard.

NOTE 1. **y** = there. Like object pronouns it usually precedes the verb.
2. **nous**, us, and **les**, them, are object pronouns.

Pronunciation and Spelling Aids

A. Practise Aloud:

1 **vous savez demander des renseignements sur les séances des cinémas**
1 (vu sa-ve də-mɑ̃-de dɛ rɑ̃-sɛ-ɲə-mɑ̃ syr lɛ se-ɑ̃:s dɛ si-ne-**ma**)
2 **êtes-vous amateur de cinéma?**
2 (ɛt vu za-ma-tœːr də si-ne-**ma**)
3 **ils adorent les films policiers et les opérettes en couleurs**
3 (il za-dɔr lɛ film pɔ-li-sje e lɛ zɔ-pe-rɛt ɑ̃ ku-**lœːr**)

B. Remember â = ɑ, ô = o, ê = ɛ. Thus:

   rôle (roːl)   **grâce** (grɑːs)   **êtes-vous** (ɛt-vu)

Building Vocabulary

A. Words Dealing with the cinema

1 **le cinéma** (si-ne-**ma**), pictures, cinema
2 **le ciné** (short for **cinéma**)
3 **le film** (film), film
4 **la séance** (se-ɑ̃:s), performance
5 **un écran** (œ̃-ne-krɑ̃), screen
6 **la vedette** (və-dɛːt), film star
7 **la pièce** (pjɛs), play
8 **les actualités** (lɛ zak-tɥa-li-te), news
9 **le rôle** (roːl), role
10 **le rang** (rɑ̃), row
11 **la place** (plas), seat
12 **une ouvreuse** (y-nu-vrœːz), usherette

Locutions françaises

1 **pour la plupart,** for the most part
2 **ils nous ennuient à mourir,** they bore us to death
3 **près de chez vous,** near your home
4 **à pied** (a pje), on foot
5 **faire mal aux yeux** (o zjø), to hurt the eyes
6 **rester** (*or* **être**) **debout,** to stand
7 **la plupart des places,** most of the seats
8 **n'importe** (nɛ̃-pɔrt), it doesn't matter
9 **grâce à vous,** thanks to you
10 **je vous remercie,** I thank you

Exercise No. 79—Completion of Text

1 (I like very much to see) **un bon film.**
2 **Les films** (do not interest me).
3 (They adore) **les films policiers.**
4 **Connaissent-ils** (all the film stars)?
5 (They know them) **bien.**
6 **Y a-t-il un ciné** (near your home)?
7 **Nous y allons** (on foot).
8 (We prefer) **les places des premiers rangs.**
9 **Nous n'aimons pas** (to stand).
10 (Therefore) **nous arrivons** (early).

Grammar Notes

1 Present Tense of **venir**, to come

I come, I am coming, you come, you are coming, etc.

je viens (vjɛ̃)	nous venons (vnɔ̃)
tu viens (vjɛ̃)	vous venez (vne)
il, elle vient (vjɛ̃)	ils, elles viennent (vjɛːn)

Imperative: **viens,** come; **venons,** let's come; **venez,** come.
Like **venir: revenir,** to come back; **devenir,** to become.

Exercise No. 80 Translate each verb into French. Read each sentence aloud.

1 (I am coming) **aujourd'hui.**
2 (They do not come) **de bonne heure.**
3 **Qui** (is coming) **avec vous?**
4 **Les petits garçons** (come) **avec leurs pères.**
5 (Come) **ici, mes enfants.**
6 (Are you coming) **à sept heures?**
7 (We are coming back) **de bonne heure ce soir.**
8 **Quand** (is he coming back)?
9 (She is not coming) **ici ce matin.**
10 **M. Martin, à quelle heure** (are you coming)?
11 **Que voulez-vous** (to become)?
12 (I want to become) **professeur.**

2 Direct Object Pronouns

Study the following sentences. They illustrate the direct object pronouns. You are already familiar with most of them.

1 M. Picard *me* connaît.	1 Mr. Picard knows *me.*
2 Il *te* connaît aussi, Annette.	2 He knows *you* too, Annette.
3 Qui *vous* aide à trouver une bonne place?	3 Who helps *you* to find a good seat?
4 L'ouvreuse *nous* aide.	4 The usherette helps *us.*
5 Qui salue M. Picard? M. Davis *le* salue.	5 Who greets Mr. Picard? Mr. Davis greets *him.*
6 Connaissez-vous Mlle Picard? Je ne *la* connais pas.	6 Do you know Miss Picard? I do not know *her.*
7 Avez-vous le journal français? Nous ne *l'*avons pas.	7 Have you the French newspaper? We do not have *it.*
8 Connaissent-ils les vedettes de l'écran? Oui, ils *les* connaissent bien.	8 Do they know the film stars? Yes, they know *them* well.

(*a*) The direct object pronouns are:

me (m'), me	**nous,** us	**le (l'),** him, it	**les,** them
te (t'), you (*fam.*)	**vous,** you	**la (l'),** her, it	

(*b*) **me** and **te** become **m'** and **t',** and **le** and **la** become **l',** when they precede a verb beginning with a vowel or **h** (usually).

(*c*) Object pronouns *precede* the verb except in the affirmative imperative when they follow the verb and are joined to it by a hyphen. In the negative imperative the object pronouns precede the verb:

Prenez la fleur. Prenez-*la*.   Take the flower. Take *it.*
Ne prenez pas la fleur. Ne *la* prenez pas.   Do not take the flower. Do not take *it.*

(*d*) **me** when used after the verb in the imperative becomes **moi.**
     Dites-moi.   Écoutez-moi.   Tell *me.*   Listen to *me.*

3 The Use of **y,** there.

The word **y,** there, is used to indicate a place already mentioned, and like the object pronouns always precedes the verb, except in the affirmative imperative.

Quand est-ce que M. Davis va en France?   When is Mr. Davis going to France?

Il *y* va au printemps.   He is going *there* in the spring.
Allons-*y* avec lui.   Let's go *there* with him.

Exercise No. 81 Read each question. Write each answer filling in the correct object pronoun in French. Finally read the questions and complete answers aloud.

1 **Prenez-vous les billets?**
2 **Connaissez-vous cette rue?**
3 **Est-ce que Jean attend son ami, Louis?**
4 **Les enfants adorent-ils les vedettes de l'écran?**
5 **Préfèrent-ils le premier rang?**
6 **Comment trouvez-vous cette tasse?**
7 **Allez-vous voir M. Davis?**
8 **Est-ce que le professeur m'attend?**
9 **Qui vient vous aider au cinéma?**
10 **Qui vous écoute parler français?**
11 **Vont-ils au cinéma à pied ou en autobus?**
12 **Demeure-t-il dans cette maison-là?**
13 **Quand allez-vous nous aider?**
14 **Est-ce que les films vous intéressent?**
15 **Est-ce que tu m'aimes, maman?**

1 Oui, je (them) prend.
2 Non, nous ne (it) connaissons pas.
3 Oui, il (him) attend dans le salon.
4 Certainement! Ils (them) adorent.
5 Non, ils ne (it) préfèrent pas.
6 Je (it) trouve charmante.
7 Nous allons (him) voir ce soir.
8 Bien sûr, il (you) attend.
9 L'ouvreuse vient (us) aider.
10 M. Picard (us) écoute parler français.
11 Ils (there) vont en autobus.
12 Oui, il (there) demeure.
13 Nous allons (you) aider demain.
14 Non, ils ne (me) intéressent pas.
15 Je (you) aime beaucoup, mon enfant.

Exercise No. 82—Questionnaire

1 Qui sait demander des renseignements?
2 Qu'est-ce que M. et Mme Davis préfèrent, le théâtre ou le cinéma?
3 Qu'est-ce que les enfants préfèrent?
4 Est-ce que les enfants connaissent les vedettes de l'écran?
5 Où est-ce que la famille Davis habite?
6 Le cinéma est-il près de la maison de M. Davis ou loin de sa maison?
7 Quelles places préfèrent-ils au cinéma?
8 Est-il possible de bien voir et bien entendre de là?
9 Qui vient les aider au cinéma?
10 Est-ce qu'ils arrivent de bonne heure ou en retard (late)?

CHAPITRE 16 (SEIZE)

QUELQUES DATES DE L'HISTOIRE DE LA FRANCE

1 — M. Davis, vous connaissez bien les nombres. Je vois que vous savez les employer correctement et rapidement. Voyons si vous connaissez les nombres en forme de dates.

2 — Avec plaisir, M. Picard. J'aime beaucoup les questionnaires en français.

3 — C'est pourquoi vous apprenez vite. Je vais citer quelques dates de l'histoire de la France et vous allez citer un événement important pour chacune.

4 — Bon. Commençons.

5 — Le quatorze juillet, 1789 (dix-sept cent quatre-vingt-neuf).

6 — Comme vous êtes gentil! C'est facile: la prise de la Bastille pendant la Révolution Française.

7 — Très bien. 1815 (dix-huit cent quinze).

8 — C'est sans doute Napoléon. Voyons. C'est la bataille de Waterloo, n'est-ce pas?

9 — Correct. 1870 (dix-huit cent soixante-dix).

10 — Ah, c'est une date triste pour la France: la défaite de l'armée pendant la guerre franco-prussienne.

11 — Voici une date victorieuse: 1918 (dix-neuf cent dix-huit).

12 — La victoire des Alliés à la fin de la première guerre mondiale.

13 — Finissons le questionnaire. Encore une date, la dernière: 1944 (dix-neuf cent quarante-quatre).

14 — C'est une date glorieuse pour les Parisiens: la libération de Paris par les Parisiens et la fin de l'occupation nazie.

15 — Merveilleux, M. Davis. Je vois que vous connaissez l'histoire de France aussi bien que son système monétaire.

16 — Mais, M. Picard, je n'ai pas passé[1] treize ans en classe pour rien. D'ailleurs, j'ai un professeur qui m'apprend à aimer la France.

17 — C'est vous maintenant qui êtes trop aimable.

18 — Pas du tout. C'est la vérité.

1 Mr. Davis, you know the numbers well. I see that you know how to use them correctly and rapidly. Let us see if you know the numbers in the form of dates.

2 With pleasure, Mr. Picard. I like questionnaires in French.

3 That's why you learn quickly. I am going to mention some dates in the history of France and you will mention an important event for each one.

4 Good. Let's begin.

5 14 July 1789.

6 How kind you are! That's easy: the storming of the Bastille during the revolution.

7 Very good. 1815.

8 That's Napoleon, no doubt. Let's see. It's the battle of Waterloo, isn't it?

9 Correct. 1870.

10 Ah, that's a sad date for France: the defeat of the army in the Franco-Prussian war.

11 Here is a victory date: 1918.

12 The victory of the Allies at the end of the First World War.

13 Let us finish the quiz. One more date, the last: 1944.

14 This is a glorious date for Parisians: the liberation of Paris by the Parisians and the end of the Nazi occupation.

15 Marvellous, Mr. Davis. I see that you know the history of France as well as its monetary system.

16 Well, Mr. Picard, I didn't spend thirteen years in school for nothing. Besides I have a teacher who teaches me to love France.

17 Now it is you who flatter me.

18 Not at all. It's the truth.

NOTE 1. **je n'ai pas passé** = I have not spent or did not spend. This is the conversational past tense. You will learn more about this tense later.

Pronunciation and Spelling Aids

Practise Aloud:

1 **voyons si vous connaissez les nombres en forme de dates**
1 (vwa-jɔ̃ si vu kɔ-nɛ-se lɛ nɔ̃br ɑ̃ fɔrm də dat)
2 **avec plaisir, Monsieur Picard**
2 (a-vɛk plɛ-ziːr mə-sjø pi-kaːr)
3 **j'aime beaucoup les questionnaires en français**
3 (ʒɛm bo-ku lɛ kɛs-tjɔ-nɛːr ɑ̃ frɑ̃-sɛ)

Vocabulary Building

A. Les mois de l'année (le mwa dla-ne) The Months of the Year

janvier (ʒɑ̃-vje), January	**juillet** (ʒɥi-jɛ), July
février (fe-vri-je), February	**août** (u), August
mars (mars), March	**septembre** (sɛp-tɑ̃ːbr), September
avril (a-vril), April	**octobre** (ɔk-tɔbr), October
mai (mɛ), May	**novembre** (nɔ-vɑ̃ːbr), November
juin (ʒɥɛ̃), June	**décembre** (de-sɑ̃ːbr), December

B. l'an, l'année, le jour, la journée

l'année and **la journée** are used instead of **l'an** and **le jour** when one has in mind the events that take place during the year or during the day. Thus:

j'étudie toute la journée (toute l'année), I study all day (all year)

but: **je vais rester trois jours (ans) à Paris,** I am going to stay in Paris for three days (years)

NOTE all months are masculine

Exercise No. 83—Completion of Text

1 (You know how) **employer correctement les nombres.**
2 **Vous allez citer** (an important event).
3 Let's begin.
4 (How) **vous êtes gentil!**
5 **L'année 1870 est** (a sad date) **pour la France.**
6 **Voici** (a victorious date).
7 (Let us finish) **le questionnaire.**
8 **Vous connaissez l'histoire de France** (as well as) **son système monétaire.**
9 (Besides), **j'ai un bon professeur.**
10 (He teaches me) **à aimer la France.**
11 (It is you) **qui êtes trop aimable.**
12 (Not at all.) **C'est la vérité.**

Locutions Françaises

1 **comme vous êtes gentil!** how kind you are!
2 **sans doute** (sã dut), without doubt
3 **en classe** (ã klã:s), in school, in class
4 **il m'apprend à aimer la France,** he teaches me to love France; **apprendre** may mean either *to learn* or *to teach*

Grammar Notes

1 Present Tense of **finir**, to finish. Regular **-ir** verb.

I finish, am finishing, do finish, you finish, you are finishing, etc.

je finis (fi-ni)	**nous finissons** (fi-ni-sɔ̃)
tu finis (fi-ni)	**vous finissez** (fi-ni-se)
il, elle finit (fi-ni)	**ils, elles finissent** (fi-ni:s)

Imperative: **finis,** finish; **finissons,** let us finish; **finissez,** finish.
Interrogative: **finit-il?** does he finish?
Negative: **il ne finit pas,** he does not finish.
Neg. Interrog.: **ne finit-il pas?** does he not finish?

2 Some common regular **-ir** verbs like **finir** are:

bâtir,	to build	**je bâtis**	**tu bâtis**	**il bâtit**	**nous bâtissons,** etc.
choisir,	to choose	**je choisis**	**tu choisis**	**il choisit**	**nous choisissons,** etc.
obéir,	to obey	**j'obéis**	**tu obéis**	**il obéit**	**nous obéissons,** etc.
punir,	to punish	**je punis**	**tu punis**	**il punit**	**nous punissons,** etc.
remplir,	to fill	**je remplis**	**tu remplis**	**il remplit**	**nous remplissons,** etc.
saisir,	to seize	**je saisis**	**tu saisis**	**il saisit**	**nous saisissons,** etc.

Exercise No. 84 Write the correct form of the verbs indicated. Read each completed sentence aloud in French.

1 **À quelle heure** (do you finish) **votre journée?**
2 (We finish) **notre journée à cinq heures.**
3 **Quelle place** (do you choose)?
4 (I choose) **une place au premier rang.**
5 **Pourquoi est-ce que le maître** (punishes) **Jacques?**

6 **Parce qu'** (he does not obey).
7 **Les enfants** (are building) **une petite maison.**
8 (Fill) **ma tasse de café, s'il vous plaît.**
9 (They are not finishing) **leurs exercices.**
10 **Elle** (is filling) **son panier de fruits.**
11 (Let us choose) **nos places maintenant.**
12 **La police va** (to seize) **le voleur** (thief).

3 Ordinal Numbers.

1st **premier** (*m*) (prə-mje)	6th **sixième** (si-zjɛm)
1st **première** (*f*) (prə-mjɛːr)	7th **septième** (sɛ-tjɛm)
2nd **deuxième** (dø-zjem)	8th **huitième** (ɥi-tjɛm)
3rd **troisième** (trwa-zjɛm)	9th **neuvième** (nœ-vjɛm)
4th **quatrième** (ka-tri-jɛm)	10th **dixième** (di-zjɛm)
5th **cinquième** (sɛ̃-kjɛm)	last **dernier** (*m*) **dernière** (*f*)

Ordinal numbers are formed by adding **-ième** to the cardinals with the exception of **premier**, first. Final e is dropped before adding -ième (**quatrième**); u is added after **q** (**cinquième**) and **f** becomes **v** (**neuvième**); second (zgɔ̃) is used instead of **deuxième** in a number of set phrases.

Exercise No. 85 Complete in French. Read the completed expressions aloud.

1 **la** (first) **leçon**	4 **la** (fifth) **semaine**	7 **la** (last) **classe**
2 **la** (third) **place**	5 **le** (twelfth) **jour**	8 **la** (ninth) **rue**
3 **le** (fourteenth) **chapitre**	6 **le** (first) **mois**	9 **les** (last) **rangs**

4. Dates

(*a*) **Quel jour du mois est-ce aujourd'hui?** *or* **Quel jour du mois sommes-nous aujourd'hui?**
What is today's date? (*Lit.* What day of the month is it today? *or* What day of the month are we today?)
C'est aujourd'hui le vingt mai. Today is 20 May.

(*b*) **le 1ᵉʳ (premier) janvier 1966 (dix-neuf cent soixante-six)**, 1 January 1966.
le 2 (deux) février 1950 (dix-neuf cent cinquante), 2 February 1950.
le 14 (quatorze) juillet 1789 (dix-sept cent quatre-vingt-neuf), 14 July 1789.

premier is used for the first day of the month. For the other days the cardinal numbers **deux, trois**, etc., are used.

In dates, **mil** (instead of **mille** for thousand) may be used: **mil neuf cent** instead of **dix-neuf cent**.

Exercise No. 86 Write out the following dates in full. Read each date aloud in French.

Exemple: le 4 juillet 1776 le quatre juillet, dix-sept cent (*or* mil sept cent) soixante-seize

1 **le 18 avril 1775**	3 **le 22 février 1809**
2 **le 12 octobre 1492**	4 **le 1ᵉʳ mai 1956**

Exercise No. 87—Questionnaire

1 Pourquoi est-ce que M. Davis apprend vite?
2 Qu'est-ce que M. Picard va citer?
3 Qu'est-ce que M. Davis va citer?
4 Quel événement important M. Davis cite-t-il pour 1789?
5 Quel événement important cite-t-il pour 1815?
6 Est-ce que 1870 est une date triste ou une date glorieuse pour la France?
7 Quel événement est-ce que M. Davis cite pour 1918?
8 Est-ce que 1944 est une date glorieuse ou une date triste pour les Parisiens?
9 Est-ce que M. Davis connaît bien l'histoire de France?
10 Qui lui apprend à aimer la France?

CHAPITRE 17 (DIX-SEPT)

QUELQUES QUESTIONS SUR LA GÉOGRAPHIE DE LA FRANCE

1 — M. Davis, aujourd'hui voyons si vous connaissez la géographie de la France aussi bien que son histoire. Vous permettez que je vous pose quelques questions?

2 — Certainement. Est-ce que je vais recevoir un prix si mes réponses sont correctes?

3 — Non, M. Davis. Ce n'est pas une émission de radio. Commençons par la question la plus facile. Sur quel grand fleuve est-ce que la ville de Paris est située?

4 — C'est vraiment trop facile. Sur la Seine.

5 — Et quel port très important est situé à l'embouchure de la Seine?

6 — C'est Le Havre, grand marché de café, de coton et de sucre. La plus grande partie du commerce entre la France et l'Amérique du Nord passe par ce port.

7 — Quel est le fleuve le plus long de France?

8 — Voyons. Est-ce le Rhône?

9 — Non, pas tout à fait exact. La Loire est le fleuve le plus long de France. Il n'est pas beaucoup plus long que le Rhône, d'une centaine de kilomètres plus ou moins.

10 — En tout cas, il est bien plus petit que la Volga.

11 — Oh incontestablement. La Volga est plus longue et plus large que la Loire. Savez-vous quelle est la plus haute montagne de France?

12 — Ça oui, je le sais, le Mont Blanc.

13 — Savez-vous s'il y a une montagne aussi haute que le Mont Blanc ici en Grande-Bretagne?

14 — Je sais que le Mont Blanc est plus haut que le Ben Nevis, qui est la montagne la plus haute de la Grande-Bretagne, mais je ne sais pas exactement sa hauteur.

15 — Ni moi non plus, M. Davis, mais je sais que vous avez raison. Alors, voilà: l'examen est terminé. Je vous en[1] félicite.

16 — Merci. J'attends mon diplôme la semaine prochaine.

17 — Oh non, M. Davis. Pas encore. Ce n'est que[2] la partie élémentaire du cours.

18 — Eh bien, nous pouvons entreprendre la deuxième partie plus tard.

1 Mr. Davis, today let us see if you know French geography as well as French history. Will you allow me to ask you a few questions?

2 Certainly. Shall I receive a prize if my answers are correct?

3 No, Mr. Davis. This is not a radio programme. Let us begin with the easiest question. On what great river is the city of Paris situated?

4 That is really too easy. On the Seine.

5 And what very important port is situated at the mouth of the Seine?

6 It is Le Havre, a big market for coffee, cotton and sugar. The largest part of the trade between France and North America passes through this port.

7 What is the longest river in France?

8 Let's see. Is it the Rhône?

9 No, not quite right. The Loire is the longest river in France. It is not very much longer than the Rhône, one hundred kilometres, more or less.

10 In any case, it is very much smaller than the Volga.

11 Oh, decidedly. The Volga is longer and wider than the Loire. Do you know which is the highest mountain in France?

12 That I do know, Mont Blanc.

13 Do you know if there is a mountain as high as Mont Blanc here in Great Britain?

14 I do know that Mont Blanc is higher than Ben Nevis, which is the highest mountain in Britain, but I don't know exactly its height.

15 Neither do I, Mr. Davis, but I know that you're right. Well, Mr. Davis, the examination is over. I congratulate you.

16 Thank you. I will expect my diploma next week.

17 Oh, no, Mr. Davis. Not yet. This is only[2] the elementary part of the course.

18 Well, we can take the second part later.

NOTE 1. **en** is not translated here. It means *on it*.

2. **ne** *verb* **que** is one way of saying *only*. Another way of saying this sentence is: **C'est seulement** (only) **la première partie,** etc.

Pronunciation and Spelling Aids

A. Practise Aloud:

1 **voyons si vous connaissez la géographie de la France aussi bien que son histoire**

1 (vwa-jɔ̃ si vu kɔ-nɛ-se la ʒe-ɔ-gra-fi də la frɑ̃ o-si bjɛ̃ kə sɔ̃ nis-twaːr)

2 **vous permettez que je vous pose quelques questions?**

2 (vu pɛr-mɛ-te kə ʒə vu poːz kɛlk kɛs-tjɔ̃)

B. 1 **le** and **la** become **l'** before words beginning with a vowel and usually before **h**. However, there are exceptions. Thus:

According to rule: **l'hôtel   l'homme   l'histoire   l'heure   l'habitude**

Some exceptions: **la hauteur   la haute montagne   le huitième jour   le Havre**

2 **si** (if) plus **il** becomes **s'il**.

Building Vocabulary

Related Words

1 **grand**, great; **la grandeur**, greatness
2 **haut**, high; **la hauteur**, height
3 **long**, long; **la longueur**, length
4 **large**, wide; **la largeur**, width

5 **visiter**, to visit; **le visiteur**, visitor
6 **porter**, to carry; **le porteur**, porter
7 **penser**, to think; **le penseur**, thinker
8 **vendre**, to sell; **le vendeur**, seller

Locutions françaises

1 **pas tout à fait** (pɑ tu ta fɛ), not quite
2 **en tout cas** (ɑ̃ tu kɑ), in any case
3 **ni moi non plus** (ni mwa nɔ̃ ply), neither do I

4 **pas encore** (pɑ zɑ̃-kɔːr), not yet
5 **alors** (a-lɔːr), well, then, in that case, and so
6 **voilà** (vwa-la), is used in the sense of *there is* or *there are* (pointing); also as an exclamation translated in various ways: *there! there now! that's that! behold!* etc.

Exercise No. 88—Completion of Text

1 (Let us see) **si vous connaissez** (French geography).
2 **Vous permettez** (that I ask you) **quelques questions?**
3 **Vous n'allez pas** (to receive a prize).
4 **Le Havre** (is situated) **à l'embouchure de la Seine.**
5 **C'est un grand marché** (of coffee, cotton and sugar).
6 **Quel est** (the longest river) **de France.**
7 **Il n'est pas** (much longer than) **le Rhône.**
8 **Il est** (smaller than) **la Volga.**
9 **Le Mont Blanc est** (the highest mountain) **de France.**
10 **Le Mont Blanc est** (higher than) **le Ben Nevis.**
11 **Je sais** (that you are right).
12 **L'examen** (is finished).

Grammar Notes

1 Present Tense of **mettre**, to put.
   I put, I am putting, you put, you are putting, etc.

je mets (mɛ)	**nous mettons** (mɛ-tɔ̃)
tu mets (mɛ)	**vous mettez** (mɛ-te)
il, elle met (mɛ)	**ils, elles mettent** (mɛːt)

Imperative: **mets**, put; **mettons**, let us put; **mettez**, put.

Like **mettre** are: **permettre**, to permit; **admettre**, to admit; **remettre**, to put back.

Exercise No. 89 Translate into French:

1 I am putting
2 Who puts?
3 Why do you put?
4 What do you (**tu**) put?
5 we are putting
6 they do not put
7 I do not permit
8 Does he permit?
9 Why do you permit?
10 we permit
11 Does he not permit?
12 permit me

2. The Comparison of Adjectives and Adverbs.

Observe the positive, comparative and superlative forms of the adjectives **grand** and **assidu**, and of the adverb **vite**:

La Seine est un *grand* fleuve.   The Seine is a *large* river.
Le Rhin est *plus grand* que la Seine.   The Rhine is *larger* than the Seine.
La Volga est *le plus grand* fleuve d'Europe.   The Volga is *the largest* river in Europe.

Hélène est très *assidue*.   Helen is very *diligent*.
Marie est *moins assidue* qu'Hélène.   Mary is *less diligent* than Helen.
Anne est l'élève *la moins assidue* de cette classe.   Anne is *the least diligent* pupil in this class.

Le paquebot marche *vite*. The steamer travels *fast*,
Le train marche *plus vite* que le paquebot. The train travels *faster* than the steamer.
L'avion va *le plus vite* de tous. The aeroplane travels *fastest* of all.

Positive	Comparative	Superlative
grand, tall, big, great	**plus grand**, taller	**le plus grand**, tallest
assidu, diligent	**moins assidu**, less diligent	**le moins assidu**, least diligent
vite, fast	**plus vite**, faster	**le plus vite**, fastest

(*a*) The comparative of an adjective or adverb is formed by placing **plus** (*more*) or **moins** (*less*) before the positive. The superlative of an adjective is formed by placing the definite article (**le, la** or **les**) before the comparative. In the superlative of an adverb only **le** is used.

(*b*) The superlative of the adjective may be preceded by a possessive adjective instead of by the definite article.

> **mon plus jeune frère, ma plus jeune sœur,** my youngest brother, my youngest sister

(*c*) After a superlative use **de (d')** not **dans** for **in**.

> **la montagne la plus haute d'Europe,** the highest mountain *in* Europe.

3 Expressions of Comparison

(*a*) When unequals are compared **que** is used for *than*, except with numbers, when **de** replaces **que**.

La Loire est *plus longue que* le Rhône. The Loire is *longer than* the Rhône.
Cette excursion coûte *plus (moins) de* trois livres. This tour costs *more (less) than* £3.

(*b*) When equals are compared **aussi . . . que** (*as . . . as*) is used. After a negative **si . . . que** is used instead of **aussi . . . que**.

M. Davis connaît l'histoire de la France *aussi bien que* sa géographie. Mr. Davis knows the history of France *as well as* its geography.
Guillaume n'est *pas si grand qu'*Henri. William is *not as tall as* Henry.

4 Some Irregular Comparisons

Adjectives	Adverbs
bon (bonne), good	**bien**, well
meilleur, better	**mieux**, better
le meilleur, the best	**le mieux**, best
mauvais, bad	**mal**, badly
pire (or plus mauvais), worse	**pis**[1] **(plus mal)**, worse
le pire (or le plus mauvais), the worst	**le pis**[1] **(le plus mal)**, worst

NOTE 1. **plus mal** and **le plus mal** are the usual forms. **Pis** and **le pis** are used chiefly in a number of set phrases.

Exercise No. 90 Translate the following sentences. Read them aloud three times.

1 Les films français sont-ils *meilleurs* que les films américains?
2 Quelques-uns sont *meilleurs*, d'autres sont *pires* (*plus mauvais*). En France et aux États-Unis on peut voir *les meilleurs* et aussi *les pires* (*plus mauvais*) films. En général j'aime *mieux* les films français.
3 Georges chante *mal*. Henri chante *plus mal* que Georges. Mais Guillaume chante *le plus mal* de tous.
4 Philippe écrit *bien*, mais vous écrivez *mieux* que lui. Jeanne écrit *le mieux* de tous.
5 Où fait-on *la meilleure porcelaine*? — On la fait à Limoges.
6 Mieux vaut tard que jamais.

Exercise No. 91 Complete the French sentences so that they correspond fully to the English. Read each completed French sentence aloud.

Exemple 1. Les verbes sont aussi importants que les noms.

1 The verbs are as important as the nouns.
2 Mary is nicer than Susan.
3 I have the best pen.
4 The black ink is not as good as the blue.
5 Theresa is taller than Julia.
6 John is the most diligent boy in the class.
7 Annette is the youngest child in the family.
8 I find French more interesting than Spanish.
9 Which is the longest river in France?
10 London is one of the largest cities in the world.
11 The Rhine is longer and wider than the Loire.
12 Why do you answer so badly?
13 We like the best films.
14 I have the worst pen.
15 This watch costs more than twelve pounds.

1 Les verbes sont ...... importants ...... les noms.
2 Marie est ...... aimable ...... Suzanne.
3 J'ai ...... plume.
4 L'encre noire n'est pas ...... bonne ...... la bleue.
5 Thérèse est ...... que Julie.
6 Jean est l'élève ...... de la classe.
7 Annette est la ...... enfant de la famille.
8 Je trouve le français ...... l'espagnol.
9 Quel est le fleuve ...... de France?
10 Londres est ...... du monde.
11 Le Rhin est ...... long et ...... large ...... la Loire.
12 Pourquoi répondez-vous si ......?
13 Nous aimons les ...... films.
14 J'ai le .... stylo.
15 Cette montre coûte .... douze livres.

Exercise No. 92—Questionnaire

1 Par quelle question facile est-ce que M. Picard commence?
2 Où est-ce que le port du Havre est situé?

3 Le port du Havre est-il un grand marché?

4 Quel fleuve est plus long et plus large que la Loire?

5 Quelle montagne est la plus haute, le Mont Blanc ou le Ben Nevis?

6 M. Dupont est un homme de quarante-cinq ans. Il a £35 000 (trente-cinq mille livres).

　M. Millet est un homme de cinquante ans. Il a £28 000 (vingt-huit mille livres).

　M. Arnaud est un homme de soixante ans. Il a £17 000 (dix-sept mille livres).

(a) Lequel[1] est le plus jeune des trois?

(b) Lequel est le plus âgé des trois?

(c) Est-ce que M. Millet est plus âgé que M. Dupont?

(d) Lequel est le plus riche?

(e) Lequel est le moins riche?

(f) Est-ce que M. Millet est aussi riche que M. Dupont?

NOTE 1. lequel, laquelle (*f*)?　which one?　lesquels, lesquelles (*f*)?　which ones?

CHAPITRE 18 (DIX-HUIT)

LA JOURNÉE DE M. DAVIS

1 — M. Davis, vous permettez que je vous demande comment vous passez une journée typique?

2 — Certainement. Quand je vais à mon bureau je me lève à six heures et demie. Vous voyez que je suis matinal. Je me lave et je m'habille en une demi-heure environ. Vers sept heures je me mets à table dans la salle à manger pour prendre mon petit déjeuner.

Ma femme, qui est matinale aussi, se lève de bonne heure et nous déjeunons ensemble. Naturellement cela me plaît beaucoup. Nous avons là une belle occasion de parler des enfants et d'autres choses qui nous intéressent.

3 — Qu'est-ce que vous prenez au petit déjeuner?

4 — Je bois du¹ jus d'orange, du café et je mange des petits pains et des œufs. Parfois je mange des céréales au lieu d'œufs.

5 — Je vois que vous aimez un petit déjeuner copieux. Et ensuite?

6 — À sept heures et demie je suis prêt à partir pour prendre le train. Parfois les enfants se lèvent de bonne heure pour m'embrasser avant mon départ.

7 — À quelle heure arrivez-vous au bureau?

8 — J'arrive vers neuf heures. Au bureau je lis mon courrier, je dicte les réponses à la sténo-dactylo, je parle au téléphone avec certains clients et je fais les choses qu'un commerçant doit faire.

9 — Et quand est-ce que vous déjeunez?²

10 — Presque toujours à une heure. Il me faut à peu près vingt minutes pour manger.

11 — C'est très peu. En France vous allez voir que les habitudes de manger sont tout autres. Le Français passe beaucoup plus de temps à table. Mais parlons de cela une autre fois. Qu'est-ce que vous mangez au déjeuner?

12 — D'habitude je prends un sandwich, un café et un dessert quelconque— une pomme cuite ou un gâteau.

13 — Que faites-vous après le déjeuner?

14 — Il y a souvent des clients qui viennent me voir et de temps en temps je sors pour voir d'autres clients.

15 — À quelle heure finissez-vous votre journée?

16 — À cinq heures précises je quitte le bureau. J'arrive chez moi vers sept heures moins le quart. Je fais un bout de toilette, je joue un peu avec les enfants et puis nous nous mettons à table pour dîner.

17 — Vous devez être fatigué après une journée pareille.

18 — Je pense bien, répond M. Davis.

1 Mr. Davis, may I ask you how you spend a typical day?

2 Certainly. When I go to my office I get up at six thirty. You see that I am an early riser. I wash and dress in about half an hour. At about seven I sit down at the table in the dining-room to have breakfast.

My wife, who is also an early riser, gets up early and we have breakfast together. Naturally I like that very much. We have a fine opportunity to talk about the children and other things which interest us.

3 What do you have for breakfast?

4 I drink (some)[1] orange juice, coffee and I eat rolls and eggs. Sometimes I eat cereals instead of eggs.

5 I see that you like a substantial breakfast. And afterwards?

6 At seven-thirty I am ready to leave to take the train. Sometimes the children get up early to kiss me before I go.

7 At what time do you arrive at the office?

8 I arrive at about nine o'clock. In the office I read my mail, dictate answers to the shorthand typist, talk on the telephone to various clients and do the things that a businessman has to do.

9 And when do you have lunch?[2]

10 Almost always at one. I need about twenty minutes to eat.

11 It is very little. In France you will see that eating habits are very different. The Frenchman spends much more time at meals. But let us speak of this at some other time. What do you have for lunch?

12 Usually I have a sandwich, coffee and some sweet or other—a baked apple or a cake.

13 What do you do after lunch?

14 Often customers come to visit me and from time to time I go out to visit other customers.

15 At what time do you finish your day's work?

16 At five o'clock sharp I leave the office. I arrive home at about a quarter to seven. I have a wash, play a little with the children and then we sit down at table to have dinner.

17 You must be tired after such a day.

18 'Yes indeed,' answers Mr. Davis.

NOTE 1. The idea *some* is expressed in French by **du, de la, de l'** and **des**. This usage is fully treated in the next chapter.

2. See 'Building Vocabulary' A 1, 2, 3.

Pronunciation and Spelling Aids

Practise Aloud:

1 je me lève (ʒə mlɛːv)
2 je me lave (ʒə mlaːv)
3 je m'habille (ʒə ma-bij)
4 je me mets à table (ʒəm mɛ a tabl)
5 je prends du café (ʒə prã dy ka-fe)
6 des petits pains (dɛ pti pɛ̃)
7 des oranges (dɛ zɔ-rãːʒ)
8 des œufs (dɛ zø)

Building Vocabulary

A. Les repas (lɛ rə-pa) Meals

1 le déjeuner (de-ʒœ-ne), breakfast or lunch
2 prendre le petit déjeuner, déjeuner, to have breakfast or lunch
3 le petit déjeuner, breakfast (of coffee and rolls)
4 un petit déjeuner copieux, substantial breakfast (of eggs, meat, etc.)
5 le dîner, dinner; dîner, to dine
6 le souper, supper

B. Quelques Aliments Some Foods

1 **le pain,** the bread; **du pain,** (some) bread
2 **un œuf** (ŏ-nœf), an egg; **des œufs** (dɛ zø), (some) eggs
3 **le petit pain,** the roll
4 **le café,** the coffee; **du café,** (some) coffee
5 **les céréales** (*f*), cereals; **des céréales,** (some) cereals
6 **le beurre,** the butter; **du beurre,** (some) butter
7 **le lait,** the milk; **du lait,** (some) milk
8 **la pomme,** the apple
9 **le gâteau (les gâteaux),** the cake
10 **la crème,** the cream; **de la crème,** (some) cream
11 **la viande,** the meat; **de la viande,** (some) meat
12 **le jus d'orange,** the orange juice
13 **la soupe,** soup; **de la soupe,** (some) soup
14 **le légume,** vegetable

Locutions françaises

1 **cela me plaît,** that pleases me, I like that
2 **il me faut 20 minutes,** I need 20 minutes (*Lit.* it is necessary to me 20 minutes)
3 **de temps en temps,** at times, from time to time
4 **je fais un bout de toilette,** I have a wash
5 **je pense bien,** yes, indeed
6 **se mettre à table,** to sit down at table

Exercise No. 93—Completion of Text

1 **Comment passez-vous** (a typical day)?
2 **Je me lève** (at six-thirty).
3 **Je suis** (an early riser).
4 **Ma femme se lève** (early).
5 (What do you eat) **au petit déjeuner?**
6 **Je prends** (coffee, rolls and eggs).
7 (At times) **les enfants se lèvent de bonne heure.**
8 **J'arrive** (at the office) **à neuf heures.**
9 **Je lis** (my mail) **et je dicte** (the answers).
10 (What do you do) **après le déjeuner?**
11 **Des clients viennent souvent** (to see me).
12 **À quelle heure** (do you finish) **votre journée?**
13 (I leave) **le bureau à cinq heures.**
14 (We sit down) **à table.**

Grammar Notes

1 Present Tense of the Reflexive Verb **se laver,** to wash oneself

je me lave (lav)	I wash myself, I am washing myself
tu te laves (lav)	you wash yourself
il se lave (lav)	he washes himself
elle se lave (lav)	she washes herself
nous nous lavons (la-vɔ̃)	we wash ourselves

vous vous lavez (la-ve)	you wash yourselves
ils se lavent (lav)	they wash themselves
elles se lavent (lav)	they wash themselves

Interrogative: **Vous lavez-vous?** or **Est-ce que vous vous lavez?**
Do you wash yourself?

Negative: **Je ne me lave pas,** I do not wash myself.

(*a*) The reflexive pronouns are: **me,** myself; **te,** yourself; **nous,** ourselves; **vous,** yourself, yourselves; **se,** himself, herself, itself, oneself, themselves.

(*b*) Like all object pronouns, the reflexive pronouns always precede the verb except in the affirmative imperative, when they follow it. Note that te becomes **toi** when after the verb.

Imperative (Affirmative)	*Imperative (Negative)*
lave-toi (*fam.*), wash yourself;	**ne te lave pas,** do not wash yourself;
lavons-nous, let us wash ourselves;	**ne nous lavons pas,** let us not wash ourselves;
lavez-vous, wash yourself (yourselves).	**ne vous lavez pas,** do not wash yourself (yourselves).

2 Some Common Reflexive Verbs.

Note that the French reflexive verb is not always translated by a reflexive verb in English.

1 **s'appeler,** to be called, named (*Lit.* to call oneself)
2 **s'amuser,** to enjoy oneself (*Lit.* to amuse oneself)
3 **se lever,** to get up (*Lit.* to raise oneself)
4 **s'asseoir** (sa-swaːr), to sit down (*Lit.* to seat oneself)
5 **se mettre à** (table), to sit down at (*Lit.* to put oneself at)
6 **se porter,** to feel (health) (*Lit.* to carry oneself)
7 **se coucher,** to go to bed (*Lit.* to lay oneself down)
8 **s'habiller,** to get dressed (*Lit.* to dress oneself)

Exercise No. 94 Complete each French sentence by inserting the correct reflexive pronoun. Read the completed sentences aloud.

Exemple: M. Davis va se mettre à table.

1 Mr. Davis is going to sit down at the table.
2 He gets up at seven o'clock.
3 He washes (himself) and dresses (himself).
4 At what time do you go to bed?
5 How do you feel? (How are you?)
6 She is feeling well.
7 My mother is feeling better today.
8 We enjoy ourselves at the cinema.
9 What is your name? (How do you call yourself?)
10 What are their names?
11 My name is John Martin.
12 Dress yourself quickly, Annette.
13 Do not get up late, children.
14 I do not go to bed before ten o'clock.
15 The children do not want to get up.

1 M. Davis va ...... mettre à table.
2 Il ...... lève à sept heures.
3 Il ...... lave et ...... habille.
4 A quelle heure ...... couchez-vous?
5 Comment ...... portez-vous?
6 Elle ...... porte bien.
7 Ma mère ...... porte mieux aujourd'hui.
8 Nous ...... amusons au ciné.
9 Comment ...... appelez-vous?
10 Comment ...... appellent-ils?
11 Je ...... appelle Jean Martin.
12 Habille- ...... vite, Annette.
13 Ne ...... levez pas tard, mes enfants.
14 Je ne ...... couche pas avant dix heures.
15 Les enfants ne veulent pas ...... lever.

Exercise No. 95 Translate the questions and answers. Read the questions and answers aloud several times.

1 — Comment vous appelez-vous?
   — Je m'appelle Jean Martin.
2 — À quelle heure est-ce que vous vous levez?
   — Je me lève à sept heures du matin.
3 — À quelle heure est-ce que vous vous couchez?
   — Je me couche à onze heures du soir.
4 — Est-ce que vous vous habillez vite?
   — Je m'habille très vite.
5 — Comment vous portez-vous?
   — Je me porte bien, merci.
6 — Comment votre père se porte-t-il?
   — Il ne se porte pas bien. Il est enrhumé.
7 — À quelle heure est-ce que M. Davis se met à table?
   — Il se met à table à sept heures du soir.
8 — Est-ce que les garçons s'amusent bien en jouant au football?
   — Ils s'amusent très bien.

Exercise No. 96—Questionnaire

1 À quelle heure est-ce que M. Davis se lève?
2 Ensuite que fait-il?
3 En combien de temps s'habille-t-il?
4 Que fait-il vers sept heures?
5 Est-ce que sa femme se lève de bonne heure?
6 Est-ce qu'ils déjeunent ensemble?
7 Qu'est-ce qu'il prend au petit déjeuner?
8 Qu'est-ce qu'il mange parfois au lieu d'œufs?
9 À quelle heure est-il prêt à partir?
10 À quelle heure arrive-t-il à son bureau?
11 À quelle heure déjeune-t-il?
12 Qu'est-ce qu'il prend au déjeuner?
13 Quelles personnes viennent le voir l'après-midi?
14 À quelle heure est-ce qu'il finit sa journée?

CHAPITRE 19 (DIX-NEUF)

LA VIE EN BANLIEUE

1 — Maintenant je suis bien renseigné sur votre journée en ville. Mais je suis toujours curieux. Dites-moi, M. Davis, comment passez-vous le temps chez vous dans la banlieue où vous habitez?

2 — Comment je passe mon temps? Mais, c'est bien simple. Vous savez déjà que je rentre assez tard. Nous ne finissons pas de dîner bien avant huit heures et demie. Alors il ne nous reste pas trop de temps pour de grandes entreprises.

3 — Tout de même, vous vous permettez quelques distractions, le cinéma, par exemple?

4 — Évidemment. Mais, d'habitude nous restons sagement chez nous, en famille. Nous causons, nous lisons, nous regardons la télévision et nous faisons la guerre aux enfants quand ils ne veulent pas se coucher.

5 — Et quant aux achats, est-ce que madame Davis peut faire son marché commodément?

6 — Oh, tout à fait. Tout près de chez nous il y a un de ces palais de ravitaillement qui s'appelle supermarché. On y achète non seulement des fruits, des légumes, du lait, du fromage, du beurre, du café, des conserves de toutes sortes, de la viande, des bonbons et des gâteaux mais aussi des collants, et des casseroles.

7 — Tout de même, vous n'y trouvez pas de pardessus.

8 — Pas encore. Mais nous avons un quartier commerçant très important. Plusieurs grands magasins de Londres ont des succursales qui peuvent nous fournir presque tout ce qu'il nous faut.

9 — Vous avez de la chance.

10 — Et le plus beau de l'affaire c'est qu'on peut toujours stationner, on n'est pas bousculé, et on peut causer à son aise avec les vendeurs.

11 — Et les enfants, sont-ils contents à l'école?

12 — Si on peut jamais dire qu'un enfant est content à l'école, alors oui, ils sont contents. Ils aiment bien leurs maîtres d'école, ils ont de bons camarades.

13 — Vous faites si bien la propagande pour la banlieue que j'ai envie de déménager?

14 — Venez donc! Vous serez le bienvenu!

1 Now I am well informed about your day in town. But I am still inquisitive. Tell me, Mr. Davis, how do you pass the time at home in the suburbs where you live?

2 How I pass the time? Well, it's very simple. You know already that I get home rather late. We don't finish our dinner much before 8.30, so that there is not too much time left for great undertakings.

3 All the same, you do allow yourselves some amusements, the cinema for example?

4 Of course. But generally we stay quietly at home with the family. We

talk, we read, we watch television and we battle with the children when they don't want to go to bed.

5 And as for shopping, can Mrs. Davis do it conveniently?

6 Oh, quite. Very near us there is one of those palaces for provisions which is called a 'supermarket'. There one can buy not only fruit, vegetables, milk, cheese, butter, coffee, all sorts of tinned goods, meat, sweets and cakes, but also tights and saucepans.

7 Just the same you don't find overcoats there.

8 Not yet. But we have a very large business area. Several of the London stores have branches which can supply us with nearly everything we need (*Lit.* everything that is necessary to us).

9 You're lucky (*Lit.* You have luck).

10 And the best part of it is that one can always park, one is not pushed around and one can talk at one's ease with the salespeople.

11 And the children, are they happy at school?

12 If one can ever say that a child is happy at school, then yes, they are very happy. They like their teachers, they have good friends.

13 You make life in the suburbs sound so attractive that I feel like moving.

14 Come on, then. You will be very welcome.

Pronunciation and Spelling Aids

Practise Aloud:

maintenant je suis bien renseigné sur votre journée en ville (mɑ̃t-nɑ̃ ʒə sɥi bjɛ̃ rɑ̃-sɛ-ɲe syr vɔtr ʒur-ne ɑ̃ vil)

mais je suis toujours curieux (mɛ ʒə sɥi tu-ʒuːr ky-rjø)

dites-moi, monsieur Davis, comment passez-vous le temps chez vous dans la banlieue où vous habitez? (dit-mwa mə-sjø da-vis kɔ-mɑ̃ pa-se-vu ltɑ̃ ʃe vu dɑ̃ la bɑ̃-ljø u vu za-bi-te)

Building Vocabulary

Quelques fruits et légumes Some Fruits and Vegetables

la banane (ba-nan), banana
le citron (si-trɔ̃), lemon
une orange (y-nɔ-rɑ̃ːʒ), orange
la poire (pwar), pear
la pêche (pɛːʃ), peach
la pomme (pɔm), apple
la tomate (tɔ-mat), tomato
les raisins (*m*) (rɛ-zɛ̃), grapes
la betterave (bɛt-rav), beetroot

la carotte (ka-rɔt), carrot
le chou (ʃu), cabbage
les épinards (*m*) (lɛ ʒe-pi-naːr), spinach
les petits pois (*m*) (pti pwa), peas
les haricots (*m*) (lɛ a-ri-ko), haricot beans
un oignon (ɔ-ɲɔ̃), onion
la pomme de terre (pɔm də tɛːr), potato

Locutions françaises

1 tout de même (tud mɛːm), all the same, nevertheless
2 en famille (ɑ̃ fa-miːj), with the family
3 faire son marché, to do one's shopping
4 le plus beau de l'affaire, the best part of it
5 être à son aise, to be at one's ease, comfortable
6 j'ai envie de (ʒɛ ɑ̃-vi də) I desire, have a mind to
7 être le bienvenu (bjɛ̃-vny), to be welcome

Exercise No. 97—Completion of Text

1 Je suis (well informed).
2 (All the same) **vous vous permettez quelques distractions?**
3 (We remain) **sagement chez nous.**
4 **Mme Davis peut faire** (her shopping) **commodément.**
5 **On achète** (fruits, vegetables, milk, butter, cheese and coffee) **au super-marché.**
6 **On y achète aussi** (tights and saucepans).
7 **On peut toujours** (park).
8 **On peut causer** (at one's ease).
9 **Les enfants ont** (good friends).
10 I feel like moving.

Grammar Notes

1 Some or Any

Observe in the following sentences how *some* or *any* is expressed in French:

1 Je prends *du* jus d'orange.
2 J'achète *de la* crème.
3 Avez-vous *de l'*argent?
4 **M. Davis importe *des* objets d'art.**

1 I take (*some*) orange juice.
2 I buy (*some*) cream.
3 Have you (*any*) money?
4 Mr. Davis imports (*some*) art objects.

(*a*) The idea *some* or *any* preceding a noun is usually expressed in French by de plus the definite article, that is: **du, de la, de l'**, or **des**. This construction is called the *partitive* because it indicates *part*, not all of the thing or things.

(*b*) The words *some* and *any* are often omitted in English, but the corresponding words in French are almost never omitted.

2 Omissions of the Definite Article in the Partitive.

The partitive (*some* or *any*) is usually expressed by de without the definite article; (*a*) after a negative verb; (*b*) when a plural adjective precedes the noun.

(*a*) Je n'achète pas *de* café, *de* crème ni[1] *d'*œufs.
(*b*) M. Davis importe *de* beaux objets d'art.

(*a*) I am not buying (*any*) coffee, (*any*) cream or (*any*) eggs.
(*b*) Mr. Davis imports (*some*) beautiful art objects.

NOTE 1. **ni,** nor.

Exercise No. 98 In these sentences substitute the French words for *some* or *any* (du, de la, de l', des or de):

1 **Pour le petit déjeuner je prends** (some) **café et** (some) **jus d'orange.**
2 **Voulez-vous** (some) **lait,** (some) **beurre et** (some) **œufs?**
3 **N'avez-vous pas** (any) **porcelaine de Limoges?**
4 **Les enfants mangent** (some) **gâteaux.**
5 **Mangez-vous** (some) **céréales au lieu d'œufs?**
6 **M. Davis ne vend pas** (any) **auto.**
7 **Pour le dîner M. Davis prend** (some) **soupe,** (some) **viande et** (some) **légumes.**
8 **Est-ce qu'il y a** (any) **bons restaurants près d'ici?**
9 **Je veux acheter** (some) **encre rouge.**
10 **Les enfants ont** (some) **bons camarades.**

3 The Partitive Pronoun **en** (some of it, any of it, etc.)
You are familiar with the word **en** as a preposition. Thus:

En été il fait chaud. It is warm in summer.
Ils voyagent en France. They are travelling in France.
Répétez ces mots en français. Repeat these words in French.

Study the use of the pronoun **en** in the following sentences:

Voulez-vous de la crème? Do you want any cream?
Merci. J'*en* ai déjà. Thanks. I have *some* (*of it*) already.
Avez-vous des stylos? Have you any fountain pens?
Moi, je n'*en* ai pas. Louis en a trois. I haven't *any* (*of them*). Louis has three.
Achetez-vous des œufs? Are you buying any eggs?
Oui, j'*en* achète deux douzaines. Yes, I am buying two dozen (*of them*).
A-t-il beaucoup d'argent? Has he a great deal of money?
Non. Il n'*en* a qu'un peu. He has only a little (*of it*).

(*a*) en is used as a pronoun meaning *some* or *any*. en may be translated as *some, any, some of it, any of it, some of them, any of them.*

(*b*) In English the above words may be expressed or understood. In French the en must not be omitted. Thus:
Voici des gâteaux. Here are some cakes.
N'*en* mangez pas trop. Do not eat too many (*of them*).

(*c*) Like all object pronouns en precedes the verb except in the affirmative imperative.

Voici des gâteaux. Here are some cakes.
Prenez-*en*. N'*en* prenez pas. Take *some*. Do not take *any* (*of them*).

Exercise No. 99 Read each question. Then give the indicated answer in French.

Exemple 1. Oui, nous en vendons beaucoup.

1 Vendez-vous beaucoup de porcelaine?	1 Yes, we sell a good deal of it.
2 Achète-t-elle des conserves?	2 Yes, she is buying some.
3 Avez-vous un pardessus?	3 No, I haven't any.
4 Voici de la soupe.	4 Take some.
5 Les pommes ne sont pas mûres (ripe).	5 Do not eat any (of them).
6 Combien d'élèves a-t-il?	6 He has thirty (of them).
7 Prenez quelques poires.	7 Thanks. I don't want any.
8 Ont-ils assez de livres?	8 Yes, they have enough (of them).

Exercise No. 100—Questionnaire

1 Qui est toujours curieux?
2 Qu'est-ce que M. Picard sait déjà?
3 À quelle heure est-ce que la famille Davis finit de dîner?
4 Pourquoi les parents font-ils la guerre aux enfants?
5 Comment le palais de ravitaillements s'appelle-t-il?
6 Qu'est-ce qu'on achète au 'supermarché'?
7 Qu'est-ce qu'on ne trouve pas au 'supermarché'?
8 Est-ce que les grands magasins de Londres ont des succursales dans la banlieue?
9 Qui est-ce que les enfants aiment?
10 Qui a envie de déménager en banlieue?

RÉVISION 4

CHAPITRES 15–19 PREMIÈRE PARTIE

Révision de mots

NOUNS

1 un amateur	11 le dîner	21 la plupart (de)
2 le beurre	12 le film	22 la pomme
3 le ciné (*fam.*)	13 la glace	23 une émission
4 le cinéma	14 une histoire	24 le rang
5 le côté	15 la lumière	25 le fleuve
6 le cours	16 la montagne	26 la sténo-dactylo
7 la date	17 un œil (des yeux)	27 le téléphone
8 le départ	18 un œuf	28 la télévision
9 le petit déjeuner	19 le pain	29 la viande
10 le déjeuner	20 le petit pain	30 la voiture

1 lover (of things)	11 dinner	21 the majority of, most
2 butter	12 film	22 apple
3 cinema	13 ice-cream	23 broadcast
4 cinema	14 history, story	24 row
5 side	15 light	25 river (large)
6 course, lesson	16 mountain	26 shorthand typist
7 date	17 eye (eyes)	27 telephone
8 departure	18 egg	28 television
9 breakfast	19 bread	29 meat
10 lunch	20 roll	30 car, carriage

VERBS

1 adorer	14 finir	27 s'amuser
2 aider	15 nous finissons	28 je m'amuse
3 déjeuner	16 bâtir	29 s'appeler
4 embrasser	17 choisir	30 il s'appelle
5 ennuyer	18 obéir	31 se coucher
6 féliciter	19 punir	32 s'habiller
7 intéresser	20 remplir	33 se laver
8 remercier	21 saisir	34 se lever
9 préférer	22 mourir	35 levez-vous
10 rester	23 venir	36 se reposer
11 mettre	24 il vient	37 boire
12 je mets	25 devenir	38 je bois
13 permettre	26 revenir	

1 to adore	10 to remain, stay	19 to punish
2 to help	11 to put	20 to fill
3 to breakfast, lunch	12 I put	21 to seize
4 to kiss	13 to permit, allow	22 to die
5 to bore	14 to finish	23 to come
6 to congratulate	15 we finish	24 he comes
7 to interest	16 to build	25 to become
8 to thank	17 to choose	26 to come back
9 to prefer	18 to obey	27 to enjoy oneself

28 I enjoy myself	32 to dress oneself	36 to rest
29 to be called	33 to wash oneself	37 to drink
30 his name is	34 to get up	38 I drink
31 to go to bed	35 get up	

ADJECTIVES

1 fatigué	**4** occupé	**7** quelconque
2 gentil (ille *f*)	**5** pareil (eille *f*)	**8** terminé
3 glorieux (ieuse *f*)	**6** mûr	**9** triste

1 tired	4 busy	7 any, some sort of
2 kind, nice	5 like, such	8 finished
3 glorious	6 ripe	9 sad

ADVERBS

1 alors	**4** exactement	**7** seulement
2 ensemble	**5** parfois	**8** souvent
3 d'ailleurs	**6** puis	**9** toujours

1 well, then	4 exactly	7 only
2 together	5 at times	8 often
3 besides	6 then	9 always

PREPOSITIONS

1 au lieu (de)	**2** jusqu'à	**3** pendant	**4** sans
1 instead of	2 up to, until, as far as	3 during	4 without

FRENCH EXPRESSIONS

1 attraper un rhume	**9** pas encore
2 être le bienvenu	**10** cela me plaît
3 bien entendu	**11** rester (être) debout
4 à l'heure	**12** de temps en temps
5 de bonne heure	**13** (pas) tout à fait
6 n'importe	**14** tout de même
7 se mettre à table	**15** voilà
8 ni moi non plus	**16** en tout cas

1 to catch a cold	9 not yet
2 to be welcome	10 I like that
3 of course	11 to stand
4 on time	12 from time to time
5 early	13 (not) quite
6 never mind	14 all the same
7 to sit at table	15 there is (are)
8 neither do I	16 in any case

Exercise No. 101 Select the group of words in Column II which best completes each sentence begun in Column I.

I	II
1 Les enfants de M. Davis connaissent	(a) que je me lève de bonne heure.
2 Au quatorzième rang	(b) M. Davis prend du jus d'orange.
3 Le quatorze juillet 1789 est la date	(c) à sept heures du soir.
4 M. Davis connaît l'histoire de la France	(d) et moi nous déjeunons ensemble.
5 La Loire est le fleuve	(e) on peut bien voir et bien entendre.
6 'Je suis matinal' veut dire	(f) de la prise de la Bastille.

7 Toute la famille se met à table

8 Pour arriver à son bureau M. Davis fait le trajet[1]

9 Pour commencer le petit déjeuner

10 Cela me plaît beaucoup quand ma femme

(g) le plus long de la France.

(h) aussi bien que son système monétaire.

(i) toutes les vedettes de l'écran.

(j) en voiture, par le train et par le métro (underground).

NOTE 1. **Faire le trajet**, to travel.

Exercise No. 102 Complete these sentences in French:

1 La Loire est (the longest river) **de la France.**

2 Londres est (bigger than) **Paris.**

3 Philippe est (more tired than) **moi.**

4 Je ne suis pas (as tall as) **mon frère.**

5 Le Mont Blanc est (higher than) **le Ben Nevis.**

6 Le Mont Everest est (the highest mountain) **du monde.**

7 Lundi est (the first day) **de la semaine.**

8 January 30, 1956.

9 Annette est **la plus jeune** (in the family).

10 Georges est (my best friend).

Exercise No. 103 Translate the following brief dialogues. Practise them aloud. Note the various examples of the partitive.

1 — **Pour votre déjeuner prenez-vous du café ou du chocolat? — Je ne prends ni l'un ni l'autre. Je bois un verre d'eau.**

2 — **Désirez-vous de la crème et du sucre dans votre café? — Je voudrais**[1] **de la crème, mais je ne veux pas de sucre.**

3 — **Qu'est-ce qu'on mange au petit déjeuner en France? — On mange très peu, en général on mange des petits pains**[2] **et on boit du café.**

4 — **Que prend-on le matin au petit déjeuner en Grande-Bretagne? — Quelque fois on commence par du jus d'orange. Puis on mange des céréales, des œufs ou du bacon, souvent tous les deux. Les Anglais sont aussi très friands** (fond) **de pain grillé. Bien entendu il y a aussi du thé, du café, du lait, du pain ou des petits pains.**

NOTE 1. **je voudrais**, I would like, is more polite than **je veux**, I want.

2. **des** (not **de**) **petits pains**, since **petits pains**, like **petits pois**, is considered as a single noun, and not as an adjective plus noun.

Exercise No. 104 Read each French question. Then make your answer in French correspond to the English answer that follows the question.

Exemple 1. Oui, je les invite.

1 Invitez-vous vos amis à dîner chez vous?

2 Préférez-vous le ciné?

3 Est-ce que les enfants connaissent les vedettes du cinéma?

4 Est-ce que vous nous attendez?

5 Vous levez-vous de bonne heure?

6 À quelle heure est-ce que vous vous couchez?

1 Yes, I am inviting them.

2 No, I do not prefer it.

3 Yes, they know them well.

4 Yes, we are waiting for you.

5 No, I get up late.

6 We go to bed at eleven o'clock.

7 Les enfants s'habillent-ils rapide-ment le matin?	7 Yes, they dress themselves very quickly.
8 Comment vous appelez-vous?	8 My name is John Martin.
9 À quelle heure finissez-vous vos examens?	9 We finish them at four o'clock in the afternoon.
10 Finissent-ils maintenant le travail?	10 Yes, they are finishing it now.

Exercise No. 105 Complete these sentences by choosing the correct expression from those listed below. Be sure to use the correct form of the verbs and adjectives.

1 Elle doit être (tired) **après une journée** (such).
2 (They sit down at table) **à sept heures.**
3 (They are standing) **devant la maison.**
4 Les messieurs (are sitting) **dans le salon.**
5 (From time to time) **nous prenons du chocolat** (instead of) **café.**
6 Nous ne voulons pas (to catch cold).
7 Je vois (the majority of) **mes clients le matin.**
8 Le train arrive rarement (on time).
9 (We are) **toujours** (welcome) **chez M. Davis.**
10 Nous nous levons (early); ils se lèvent (late).

(a) au lieu (de)	(g) de temps en temps
(b) pareil (eille *f.*)	(h) attraper un rhume
(c) tard; à l'heure	(i) se mettre à table
(d) fatigué	(j) être le bienvenu
(e) la plupart (de)	(k) être debout
(f) de bonne heure	(l) être assis

Dialogue

Au Marché aux Puces   At the Flea Market

Nous sommes près d'un étalage de dessus de lit.

L'acheteur: Combien coûte ce dessus blanc brodé en bleu?

Le vendeur: Il coûte cent cinquante francs.

L'acheteur: C'est beaucoup trop. Je vais vous en donner cent trente.

Le vendeur: Mais monsieur, vous n'y pensez pas! Regardez ce travail, comme il est fin. Regardez la qualité du tissu. Enfin, ça va doucement aujourd'hui. Je vous le laisse à quarante-cinq.

L'acheteur: C'est encore beaucoup. Je vous en donne cent trente-cinq.

Le vendeur: Mais regardez, monsieur, comme il est grand. Il est assez grand pour un lit à deux places. Donnez-m'en cent quarante-deux.

L'acheteur: Je dors dans un lit à une place. Je suis célibataire. Je ne vais pas me marier. Je vous en donne cent trente-sept.

Le vendeur: Impossible, monsieur. Je suis marié, moi, et j'ai des enfants à nourrir. Cent quarante francs. C'est mon dernier prix.

L'acheteur: Bon, d'accord. Voici, monsieur.

(Il donne cent quarante francs au vendeur et il s'en va[1] avec le dessus blanc brodé en bleu. C'est la coutume de marchander au Marché aux Puces, et tous les deux sont contents.)

We are near a display of bedspreads.

Customer: What is the price of this white bedspread embroidered in blue?
Salesman: It costs hundred and fifty francs.
Customer: That's much too much. I'll give you hundred and thirty francs.
Salesman: But, sir, you can't mean it! Look at this fine work. Look at the quality of the cloth. Well, things are slow today. I'll let you have it for hundred and forty-five.
Customer: It's still high. I'll give you hundred and thirty-five.
Salesman: But look, sir, how big it is. It is big enough for a double bed. Make it hundred and forty-two.
Customer: I sleep in a single bed. I am a bachelor. I am not going to get married. I'll give you hundred and thirty-seven.
Salesman: Can't be done, sir. I am married, and I have children to feed. Hundred and forty francs. That's my final price.
Customer: All right, agreed. Here you are.

(He gives the seller hundred and forty francs, and he goes away with the white bedspread embroidered in blue. It is the custom to bargain at the flea market, and they are both pleased.)

NOTE 1. s'en aller, to go away, il s'en va, he goes away.

LECTURE
Exercise No. 106—Une visite au paquebot[1]
Île de France

C'est samedi. M. Davis se lève à huit heures et il regarde par la fenêtre. Le ciel est bleu. Le soleil brille. Il dit à sa femme: — Aujourd'hui allons visiter le paquebot *Île de France* qui est arrivé[2] ce matin. J'ai de la marchandise à bord. Nous allons avoir une belle occasion[3] de visiter le bateau.

— Très bien, dit Mme Davis.

À neuf heures ils partent en voiture et quelques heures plus tard ils arrivent sur le quai. À l'entrée, ils voient un groupe de garçons qui mangent des glaces et qui causent en français.

M. Davis dit bonjour aux garçons et cause un peu avec le plus proche.[4] Voici la conversation:

— Bonjour, jeune homme! Êtes-vous français?

— Non, monsieur, je suis anglais.

— Mais vous parlez très bien le français.

— Eh bien, ces garçons qui travaillent sur le paquebot *Île de France* sont mes amis, et ils m'apprennent à parler correctement. Ils sont mes professeurs. D'ailleurs, j'étudie le français au lycée[5] et tous les jours je lis quelques pages de français. À propos, êtes-vous français?

— Merci pour le compliment. Non, mon petit, je suis anglais et comme[6] vous j'étudie le français. Mais moi je n'ai qu'un professeur.[7]

— Ah bon. Mais vous parlez très bien.

— Merci encore une fois. Au revoir et bonne chance.

— Au revoir monsieur, au plaisir.

M. Davis rejoint sa femme qui l'attend en souriant, et ils se remettent en route[8] pour visiter le paquebot.

— Il est sympathique, ce garçon, dit M. Davis à sa femme. Et puis il traduit[9] la phrase, parce qu'elle ne comprend pas le français: 'He's a likeable boy.'

NOTE 1. steamship.
2. arrived.
3. opportunity.
4. the nearest one.
5. grammar school.
6. like.
7. I have only one teacher.
8. **ils . . . route,** they continue on their way.
9. **traduire,** to translate; **il traduit,** he translates.

CHAPITRE 20 (VINGT)

QUEL SALE TEMPS!

1 Il pleut à verse. La bonne ouvre la porte de la maison de M. et de Mme Davis. M. Picard entre.

2 La bonne dit: — Bonsoir, M. Picard. Quel sale temps! Entrez, entrez. Vous êtes trempé. Donnez-moi votre imperméable et votre chapeau, s'il vous plaît. Mettez votre parapluie dans le porte-parapluies. Vous pouvez laisser vos paquets ici dans l'entrée.

3 M. Picard répond: — Merci. Maintenant ça va mieux. Il pleut à verse, mais il ne fait pas froid. Je suis sûr que je ne vais pas attraper un rhume. Est-ce que M. Davis est là?

4 — Oui, oui, monsieur. Il vous attend dans le salon. Le voilà lui-même.

5 — Bonsoir M. Picard. Je suis très content de vous voir, mais par un sale temps pareil on ne doit pas sortir. Venez dans la salle à manger et prenez une tasse de thé au rhum pour vous réchauffer un peu.

6 — Merci infiniment, M. Davis. J'ai un peu froid. Une tasse de thé au rhum fera mon affaire, et pendant que nous prenons le thé nous allons causer du temps qu'il fait. C'est un sujet de conversation très courant et tout à fait à propos.

7 Les messieurs entrent dans la salle à manger en causant d'un ton animé. Ils s'asseyent et la bonne leur¹ apporte un plateau chargé de deux tasses et de deux soucoupes, d'une théière pleine de thé chaud, d'un sucrier, et de cuillers à thé. Elle met le plateau sur la table avec une bouteille de rhum qu'elle va chercher dans le buffet. Puis, elle sort de la salle à manger.

8 — Permettez-moi de vous servir, M. Picard, dit M. Davis. Il verse le thé dans les tasses avec une portion libérale de rhum pour chacun.

9 Pendant qu'ils prennent le thé au rhum les messieurs causent toujours d'un ton animé.

10 Dehors il pleut toujours.

1 It is pouring with rain. The maid opens the door of the house of Mr. and Mrs. Davis. Mr. Picard enters.

2 The maid says: Good evening, Mr. Picard. What nasty weather! Come in, come in. You are wet through. Give me your raincoat and hat. Put your umbrella in the umbrella stand. You can leave your parcels here in the hall.

3 Mr. Picard answers: Thank you. Now I feel better. It is raining hard, but it is not cold. I am sure that I shall not catch cold. Is Mr. Davis at home?

4 Yes, sir, yes. He is waiting for you in the living-room. There he is himself.

5 Good evening, Mr. Picard. I am very glad to see you, but in nasty weather like this one should not go out. Come to the dining-room and drink a cup of tea with rum to warm yourself a bit.

6 Thank you, thank you, Mr. Davis. I am a little cold. A cup of tea with rum will suit me very well, and while we drink tea with rum we will chat about the weather. It is a very common topic of conversation and just now is quite appropriate.

7 The gentlemen go into the dining-room chatting in animated voices. They sit down and the maid brings them[1] a tray loaded with two cups and saucers, a teapot full of hot tea, a sugar bowl and some teaspoons. She puts them on the table together with a bottle of rum which she takes from (*Lit.* goes to look for in) the sideboard. Then she leaves the dining-room.

8 Allow me to serve you, Mr. Picard, says Mr. Davis. He pours tea into the cups, with a generous portion of rum for each.

9 While they are drinking tea with rum the gentlemen continue chatting in a lively way.

10 Outside it is still raining.

NOTE 1. **leur.** (to) them. It is an indirect object pronoun.

Pronunciation and Spelling Aids

A. Practise Aloud:

bonsoir, M. Picard, je suis très content de vous voir, mais par un sale temps pareil on ne doit pas sortir (bɔ̃-swaːr mə-sjø pi-kaːr ʒə sɥi trɛ̃ kɔ̃-tɑ̃ dvu vwaːr mɛ par œ̃ saːl tɑ̃ pa-rɛj ɔ̃ ndwa pɑ sɔr tiːr)

venez dans la salle à manger et prenez une tasse de thé au rhum pour vous réchauffer (vne dɑ̃ la sa-la mɑ̃-ʒe e prə-ne yn taːs də te o rɔm pur vu re-ʃo-fe)

Building Vocabulary

A. **quel temps fait-il?** (kɛl tɑ̃ fɛ-til) what is the weather like?

1 **il fait beau** (il fɛ bo)	1 it is nice (weather)
2 **il fait mauvais** (mɔ-vɛ)	2 it is bad (weather)
3 **il fait (très) chaud** (ʃo)	3 it is (very) hot
4 **il fait (très) froid, frais** (frwa, frɛ)	4 it is (very) cold, cool
5 **il fait du vent** (dy vɑ̃)	5 it is windy
6 **il pleut, il neige, le soleil brille** (il plø il nɛːʒ lə sɔlɛːj brij)	6 it is raining, it is snowing, the sun is shining
7 **la pluie (la neige) tombe** (la plɥi, la nɛːʒ tɔ̃ːb)	7 the rain (the snow) is falling
8 **il pleut à verse** (il plø ta-vɛrs)	8 it is raining hard
9 **avez-vous froid? j'ai froid**	9 are you cold? I am cold
10 **avez-vous chaud? je n'ai pas chaud**	10 are you warm? I am not warm

NOTE: in French we say: what weather does it *make*? *not*, what *is* the weather like? it *makes* (**fait**) warmth, cold, etc. *not*, it *is* warm, cold, etc. We say: I *have* warmth, I *have* cold, etc. not, I *am* warm, I *am* cold, etc.

B. For Various Kinds of Weather

le pardessus (par-də-sy), overcoat
un imperméable (œ̃-nɛ̃-pɛr-me-abl), raincoat
le chandail (ʃɑ̃-daj), sweater
le parapluie (pa-ra-plɥi), umbrella
une ombrelle (y-nɔ̃ brɛl), parasol

Locutions françaises

1 **quel sale temps!** (kɛl saːl tɑ̃) what nasty weather!
2 **attraper un rhume** (a-tra-pe œ̃ rym), to catch a cold

3 **le voilà**, there he is
4 **une tasse de thé fera mon affaire**, a cup of tea will suit me (*Lit.* will make my business)
5 **en causant**, while chatting
6 **lui-même**, he himself
7 **elle-même**, she herself
8 **moi-même**, I myself

Exercise No. 107—Completion of Text

1 **La bonne dit:** — (What nasty weather!)
2 (Come in, come in.) **Vous êtes** (wet through).
3 **Donnez-moi** (your raincoat).
4 (Put) **votre parapluie dans le porte-parapluies.**
5 **Maintenant** (I feel better).
6 **Je ne vais pas** (to catch a cold).
7 **Par un sale temps pareil** (one should not go out).
8 (Come) **à la salle à manger.**
9 **La bonne** (brings them) **un plateau.**
10 (Drink) **une tasse de thé au rhum.**
11 (Permit me) **de vous servir.**
12 **Dehors** (it continues to rain).

Grammar Notes

1 The Present Tense of **ouvrir**, to open

I open, I am opening, you open, you are opening, etc.

j'ouvre (ʒuvr)	**nous ouvrons** (u-vrɔ̃)
tu ouvres (uvr)	**vous ouvrez** (u-vre)
il, elle ouvre (uvr)	**ils, elles ouvrent** (uvr)

Like ouvrir are: **couvrir**, to cover; **découvrir**, to discover; **offrir**, to offer

2 The Indirect Object Pronouns

The indirect object may be called the *to* (sometimes *for*) object. It indicates the person *to* or *for* whom the action is performed. Thus:

He writes a letter *to* his agent. He writes (*to*) him a letter. Observe carefully the indirect object pronouns in the following sentences:

1 Charles *me* donne un cadeau.
1 Charles is giving *me* a gift.

2 Ton père *t'*achète un chandail.
2 Your father is buying (*for*) *you* a sweater.

3 Qui *vous* apprend le français?
3 Who is teaching *you* French?

4 M. Picard *nous* apprend le français.
4 Mr. Picard is teaching *us* French.

5 Voilà M. Davis. Qui *lui* parle?
5 There is Mr. Davis. Who is speaking *to him*?

6 Voilà Mme Davis. Qui *lui* parle?
6 There is Mrs. Davis. Who is speaking *to her*?

7 Nous *leur* apportons les parapluies.
7 We are bringing *them* the umbrellas.

Compare the *direct object* pronouns with the *indirect object* pronouns.

Direct		*Indirect*	
me, m', me	nous, us	me, m', (to) me	nous, (to) us
te, t', you (*fam.*)	vous, you	te, t', (to) you (*fam.*)	vous, (to) you
le, l', him, it			
la, l', her, it	les, them	lui, (to) him, (to) her	leur, (to) them

(*a*) The direct and indirect objects are alike except in the third persons. Direct: **le**, him, it, **la**, her, it, **les**, them. Indirect: **lui**, to him, to her; **leur**, to them.

(*b*) Like the direct object, the indirect object precedes the verb except in the affirmative imperative.

> Donnez-*lui* le livre.   Give *him* the book.
> Ne *lui* donnez pas le livre.   Do not give *him* the book.

3 Some Common Verbs Which Take Indirect Objects When Mainly Referring to People:

apporter, to bring	prêter, to lend	rendre, to give back
acheter, to buy	présenter, to present	répéter, to repeat
dire, to say	montrer, to show	apporter, to bring
donner, to give	envoyer, to send	rapporter, to bring back
demander, to ask	écrire, to write	servir, to serve
parler, to speak	lire, to read	vendre, to sell
poser une question,[1] to ask a question		

Exercise No. 108 Complete the French sentences with the missing indirect objects. Read aloud. Remember **lui** = to him, to her, **leur** = to them.

Exemple 1. Je ne lui prête pas d'argent.

1 I am not lending *him* any money.
1 Je ne ...... prête pas d'argent.

2 They are bringing *us* some sweets.
2 Ils ...... apportent des bonbons.

3 We are teaching *her* French.
3 Nous ...... enseignons (*or* apprenons) le français.

4 The maid is serving *them* some tea.
4 La bonne ...... sert du thé.

5 He is showing *them* the samples.
5 Il ...... montre les échantillons.

6 Are you sending *her* a gift?
6 ...... envoyez-vous un cadeau?

7 She is buying *me* a raincoat.
7 Elle ...... achète un imperméable.

8 Do not speak *to her*.
8 Ne ...... parlez pas.

9 Bring the umbrella back *to him*.
9 Rapportez- ...... le parapluie.

10 They are asking *us* for our tickets.
10 Ils ...... demandent nos billets.

11 Give *us* more time.
11 Donnez- ...... plus de temps.

12 Return my fountain-pen *to me* please.
12 Rendez- ...... mon stylo, s'il vous plaît.

13 You may repeat my words *to them*.
13 Vous pouvez ...... répéter mes paroles.[2]

14 I am going to introduce my friend *to her*.
14 Je vais ...... présenter mon ami.

15 Do not sell *him* your bicycle.
15 Ne ...... vendez pas votre bicyclette.

NOTE 1. **poser une question**, to ask a question. **demander**, to ask or ask for something. The person asked is the indirect object. The thing asked or asked for is the direct object. Thus:

M. Picard demande à M. Davis (lui demande) le nom de son représentant. Mr. Picard asks Mr. Davis (asks him) the name of his agent.

demander does not mean *to demand*. **exiger**, to demand.

2. **la parole**, the spoken word.

Exercise No. 109—Questionnaire

1 Quel temps fait-il quand M. Picard arrive chez M. Davis?
2 Qui ouvre la porte?
3 Où est-ce que M. Picard met son parapluie?
4 Où est-ce qu'il laisse ses paquets?
5 Où est-ce que les deux messieurs entrent?
6 Qu'est-ce qu'ils prennent dans la salle à manger?
7 Qu'est-ce que la bonne met sur la table?
8 Et après, (afterwards) que fait-elle?
9 Qui sert M. Picard?
10 Qu'est-ce que M. Davis verse dans les tasses?

CHAPITRE 21 (VINGT ET UN)

LE CLIMAT DE LA FRANCE

1 Les deux messieurs sont toujours assis dans la salle à manger. Ils causent toujours en prenant du thé au rhum. Dehors il continue à pleuvoir. M. Picard n'a plus froid.

2 M. Picard dit: — Le climat de Londres et le climat de Paris sont peu différents et ne passent pas d'un extrême à l'autre.

3 — C'est vrai, M. Picard. Ici à Londres il fait assez chaud en été; quelquefois il fait très chaud. En hiver, il fait froid, parfois il fait très froid et de temps en temps il neige.

Au printemps il commence à faire beau, mais il fait plus doux et quand vient l'été il fait chaud. Quelle saison préférez-vous, M. Picard?

4 — Je préfère l'automne. L'air est frais et vif. Le ciel est lumineux. Le soleil brille de tout son éclat. Et vous, M. Davis, quelle saison préférez-vous?

5 — Je préfère le printemps quand petit à petit tout devient vert. Mais parlons plutôt du climat de la France. Y a-t-il en France une différence marquée entre les saisons?

6 Pour la plupart, oui, assez marquée; mais nous avons moins d'humidité et de brouillard qu'en Angleterre.

7 — Cela doit être beaucoup plus agréable.

8 — Pas tout à fait. Il est vrai qu'à Paris par exemple il fait rarement très froid en hiver. Mais par contre, il pleut beaucoup, il fait du vent, le ciel est gris pâle, et on commence à se demander: — le printemps ne revient-il jamais?

9 — Ah oui, le printemps à Paris est célèbre.

10 — Vous qui préférez le printemps, vous allez être heureux à Paris. Au printemps il fait presque toujours beau. Le ciel est bleu clair avec de gros nuages blancs; les grands platanes des boulevards commencent à se feuiller; l'air est doux, embaumé. Toute la ville sourit.

11 — Mais vous faites un poème, M. Picard!

12 — Ce n'est pas pour rien que le printemps à Paris est célèbre.

13 — Tant mieux pour moi, car je compte partir au mois de mai. Et les autres saisons?

14 — Il est déjà tard. Laissons le reste pour la semaine prochaine.

1 The two gentlemen are still sitting in the dining-room. They are still chatting while drinking tea with rum. Outside it goes on raining. Mr. Picard is no longer cold.

2 Mr. Picard says: The climate of London and the climate of Paris are little different and do not pass from one extreme to the other.

3 That's true, Mr. Picard. Here in London it is fairly hot in summer; sometimes it is very hot. In winter it is cold, at times it is very cold and it snows now and then.

In spring it begins to be fine, it gets milder, and when summer comes, it is warm. Which season do you prefer, Mr. Picard?

4 I prefer the autumn. The air is cool and crisp. The sky is bright. The sun shines brilliantly. And you, Mr. Davis, which season do you prefer?

5 I prefer the spring when little by little everything becomes green. But let us talk rather about the climate of France. Is there a marked difference in France among the seasons?

6 For the most part, yes, quite marked; but we have less damp and fog than in England.

7 That must be very much nicer.

8 Not quite. It is true that in Paris, for example, it is rarely extremely cold in winter. But, on the other hand, it rains a great deal, it is windy, the sky is a pale grey and one begins to wonder: will spring ever come again?

9 Ah, yes, spring in Paris is famous.

10 You who prefer the spring will be happy in Paris. In spring the weather is almost always fine. The sky is blue with thick white clouds; the big plane-trees on the boulevards begin to come into leaf, the air is mild and balmy. The whole city smiles.

11 But you're composing a poem, Mr. Picard!

12 It's not for nothing that spring in Paris is famous.

13 All the better for me, as I expect to leave in May. And the other seasons?

14 It is already late. Let us leave the rest for next week.

Pronunciation and Spelling Aids

Practise Aloud:

les deux messieurs sont toujours assis dans la salle à manger (lɛ dø mɛ-sjø sɔ̃ tu-ʒuːr a-si dɑ̃ la sa-la-mɑ̃-ʒe)

ils causent toujours en prenant du thé au rhum (il koːz tu-ʒuːr ɑ̃ prə-nɑ̃ dy te o rɔm)

dehors il continue à pleuvoir (də-ɔr il kɔ̃-ti-ny a plø-vwaːr)

monsieur Picard n'a plus froid (mə-sjø pi-kaːr na ply frwa)

Building Vocabulary

A. Les Quatre Saisons[1]

le printemps (prɛ̃-tɑ̃), spring	**au printemps**, in spring
l'été (le-te), summer	**en été**, in summer
l'automne (lo-tɔn), autumn	**en automne**, in autumn
l'hiver (li-vɛːr), winter	**en hiver**, in winter

B. Related Words

1 **différent**, la **différence**	4 **évident**, une **évidence**
2 **intelligent**, une **intelligence**	5 **content**, le **contentement**
3 **assidu**, une **assiduité**	6 **intéressant**, un **intérêt**

NOTE 1. all seasons are masculine.

Locutions françaises

1 **tout à coup** (tu ta **ku**), all of a sudden
2 **de tout son éclat** (e-**kla**), in all its brilliance
3 **petit à petit**, little by little
4 **pour la plupart**, for the most part
5 **par contre** (par kɔ̃ːtr), on the other hand
6 **se demander**, to wonder (*Lit.* to ask oneself)

Exercise No. 110—Completion of Text

1 **Ils causent** (while drinking) **du thé au rhum.**
2 **Dehors il continue** (to rain).
3 **En été** (it is hot).
4 **En hiver** (it is very cold).
5 **Au printemps** (it often rains).
6 (I prefer) **l'automne.**
7 **Quelle saison** (do you prefer)?
8 **Mais** (let us talk rather) **du climat de la France.**
9 **Nous avons moins** (of damp and of fog).
10 **Cela** (ought) **être plus agréable.**
11 **Au printemps** (the weather is fine) **à Paris.**
12 **Le ciel est** (blue). **L'air est** (mild). **Toute la ville** (smiles).

Grammar Notes

1 Present Tense of **devoir**, to owe, must, to be obliged to, to have to; **recevoir**, to receive

I owe, am obliged to, have to, etc.

I receive, you receive, etc.

je dois (dwa)	**nous devons** (dvɔ̃)	**je reçois**	**nous recevons**
tu dois (dwa)	**vous devez** (dve)	**tu reçois**	**vous recevez**
il doit (dwa)	**ils doivent** (dwaːv)	**il reçoit**	**ils reçoivent**
elle doit (dwa)	**elles doivent** (dwaːv)	**elle reçoit**	**elles reçoivent**

Like **recevoir: apercevoir**, to perceive; **décevoir**, to deceive.

The verb **devoir** is a very important verb with various shades of meaning. It expresses the idea of *must, ought, should,* in the sense of duty or obligation; also *must* in the sense of *is supposed to, is probably.*

Exercise No. 111. In the following sentences note the various meaning of devoir. Repeat each French sentence aloud five times.

1 **Nous leur devons sept livres.**
2 **M. Davis doit ses grands progrès dans l'étude du français à M. Picard.**
3 **Les élèves doivent faire leurs devoirs tous les jours.**
4 **Le train doit arriver à six heures.**
5 **Le climat de la France doit être plus agréable que le climat de notre pays.**
6 **Cela doit être vraiment beau.**
7 **Par un sale temps pareil on ne doit pas sortir.**
8 **Vous devez être fatigué après une journée pareille.**

1 We owe them seven pounds.
2 Mr. Davis owes his great progress in the study of French to Mr. Picard.
3 The pupils must do their homework every day.
4 The train should arrive (is due) at six o'clock.
5 The climate of France must be (is probably) more agreeable than the climate of our country.
6 That must be really beautiful.
7 One should not go out in such nasty weather.
8 You must be tired after such a day.

2 Some Negative Expressions.

You have learned that the negative *not* is expressed in French by ne before the verb and pas after the verb. Thus:

Je *ne* sais *pas*. Est-ce que vous *ne* savez *pas*? *Ne* savez-vous *pas*?

Study in the following sentences other negative expressions which also have two parts:

1 Le professeur *n'*est *pas encore* ici.	1 The teacher is *not yet* here.
2 Ces élèves *ne* sont *jamais* en retard.	2 These pupils are *never* late.
3 M. Martin *ne* me doit *rien*.	3 Mr. Martin owes me *nothing*.
4 Nous *ne* pouvons *pas* y aller *non plus*.	4 We can *not* go *either*.
5 Est-ce que vous n'avez *que* trente-cinq francs?	5 Do you have *only* thirty-five francs?
6 Ils *ne* viennent *plus* ici.	6 They do *not* come here *any more*.
7 Il *ne* sait *ni* parler *ni* écrire le français.	7 He can *neither* speak *nor* write French.
8 Il *ne* connaît personne à Paris.	8 He *doesn't* know anybody in Paris.

Negative expressions usually have two parts, ne before the verb and the rest of each expression after it. Learn:

1 ne . . . pas encore, not yet	5 ne . . . que, only
2 ne . . . jamais, never, not ever	6 ne . . . plus, no longer, not any more
3 ne . . . rien, nothing, not anything	7 ne . . . ni . . . ni, neither . . . nor
4 ne . . . pas . . . non plus, not . . . either	8 ne . . . personne, nobody, not anybody

The word jamais used in a sentence without ne means ever.

Lisez-vous *jamais* les journaux français?   Do you *ever* read the French newspapers?

Negatives when used without a verb drop the ne.

Que faites-vous? *Rien*.   What are you doing? *Nothing*.
Quand le voyez-vous? *Jamais*.   When do you see him? *Never*.
Est-ce que Jean est ici? *Pas encore*.   Is John here? *Not yet*.
Je ne l'aime pas. *Ni moi non plus*.   I don't like him. *Neither* do I. (*nor I either*)
Qui est là? *Personne*.   Who is there? *Nobody*.

Exercise No. 112 Complete each French sentence with the correct negative. Read each sentence aloud twice.

Exemple 1. Je ne sais rien de cette affaire.

1 I know nothing about that matter.
2 The examination is not yet finished.
3 We never travel in winter.
4 They do not like detective films either.
5 He says nothing and he does nothing.
6 Don't you want to take a trip to France?
7 She is no longer satisfied with her radio set.
8 I am not working either.

9 We have nothing to say to you.
10 I have only one notebook.
11 What you are bringing me? Nothing.
12 Is the lesson finished? Not yet.
13 Better late than never.
14 Is spring never coming?
15 We have neither the time nor the money.

1 Je ...... sais ...... de cette affaire.
2 L'examen ...... est ...... terminé.
3 Nous ...... voyageons ...... en hiver.
4 Ils ...... aiment ...... les films policiers ......
5 Il ...... dit ...... et il ...... fait ......
6 ...... voulez-vous ...... faire un voyage en France?
7 Elle ...... est ...... contente de son poste de radio.
8 Je ...... travaille ......
9 Nous ...... avons ...... à vous dire.
10 Je ...... ai ...... un carnet.
11 Qu'est-ce que vous m'apportez? ......
12 La leçon est-elle finie? ......
13 Mieux vaut tard que ......
14 Le printemps ...... vient-il ......?
15 Nous ...... avons ...... le temps ...... l'argent.

Exercise No. 113—Questionnaire

1 De quoi les messieurs parlent-ils?
2 Est-ce que le climat de la France est pareil (like) au climat de la Grande-Bretagne?
3 Quel temps fait-il en été à Londres?
4 Quelle saison M. Picard préfère-t-il?
5 Et M. Davis, quelle saison préfère-t-il?
6 Y a-t-il une différence marquée entre les saisons en France?
7 Comment est l'hiver à Paris?
8 Comment est le printemps à Paris?
9 Pourquoi est-ce que M. Davis est content?
10 En quel mois est-ce que M. Davis compte partir?

CHAPITRE 22 (VINGT-DEUX)

LE CLIMAT DE LA FRANCE (SUITE)

1 — Ce soir nous allons continuer à parler du climat de la France.

2 — Vous savez maintenant que le climat de Paris est très désagréable en hiver. C'est pour cela que ceux qui ont les moyens quittent Paris en hiver pour aller en Suisse ou sur la Côte d'Azur.

3 — Est-ce que le climat de la Suisse est moins sévère en hiver que celui de Paris?

4 — Au contraire, il est plus sévère, mais il est beaucoup plus agréable.

5 — Est-ce qu'il n'y a pas d'hiver sur la Côte d'Azur?

6 — L'hiver est doux. Le soleil brille presque tous les jours. Il fait bon. En été il fait plus chaud, mais il y a toujours une jolie brise de mer. En fait, ce climat ressemble un peu à celui de la Floride.

7 — Ah bon. Mais est-ce qu'il ne fait jamais froid?

8 — Il fait frais pendant la nuit. Il faut se mettre un lainage quelconque. Mais il ne fait jamais très froid, sauf dans les montagnes.

9 — Est-ce vrai qu'on peut nager le matin et faire du ski l'après-midi sur la Côte d'Azur?

10 — Mais oui. Ceux qui sont jeunes et forts le font tout le temps. De la plage on voit les hautes montagnes des Alpes Maritimes couvertes de neige. Elles sont à une distance d'environ quatre-vingts kilomètres.

11 — Ah, cela doit être vraiment beau!

12 — C'est un coin délicieux. Si vous avez le temps de faire un saut jusqu'à Nice ou Cannes vous allez être enchanté de votre visite.

13 — Merci bien pour le bon conseil. Je vais tâcher de faire ce petit voyage au mois de juin.

14 — Vous n'allez pas le regretter, je vous assure.

1 This evening we are going to continue to talk about the climate of France.

2 Now you know that the climate of Paris in winter is very disagreeable. That is why those who have the means leave Paris in winter to go to Switzerland or to the Riviera (the Blue Coast).

3 Is the climate of Switzerland less severe in winter than that of Paris?

4 On the contrary, it is more severe, but it is much more agreeable.

5 Is there no winter on the Riviera?

6 The winter is mild. The sun shines nearly every day. The weather is fine. In summer it's warmer, but there is always a good sea breeze. In fact, this climate resembles somewhat that of Florida.

7 Oh, I see. But isn't it ever cold?

8 It is cool during the night. One must put on some woollen garment or other. But it is never very cold except in the mountains.

9 Is it true that one can go swimming in the morning and ski-ing in the afternoon on the Riviera?

10 Yes, indeed. Those who are young and strong do it all the time. From the beach one can see the high mountains of the Maritime Alps covered with snow. They are at a distance of about eighty kilometres.

11 That must be really beautiful!

12 It is a delightful spot. If you have the time to hop over to Nice or Cannes you will be enchanted with your visit.

13 Thank you for the good advice. I shall try to make this little trip in the month of June.

14 You won't be sorry, I assure you.

Pronunciation and Spelling Aids

Practise Aloud:

l'hiver est doux, le soleil brille presque tous les jours, il fait bon (li-vɛːr ɛ du lə sɔ-lɛːj briːj prɛsk tu lɛ ʒuːr il fɛ bɔ̃)

en été il fait plus chaud, mais il y a toujours une jolie brise de mer (ã-ne-te il fɛ ply ʃo mɛ zil-ja tu-ʒuːr yn ʒɔ-li briːz də mɛːr)

Building Vocabulary

A. Antonyms

1 **agréable**, agreeable; **désagréable**, disagreeable
2 **doux**, mild, soft; **sévère**, severe, harsh
3 **toujours**, always; **ne . . . jamais**, never
4 **souvent**, often; **rarement**, rarely
5 **devant**, in front of; **derrière**, behind
6 **avant**, before; **après**, after
7 **entrer (dans)**, to enter; **sortir (de)**, to leave
8 **une entrée**, entrance; **la sortie**, exit
9 **voyant**, garish

Locutions françaises

1 **au contraire**, on the contrary
2 **en fait**, in fact
3 **faire du ski**, to go ski-ing
4 **être enchanté de**, to be delighted with
5 **tâcher de faire**, to try to do
6 **il faut mettre**, one must (it is necessary to) put on
7 **il faut avoir**, one must (it is necessary) to have

Exercise No. 114—Completion of Text

1 Ce soir (we are going to continue) à parler du climat de la France.
2 Le climat en hiver à Paris est (very disagreeable).
3 Ceux (who have the means) quittent Paris en hiver.
4 (Isn't there any winter) sur la Côte d'Azur?
5 (It is never cold) sauf dans les montagnes.
6 (It is necessary to put on) un lainage quelconque.
7 On peut (swim in the morning).
8 (One can see) les hautes montagnes.
9 Cela (must be) vraiment beau.
10 (If you have the time) faites un saut jusqu'à Nice.

Grammar Notes

1 Demonstrative Pronouns.

Compare the demonstrative pronouns (**celui, celle, ceux, celles**) with the demonstrative adjectives (**ce, cette, ces**) in the following sentences:

Demonstrative Adjectives	Demonstrative Pronouns
Ce (this) **docteur-ci est français.**	**Celui-ci** (this one) **est anglais.**
Ce (that) **docteur-là est américain.**	**Celui-là** (that one) **est italien.**
Cet (this) **homme-ci habite Paris.**	**Celui-ci** (this one) **est médecin.**
Cet (that) **homme-là demeure à Rome.**	**Celui-là** (that one) **est professeur.**
Cette (this) **fleur-ci est pour Louise.**	**Celle-ci** (this one) **est pour Marie.**
Cette (that) **fleur-là est pour Anne.**	**Celle-là** (that one) **est pour Jeanne.**
Ces (these) **docteurs-ci sont français.**	**Ceux-ci** (these) **sont anglais.**
Ces (those) **docteurs-là sont américains.**	**Ceux-là** (those) **sont italiens.**
Ces (these) **fleurs-ci sont pour Louise.**	**Celles-ci** (these) **sont pour Marie.**
Ces (those) **fleurs-là sont pour Anne.**	**Celles-là** (those) **sont pour Jeanne.**

NOTE 1. **cet** is used before a noun beginning with a vowel or a silent h.

The Demonstrative Pronoun Chart

	Singular	*Plural*
masc.	**celui**, this (one), that (one)	**ceux**, these, those
fem.	**celle**, this (one), that (one)	**celles**, these, those

(*a*) The demonstrative adjectives (**ce, cet, cette, ces**) are always followed by a noun. The demonstrative pronouns (**celui, celle, ceux, celles**) are never followed by a noun.

(*b*) The demonstrative pronouns have the same gender and number as the nouns for which they stand.

(*c*) **-ci** and **-là** are used for emphasis or clarity. Omit **-ci** and **-là** before **de** and before a relative pronoun.

Le climat de la France, et *celui* de l'Italie.   The climate of France and *that* of Italy.

***Ceux* qui ont les moyens quittent Paris en hiver.**   *Those* who have the means leave Paris in winter.

Celui-ci, celui-là often translate latter, former:

M. Davis et M. Picard causent, *celui-ci* est français mais *celui-là* est anglais.

Mr. Davis and M. Picard are talking. *The latter* is French but *the former* is English.

2 Ceci, Cela (Ça), This, That

ceci and **cela** (often shortened to **ça**) mean this thing or that thing to which we are pointing; or they may refer to whole ideas or statements.

Ceci est un rasoir électrique.   This is an electric razor.
Cela est un rasoir de sûreté.   That is a safety razor.
Cela est vrai (faux).   That is true (false).
Cela ne fait rien.   That doesn't matter.
N'oubliez pas ceci: Le commerçant français n'est pas pressé.   Do not forget
this: the French businessman is not in a hurry.

Exercise No. 115 Translate these brief dialogues. Practise them aloud:

1 — Quelle poterie préférez-vous, celle de Vallauris ou celle de Biot? — Je
préfère celle de Biot.
2 — Quel chapeau aimez-vous mieux, celui-ci ou celui-là? — J'aime mieux
celui-là.
3 — Quel climat est plus doux, celui de la France ou celui du Canada? — Celui
de la France est plus doux.
4 — Comment trouvez-vous ces robes? — J'aime bien celle-ci. Je trouve les
couleurs de celle-là trop voyantes.
5 — Quelles places préférez-vous, celles aux premiers rangs ou celles au fond?
— Nous préférons celles aux premiers rangs.
6 — Quelle sorte de mouchoirs allez-vous acheter? — Je vais acheter ceux qui
sont le meilleur marché.

Exercise No. 116 Complete with the correct form of the demonstrative
pronoun.

Exemple 1: Les montagnes du Canada sont plus hautes que *celles* de l'Europe.

1 Les montagnes du Canada sont plus hautes que (those) de l'Europe.
2 Les fleuves de l'Amérique du Sud sont plus longs que (those) de l'Europe.
3 Ce pot au lait-ci est de Limoges, (that one) est de Biot.
4 Ces tasses et ces soucoupes-ci sont de la France, (those) sont du Mexique.
5 Ces robes-ci sont meilleur marché que (those).
6 Ces problèmes-ci (*m*) sont plus difficiles que (those).
7 Lequel[1] est votre parapluie, (this one) ou (that one)?
8 Laquelle[1] est votre place, (this one) ou (that)?
9 Le climat de la France est plus doux que (that) de la Suisse.
10 Ma femme et moi, nous déjeunons ensemble. (That) me plaît beaucoup.

NOTE 1. lequel (laquelle *f*) which one

Exercise No. 117—Questionnaire

1 Pourquoi est-ce que ceux qui ont les moyens quittent Paris en hiver?
2 Où vont-ils?
3 Comment est l'hiver sur la Côte d'Azur?
4 Comment est l'été sur la Côte d'Azur?
5 Où est-ce qu'on peut nager le matin et faire du ski l'après-midi?
6 Qu'est-ce qu'on peut voir de la plage?
7 Quel temps fait-il pendant la nuit?
8 Où fait-il très froid?
9 À quelle distance les montagnes sont-elles de la plage?
10 Quand est-ce que M. Davis va tâcher de faire ce petit voyage?

CHAPITRE 23 (VINGT-TROIS)

LA BONNE CUISINE FRANÇAISE

1 — Vous savez, sans doute, M. Davis, que la bonne cuisine française est un des plus grands plaisirs du touriste en France.

2 — Je le sais bien, M. Picard. Je peux même dire que je la connais un peu, la cuisine française. Quand j'ai un client important, je l'invite à déjeuner dans un des bons restaurants français ici à Londres. Et cela arrive assez souvent.

3 — La cuisine française nous fait cadeau de beaucoup d'expressions d'usage courant en anglais; par exemple: à la carte, bouillon, consommé, purée, sauté, au gratin, café, petits fours, hors-d'œuvre, soufflé, et sans doute beaucoup d'autres. À propos, M. Davis, vous êtes dans l'importation. À Paris, faites une liste de vos plats préférés, et envoyez à votre femme un bon livre de cuisine française, en anglais, bien entendu.

4 — Quelle bonne idée! Mais la cuisine française n'est-elle pas compliquée?

5 — Non, vraiment. Il y a certainement des plats célèbres qui sont très compliqués, mais il n'y a rien de mystérieux dans la bonne cuisine française. Je vais vous dire les trois secrets, gratis.

6 — Pour commencer, tout ce qui entre dans un plat doit être de bonne qualité: le beurre, les œufs, la viande, les légumes, tout, enfin; ensuite, il faut avoir[1] le goût et l'amour de la cuisine; et après, du beurre, du beurre, et encore du beurre.

7 — Merci pour les trois secrets. Je vais les dire tout de suite à ma femme.

8 — Voilà un mari modèle!

9 — M. Picard, j'ai un appétit de loup! Voulez-vous casser la croûte avec moi?

10 — Avec plaisir, M. Davis.

1 No doubt you know, Mr. Davis, that good French cooking is one of the greatest pleasures of the tourist in France.

2 Indeed I do, Mr. Picard. I can even say that I know something about French cooking. When I have an important customer, I invite him out to lunch at one of the good French restaurants here in London. And this happens quite often.

3 French cooking gives us (*Lit.* makes us a gift of) many expressions commonly used in English; for example: à la carte, bouillon, consommé, purée, sauté, au gratin, café, petits fours, hors-d'œuvres, soufflé, and no doubt many others. By the way, Mr. Davis, you are in the import business. In Paris make a list of your favourite dishes, send your wife a good French cookery book, in English of course.

4 What a good idea! But isn't French cooking complicated?

5 Not really. There are certainly some famous dishes which are very complicated, but there is nothing mysterious about good French cooking. I am going to tell you the three secrets, free of charge.

6 First, everything that goes into a dish must be of good quality; butter,

eggs, meat, vegetables, in short, everything; then, one must have a taste for and a love of cooking; then, butter, butter and more butter.

7 Thank you for the three secrets. I am going to tell them at once to my wife.

8 There's a model husband!

9 Mr. Picard, I'm as hungry as a wolf! Will you have a snack (*Lit.* break the crust) with me?

10 With pleasure, Mr. Davis.

NOTE 1. *Lit.* It is necessary to have.

Pronunciation and Spelling Aids

Practise Aloud:

vous savez, sans doute, monsieur Davis, que la bonne cuisine française est un des plus grands plaisirs du touriste en France (vu sa-ve, sã dut mə-sjø Davis kə la bɔn kɥi-zin frã-sɛːz ɛ tœ̃ dɛ ply grã plɛ-ziːr dy tu-rist ã frãːs)

Building Vocabulary

A. Some French Cooking Expressions Adopted in English.

1 le bouillon (bu-jɔ̃), broth
2 le consommé (kɔ̃-sɔ-me), clear soup
3 la purée (py-re), mashed vegetables
4 sauté (so-te), fried
5 au gratin (o gra-tɛ̃), dressed with bread crumbs or cheese, and browned in the oven.
6 les petits fours (pti fur), small cakes
7 les hors-d'œuvre (ɔr-dœːvr), starters
8 le soufflé (su-fle), puffed-up dish on egg base

B. Some Tasty French Dishes Not Difficult to Prepare.

1 la soupe à l'oignon (sup-a-lɔ-ɲɔ̃), onion soup
2 le poulet Marengo (pu-lɛ ma-rã-go), Chicken Marengo
3 le bœuf bourguignon (bœf bur-gi-ɲɔ̃), Burgundy beef
4 la blanquette de veau (blã-kɛːt də vo), veal fricassee
5 les haricots verts sautés (lɛ a-ri-ko vɛːr so-te), fried French beans
6 les épinards à la crème (lɛ ze-pi-naːr a la krɛm), creamed spinach
7 les petits pois à la française (pti pwa a la frã-sɛːz), peas French style
8 la poire Hélène (pwaːr e-lɛːn), pear Helene
9 les fraises Chantilly (frɛːz ʃã-ti-ji), strawberries with whipped cream

Locutions françaises

1 cela arrive, that happens
2 assez souvent, quite often
3 bien entendu, of course
4 faire cadeau (de), to make a gift of, to give
5 beaucoup d'autres, many others
6 quelle bonne idée! what a good idea!
7 rien de mystérieux, nothing mysterious
8 tout ce qui, everything that

Exercise No. 118—Completion of Text

1 **Je connais un peu** (good French cooking).
2 **C'est** (one of the greatest pleasures) **du touriste.**
3 **J'invite un client important** (to lunch).
4 (That happens) **assez souvent.**
5 **La cuisine française** (makes us a gift) **de beaucoup d'expressions.**
6 (Send your wife) **un bon livre de cuisine française.**
7 (I am going to tell you) **les trois secrets.**
8 (All that) **entre dans un plat doit être** (of good quality).
9 (One must have) **l'amour de la cuisine.**
10 **Et après** (butter, butter and more butter).

Grammar Notes

1 Present Tense of **envoyer**, to send

I send, I am sending, you send, you are sending, etc.

j'envoie (ʒɑ̃-vwa)	**nous envoyons** (nu zɑ̃-vwa-jɔ̃)
tu envoies (ty ɑ̃-vwa)	**vous envoyez** (vu-zɑ̃-vwa-je)
il envoie (il ɑ̃-vwa)	**ils envoient** (il zɑ̃-vwa)
elle envoie (ɛl ɑ̃-vwa)	**elles envoient** (ɛl zɑ̃-vwa)

Imperative

envoie, send; **envoyons**, let us send; **envoyez**, send.
renvoyer to send back, has the same endings as **envoyer**.

2 Independent Pronouns. Used after Prepositions.

(*a*) Note carefully the personal pronouns used after prepositions. They are called *independent* pronouns because they are usually independent of the verb. They are sometimes called *disjunctive* or *emphatic* pronouns.

après *moi*, after *me*	**près de** *nous*, near *us*
sans *toi* (*fam.*), without *you*	**loin de** *vous*, far from *you*
avec *lui*, with *him*	**excepté** *eux*, except *them* (*m*)
pour *elle*, for *her*	**derrière** *elles*, behind *them* (*f*)

(*b*) Note the independent pronouns with the preposition **chez:**

chez moi, at my house (home)	**chez nous**, at our house (home)
chez toi, at your house (home) (*fam.*)	**chez vous**, at your house (home)
chez lui, at his house (home)	**chez eux** (*m*), at their house (home)
chez elle, at her house (home)	**chez elles** (*f*), at their house (home)

(*c*) After **est** and **sont**, the independent pronouns with the preposition **à** show possession.

Ce chapeau est à moi (à toi, à lui, à elle).   This hat is mine (belongs to me) (yours (*fam.*), his, hers).
Ces chaises sont à nous (à vous, à eux, à elles).   These chairs are ours (yours, theirs (*m*), theirs (*f*)).

Exercise No. 119. Complete the following in French:

1 **Voulez-vous aller** (with me)?
2 **Cette carte est** (for you), **mon enfant.**
3 **Ils vont dîner** (at my house).
4 **Nous restons** (at home) **en famille.**

5 Mlle Martin n'est pas (at her house).
6 L'avion va partir (without them) (*m*).
7 Il est assis (near her).

8 Il y a beaucoup de choses (around us).
9 Ces places-ci sont (ours).
10 Ces places-là sont (theirs) (*f*).

3 Other Uses of the Independent Pronouns.

(*a*) When the pronoun stands alone (without a verb):

Qui a un appétit de loup?   Who is as hungry as a wolf?
Moi. Toi. Lui. Elle.   I. You (*fam.*). He. She.
Nous. Vous. Eux. Elles.   We. You. They (*m*). They (*f*).

(*b*) For emphasis and in double pronoun subjects:

Moi, j'aime le théâtre.   *I* like the theatre.
Lui et moi, nous étudions le français.   He and I (*we*) are studying French.

(*c*) With c'est and ce sont:

C'est moi.   It is I.
C'est toi.   It is you (*fam.*).
C'est lui (elle).   It is he (she).

C'est nous.   It is we (us).
C'est vous.   It is you.
Ce sont[1] eux (elles).   It is they.

NOTE 1. Ce sont is used with eux and elles.

(*d*) In the affirmative imperative, me becomes moi and te becomes toi.

Dites-moi où vous demeurez.   Tell me where you live.
Lève-toi, mon enfant.   Get up, child.

But: Ne me dites pas. Ne te lève pas.   Do not tell me. Do not get up.

Exercise No. 120 Complete the following in French:

1 Qui fait de grands progrès dans ses études? (He.) (She.)
2 (I), j'aime le français; elle, elle aime l'anglais.
3 Qui frappe (knocks) à la porte? C'est (me). C'est (we). Ce sont (they) (m).
4 Habille-(yourself), Rosette.
5 Envoyez-(me) les fleurs.
6 Vous venez plus tard que (he).
7 (She and I), nous allons au théâtre.
8 Qui étudie assidûment? (I).
9 Est-ce que ce stylo est (yours)?
10 Non, il est (his).

Exercise No. 121—Questionnaire

1 Quel est un des plus grands plaisirs du touriste en France?
2 Est-ce que M. Davis connaît la cuisine française?
3 De quoi la cuisine française nous fait-elle cadeau?
4 Qu'est-ce que M. Davis doit faire à Paris?
5 Est-ce que la cuisine française est compliquée?
6 Quel est le troisième secret de la bonne cuisine?
7 Est-ce que M. Davis va le dire à sa femme?
8 Qui est un mari modèle?
9 Qui a un appétit de loup?
10 Qui va casser la croûte avec M. Davis?

RÉVISION 5

CHAPITRES 20–23 PREMIÈRE PARTIE

Révision de mots

NOUNS

1 un amour
2 un appétit
3 le bœuf
4 le cadeau
5 le climat
6 le coin
7 le conseil
8 le dessert
9 les épinards (*m*)
10 la fraise
11 les haricots verts (*m*)
12 un hiver
13 un imperméable
14 le légume
15 la mer
16 la neige
17 les moyens (*m*)
18 le paquet
19 le parapluie
20 le pardessus
21 le plateau
22 la pluie
23 la poire
24 le poulet
25 le reste
26 la saison
27 la sortie
28 la soupe
29 le thé
30 le veau
31 la visite

1 love
2 appetite
3 beef, ox
4 gift
5 climate
6 corner
7 advice
8 dessert
9 spinach
10 strawberry
11 French beans
12 winter
13 raincoat
14 vegetable
15 sea
16 snow
17 means
18 parcel
19 umbrella
20 overcoat
21 tray
22 rain
23 pear
24 chicken
25 remainder
26 season
27 exit
28 soup
29 tea
30 veal, calf
31 visit

VERBS

1 apporter
2 briller
3 casser
4 chercher
5 envoyer
6 j'envoie
7 frapper
8 nager
9 neiger
10 oublier
11 quitter
12 raconter, dire
13 réchauffer
14 tomber
15 tâcher (de)
16 verser
17 couvrir
18 je couvre
19 devenir
20 je deviens
21 pleuvoir
22 il pleut
23 sourire
24 je souris

1 to bring
2 to shine
3 to break
4 to look for
5 to send
6 I send
7 to knock
8 to swim
9 to snow
10 to forget
11 to leave, quit
12 to tell about, say
13 to warm
14 to fall
15 to try
16 to pour
17 to cover
18 I cover
19 to become
20 I become
21 to rain
22 it is raining
23 to smile
24 I smile

ADJECTIVES

1 agréable
2 chaud
3 clair
4 couvert
5 enchanté
6 faux (fausse *f*)

136

7 froid	10 préféré	13 trempé
8 plein	11 pressé	14 sûr
9 pâle	12 sale	15 vif (vive *f*)

1 agreeable	6 false	11 in a hurry
2 hot	7 cold	12 nasty, dirty
3 clear	8 full	13 soaked
4 covered	9 pale	14 sure
5 delighted	10 favourite	15 brisk, lively

ADVERBS

| 1 dehors | 3 tôt | 5 plus tôt |
| 2 plutôt | 4 tard | 6 plus tard |

| 1 outside | 3 soon, early | 5 sooner, earlier |
| 2 rather | 4 late | 6 later |

PREPOSITIONS

| 1 à côté (de) | 2 au lieu (de) | 3 sauf |

| 1 at the side of, next to | 2 instead of | 3 except |

NEGATIVES

| 1 ne ... pas | 3 ne ... pas encore | 5 ne ... rien | 7 ne ... personne |
| 2 ne ... jamais | 4 ne ... plus | 6 ne ... que | |

| 1 not | 3 not yet | 5 nothing | 7 nobody |
| 2 never | 4 no longer, no more | 6 only | |

FRENCH EXPRESSIONS

1 cela arrive	7 ça va mieux
2 assez souvent	8 tout à coup
3 par contre	9 moi-même
4 petit à petit	10 lui-même
5 il pleut à verse	11 elle-même
6 quel sale temps!	12 le voilà

1 that happens	7 I feel better
2 quite often	8 all of a sudden
3 on the other hand	9 myself
4 little by little	10 himself
5 it is raining hard	11 herself
6 what nasty weather!	12 there he (it) is

DEUXIÈME PARTIE

Exercise No. 122. From Group II select the opposite of each word in Group I.

I		II	
1 tôt	7 agréable	(a) beaucoup de temps	(g) libre
2 vieux	8 toujours	(b) jamais	(h) rarement
3 peu de temps	9 faux	(c) tard	(i) recevoir
4 chercher	10 quelque chose	(d) vrai	(j) pas encore
5 occupé	11 souvent	(e) trouver	(k) désagréable
6 envoyer	12 déjà	(f) jeune, nouveau	(l) rien

Exercise No. 123 Complete the following sentences in French.

1 **Quand il fait froid,** (I am cold).
2 **Quand il fait chaud,** (I am warm).
3 **En été,** (it is warm).
4 **Au printemps,** (it rains a great deal).
5 **En automne,** (it is cool).
6 **En hiver,** (it is cold).
7 **Quand il pleut, je porte** (a raincoat).
8 **Quand il neige,** (I wear an overcoat).
9 **La pluie** (is falling).
10 **J'aime** (all the seasons).

Exercise No. 124 Select the group of words in Column II which best completes each sentence begun in Column I.

I

1 **Moi, je préfère le climat de la France,**
2 **Prenez du thé au rhum**
3 **Je vais vous dire**
4 **Il est vrai que l'hiver**
5 **Prenez un parapluie**
6 **Les deux messieurs entrent dans le salon**
7 **Ces places-ci sont occupées,**
8 **Il n'est pas difficile de**
9 **Je vais faire cadeau à ma femme**
10 **Le train de Lyon doit**

II

(a) **quelque chose sur le climat de la France.**
(b) **préparer quelques bons plats français.**
(c) **arriver à cinq heures de l'après-midi.**
(d) **mais elle préfère celui de la Suisse.**
(e) **mais celles-là sont libres.**
(f) **pour vous réchauffer.**
(g) **à Paris est souvent désagréable.**
(h) **en causant d'un ton animé.**
(i) **parce qu'il pleut à verse.**
(j) **d'un bon livre de cuisine française.**

Exercise No. 125 Complete the answer to each question with the correct direct or indirect object pronoun in French.

1 **Qu'est-ce que la bonne dit à M. Davis?**
2 **Qu'est-ce que M. Picard donne à la bonne?**
3 **Est-ce que M. Davis attend M. Picard?**
4 **Est-il content de voir M. Picard?**
5 **Pourquoi est-ce que M. Picard prend une tasse de thé?**
6 **Qu'est-ce que M. Davis dit à M. Picard?**
7 **Préférez-vous les films policiers?**
8 **Quand allez-vous quitter la ville?**
9 **Qui vous invite à déjeuner?**
10 **Qu'est-ce que vous donnez aux enfants?**

1 **Elle** (to him) **dit: — Quel sale temps!**
2 **Il** (to her) **donne son parapluie.**
3 **Oui, il** (him) **attend.**
4 **Il est content de** (him) **voir.**
5 **Il** (it) **prend pour** (himself) **réchauffer.**

6 Il dit: — Permettez-(me) de (you) servir.
7 Nous ne (them) préférons pas.
8 Je vais (it) quitter l'été prochain.
9 Mon ami Charles (me) invite à déjeuner.
10 Je (to them) donne une radio.

Exercise No. 126 Translate the English sentences using the negative indicated.
ne must precede the verb.

1 (ne ...... personne) I do not know anybody.
2 (ne ...... jamais) We never eat meat.
3 (ne ...... que) I have only one teacher.
4 (ne ...... plus) She no longer wants that hat.
5 (ne ...... pas encore) Annette does not go to school yet.
6 (ne ...... pas ...... non plus) I am not tired either.
7 (ne ...... plus) We have no more (le) time.
8 (ne ...... rien) Why do you say nothing?
9 (ne ...... ni ...... ni) We have neither the time nor the money.

Dialogue
Au restaurant

1 — Bonjour monsieur. Voici le menu.
2 — Merci. Qu'est-ce qu'il y a de bon aujourd'hui?
3 — Nous avons un très bon dîner à prix fixe¹ aujourd'hui: soupe à l'oignon, entrecôte aux pommes, tomates farcies, salade, fromage et une belle tarte aux pêches.
4 — Qu'y a-t-il de bon à la carte?
5 — Je vous recommande le canard à l'orange. C'est de l'extra.
6 — Très bien. J'aime beaucoup le canard. Apportez-moi de la soupe à l'oignon pour commencer.
7 — Très bien, monsieur. Voulez-vous un légume? Le canard est garni de pommes sautées.
8 — Non merci. Pas de légumes. Une salade, c'est tout.
9 — Bien, monsieur. Voulez-vous du fromage?
10 — Ça oui. Comment est le camembert? Est-il bien fait?
11 — Il est à point, monsieur, un délice!
12 — Très bien. Avec ça un café bien fort.
13 — Et comme boisson?
14 — Une demi-bouteille de Pommard.
15 — Très bien, monsieur. Tout de suite.
16 — Le repas terminé M. Davis dit: — Garçon, l'addition, s'il vous plaît.
17 — Voici, monsieur.
18 — Est-ce que le service est compris?
19 — Oui monsieur, vous voyez, là, en bas.
20 — Merci.
21 — Merci bien, monsieur.

1 Good evening, sir. Here is the menu.
2 Thank you. What's nice today?
3 We have a very good table d'hôte dinner today: onion soup, steak with potatoes, stuffed tomatoes, salad, cheese and a fine peach tart.
4 What's nice à la carte?

5 I recommend duck with orange sauce. It is especially good.

6 Very good. I like duck very much. Bring me the onion soup first.

7 Very good, sir. Do you want a vegetable? The duck is garnished with sautéd potatoes.

8 No thank you. No vegetables. A salad, that's all.

9 Very well, sir. Do you want any cheese?

10 Yes. How is the camembert? Is it ripe?

11 It is just right, sir, a treat!

12 Very good. With that, a cup of good strong coffee.

13 And what will you drink? (*Lit.* And as a beverage?)

14 A half bottle of Pommard.

15 Very good, sir. Right away.

16 At the end of the meal Mr. Davis says: Waiter, the bill, please.

17 Here you are, sir.

18 Is the service charge included?

19 Yes sir, see, down there.

20 Thank you.

21 Thank you very much, sir.

NOTE 1. à prix fixe = table d'hôte

Exercise No. 127—Lecture

Phillippe n'aime pas étudier l'arithmétique

Un jour, en revenant de l'école, Philippe dit à sa mère: — Je n'aime pas étudier l'arithmétique. C'est si difficile. Pourquoi avons-nous besoin de tant[1] d'exercices et de tant de problèmes? Nous avons des machines à calculer,[2] n'est-ce pas? Alors![3]

Mme Davis regarde son fils et dit: — Tu as tort, mon petit. On ne peut pas se passer[4] des nombres. Par exemple, on a toujours besoin de changer de l'argent, de faire des achats, d'estimer les distances, et puis, et puis. . . . La mère s'arrête en voyant que Philippe ne fait pas attention à ce qu'elle dit.

— À propos, continue-t-elle en souriant,[5] le football ne t'intéresse pas non plus,[6] mon petit?

— Par exemple! Tu veux rire.[7]

— Alors, si les Spurs ont gagné[8] quatre-vingts parties,[9] et s'ils en ont perdu[10] trente, sais-tu quel pourcentage de parties ils ont gagné?

En entendant[11] cela Philippe s'écrie: — Tu as raison, maman. Les nombres, l'arithmétique et les mathématiques sont très importants. Je crois que maintenant je vais étudier beaucoup plus.

NOTE 1. so many.

    2. adding machines.

    3. Well!

    4. se passer de, to do without.

    5. smiling.

    6. either.

    7. You are joking. (*Lit.* You wish to laugh.)

    8. have won.

    9. games.

    10. have lost.

    11. on hearing.

CHAPITRE 24 (VINGT-QUATRE)

LES FRANÇAIS

1 — M. Picard, Je vais vous poser quelques questions sur les Français. Êtes-vous prêt? Voulez-vous encore un cigare? Voici les allumettes et le cendrier.

2 — Merci, M. Davis. Je suis bien à mon aise. Continuez, s'il vous plaît.

3 — Pour commencer, est-ce que les Français se ressemblent[1] plus ou moins, ou est-ce qu'ils diffèrent de caractère selon la géographie du pays?

4 — Je vais vous dire tout de suite, M. Davis, qu'un Français est un Français partout. Il est vrai qu'il y a de très grandes différences entre tous les Français, non seulement à cause de la géographie, comme vous dites, mais aussi à cause de leurs métiers.

5 — Dites-moi, M. Picard, quelles sont quelques-unes de ces différences?

6 — Eh bien, pour commencer, au nord-ouest, il y a les pêcheurs et les marins de la Bretagne, plus souvent en mer que chez eux, très dévots et très fervents de l'eau-de-vie normande, le calvados. Ensuite, les fermiers de la Normandie, ronds et railleurs. Et puis, les mineurs et les ouvriers des usines du nord-est, débrouillards et syndiqués actifs.

7 — Tout cela, seulement pour commencer? Mais, M. Picard, nous allons rester ici toute la nuit!

8 — Je crois que nous n'avons pas besoin de continuer. Vous comprenez par exemple, que l'homme du Midi, bavard et blagueur ne ressemble pas trop au montagnard taciturne de l'Auvergne.

9 — Sans connaître trop les détails je le comprends bien.

10 — Mais, malgré toutes ces différences, ils sont tous français; c'est-à-dire, qu'ils aiment beaucoup discuter, surtout des questions politiques; qu'ils n'ont pas peur des idées; qu'ils sont fiers de leur tradition de démocratie, de belles-lettres, de philosophie et de science; et finalement qu'ils aiment tous la bonne cuisine et le bon vin.

11 — M. Picard, je les aime déjà sans les connaître.

12 — Si c'est comme ça à présent, qu'est-ce qui va se passer au mois de juin pendant votre visite?

13 — Ça va être un roman d'amour, M. Picard!

1 Mr. Picard, I am going to ask you a few questions about the French people. Are you ready? Do you want another cigar? Here are the matches and the ashtray.

2 Thank you, Mr. Davis. I am very comfortable. Please continue.

3 To begin with, are the French people more or less alike,[1] or do they differ in character according to the geography of the country?

4 I'll tell you at once, Mr. Davis, that a Frenchman is a Frenchman everywhere. It is true that there are some very great differences among all Frenchmen, not only because of the geography, as you say, but also because of their occupations.

5 Tell me, Mr. Picard, what are some of these differences?

6 Well, to begin with, in the north-west we have the fishermen and sailors of Brittany, more often at sea than at home; very devout, and very devoted to the Norman brandy, calvados. Then, the farmers of Normandy, rotund and bantering. And then the workers in the mines and factories of the north-east, resourceful and active trade-unionists.

7 All this only to begin with? But, Mr. Picard, we're going to be here all night!

8 I don't think that we need go on. You realize for example, that the talkative southerner (*Lit.* man of the south), teller of tall stories, is not much like the taciturn mountaineer of Auvergne.

9 Without knowing the details too well, I do realize that.

10 But in spite of all these differences, they are all French; that is to say that they love to argue, especially over questions of politics; that they are not afraid of ideas; that they are proud of their tradition of democracy, of literature, of philosophy, and of science; and finally that they all love good cooking and good wine.

11 Mr. Picard, I like them already without knowing them.

12 If that's the case now, what will happen in the month of June during your visit?

13 It is going to be a love story, Mr. Picard!

NOTE 1. *Lit.* Do the French people resemble each other more or less?

Pronunciation and Spelling Aids

Practise Aloud:

monsieur Picard, je vais vous poser quelques questions sur les Français (mə-sjø pi-kaːr ʒə vɛ vu po-ze kɛlk kɛs-tjɔ̃ syr lɛ frɑ̃-sɛ)

êtes-vous prêt? voulez-vous encore un cigare? (ɛt-vu prɛ vu-le vu zɑ̃-kɔːr œ̃ si-gaːr)

voici les allumettes et le cendrier (vwa-si lɛ za-ly-mɛt e lə sɑ̃-dri-je)

Building Vocabulary

A. Points cardinaux[1]   Points of the Compass

le nord (nɔr), north

le sud (syd), south

l'est (lɛst), east

l'ouest (lwɛst), west

B. Pour fumer Some Smoking Terms

le cigare (si-gaːr), cigar

la cigarette (si-ga-rɛt)

une allumette (y-na-ly-mɛt), match

la pipe (pip), pipe

le tabac (ta-ba), tobacco

le cendrier (sɑ̃-dri-je), ashtray

défense de fumer (de-fɑ̃ də fy-me), no smoking

C. Des ouvriers (*m*), ouvrières (*f*) Some Working Men, Working Women

le pêcheur (pɛ-ʃœːr), fisherman

le marin (ma-rɛ̃), seaman

le fermier (fɛr-mje), farmer

la cuisinière (kɥi-zi-njɛːr), cook

les mineurs (lɛ mi-nœːr), miners

un ouvrier (œ̃-nu-vri-e), une ouvrière (y-nu-vri-ɛːr), factory worker

la modiste (mɔ-dist), milliner

NOTE 1. All points of the compass are masculine.

Locutions françaises

1 **avoir peur (de)** (a-vwaːr pœːr də), to be afraid of
2 **se passer** (spa-se), to happen
3 **se passer (de)**, to do without
4 **qu'est-ce qui se passe?** what is happening?
5 **qu'est-ce qui arrive?** what is happening?

Exercise No. 128—Completion of Text

1 Je vais vous poser (a few) questions.
2 Voici (the matches and the ashtray).
3 Je suis (very comfortable).
4 (They are alike) plus ou moins.
5 Mais un Français est un Français (everywhere).
6 Il y a de grandes différences (as you say).
7 Quelles sont (some of these) différences?
8 (The fisherman and seaman) sont très dévots.
9 (The farmers) sont ronds et railleurs.
10 (The mine workers) sont syndiqués.
11 (We don't need) de continuer.
12 L'homme du Midi (does not resemble) au montagnard.
13 Ils aiment beaucoup (to argue).
14 Ça va être (a love story).

Grammar Notes

1 Reflexive Verbs with Reciprocal Meaning

The reflexive pronouns are sometimes translated *each other* or *one another*. This use is known as the reflexive with reciprocal meaning.

Les Français se ressemblent plus ou moins. French people resemble each other more or less.
Nous nous rencontrons tous les jeudis. We meet each other (one another) every Thursday.

To make the meaning clear **l'un (une) l'autre** and **les uns (unes) les autres,** are used after the verb. Thus:

Nous nous aimons l'un l'autre. We love one another.
Elles se donnent des cadeaux les unes aux autres. They give gifts to each other.

2 Verbs after Prepositions

(*a*) In English the present participle of the verb is used after prepositions. In French the infinitive of the verb is used after any preposition except **en.**
Sans connaître les détails je le comprends. Without knowing the details I realize it.
Avant de sortir il met son pardessus. Before leaving he puts on his overcoat.

(*b*) After the preposition **en** the French use the present participle. In this case en is translated by *while, on, by, upon, in,* or is not translated at all.
Ils entrent dans la salle à manger en causant d'un ton animé. They enter the dining-room while chatting in an animated tone.
En sortant de la gare ils appellent un taxi. On leaving the station they call a taxi.

3 Formation of the Present Participle

All French verbs, except **être**, **avoir** and **savoir** form their present participles by dropping the ending **-ons** from the **nous** form of the present tense and adding **-ant**. Thus:

nous donnons, we give	nous vendons, we sell	nous finissons, we finish
donnant, giving	vendant, selling	finissant, finishing
nous voyons, we see	*but*	
voyant, seeing		
nous avons, we have	nous sommes, we are	nous savons, we know
ayant, having	étant, being	sachant, knowing

Exercise No. 129 Write the **nous** form of the present tense, and the present participle of the following verbs.

Exemple: aller, nous allons, allant.

1 étudier	4 acheter	7 choisir	10 connaître	13 compter	16 faire
2 venir	5 vouloir	8 finir	11 apprendre	14 dormir	17 avoir
3 lire	6 dire	9 bâtir	12 appeler	15 mettre	18 être

4 quelque, quelqu'un

(*a*) **quelque**, some (*plur.* **quelques**, some, any, a few) is an adjective and therefore modifies a noun.

Voulez-vous quelque chose?   Do you want something?
Je vais poser quelques questions.   I am going to ask a few questions.

(*b*) **quelqu'un** (*fem.* **quelqu'une**), somebody, anybody (*plur.* **quelques-uns**, **quelques-unes**), some, a few, is a pronoun and therefore is not followed by a noun.

Quelqu'un sait la vérité.   Somebody knows the truth.
Quelques-uns de ces élèves apprennent le français.   A few of these pupils are learning French.
Je connais quelques-unes de ces différences.   I know a few of these differences.

Exercise No. 130 Complete these sentences with the correct form of **quelque** or of **quelqu'un**.

1 Il y a (somebody) **dans la cuisine.**
2 Nous achetons (a few) **légumes.**
3 (Some) **de ces messieurs sont français.**
4 (Some) **de ces dames sont anglaises.**
5 Quelles sont (some) **de ces différences?**
6 Nous apprenons (some) **locutions françaises.**
7 J'ai (something) **pour vous.**
8 Nous avons (a few) **cadeaux pour maman.**
9 Voulez-vous (some) **de ces poires?**
10 Est-ce que vous attendez (somebody)?

NOTE 1. **plusieurs**, several.   **Nous avons plusieurs cahiers.**

Exercise No. 131—Questionnaire

1 Qu'est-ce que M. Davis va faire?
2 Qu'est-ce que M. Davis demande pour commencer?

3 Est-il vrai qu'il y a de très grandes différences entre tous les Français?
4 Pourquoi y a-t-il des différences entre les Français?
5 Comment sont les pêcheurs de la Bretagne?
6 Comment est l'homme du Midi?
7 Est-ce qu'il ressemble au montagnard de l'Auvergne?
8 Est-ce que les Français aiment discuter?
9 De quoi les Français sont-ils fiers?
10 Qu'est-ce qu'ils aiment tous?

CHAPITRE 25 (VINGT-CINQ)

L'ART ET LA MODE

1 M. Davis vient de recevoir une grande caisse de marchandises et M. Picard est en train de regarder et d'admirer.

2 — Ce sont des échantillons de riches étoffes de soie de Lyon, de beaux tissus de polyester, de velours, et de laine. Regardez, M. Picard, cette belle étoffe de laine de la maison Cardin pour un manteau de dame.

3 — Tiens! Cardin? Mais n'est-il pas couturier?

4 — Certainement. Un des plus connus. Les grandes maisons de couture font le commerce non seulement de robes, de costumes tailleurs, de blouses, et de manteaux, mais aussi de lingerie, de parfums, de gants, de collants, et de tissus; et qui sait si l'année prochaine ils ne vont pas offrir aux élégantes des éviers de cuisine parfumés, de couleurs assorties?

5 — M. Davis, je crois que vous n'aimez pas la mode.

6 — J'aime beaucoup les belles choses telles que ces jolies étoffes aux couleurs magnifiques; mais la mode, c'est quelque chose d'autre.

7 — Pourtant, la couture est un art, n'est-ce pas? Et vous êtes amateur des arts.

8 — C'est vrai, mais je préfère les beaux-arts: la peinture, la sculpture, l'architecture. Je compte beaucoup sur le plaisir de visiter le Musée du Louvre pour étudier l'art des grands maîtres. J'espère aussi visiter les musées d'art moderne.

9 — Vous êtes un commerçant tout à fait exceptionnel. Vous vous intéressez à toutes sortes de choses: l'art, l'histoire, les belles-lettres. Je vous admire.

10 — Et moi, je vous admire aussi. Vous êtes un professeur tout à fait exceptionnel.

11 — Bon. Formons une société d'estime mutuelle.

12 — Très bien. Prochaine réunion de la société: mardi à huit heures.

13 — Entendu. Au revoir, co-sociétaire.

14 Ils se serrent la main.

1 Mr. Davis has just received a large case of merchandise and Mr. Picard is looking and admiring.

2 These are samples of rich silk materials from Lyons, and of beautiful polyester, velvet and woollen fabrics. Look, Mr. Picard, at this fine woollen material from Cardin for a lady's coat.

3 Well, well! Cardin? But isn't he a couturier? (dress designer).

4 Certainly. One of the best known. The big dressmaking houses do business not only in dresses, suits, blouses and coats but also in lingerie, perfume, gloves, tights and fabrics; and who knows if next year they won't offer the fashionable ladies perfumed kitchen sinks in assorted colours?

5 Mr. Davis, I don't think you like fashion.

6 I'm very fond of beautiful things such as these lovely materials in magnificent colours; but fashion, that's another matter.

7 And yet, dressmaking is an art, isn't it? And you love (*Lit.* are a lover of) the arts.

8 That's true, but I prefer the fine arts: painting, sculpture and architecture. I am very much looking forward to visiting the Louvre Museum to study the art of the great masters. I hope also to visit the museums of modern art.

9 You are a very unusual businessman. You take an interest in all sorts of things, art, history, literature. I admire you.

10 And I admire you too. You are a very unusual teacher.

11 Good. Let us form a mutual admiration society.

12 Very good. Next meeting of the society: Tuesday at eight o'clock.

13 Agreed. Goodbye, fellow-member.

14 They shake hands. (*Lit.* They give each other the hand.)

Pronunciation and Spelling Aids

A. Practise Aloud:

M. Davis vient de recevoir une grande caisse de marchandises et M. Picard est en train de regarder et d'admirer (mə-sjø Davis vjɛ̃ drə-sə-vwaːr yn grɑ̃ːd kɛːs də mar-ʃɑ̃-diːz e mə-sjø pi-kaːr ɛ tɑ̃ trɛ də rə-gar-de e dad-mi-re)

B. Remember: **é** = e **è** = ɛ

je préfère (ʒə pre-fɛːr) **j'achète** (ʒa-ʃɛt)
e before a double consonant equals è (ɛ)
j'appelle (ʒa-pɛl) **je iette** (ʒə ʒɛt)

Building Vocabulary

A. **Les vêtements** (vɛt-mɑ̃) Clothes

la blouse (bluːz), blouse
la ceinture (sɛ̃-tyːr), belt
le chapeau (ʃa-po), hat
la chaussette (ʃo-sɛt), sock
la chaussure (ʃo-syːr), shoe, footwear
la chemise (ʃmiz), shirt
le chemisier, woman's shirt
le collant (kɔ-lɑ̃), tights
la cravate (kra-vat), tie
le complet (kɔ̃-plɛ), suit (man's)

le costume tailleur (ta-jœːr), suit (woman's)
une écharpe (y-ne-ʃarp), scarf
le foulard (fu-laːr), scarf
le gant (gɑ̃), glove
la jupe (ʒyp), skirt
le manteau (mɑ̃-to), coat
le pantalon (pɑ̃-ta-lɔ̃), trousers
le mouchoir (mu-ʃwaːr), handkerchief
la robe (rɔb), dress

B. Noun Combinations. In English we can put two nouns together using the first one as an adjective.

Thus: *a silk dress*, *a woollen coat*, *a school teacher*, *etc.* This is not done in French, which uses instead two nouns connected by **de** (of).

une robe de soie, a silk dress
un manteau de laine, a woollen coat
un gant de cuir, leather glove
une ceinture de plastique, plastic belt
le chapeau de velours, the velvet hat

une étoffe de coton, cotton cloth
le maître d'école, the school teacher
la classe de français, the French class
l'Opéra de Paris, the Paris Opera-house
les rues de Londres, London streets

Locutions françaises

1 **venir de** + *infinitive* = to have just
2 **venir de recevoir,** to have just received
3 **il vient de recevoir,** he has just received
4 **nous venons d'écrire,** we have just written
5 **ils viennent de dîner,** they have just dined
6 **être en train de,** to be in the act of
7 **il est en train d'admirer,** he is (in the act of) admiring
8 **ils font le commerce de,** they do business in
9 **c'est quelque chose d'autre,** that's something else, another matter
10 **compter sur le plaisir de visiter,** to look forward to visiting

Exercise No. 132—Completion of Text

1 **Il** (has just received) **des échantillons.**
2 **M. Picard** (is admiring) **les étoffes de soie.**
3 **Les maisons de couture font le commerce** (not only) **de robes** (but also) **de lingerie, etc.**
4 **Je crois** (that you do not like) **la mode.**
5 **La couture est un art** (isn't it?)
6 **Je préfère** (the fine arts).
7 Painting, sculpture and architecture.
8 (I look forward) **de visiter le Musée du Louvre.**
9 **Vous êtes un commerçant** (very unusual).
10 I admire you.

Grammar Notes

1 Verbs with Spelling Changes

acheter, to buy	**préférer,** to prefer	**appeler,** to call
j'achète	**je préfère**	**j'appelle**
tu achètes	**tu préfères**	**tu appelles**
il, elle achète	**il, elle préfère**	**il, elle appelle**
nous achetons	**nous préférons**	**nous appelons**
vous achetez	**vous préférez**	**vous appelez**
ils, elles achètent	**ils, elles préfèrent**	**ils, elles appellent**

These verbs are regular **-er** verbs. Note, however, the slight changes in the spelling of the stem before silent endings.

Like **acheter** (e of stem becomes è before silent endings)

lever, to raise	**je lève**	**tu lèves**	**il, elle lève**
	nous levons	**vous levez**	**ils, elles lèvent**

Like **préférer** (é of stem becomes è before silent endings)

espérer, to hope	**j'espère**	**tu espères**	**il, elle espère**
	nous espérons	**vous espérez**	**ils, elles espèrent**
célébrer, to celebrate	**je célèbre**	**tu célèbres**	**il, elle célèbre**
	nous célébrons	**vous célébrez**	**ils, elles célèbrent**
répéter, to repeat	**je répète**	**tu répètes**	**il, elle répète**
	nous répétons	**vous répétez**	**ils, elles répètent**

Like **appeler** (consonant of stem doubles before silent endings)

jeter, to throw	je jette	tu jettes	il, elle jette
	nous jetons	vous jetez	ils, elles, jettent

Exercise No. 133 Complete each sentence into the correct French verb.

1 (She is buying) **quelques-uns de ces foulards.**

2 (Do you prefer) **les mouchoirs de soie?**

3 Non, (I prefer) **les mouchoirs de coton.**

4 (Let us repeat) **cette phrase.**

5 (I hope) **voir tout cela.**

6 À quelle heure (do you get up)?

7 (I get up) **à sept heures du matin.**

8 En France on (celebrates) **le 14 juillet.**

9 Le fils aîné (is named) **Philippe.**

10 Les enfants (are throwing) **la balle.**

11 Le maître (calls) **les élèves.**

12 (I am raising) **la fenêtre.**

Exercise No. 134—Questionnaire

1 Qu'est-ce que M. Davis vient de recevoir?

2 Que fait M. Picard?

3 Qu'y a-t-il dans la grande caisse?

4 De quelle maison est la belle étoffe de laine?

5 Qu'est-ce que M. Picard croit au sujet de M. Davis et de la mode?

6 De quoi M. Davis est-il amateur?

7 Qu'est-ce que M. Davis va étudier au Musée du Louvre?

8 Qu'est-ce qu'il espère visiter aussi?

9 À quoi M. Davis s'intéresse-t-il?

10 Qu'est-ce que les messieurs vont former?

CHAPITRE 26 (VINGT-SIX)

LES JOURS DE FÊTE DE LA FRANCE

1 — Ce soir, parlons des jours de fête de la France. Cela va nous égayer un peu, car il fait du vent et il pleut.

2 — Volontiers. Je sais que le quatorze juillet on célèbre la prise de la Bastille, et que c'est la grande fête nationale. Mais dites-moi, M. Picard, comment est-elle célébrée?

3 — Le quatorze juillet est célébré dans les rues partout en France. Tout le monde est dans la rue. À Paris, dans certains quartiers, on danse toute la journée et presque toute la nuit. On vend des beignets chauds, des gaufrettes, des glaces, et toutes sortes de friandises. Il y a des petits chevaux de bois,[1] guignol pour les enfants, et naturellement des buvettes pour les grands.

4 — J'espère voir tout cela et même danser dans les rues au mois de juillet. Et comment le Noël est-il célébré?

5 — M. Davis, je dois vous corriger. Noël est bien masculin, mais on dit *la Noël*, pas le Noël, parce que c'est *la fête de Noël* qu'on veut dire.

6 — Merci. Je recommence. Comment est-ce qu'on célèbre la Noël?

7 — Eh bien, on la célèbre en dormant.

8 — Comment!

9 — Oui, monsieur, c'est ça. On dort parce qu'on a réveillonné toute la nuit. La veille de Noël correspond à la veille du jour de l'an en Écosse. Naturellement les bons viveurs ne manquent pas de saisir l'occasion de réveillonner deux fois.

10 — Et quand est-ce que les enfants reçoivent leurs cadeaux, si tout le monde dort?

11 — Le Père Noël, lui, ne dort pas. Mais le jour de l'an est aussi le jour des cadeaux, qu'on appelle les étrennes. C'est une fête de réunion de famille. On tient table ouverte. On peut même dire qu'on tient auberge!

12 — Ça doit être très agréable. Y a-t-il d'autres grandes fêtes en France?

13 — Pendant la quinzaine de Pâques, on va à la campagne si possible. À la Pentecôte et à l'Assomption tout le monde quitte Paris. La ville est morte pour la journée.

14 — Tiens! Ça doit être intéressant à voir!

15 — Oui. Mais il n'y reste personne pour le voir.[2] Seulement un chien par-ci, par-là, au coin d'une rue un agent mécontent, et le silence.

1 This evening let's talk of the holidays of France. This will cheer us up a bit, for it's blowing and raining.

2 Gladly. I know that on the fourteenth of July they celebrate the capture of the Bastille and that it's the big national holiday. But tell me, Mr. Picard, how is it celebrated?

3 The fourteenth of July is celebrated in the streets everywhere in France. Everybody is in the street. In some Paris districts, they dance all day and nearly all night. They sell hot fritters, biscuit wafers, ice-cream and all sorts

of tit-bits. There are small roundabouts,[1] puppet shows for the children, and naturally, bars for the grown-ups.

4 I hope to see all this and even to dance in the streets in July. And how is Christmas celebrated?

5 Mr. Davis, I must correct you. Noël is masculine all right, but you say *la Noël*, not *le Noël*, because it is *la fête de Noël* that is meant (*Lit.* that one wishes to say).

6 Thank you. I begin again. How is Christmas celebrated?

7 Well, it is celebrated by sleeping.

8 What!

9 Yes, that's right. People sleep because they have been celebrating all night. Christmas Eve corresponds to New Year's Eve in Scotland. Naturally, the men about town don't miss (*Lit.* fail to seize) the opportunity to celebrate twice.

10 And when do the children receive their presents, if everyone is sleeping?

11 Father Christmas does *not* sleep. But New Year's Day is also the day for gifts which are called **étrennes**. It is a holiday for family gatherings. People keep open house. One can even say that they keep open inn!

12 That must be very pleasant. Are there other big holidays in France?

13 During the Easter fortnight, people go to the country if it's possible. At Whitsun and on the Feast of the Assumption everybody leaves Paris. The city is dead for the day.

14 Well, well! That must be interesting to see.

15 Yes. But nobody remains there to see it.[2] Only a dog here and there, at the corner of a street a disgruntled policeman, and silence.

NOTE 1. *Lit.* little wooden horses.
2. This is almost literally true. All stores are shut and boarded up. One can walk through street after street in the centre of the city and see scarcely a soul.

Pronunciation and Spelling Aids

A. Practise Aloud:

ce soir parlons des jours de fêtes de la France (sə swaːr par-lɔ dɛ ʒuːr də fɛt də la frãːs)

cela va nous égayer un peu, car il fait du vent et il pleut (sla va nu ze-gɛ-je œ̃ pœ, kaːr il fɛ dy vã e il plœ)

B. Remember: The letter **c** before **e** or **i** equals *s* as in *see*. Before **a**, **o**, or **u**, **c** equals *k*. The letter **ç** (c with a cedilla) always equals *s*.

commencer (kɔ-mã-se) **commençons** (kɔ-mã-sɔ)

The letter **g**, before **e** or **i**, is pronounced zh. Before **a**, **o**, or **u**, **g** is hard like *g* in *gate*.

manger (mã-ʒe) **mangeons** (mã-ʒɔ̃) **gant** (gã)

Building Vocabulary

la Noël (nɔ-ɛl), Christmas
le jour de l'an, New Year's Day
Pâques (paːk), Easter
la veille (vɛːj) **de Noël**, Christmas Eve
la Pentecôte (pãt-koːt), Whitsun

le quatorze juillet, Bastille Day
joyeux Noël, Merry Christmas
bonne année, Happy New Year
guignol, puppet show

Locutions françaises

1 **tout le monde,** everybody
2 **les étrennes,** New Year's gifts
3 **on tient table ouverte,** people keep open house.

4 **toute la nuit,** all night
5 **par-ci, par-là,** here and there
6 **tiens!** well!

Exercise No. 135—Completion of Text

1 **Le quatorze juillet est** (the big national holiday).
2 (People celebrate) **la prise de la Bastille.**
3 (Everybody) **est dans la rue.**
4 **On danse** (all day) **et presque** (all night).
5 **Il y a** (a puppet show) **pour les enfants.**
6 (I hope) **voir tout cela.**
7 **Comment la Noël est-elle** (celebrated)?
8 **On la célèbre** (sleeping).
9 (New Year's Day) **est le jour des cadeaux.**
10 **On appelle ces cadeaux** (the New Year's gifts).
11 **On tient** (open house).
12 **Cela** (must be) **très agréable.**
13 **À l'Assomption** (everybody leaves Paris).

Grammar Notes

1 Present Tense of **tenir,** to hold, to keep

Note that the present tense of **tenir** is exactly like that of **venir.**

I hold, I am holding, you hold, etc.   I come, I am coming, you come, etc.

je tiens (tjɛ̃)	**nous tenons** (tnɔ̃)	**je viens**	**nous venons**
tu tiens (tjɛ̃)	**vous tenez** (tne)	**tu viens**	**vous venez**
il tient (tjɛ̃)	**ils tiennent** (tjɛn)	**il vient**	**ils viennent**
elle tient (tjɛ̃)	**elles tiennent** (tjɛn)	**elle vient**	**elles viennent**

Other verbs like **tenir** are: **détenir,** to detain; **retenir,** to reserve, to hold back; **obtenir,** to obtain.

2 More Verbs with Spelling Changes. **commencer** to begin; **manger** to eat

I begin, I am beginning, etc.   I eat, I am eating, etc.

je commence	**nous commençons**	**je mange**	**nous mangeons**
tu commences	**vous commencez**	**tu manges**	**vous mangez**
il, elle commence	**ils, elles commencent**	**il, elle mange**	**ils, elles mangent**

In verbs whose infinitives end in **-cer** or **-ger,** the **c** or **g** must be softened by adding a cedilla to the **c** and an **e** to the **g**: **ç, ge,** before **a** or **o**; thus: **en commençant** (ã-kɔ-mã-sã), on beginning; **en mangeant** (ã mã-ʒã), in eating; **nous prononçons** (prɔ-nɔ̃-sɔ̃), we pronounce; **nous changeons** (ʃã-ʒɔ̃), we change.

Other verbs like **commencer** are: **placer,** to place (**nous plaçons**); **recommencer,** to begin again (**nous recommençons**); **avancer,** to advance (**nous avançons**).

Like **manger: nager,** to swim (**nous nageons**); **corriger,** to correct (**nous corrigeons**).

Exercise No. 136 Complete each sentence with the correct French verb.

1 (He is holding) **le livre mais il ne le lit pas.**
2 (We are obtaining) **des tissus fins.**
3 (I am not reserving) **les places.**
4 **Le jour de l'an on** (keeps open house).
5 (We begin to work) **à neuf heures.**
6 **Où** (do we change) **de train?**
7 **Comment** (do you pronounce) **ce mot?**
8 (We pronounce it) **'Noël'** (nɔ-ɛl).
9 (We do not eat) **de viande le matin.**
10 **Sur la Côte d'Azur** (we swim) **tous les jours.**
11 (We are correcting) **nos fautes.**
12 Let us begin again.

3 on one, people, they, you

on is an indefinite subject pronoun. Note the various ways **on** is translated.
on dit, one says, people say, you say, they say, it is said
On danse toute la journée. They (people) dance all day.

Often **on** is used instead of a passive construction:
Ici on parle français. Here French is spoken. (One speaks French.)
On célèbre la Noël. Christmas is celebrated. (One celebrates Christmas.)

4 ne . . . personne, nobody, no one, not anybody; **ne . . . rien,** nothing, not anything.

(*a*) When used as objects of the verb, **personne** and **rien**, like other negatives
(**ne . . . pas, ne . . . jamais,** etc.) require **ne** before the verb.
Je ne vois personne. I do not see anybody. (I see nobody.)
Je ne vois rien. I do not see anything. (I see nothing.)

(*b*) When used as subjects, **personne** and **rien** are followed by **ne.**

Personne ne sait où il demeure. Nobody knows where he lives.
Rien ne me plaît aujourd'hui. Nothing pleases me today.

(*c*) When **personne** and **rien** are used without a verb, **ne** is omitted.
Qui est chez vous? Personne. Who is at your house? Nobody.
Que fait-il? Rien. What is he doing? Nothing.

(*d*) The negative **ne . . . personne** must not be confused with the noun **la personne.**

Je ne connais pas cette personne-là. I don't know that person.

Exercise No. 137 Complete each sentence in French:

1 **Ici** (one) **parle français.**
2 **Ici** (nobody) **parle anglais.**
3 (People) **danse dans les rues.**
4 **Nous n'avons** (nothing).
5 **Il ne reste** (nobody) **dans la ville.**
6 **Il n'y a** (nothing) **à voir.**
7 **Que voulez-vous?** (Nothing.)
8 **Qui veut ces billets?** (Nobody.)
9 **Il n'aime** (anybody).
10 (Nobody) **l'aime.**

Exercise No. 138—Questionnaire

1 **De quoi les messieurs vont-ils parler ce soir?**
2 **Où est-ce qu'on célèbre le quatorze juillet?**

3 Qu'est-ce qu'on fait dans les rues?
4 Qu'est-ce qu'on vend dans les rues?
5 Qu'y a-t-il pour les enfants?
6 Faut-il dire *la Noël* ou *le Noël* quand on veut dire 'la fête de Noël'?
7 Pourquoi est-ce qu'on dort le jour de Noël?
8 Quand est-ce que les enfants reçoivent leurs cadeaux?
9 Comment appelle-t-on les cadeaux du jour de l'an?
10 Comment est la ville le jour de l'Assomption?

CHAPITRE 27 (VINGT-SEPT)

QUELS ENDROITS VOULEZ-VOUS VISITER, M. DAVIS?

1 — Vous allez bientôt partir pour la France, M. Davis. Avez-vous décidé quels endroits vous voulez visiter?

2 — Je ne pense à rien d'autre, et je lis beaucoup dans ma collection de guides.

3 — J'irai à Paris par avion. Je visiterai ce qu'il y a d'intéressant dans la ville, dans les environs de la ville, et autre part en France.

4 — C'est un projet ambitieux. Pour voir ce qu'il y a d'intéressant à Paris il vous faudra dix ans.

5 — Je ferai tout mon possible pour faire l'impossible. À Paris je compte visiter la cathédrale de Notre-Dame. Au Musée du Louvre, j'irai voir la Vénus de Milo, la Joconde et la salle de céramique grecque. Vous voyez que je m'intéresse toujours à la céramique.

6 — En sortant du Louvre, je traverserai le Jardin des Tuileries jusqu'à la place de la Concorde et puis je continuerai dans l'avenue des Champs-Élysées jusqu'à la place de l'Étoile. Là, je prendrai un taxi pour me promener au Bois de Boulogne. Je reviendrai par Passy pour visiter la Tour Eiffel et puis . . .

7 — Ah bon, je comprends! Vous verrez tout, voilà! Mais vous m'étonnez. Vous connaissez Paris mieux que moi.

8 — Ah non, M. Picard. Pas tout à fait. Je connais le Paris des guides. Mais il me semble qu'à Paris tout me sera familier.

9 — C'est une chose qui arrive à tout le monde. On se sent chez soi à Paris. Et que comptez-vous visiter dans les environs de la ville?

10 — Dans les environs, j'irai visiter Versailles, surtout les jardins.

11 — Il faut y aller le soir du quatorze juillet pour voir jouer les jets d'eau et regardez le feu d'artifice.

12 — Ah, très bien. Je n'y manquerai pas. Je veux voir aussi le château de Chantilly. Et puis Fontainebleau, et puis, Sens, Senlis. . . .

13 — Oh là, là! Laissons les environs, ou nous n'en sortirons jamais. Et après?

14 — Après, je ferai un grand cercle pour visiter la Normandie, surtout le Mont-Saint-Michel, où je mangerai trois omelettes, la spécialité du Mont. Puis, je visiterai la Bretagne, et en revenant à Paris, les châteaux de la Loire.

15 — Et quand irez-vous sur cette célèbre Côte d'Azur?

16 — Tout de suite après, j'irai sur la Côte d'Azur, pour me tremper dans la mer et prendre des bains de soleil, et je reviendrai à Paris par la route des Alpes. Qu'en pensez-vous?

17 — Ce que j'en pense? J'ai grande envie de vous accompagner! Mais ce n'est pas possible.

18 — Quel dommage, M. Picard.

1 Soon you are going to leave for France, Mr. Davis. Have you decided what places you want to visit?

2 I think of nothing else and I am reading a great deal in my collection of guide books.

3 I'll travel by plane to Paris. I'll visit what is interesting in the city, in the outskirts of the city, and elsewhere in France.

4 It's an ambitious project. To see what is interesting in Paris you'll need ten years.

5 I'll do my best to do the impossible. In Paris I expect to visit Notre Dame Cathedral. At the Louvre Museum, I'll go to see the Venus de Milo, the Mona Lisa and the Greek ceramics room. You see that I'm always interested in ceramics.

6 Leaving the Louvre, I shall pass through the Tuileries Garden to the Place de la Concorde and then I'll continue on the Champs-Élysées up to the Place de l'Étoile. There I'll take a taxi around the Bois de Boulogne. I'll come back by way of Passy to visit the Eiffel Tower and then . . .

7 Ah now I understand. You'll see everything, that's it! But you surprise me. You know Paris better than I.

8 Oh, no, Mr. Picard. Not quite. I know the Paris of the guide-books. But it seems to me that in Paris everything will be familiar.

9 It's a thing that happens to everybody. One feels at home in Paris. And what do you intend to visit in the outskirts of the city?

10 In the outskirts I'll go to visit Versailles, especially the gardens.

11 You must go there on the evening of the fourteenth of July to see the fountains play and watch the fireworks.

12 Ah, very good. I'll not fail to do so. I want to see also the Chantilly Castle. Then, Fontainebleau, and then, Sens, Senlis. . . .

13 Help! Let's leave the outskirts or we'll never get out of them. And afterwards?

14 Afterwards, I'll make a large circle to visit Normandy, especially the Mont-Saint-Michel, where I'll eat three omelettes, the speciality of the Mont. Then I shall visit Brittany, and on the way back to Paris, the castles on the Loire.

15 And when will you go to that famous Riviera (Blue Coast)?

16 Immediately after I'll go to the Riviera, to soak myself in the sea and to sunbathe, and I'll come back to Paris through the Alps. What do you think of it?

17 What do I think of it? I have a great mind to accompany you. But that isn't possible.

18 What a pity, Mr. Picard.

Pronunciation and Spelling Aids

Practise Aloud:

vous allez bientôt partir pour la France, monsieur Davis (vu za-le bjɛ̃-to par-tir pur la frɑ̃ːs, mə-sjø Davis)

avez-vous décidé quels endroits vous voulez visiter? (a-ve vu de-ci-de kɛl zɑ̃-drwa vu vu-le vi-si-te)

je ne pense à rien d'autre (ʒən pɑ̃s a rjɛ̃ doːtr)

c'est un projet ambitieux (sɛ tœ̃ prɔ-ʒɛ ɑ̃-bi-sjø)

Building Vocabulary

Expressions Indicating Future Time.

1 **demain (də-mɛ̃),** tomorrow
2 **après-demain,** day after tomorrow
3 **le mois prochain (prɔ-ʃɛ̃),** next month
4 **lundi (mardi) prochain,** next Monday (Tuesday)
5 **la semaine prochaine (smɛn prɔ-ʃɛn),** next week
6 **l'année prochaine,** next year

Locutions françaises

1 **il vous faudra dix ans,** you will need ten years (*Lit.* it will be necessary to you ten years)
2 **je ferai tout mon possible,** I shall do everything possible
3 **d'abord,** first, at first
4 **chez soi,** at home
5 **se promener,** to go for a walk, drive, sail, to promenade
6 **je me promène en voiture (en bateau),** I go for a drive (for a sail)
7 **je n'y manquerai pas,** I shall not fail to do so (*Lit.* I shall not fail there)
8 **j'ai envie de vous accompagner,** I have a mind (desire) to accompany you; I feel like accompanying you

Exercise No. 139—Completion of Text

1 (I shall travel) **l'avion.**
2 (I shall visit) **ce qu'il y a d'intéressant.**
3 **Il vous** (will be necessary) **dix ans.**
4 (I shall do) **tout mon possible.**
5 (I shall go) **voir d'abord la Vénus de Milo.**
6 (I shall pass) **par le jardin des Tuileries.**
7 **Là,** (I shall take) **un taxi.**
8 (I shall return) **par Passy.**
9 **Vous connaissez Paris** (better than I).
10 **À Paris tout me** (will be) **familier.**
11 **C'est une chose** (which happens to everybody).
12 **On se sent** (at home) **à Paris.**
13 (Let's leave) **les environs.**
14 (I have a great mind) **de vous accompagner.**

Grammar Notes

1 The Future Tense. What *shall* or *will* happen. **Parler, finir, vendre.**

I shall speak, you will speak, etc.	I shall finish, etc.	I shall sell, etc.
je parlerai (par-lre)	**je finirai**	**je vendrai**
tu parleras (par-lra)	**tu finiras**	**tu vendras**
il parlera (par-lra)	**il finira**	**il vendra**
elle parlera (par-lra)	**elle finira**	**elle vendra**
nous parlerons (par-lrɔ̃)	**nous finirons**	**nous vendrons**
vous parlerez (par-lre)	**vous finirez**	**vous vendrez**
ils parleront (par-lrɔ̃)	**ils finiront**	**ils vendront**
elles parleront (par-lrɔ̃)	**elles finiront**	**elles vendront**

parlera-t-il? will he speak? **finira-t-il?** will he finish? **vendra-t-il?** will he sell?

(*a*) The personal endings of the future tense of all verbs are: **-ai, -as, -a; -ons, -ez, -ont**. They are exactly like the present tense endings of **avoir**.

(*b*) To form the future tense, add the future endings to the infinitive as a base:

    parler: je parler-ai, etc.   **finir: je finir-ai,** etc.   **ouvrir: j'ouvrir-ai,** etc.

(*c*) If the infinitive ends in **-re** as in **vendre**, drop the final e before adding the future endings:

vendre: je vendr-ai, etc.   **apprendre: j'apprendr-ai,** etc.   **lire: je lir-ai,** etc.

2 Some Verbs with an Irregular Future

In a number of common verbs there is a change in the infinitive base to which the future endings are added. Among these verbs are:

avoir, to have	**j'aurai**	**tu auras**	**il aura**	**nous aurons,** etc.
être, to be	**je serai**	**tu seras**	**il sera**	**nous serons,** etc.
aller, to go	**j'irai**	**tu iras**	**il ira**	**nous irons,** etc.
voir, to see	**je verrai**	**tu verras**	**il verra**	**nous verrons,** etc.
venir, to come	**je viendrai**	**tu viendras**	**il viendra**	**nous viendrons,** etc.
faire, to do, make	**je ferai**	**tu feras**	**il fera**	**nous ferons,** etc.
pouvoir, to be able	**je pourrai**	**tu pourras**	**il pourra**	**nous pourrons,** etc.
falloir, to be necessary	**il faut,** it is necessary		**il faudra,** it will be necessary	

Exercise No. 140 Translate each dialogue. Read each aloud three times.

1 — Où irez-vous l'été prochain?
— J'irai en France.
— Quand partirez-vous de Londres?
— Je partirai le 31 mai.
2 — Combien de temps passerez-vous en France?
— J'y passerai trois mois.
— Est-ce que vous prendrez l'avion ou le bateau?
— Je prendrai l'avion.
3 — Est-ce que vous ferez un voyage au Maroc?
— Oui. Je ferai un voyage au Maroc et peut-être aussi en Corse.
— M. Picard pourra-t-il vous accompagner?
— Hélas! Il ne pourra pas m'accompagner.
4 — Est-ce que vous verrez votre représentant à Paris?
— Mais oui. Il m'attendra à l'aéroport.
— Combien de temps resterez-vous à Paris?
— J'y resterai quinze jours.[1]
5 — Est-ce que vous visiterez la célèbre Côte d'Azur?
— Bien entendu, je la visiterai.
— Quand reviendrez-vous en Angleterre?
— Je reviendrai le premier septembre.

NOTE 1. Very often, one says **huit jours** instead of **une semaine** and **quinze jours** instead of **deux semaines**.

Exercise No. 141 Translate:

1 he will visit	3 we shall go
2 I shall travel	4 they will not write

 5 It will be necessary
 6 will you see?
 7 they will not leave
 8 we shall sell
 9 will he not finish?
10 she will not learn
11 he will be

12 will you come?
13 I shall have
14 you (tu) will not listen
15 we shall study
16 I shall not make
17 will you be able?
18 will you go?

Exercise No. 142—Questionnaire

1 M. Davis prendra-t-il l'avion ou le bateau?
2 Qu'est-ce que M. Davis verra au Louvre?
3 En sortant du Louvre par quel jardin passera-t-il?
4 Où prendra-t-il un taxi?
5 Quelle tour visitera-t-il?
6 Où se promènera-t-il?
7 Quel est le Paris que M. Davis connaît?
8 Qu'est-ce qui arrive à tout le monde?
9 Quand est-ce qu'on voit jouer les grands jets d'eau à Versailles?
10 Où M. Davis mangera-t-il trois omelettes?
11 Que fera M. Davis sur la Côte d'Azur?
12 Par quelle route est-ce que M. Davis reviendra à Paris?

RÉVISION 6

CHAPITRES 24–27 PREMIÈRE PARTIE

Révision de mots

NOUNS

1 une allumette	14 une étoffe	27 le nord
2 le bas	15 le feu	28 l'ouest (*m*)
3 le bois	16 la fête	29 un ouvrier
4 le cercle	17 le foulard	30 le pêcheur
5 le cheval	18 le gant	31 la peinture
6 les chevaux	19 le jardin	32 le projet
7 le chien	20 le lin	33 la robe
8 le collant	21 la laine	34 la soie
9 le costume	22 le marin	35 la sorte
10 le couturier	23 la marchandise	36 le sud
11 la couturière	24 la mode	37 le tissu
12 une eau de vie	25 le musicien	38 le tabac
13 une écharpe	26 la musicienne	39 le vin

1 match	14 material	27 north
2 stocking	15 fire	28 west
3 wood	16 holiday	29 workman
4 circle	17 scarf	30 fisherman
5 horse	18 glove	31 painting (art of)
6 horses	19 garden	32 project, plan
7 dog	20 linen	33 dress
8 tights	21 wool	34 silk
9 costume	22 seaman	35 kind, sort
10 dress-designer	23 merchandise	36 south
11 dressmaker	24 fashion	37 fabric
12 brandy	25 musician (*m*)	38 tobacco
13 scarf	26 musician (*f*)	39 wine

VERBS

1 accompagner	8 étonner	14 se promener
2 admirer	9 étudier	15 rester
3 célébrer	10 manquer	16 recommencer
4 corriger	11 se passer	17 regarder
5 danser	12 se passer (de)	18 ressembler (à)
6 décider	13 s'intéresser (à)	19 sembler
7 discuter		

1 to accompany	8 to astonish	14 to take a walk
2 to admire	9 to study	15 to remain
3 to celebrate	10 to lack, miss	16 to begin again
4 to correct	11 to happen	17 to look at
5 to dance	12 to do without	18 to resemble
6 to decide	13 to be interested in	19 to seem
7 to discuss, argue		

ADJECTIVES

1 ambitieux	5 bavard	9 parfumé
2 droit	6 magnifique	10 politique
3 entendu	7 mort	11 tel (telle *f*)
4 fier (fière *f*)	8 mécontent	

160

1 ambitious	5 talkative	9 perfumed
2 straight, right	6 magnificent	10 political
3 agreed	7 dead	11 such
4 proud	8 discontented	

ADVERBS

1 alors	3 bientôt	5 partout	7 volontiers
2 autre part	4 même	6 trop	

1 then, well	3 soon	5 everywhere	7 gladly
2 elsewhere	4 even	6 too much	

PREPOSITIONS

1 à cause (de)	2 malgré	3 selon
1 because of	2 in spite of	3 according to

FRENCH EXPRESSIONS

1 avoir peur (de)	9 mieux que moi
2 avoir envie (de)	10 par-ci, par-là
3 être en train (de)	11 quelque chose d'autre
4 faire tout mon possible	12 tiens!
5 faire le commerce	13 défense de fumer
6 se passer (de)	14 joyeux Noël
7 venir (de)	15 bonne année
8 plus ou moins	16 encore un (une)

1 to be afraid of	9 better than I
2 to have a mind to	10 this way and that
3 to be in the act of	11 something else
4 to do my best	12 well!
5 to do business	13 Smoking Prohibited
6 to do without	14 Merry Christmas
7 to have just	15 Happy New Year
8 more or less	16 one more

DEUXIÈME PARTIE

Exercise No. 143 In Group II find the words that correspond to the words in Group I.

I

1 the handkerchief	9 the shirt
2 the overcoat	10 the socks
3 the suit (man's)	11 the tights
4 the suit (woman's)	12 the belt
5 the coat	13 the dress
6 the scarf	14 the trousers
7 the shoes	15 the skirt
8 the tie	

II

(a) le pantalon	(i) les chaussures
(b) le manteau	(j) les chaussettes
(c) l'écharpe	(k) la ceinture
(d) la robe	(l) le complet
(e) le mouchoir	(m) la chemise
(f) la jupe	(n) le costume tailleur
(g) le pardessus	(o) la cravate
(h) le collant	

Exercise No. 144 Combine each pair of nouns to form compound nouns and give the meaning of each.

Exemple: le chapeau — le velours   le chapeau de velours   the velvet hat

1 la ceinture—le cuir   5 la chemise—le nylon   9 le tissu—le coton
2 la robe—la soie   6 le bureau—la poste   10 le bracelet—l'argent
3 la montre—l'or (gold)   7 le voyage—les affaires   11 l'objet—l'art
4 la salle—le bain   8 le cahier—la musique   12 le chapeau—la paille
                                                          (straw)

Exercise No. 145 Answer these questions in complete sentences (in the future) with the help of the words in parenthesis.

Exemple: J'achèterai une cravate.

1 Qu'est-ce que vous achèterez? (une cravate)
2 Combien coûtera-t-elle? (cinquante francs)
3 Où irez-vous l'été prochain? (en France)
4 Quand reviendrez-vous en Angleterre? (le 31 décembre)
5 À quelle heure vous coucherez-vous? (à minuit)
6 À quelle heure vous lèverez-vous? (à six heures du matin)
7 Que lui direz-vous? (rien)
8 Qui ira avec vous? (personne ne)
9 Combien de temps travaillerez-vous? (toute la journée)
10 Où nous rencontrerons-nous? (à l'entrée du théâtre)

Exercise No. 146 Complete these sentences with the help of the French expressions listed below.

Exemple: Ils n'ont pas peur d'exprimer leurs idées.

1 (They are not afraid) d'exprimer leurs idées.
2 (We do not need) de continuer.
3 (She intends) de porter son manteau neuf (brand new).
4 (Have you a mind to) m'accompagner?
5 (He will do his best) pour vous aider.
6 (Will you go shopping) au Marché aux Puces?
7 (Mr. Davis is opening) la caisse.
8 (Are you afraid) de dire la vérité?
9 Allez-vous (to go for a walk) au Bois de Boulogne?
10 Vous savez que M. Davis (is not interested in) la mode.

(a) avoir peur (de)   (d) avoir l'intention (de)   (g) se promener
(b) avoir besoin (de)   (e) faire des achats   (h) faire tout son possible
(c) avoir envie (de)   (f) s'intéresser (à)   (i) être en train (de)

Exercise No. 147 Complete these sentences in French. mettre here means *to put on*. aller bien à means *to be becoming to*.

1 Je mets (my hat).   7 Ils mettent (their raincoats[1]).
2 Tu mets (your coat).   8 Elles mettent (their scarves[1]).
3 Il met (his nylon shirt).   9 (This dress) me va bien.
4 Elle met (her silk dress).   10 (This tie) lui va bien.
5 Nous mettons (our leather belts[1]). 11 (These gloves) nous vont bien.
6 Vous mettez (your red gloves).   12 (This skirt) ne va pas bien à Jeanne.

NOTE 1. Use the singular. The idea is that each one puts on one item of clothing.

Dialogue 1

Dans l'autobus

1 — Pardon monsieur, où est-ce que je descends pour aller à l'Hôtel des Postes?¹ (au boulevard St. Michel)? (au Jardin du Luxembourg)? (à l'ambassade d'Angleterre)? (au Marché aux Puces)? (à la gare)?

2 — Vous descendez au coin de la rue du Louvre et de la rue Étienne-Marcel, (etc.).

3 — Est-ce que c'est loin d'ici?

4 — Non monsieur, pas trop loin.

5 — Quand est-ce que nous y arriverons?

6 — Dans un quart d'heure à peu près.

7 — Merci beaucoup, monsieur.

8 — De rien.

In the Bus

1 Excuse me, where do I get off for the Main Post Office? (for the Boulevard St. Michel)? (for the Luxembourg Gardens)? (for the British Embassy)? (for the Flea Market)? (for the railway station)?

2 You get off at the corner of the Rue du Louvre and of Rue Étienne-Marcel (etc.).

3 Is it far from here?

4 No, not too far.

5 When will we get there?

6 In about a quarter of an hour.

7 Thank you very much.

8 Don't mention it.

NOTE 1. **L'Hôtel des Postes**, main post office in Paris; **le bureau de poste**, post office or **la poste**, more usually.

Dialogue 2

Le courrier

1 — M. Davis, vous avez sans doute une grosse correspondance. Y a-t-il une boîte aux lettres dans votre immeuble?

2 — Naturellement. Nous en avons une à chaque étage, où nous jetons nos lettres. Mais nous envoyons les colis postaux au bureau central des postes.

3 — Qui est-ce qui les porte?

4 — Le garçon de bureau. Il nous achète aussi la quantité de timbres dont nous avons besoin, les timbres par avion, les timbres d'envoi par exprès, les mandats etc.

5 — Où est le bureau central des postes?

6 — Il n'est pas loin d'ici.

The Mail

1 Mr. Davis, of course you have a large correspondence. Is there a letter-box in your building?

2 Naturally. We have one at each floor where we drop our letters. But we send parcel post packages to the main post office.

3 Who takes them?

4 The office boy. He also buys us the many stamps that we need, the air mail stamps, the special delivery stamps, money orders, etc.

5 Where is the main post office?

6 It isn't far from here.

Exercise No. 148—Lecture

L'anniversaire[1] de Mme Davis

C'est le vingt-deux mars, jour de l'anniversaire de Mme Davis. Elle a trente-cinq ans aujourd'hui. Pour célébrer cette fête la famille Davis va dîner dans un restaurant élégant de Soho à Londres.

Quand ils entrent dans le restaurant ils voient, sur la table réservée pour les Davis, une jolie corbeille[2] remplie de[3] roses blanches. Naturellement Mme Davis est tout à fait surprise. Elle remercie[4] et embrasse[5] son cher mari avec empressement.[6]

A la fin d'un dîner exquis Annette, la plus jeune, dit tout bas[7] aux autres enfants, — Maintenant! Et chacun des quatre enfants sort de dessous[8] la table une jolie petite boîte.[9] Ce sont des cadeaux pour leur mère.

Annette lui donne un mouchoir de soie; Rosette, une blouse de nylon; Henri, une paire de gants; et Philippe, un foulard de polyester.

La semaine d'après, M. Davis fait le calcul du compte de cette journée, qui suit:[10]

Dîner (service compris) ....cent vingt livres	£120·00
Pourboire........................cinq livres	5·00
Fleurs ....trente livres	30·00
Cadeaux ....vingt-trois livres	23·00
Total	£178·00

NOTE 1. birthday.
2. basket.
3. filled with.
4. she thanks.
5. kisses.
6. warmly.
7. in a low voice.
8. from under.
9. box.
10. follows.

CHAPITRE 28 (VINGT-HUIT)

M. DAVIS ÉCRIT UNE LETTRE À SON REPRÉSENTANT

1 M. Davis et M. Picard sont assis dans le salon chez M. Davis. M. Davis tient deux lettres à la main: une copie de sa lettre à son représentant, M. Parmentier, et la réponse qui vient d'arriver.

2 — M. Picard, je vais vous lire ma lettre à M. Parmentier.

3 — Cela me fera plaisir.

4 — M. Davis lit la lettre qui suit:

Londres, le 4 mai, 1985,

M. Georges Parmentier,
76 rue de Vaugirard,
75006 Paris, France.

Cher Monsieur Parmentier,

J'ai le plaisir de vous informer que je vais bientôt faire un voyage en France. Je partirai de Londres en avion le 31 mai à dix-huit heures et j'arriverai à Orly à dix-neuf heures cinquante-cinq.

J'ai l'intention de rester deux mois en France. Je compte faire un voyage d'agrément aussi bien que d'affaires. Je passerai trois semaines environ à Paris.

En partant de Paris, je ferai quelques excursions pour voir les endroits intéressants en France. J'espère aussi aller en avion au Maroc et peut-être en Corse.

Pendant mon séjour à Paris, j'espère profiter de l'occasion pour faire votre connaissance, car j'ai toujours beaucoup apprécié vos services dévoués, qui ont tant contribué, à notre réussite.

Je sais que vous êtes très occupé et que vous êtes souvent en voyage. Par conséquent je vous écris d'avance dans l'espoir de pouvoir fixer un rendez-vous. Je vous prie de me faire savoir si j'aurai le plaisir de vous voir à Paris.

Il y a cinq mois que je prends des leçons de français. Cela vous surprendra peut-être. J'espère pouvoir vous parler dans votre belle langue, car depuis quelque temps je cause deux fois par semaine avec mon professeur, M. Auguste Picard, un de vos compatriotes.

Dans l'espoir de vous lire bientôt, agréez, monsieur, l'assurance de ma considération distinguée.

Jean Davis

5 — Merveilleux, M. Davis, Il n'y pas une seule faute dans toute la lettre.

6 — M. Picard, je dois vous avouer quelque chose. Il y a un livre qui s'appelle 'La Correspondance Commerciale'. Ce livre me rend grand service en tout ce qui regarde les en-têtes, les conclusions, et les diverses formules de politesse. Naturellement, c'est surtout à vous que je dois les plus vifs remerciements.

7 — Vous êtes très aimable. Et maintenant, voulez-vous bien me lire la réponse que vous venez de recevoir de M. Parmentier?

8 — Avec plaisir, Monsieur.

(La suite au Chapitre 29.)

165

1 Mr. Davis and Mr. Picard are sitting in the living-room at Mr. Davis' house. Mr. Davis has two letters in his hand: a copy of his letter to his agent, Mr. Parmentier, and the answer which has just arrived.

2 Mr. Picard, I am going to read you my letter to Mr. Parmentier.

3 That will please me.

4 Mr. Davis reads the letter which follows:

London, 4 May, 1982.

Mr. Georges Parmentier,
76 Rue de Vaugirard,
75006 Paris, France.

Dear Mr. Parmentier,

I am pleased to inform you that I am soon going to make a trip to France. I shall leave London by plane on 31 May at 18.00 and will arrive at Orly at 19.55.

I intend to stay two months in France. I expect to make it a pleasure trip as well as a business trip. I shall spend about three weeks in Paris.

On leaving Paris, I shall make a few excursions to see places of interest in France. I hope also to go by plane to Morocco and perhaps to Corsica.

During my stay in Paris I hope to take advantage of the opportunity to meet you personally, for I have always appreciated very much your devoted services which have contributed so much to our success.

I know that you are very busy and that you travel a great deal. For this reason I am writing you beforehand in the hope of being able to arrange an appointment. Please (*Lit.* I beg you to) let me know if I shall have the pleasure of seeing you in Paris.

I have been studying French for the last five months. This will surprise you perhaps. I hope to be able to talk with you in your beautiful language, because for some time I have been conversing twice a week with my teacher, Mr. Auguste Picard, a fellow-countryman of yours (*Lit.* one of your fellow-countrymen).

Awaiting your early reply I remain sincerely yours (*Lit.* In the hope of reading you soon, accept, Sir, the assurance of my marked esteem).

John Davis

5 Marvellous, Mr. Davis. There is not a single mistake in the whole letter.

6 Mr. Picard, I must confess something to you. There is a book entitled, 'Commercial Correspondence'. This book helps me a great deal in everything that concerns headings, conclusions and various expressions of courtesy. Of course, to you especially I owe the most sincere thanks.

7 You are very kind. And now will you kindly read me the answer which you have received from Mr. Parmentier?

8 With pleasure.

(Continued in Chapter 29.)

Pronunciation and Spelling Aids

Practise Aloud:

j'ai le plaisir de vous informer que je vais bientôt faire un voyage en France (ʒel plɛ-ziːr də vu zɛ̃-fɔr-me kə ʒə vɛ bjɛ̃-to fɛːr œ̃ vwa-jaːʒ ɑ̃ frɑ̃ːs)

je partirai de Londres en avion le 31 (trente et un) mai à dix-huit heures (ʒpar-ti-re dlɔ̃-dr ɑ̃ na-vjɔ̃ lə trɑ̃-te-œ̃ mɛ a di-ʒɥi-tœːr)

Building Vocabulary

Related Expressions

1 **la main,** hand
2 **la main droite,** the right hand
3 **la main gauche,** the left hand
4 **à droite,** on, to the right
5 **à gauche,** on, to the left

6 **tourner** or **prendre la droite (gauche),** to turn to the right (left)
7 **à la main,** in his or her hand, by hand
8 **ils se serrent la main,** they shake hands

NOTE: in certain expressions referring to parts of the body, French uses the definite article instead of **mon, ton, son,** etc. thus:

il tient deux lettres à la main, he has two letters in his hand
elle a un panier sur la tête, she has a basket on her head

Locutions françaises

1 **avoir l'intention (de),** to intend to
2 **profiter de l'occasion (pour),** to take advantage of the opportunity
3 **par conséquent,** consequently
4 **d'avance,** in advance, beforehand
5 **faire la connaissance (de),** to make the acquaintance of, to get to know
6 **faire savoir,** to let know, to inform
7 **deux fois par semaine,** twice a week
8 **voulez-vous bien,** will you kindly
9 **cela me fera plaisir,** that will please me
10 **être occupé,** to be busy

Exercise No. 149—Completion of Text

1 **M. Davis a deux lettres** (in his hand).
2 **Voici la réponse qui** (has just arrived).
3 **M. Davis lit la lettre** (which follows).
4 (I shall leave) **le 31 mai.**
5 (I intend) **de rester deux mois en France.**
6 **Je sais que vous êtes** (very busy).
7 (Consequently) **je vous écris d'avance.**
8 (For some time) **je cause** (twice a week) **avec mon professeur.**
9 **Il n'y a pas** (a single mistake) **dans toute la lettre.**
10 (Will you kindly) **me lire la réponse de M. Parmentier.**

Grammar Notes

1 Present Tense of **suivre,** to follow; **traduire,** to translate

I follow, I am following, etc.

je suis	nous suivons
tu suis	vous suivez
il, elle suit	ils, elles suivent

Imperative

suis, follow;
suivons, let us follow;
suivez, follow.

I translate, I am translating, etc.

je traduis	nous traduisons
tu traduis	vous traduisez
il, elle traduit	ils, elles traduisent

Imperative

traduis, translate;
traduisons, let us translate;
traduisez, translate.

Like **suivre** is: **poursuivre**, to pursue. Like **traduire**: **conduire**, to lead, to conduct, to drive; **produire**, to produce; **construire**, to construct, to build.

2 More Verbs with Irregular Future.

tenir, to hold	**je tiendrai**, etc.	**valoir**, to be worth	**je vaudrai**, etc.
devoir, to owe	**je devrai**, etc.	**envoyer**, to send	**j'enverrai**, etc.
recevoir, to receive	**je recevrai**, etc.	**courir**, to run	**je courrai**, etc.
vouloir, to want	**je voudrai**, etc.	**savoir**, to know	**je saurai**, etc.

Exercise No. 150 Complete the following sentences in French:

Exemple 1. Je leur enverrai des journaux français.

1 (I shall send them) **des journaux français.**
2 **Mme Davis** (will receive) **beaucoup de cadeaux.**
3 (They will know) **où me trouver.**
4 (He will not want) **nous accompagner.**
5 **Les enfants** (will run) **voir guignol.**
6 **Les billets** (will not be worth) **plus de cinq livres.**
7 (They will owe us) **moins de dix francs.**
8 (They will hold) **table ouverte.**
9 (Will you translate) **cet exercice?**
10 (We shall not follow) **la mode.**
11 (I shall make) **la connaissance de M. Parmentier.**
12 (We shall be able) **fixer un rendez-vous.**

3 depuis, depuis quand, depuis combien de temps, pendant.

(*a*) When an action began in the past and is continuing in the present, French uses **depuis** (*since, for*), **depuis quand?** (*since when?*), **depuis combien de temps?** (*how long?*), with the present tense of the verb. English uses the present perfect.

Depuis quand est-ce que M. Davis étudie le français? Since when has Mr. Davis been studying French?

Il étudie le français depuis cinq mois. He has been studying French for (since) five months.

Depuis combien de temps M. Davis étudie-t-il le français? How long is it that Mr. Davis has been studying French?

Il y a cinq mois qu'il étudie le français. It is five months that (since) he has been studying French.

(*b*) If the action is future, French uses **combien de temps?** (how long?) and **pendant** (for, during). Like the word *for* in English, **pendant** is often omitted.

Combien de temps restera-t-il à Paris? How long will he remain in Paris?
Il y restera (pendant) trois semaines. He will remain there (for) three weeks.

Exercise No. 151 Complete the following sentences in French

Exemple 1. Combien de temps resterez-vous à Paris?

1 (How long) **resterez-vous à Paris?**
2 **Nous resterons à Paris** (during the months) **de juin et juillet.**
3 (Since when) **le connaissez-vous?**
4 **Nous le connaissons** (for ten years).

5 J'étudie le français (for two years).
6 Il écrit des lettres (for three hours).
7 (How long) m'attendrez-vous?
8 (It is three days) qu'elle est malade.
9 (Since when have you been living) dans cette maison?
10 (We have been living there) depuis trois ans.

Exercise No. 152—Questionnaire

1 Où est-ce que les messieurs sont assis?
2 Qu'est-ce que M. Davis tient à la main?
3 Qu'est-ce qu'il va lire à M. Picard?
4 Quand est-ce que M. Davis partira de Londres?
5 Combien de temps passera-t-il en France?
6 Combien de temps restera-t-il à Paris?
7 Qu'est-ce qu'il fera en partant de Paris?
8 Où espère-t-il aller par avion?
9 Qui est très occupé?
10 De qui est-ce que M. Davis veut faire la connaissance?
11 Pourquoi écrit-il d'avance?
12 Combien de temps y a-t-il que M. Davis prend des leçons de français?

CHAPITRE 29 (VINGT-NEUF)

M. DAVIS REÇOIT UNE LETTRE

M. Davis a écrit une lettre à son représentant à Paris. Dans le dernier chapitre il a lu une copie de cette lettre à son professeur, M. Picard. Celui-ci n'a pas trouvé une seule faute dans la lettre.

Le commerçant a reçu une réponse de son représentant. Maintenant il la tient à la main et il est en train de la lire.

Mr. Davis has written a letter to his agent in Paris. In the last chapter he read a copy of that letter to his teacher, Mr. Picard. Mr. Picard did not find a single mistake in the letter.

The businessman has received an answer from his agent. Now he has it in his hand and is reading it.

1 Cher M. Davis,

2 J'ai reçu avec beaucoup de plaisir votre lettre du 4 mai dans laquelle[1] vous m'informez que vous allez bientôt faire un voyage en France.

3 Heureusement, je serai à Paris pendant les mois de juin et juillet, et je serai tout à fait à votre disposition.

4 Je compte sur le plaisir de vous rencontrer à l'aéroport d'Orly à dix-neuf heures cinquante-cinq, le 31 mai. J'espère pouvoir rendre votre séjour agréable quant aux distractions, aussi bien que profitable quant aux affaires.

5 C'est avec plaisir que je causerai en français avec vous et je suis sûr que vous le parlez à la perfection. En vérité vous écrivez le français à merveille. Je veux vous féliciter ainsi que votre professeur. Comme M. Picard est Français, je comprends bien votre connaissance de beaucoup de gallicismes.

6 Dans l'attente de faire votre connaissance, je vous prie de croire, monsieur, à ma parfaite considération.

Georges Parmentier

7 — C'est une gentille lettre, dit M. Picard. Jusqu'à présent vous avez connu M. Parmentier en tant que représentant sérieux. Sans doute vous allez voir qu'il est aussi très sympathique comme bon nombre de ses compatriotes. Pardonnez-moi si je suis fier des Français, mais vous verrez vous-même.

8 — Je suis certain que je serai très content de me trouver parmi les Français; et le plus beau de l'affaire c'est que je pourrai parler avec eux dans leur propre langue.

9 — C'est certain. Alors, M. Davis, mardi prochain c'est le dernier rendez-vous avant votre départ. Nous nous rencontrerons à votre bureau, n'est-ce pas?

10 — Oui, monsieur. Et vous me donnerez quelques derniers conseils?

11 — Avec plaisir, M. Davis.

1 Dear Mr. Davis,

2 I have received with great pleasure your letter of 4 May in which[1] you inform me that you will soon be making a trip to France.

3 Fortunately I shall be in Paris during the months of June and July, and I shall be entirely at your service.

4 I am looking forward to meeting you at Orly airport at 19.55, 31 May. I hope to be able to make your stay pleasant in the way of entertainment as well as profitable in the way of business.

5 I shall be happy to talk with you in French, and I am sure that you speak it perfectly. Indeed, you write French extremely well. I want to congratulate you as well as your teacher. Since M. Picard is French, I understand very well your familiarity with many French idioms.

6 Looking forward to making your acquaintance I remain,

Sincerely yours,

(*Lit.* I beg you to believe, sir, in my complete esteem)

George Parmentier

7 It's a very nice letter, says Mr. Picard. Until now you have known Mr. Parmentier as a reliable agent. No doubt, you will see that he is also very likeable like a good number of his fellow-countrymen. Forgive me if I am proud of the French people, but you will see for yourself.

8 I am certain that I shall be very happy to be among the French; and the best thing is that I'll be able to converse with them in their own language.

9 That's right. Well, Mr. Davis, Tuesday next is the last appointment before your departure. We'll meet in your office, shall we not?

10 Yes. And you will give me some final advice?

11 With pleasure, Mr. Davis.

NOTE 1. **lequel (laquelle, lesquels, lesquelles),** which, is a relative pronoun used after prepositions. It agrees with its antecedent in number and gender.

Pronunciation and Spelling Aids

Practise Aloud:

j'ai reçu avec beaucoup de plaisir votre lettre du 4 (quatre) mai dans laquelle vous m'informez que vous allez bientôt faire un voyage en France (ʒe rsy a-vɛk bo-kud plɛ-ziːr vɔtr lɛtr dy katr mɛ dɑ̃ la-kɛl vu mɛ̃-fɔr-me kə vu za-le bjɛ̃-to fɛːr œ vwa-jaːʒ ɑ̃ frɑ̃ːs)

Building Vocabulary

Expressions Referring to Past Time.

1 **hier** (iɛːr), yesterday
2 **hier soir,** yesterday evening
3 **hier matin,** yesterday morning
4 **avant-hier,** day before yesterday
5 **la semaine dernière,** last week
6 **l'année dernière,** last year
7 **le mois dernier,** last month
8 **il y a deux jours (mois, ans),** two days (months, years) ago
9 **il y a huit jours,** a week ago
10 **il y a quinze jours,** two weeks ago

Locutions françaises

1 **je compte sur le plaisir de,** I look forward to
2 **quant à,** in the matter of, as for
3 **en vérité,** indeed
4 **jusqu'à présent,** until now
5 **ma (sa, leur) propre langue,** my (his, their) own language
6 **c'est certain,** that's right
7 **en tant que,** as

Salutations—Business Letters

1 **monsieur,** dear Sir
2 **messieurs,** gentlemen

3 **cher monsieur A,** my dear Mr. A
4 **chère madame B,** my dear Mrs. B

Closings—Business Letters

1 **agréez, monsieur, mes salutations distinguées,** accept, sir, my distinguished greetings; yours truly.
2 **agréez, monsieur, mes salutations empressées,** accept, sir, my earnest greetings; yours truly.
3 **agréez, je vous prie, l'expression de mes salutations les plus distinguées,** please accept the expression of my most distinguished greetings; yours truly.
4 **veuillez agréer, monsieur, mes sincères salutations,** please accept, sir, my sincere greetings; yours truly.

Exercise No. 153—Completion of Text

1 (He is in the act of reading) **la lettre.**
2 (I have received) **votre lettre du 4 mai.**
3 **Je serai à Paris** (during the months) **de juin et juillet.**
4 (I am looking forward) **de vous rencontrer à l'aéroport.**
5 **C'est avec plaisir** (that I shall talk in French) **avec vous.**
6 **Je veux** (to congratulate you).
7 (You have known) **M. Parmentier en tant que représentant sérieux.**
8 **Pardonnez-moi** (if I am proud) **des Français.**
9 (You will see) **vous-même.**
10 (I shall be able) **parler avec eux en français.**

Grammar Notes

1 Conversational Past Tense. What has happened, what happened, what did happen. Model verbs **parler, finir, vendre.**

I have spoken, spoke, did speak, etc.

j'ai parlé	**nous avons parlé**
tu as parlé	**vous avez parlé**
il, elle a parlé	**ils, elles ont parlé**

I have not finished, did not finish, etc.

je n'ai pas fini	**nous n'avons pas fini**
tu n'as pas fini	**vous n'avez pas fini**
il, elle n'a pas fini	**ils, elles n'ont pas fini**

have I sold? did I sell? etc.

est-ce que j'ai vendu?	**avons-nous vendu?**
as-tu vendu?	**avez-vous vendu?**
a-t-il vendu?	**ont-ils vendu?**
a-t-elle vendu?	**ont-elles vendu?**

have you not sold? did you not sell?

n'as-tu pas vendu?	**n'avez-vous pas vendu?**

Like the present perfect tense in English, the conversational past tense in

French is formed by means of an auxiliary verb (usually **avoir**, have) plus a past participle.

2 How to Form the Regular Past Participle.

-er verbs drop **-er** and add **é**.

Infinitive	*Past Participle*
parler, to speak	**parlé**, spoken
trouver, to find	**trouvé**, found
demander, to ask	**demandé**, asked
casser, to break	**cassé**, broken
fermer, to close	**fermé**, closed
apporter, to bring	**apporté**, brought
écouter, to listen to	**écouté**, listened to
envoyer, to send	**envoyé**, sent
manger, to eat	**mangé**, eaten
porter, to carry	**porté**, carried

-ir verbs (with some exceptions) drop **-ir** and add **-i**.

Infinitive	*Past Participle*
finir, to finish	**fini**, finished
choisir, to choose	**choisi**, chosen
bâtir, to build	**bâti**, built
obéir, to obey	**obéi**, obeyed
saisir, to seize	**saisi**, seized
dormir, to sleep	**dormi**, slept
sentir, to feel	**senti**, felt
servir, to serve	**servi**, served
punir, to punish	**puni**, punished
remplir, to fill	**rempli**, filled

-re verbs (with some exceptions) drop **-re** and add **-u**.

Infinitive	*Past Participle*
vendre, to sell	**vendu**, sold
répondre, to answer	**répondu**, answered
perdre, to lose	**perdu**, lost
entendre, to hear	**entendu**, heard
rendre, to give back	**rendu**, given back
attendre, to wait for	**attendu**, waited for

3 Some Irregular Past Participles

Infinitive	*Past Participle*
connaître, to know	**connu**, known
lire, to read	**lu**, read
dire, to say	**dit**, said
écrire, to write	**écrit**, written
faire, to make	**fait**, made
recevoir, to receive	**reçu**, received

Exercise No. 154 Translate each dialogue. Read each dialogue aloud three times.

1 — M. Picard a-t-il posé des questions difficiles à M. Davis?
— Oui. Il lui a posé des questions difficiles.

— Est-ce que M. Davis a bien[1] répondu?
— Oui, il a bien répondu à toutes les questions.
2 — Quand est-ce que M. Davis a écrit la lettre à son représentant?
— Il y a aujourd'hui quinze jours qu'il a écrit la lettre.
— À qui a-t-il lu une copie de cette lettre?
— Il a lu la copie à M. Picard.
3 — Est-ce que M. Picard a trouvé beaucoup de fautes dans la lettre?
— Non. Il n'a pas trouvé une seule faute.
— Quel livre a rendu grand service à M. Davis?
— Le livre, *La Correspondance Commerciale*, lui a rendu grand service.
4 — M. Davis a-t-il apprécié les services de M. Parmentier?
— Oui. Il a toujours[1] apprécié ses services dévoués.
— Qu'est-ce que M. Picard a dit quand M. Davis a fini de lire la lettre?
— Il a dit: C'est une gentille lettre.

NOTE 1. Adverbs (bien, déjà, encore, toujours, souvent, etc.) generally
precede the past participle. The adverbs hier, aujourd'hui, demain,
ici, là, tôt, tard follow the past participle.

Il a déjà écrit la lettre.   He has already written the letter.
Il a écrit la lettre hier.   He wrote the letter yesterday.

Exercise No. 155 Complete the following sentences with the past participle
of the verb indicated. Read each completed sentence aloud.

Exemple 1: J'ai reçu votre lettre du 4 mai.

1 J'ai (recevoir) votre lettre du 4 mai.
2 Nous avons (décider) de visiter le Musée du Louvre.
3 Il a toujours (apprécier) vos services dévoués.
4 Ces services ont (contribuer) à notre réussite.
5 M. Davis a (vendre) beaucoup d'objets d'art.
6 Nous n'avons pas (écrire) beaucoup de lettres.
7 N'avez-vous pas (lire) tous les guides?
8 Ont-ils (rendre) les livres à la bibliothèque?
9 Avez-vous (faire) la connaissance de votre représentant?
10 Je n'ai pas (entendre) ce qu'il a (dire).
11 Elles n'ont pas encore (finir) l'examen.
12 La bonne a déjà (servir) le thé au rhum.

Exercise No. 156—Questionnaire

1 Qui a écrit une lettre à son représentant?
2 À qui a-t-il lu une copie de cette lettre?
3 M. Picard a-t-il trouvé beaucoup de fautes dans la lettre de M. Davis?
4 Quand est-ce que M. Parmentier sera à Paris?
5 Où est-ce qu'il va rencontrer M. Davis?
6 Dans quelle langue va-t-il causer avec lui?
7 Qui est-ce que M. Parmentier veut féliciter?
8 Comment est-ce que M. Davis a connu M. Parmentier jusqu'à présent?
9 De quoi M. Davis est-il certain?
10 Quand est-ce que les deux messieurs auront leur dernier rendez-vous?
11 Où est-ce qu'ils se rencontreront?
12 Qu'est-ce que M. Picard donnera à M. Davis?

CHAPITRE 30 (TRENTE)

LES DERNIERS CONSEILS DE M. PICARD

1 Il fait chaud dans le bureau de M. Davis. Il n'y a pas un souffle d'air. Par la fenêtre ouverte on entend les bruits de la rue.

2 — Je suis content de quitter la ville, dit M. Davis à M. Picard.

3 — J'ai envie de vous accompagner, répond M. Picard.

4 — Pourrez-vous venir avec moi?

5 — Malheureusement, ce n'est pas possible.

6 — Quel dommage! Eh bien, voulez-vous bien me donner quelques derniers conseils? Est-ce que la vie en France est différente de la vie en Angleterre?

7 — Oui, M. Davis, les coutumes du pays sont assez différentes. En général on fait les choses avec plus de formalité qu'ici. La question de politesse, il me semble, a une profonde signification; c'est-à-dire que chaque homme est digne d'estime.

8 — C'est vrai, répond M. Davis.

9 — J'ai remarqué que les affaires se traitent en France avec plus de formalité qu'en Angleterre. Les hommes d'affaires aiment bien causer un peu avant d'entamer une affaire. Ils désirent se connaître les uns les autres.

10 — Je serai très content d'être en France.

11 — Il faudra vous habituer à un train de vie moins agité. En général la vie en France est plus tranquille.

12 — Je l'espère. Je suis las d'être toujours bousculé.

13 — Pour parler d'autre chose, avez-vous lu les livres sur la France que je vous ai recommandés?

14 — Oui, je les ai tous lus avec beaucoup d'intérêt. J'ai parcouru aussi les deux guides que vous m'avez prêtés. Le Guide Michelin et le Guide Bleu. Il me semble que ces deux guides me rendront grand service.

15 — Sans aucun[1] doute. Quant à moi, je passerai l'été à Londres. Nos conversations m'ont donné beaucoup de plaisir. Vous allez me manquer.

16 — Je penserai à vous très souvent et de temps en temps je vous écrirai.

17 — Je serai content de recevoir vos lettres. Alors, voilà, il faut nous dire au revoir. Vous serez bien gentil de faire mes amitiés à Mme Davis et d'embrasser les enfants de ma part.

18 — Merci, et bonne chance!

19 — Bon voyage, M. Davis.

20 — Ils se serrent la main.

1 It is hot in Mr. Davis' office. There is not a breath of air. Through the open window one hears the noises of the street.

2 I am happy to leave the city, says Mr. Davis to Mr. Picard.

3 I have a mind to go with you, answers Mr. Picard.

4 Will you be able to go with me?

5 Unfortunately, it isn't possible.

6 What a pity! Well then, will you kindly give me some final advice? Is life in France different from life in Britain?

7 Yes, Mr. Davis, the customs of the country are quite different. In general, things are done with more formality than they are here. The question of courtesy, it seems to me, has a profound meaning; that is, every man is worthy of respect.

8 That's true, answers Mr. Davis.

9 I have noticed that in France business is done with more formality than it is in England. Businessmen like to chat a little with each other before taking up a business matter. They want to get to know one another.

10 I'll be very happy to be in France.

11 You'll have to (*Lit*. It will be necessary to) get used to a less turbulent way of life. In general, life in France is quieter.

12 I hope so. (*Lit*. I hope it.) I am tired of always being so rushed.

13 To speak of something else; did you read the books on France which I recommended to you?

14 Yes. I read them all with much interest. I have also glanced through the two guides which you lent me: the Michelin Guide and the Blue Guide. It seems to me that these two guides will be very useful.

15 Without any doubt. As for me, I'll spend the summer in London. I have enjoyed our conversations very much. I shall miss you.

16 I'll think of you often and from time to time I'll write to you.

17 I'll be happy to receive your letters. Well, then we must say goodbye. Kindly give my regards to Mrs. Davis and kiss the children for me.

18 Thank you, and good luck!

19 Happy journey, Mr. Davis.

20 They shake hands.

NOTE 1. **aucun** (**aucune** *f*) not any, none, no one. Except after **sans**, it is used with **ne**.

Je n'ai aucun doute. I haven't any doubt.
Aucun de ces élèves n'est français. None of these pupils is French.

Pronunciation and Spelling Aids

Practise Aloud:

—— je suis content de quitter la ville, dit M. Davis à M. Picard (ʒə sɥi kɔ̃-tɑ̃d ki-te la vil di mə-sø Davis a mə-sø pi-kaːr)

— j'ai envie de vous accompagner, répond M. Picard (ʒə ɑ̃-vid vu za-kɔ̃-pa-ɲe re-pɔ̃ mə-sø pi-kaːr)

— ne pouvez-vous pas venir avec moi? (nə pu-ve vu pa vniːr a-vɛk mwa)

— malheureusement, ce n'est pas possible (ma-lœ-røz-mɑ̃ snɛ pa po-sibl)

Building Vocabulary

Words whose appearance deceives

demander = to ask, ask for *not* to demand	**exiger** = to demand
rester = to stay, remain *not* to rest	**se reposer** = to rest
le crayon = the pencil *not* the crayon	**le pastel** = the crayon
la fabrique = the factory *not* the fabric	**le tissu** = the fabric

la lecture = reading *not* lecture
la librairie = the bookshop *not* the library
le magasin = the store *not* the magazine
actuellement = now, at present *not* actually
large = wide *not* large
les nouvelles = the news *not* novels
la conférence = the lecture
la bibliothèque = the library
la revue = the magazine
réellement = actually
grand = large
le roman = the novel
point de nouvelles, bonnes nouvelles, no news is good news.

Locutions françaises

1 **les affaires se traitent,** business is done
2 **entamer une affaire,** to take up a business matter
3 **sans aucun doute,** without any doubt
4 **manquer,** to miss, to be lacking, to fail, to be in need of
5 **vous allez me manquer,** I shall miss you (you will be missing to me)
6 **l'argent lui manque,** he lacks money (money is lacking to him)
7 **je n'y manquerai pas,** I shall not fail to do so
8 **faire ses amités,** to give one's regards
9 **faites-lui mes amitiés,** give him my regards
10 **mes amitiés à tout le monde,** love to all

Exercise No. 157—Completion of Text

1 (Through the open window) **on entend les bruits de la rue.**
2 (I have a mind) **de vous accompagner.**
3 (Will you give me) **quelques derniers conseils?**
4 **On fait les choses** (with more formality) **qu'ici.**
5 (Each man is worthy) **d'estime.**
6 **Ils désirent** (want to get to know one another).
7 **En général la vie en France** (is quieter).
8 (Have you read) **les livres sur la France?**
9 (I have also glanced through) **les deux guides.**
10 (I shall spend) **l'été à Londres.**
11 I shall miss you.
12 (I shall be happy) **de recevoir vos lettres.**

Grammar Notes

1 More Irregular Past Participles

courir, to run; **couru,** run
mettre, to put; **mis,** put
prendre, to take; **pris,** taken
voir, to see; **vu,** seen
parcourir, to scan; **parcouru,** scanned
promettre, to promise; **promis,** promised
apprendre, to learn; **appris,** learned
comprendre, to understand; **compris,** understood

Exercise No. 158 Complete each of the following sentences with the correct past participle. Read each completed sentence aloud.

1 **J'ai déjà** (glanced through) **tous les guides.**
2 **Avez-vous** (understood) **tout ce que le maître a** (said)?
3 **A-t-il** (put on) **son pardessus?**
4 **Elle a** (promised) **de nous rencontrer à l'aéroport.**
5 **J'ai tout** (heard) **mais je n'ai pas tout** (understood).

6 **Avez-vous (seen) Mme Picard?**
7 **Les enfants ont (run) pour aller à l'école.**
8 **Les élèves ont (learned) beaucoup de locutions françaises.**
9 **Ils n'ont pas (taken) leurs paquets.**
10 **Nous n'avons pas (taken) la bouteille.**

2 Agreement of the Past Participle

When a direct object precedes the verb the past participle must agree with that direct object in number and gender.

Direct Object After verb. (*No agreement*)	Direct Object Before Verb (*Agreement*)
Avez-vous trouvé *le livre*?	**Je** *l'***ai trouvé.** (*masc. sing.*)
Avez-vous trouvé *la lettre*?	**Je** *l'***ai trouvée.** (*fem. sing.*)
Avez-vous trouvé *les livres*?	**Je** *les* **ai trouvés.** (*masc. plur.*)
Avez-vous trouvé *les lettres*?	**Je** *les* **ai trouvées.** (*fem. plur.*)

The past participle does not agree with an *indirect* object preceding the verb.

Nous ne *leur* **avons pas donné de cadeaux.** We did not give *them* any gifts.

Exercise No. 159 Translate each question and answer. Read each question and answer aloud in French three times. Note the agreement of the past participle.

1 — Avez-vous recommandé ces guides (*m*)?
2 — Est-ce qu'il a écrit la réponse?
3 — Où a-t-il trouvé l'argent (*m*)?
4 — Avez-vous compris la question?
5 — A-t-elle appris le proverbe?
6 — Qui a réservé les deux places (*f*)?
7 — Quand avez-vous vu votre amie?
8 — Quand ont-ils fini l'examen (*m*)?
9 — Quand est-ce que le facteur (postman) a apporté les lettres?
10 — Avez-vous entendu la sonnette (bell)?
11 — M. Davis a-t-il parcouru tous les guides?
12 — Quelle lettre a-t-il lue[1] à M. Picard?

1 — Oui, monsieur, je les ai *recommandés.*
2 — Oui monsieur, il l'a *écrite.*
3 — Il l'a *trouvé* sur le bureau.
4 — Non monsieur, je ne l'ai pas *comprise.*
5 — Non madame, elle ne l'a pas *appris.*
6 — Mon père les a *réservées* hier.
7 — Je l'ai *vue* hier soir,
8 — Ils l'ont *fini* à deux heures.
9 — Il les a *apportées* ce matin.
10 — Non, monsieur, je ne l'ai pas *entendue.*
11 — Il les a tous *parcourus.*
12 — Il a *lu* la lettre qu'il a *reçue*[2] de M. Parmentier.

NOTE 1. The direct object preceding the verb, with which **lue** agrees is **quelle lettre**.

2. The direct object preceding the verb, with which **reçue** agrees is the relative pronoun **qu'**, which is feminine. **qu'** refers to **lettre** (*f*).

Exercise No. 160—Questionnaire

1 Où se trouvent M. Davis et M. Picard?
2 Quel temps fait-il?
3 Qu'est-ce qu'on entend par la fenêtre?
4 Qui est content de quitter la ville?
5 Qui a envie d'accompagner M. Davis?
6 Qu'est-ce que M. Picard répond à la question: 'Ne pourrez-vous pas venir avec moi'?
7 Comment fait-on les choses en France?
8 Quelle est la profonde signification de la politesse?
9 Qu'est-ce que M. Picard a remarqué en France?
10 Qui est las d'être bousculé?
11 Oui a lu des livres sur la France?
12 Qui les a recommandés?
13 Quant à M. Picard, où passera-t-il l'été?
14 À qui M. Davis pensera-t-il souvent?
15 Est-ce qu'il écrira des lettres à M. Picard de temps en temps?

CHAPITRE 31 (TRENTE ET UN)

M. DAVIS PART POUR LA FRANCE

1 Il y a cinq mois que M. Davis étudie le français. Il a passé beaucoup de temps à converser avec son professeur, M. Picard. Il a appris les règles essentielles de la grammaire et il a lu beaucoup de livres sur la France. Il a vraiment travaillé dur. Maintenant il parle bien le français et il compte se tirer d'affaire en France sans difficulté.

2 M. Davis a obtenu son passeport et son billet pour le trajet. Il a tout ce qu'il lui faut.

3 Naturellement M. Davis a écrit une lettre à son représentant en France pour lui faire savoir l'heure de son arrivée. M. Parmentier, le représentant, a promis de le rencontrer à l'aéroport.

4 C'est enfin le 31 mai, ce jour entre tous. L'avion de M. Davis quitte l'aéroport à dix-huit heures précises. M. Davis doit être à l'aéroport une heure d'avance pour faire contrôler son billet et son passeport et pour faire peser ses bagages.

5 La famille ne l'accompagne pas en France parce que les enfants doivent finir l'année scolaire, et sa femme doit rester à la maison pour s'occuper des enfants. D'ailleurs, voyager avec quatre enfants entre cinq et dix ans est non seulement difficile, mais aussi assez coûteux.

6 Naturellement la famille est dans tous ses états. Les enfants ont très peu dormi et à sept heures du matin ils sont tous levés, lavés, et habillés.

7 À quatre heures de l'après-midi la famille est prête à partir pour l'aéroport. M. Davis a fait ses deux valises et il les a déjà mises dans le coffre de l'auto. Ils montent tous en voiture. M. Davis se met en route et ils arrivent à l'aéroport vers cinq heures.

8 M. Davis fait contrôler son billet et son passeport, et il fait peser ses bagages. Il doit payer trois livres de supplément parce que le poids total dépasse les vingt kilos auxquels il a droit.

9 Alors M. Davis fait ses adieux à sa femme et aux enfants qui lui souhaitent 'bon voyage'. Il monte dans l'avion, saluant de la main son petit monde qui le regarde d'un air ému. À dix-huit heures précises l'avion prend son vol.

10 M. Davis est en route.

1 Mr. Davis has been studying French for five months. He has spent a lot of time conversing with his teacher, Mr. Picard. He has learned the essential rules of grammar and he has read many books on France. He really has worked very hard. Now he speaks French quite well and he expects to get along in France without difficulty.

2 Mr. Davis has obtained his passport and his ticket for the flight. He has everything he needs.

3 Of course Mr. Davis has written a letter to his agent in France letting him know the time of his arrival. Mr. Parmentier, the agent, has promised to meet him at the airport.

4 It is 31 May at last, the day of days. Mr. Davis' plane leaves the airport at 18.00 sharp. He must be at the airport one hour before to have his ticket checked and his baggage weighed.

5 The family is not going with him to France, because the children have to finish the school year and his wife has to remain at home to take care of the children. Besides, to travel with four children from five to ten years of age is not only difficult but also quite expensive.

6 Of course the family is extremely excited. The children have not slept very much, and at seven in the morning they are all awake, washed and dressed.

7 At four in the afternoon the whole family is ready to leave for the airport. Mr. Davis has packed two suitcases and he has already put them in the boot of the car. They all get into the car. Mr. Davis starts off and they arrive at the airport at about five.

8 Mr. Davis has his ticket and his passport checked and he has his baggage weighed. He has to pay £3 extra, because the total weight exceeds the 20 kilos to which he is entitled.

9 Then Mr. Davis takes leave of his wife and children who wish him 'a happy journey'. He goes up into the plane waving his hand to his family[1] who are watching him with emotion. At 18.00 sharp the plane takes off.

10 Mr. Davis is on his way.

NOTE 1. *Lit.* little world.

Building Vocabulary

Antonyms

1 **il a ouvert**, he opened; **il a fermé**, he closed
2 **j'ai commencé**, I began; **j'ai fini**, I finished
3 **nous avons trouvé**, we found; **nous avons perdu**, we lost
4 **vous avez envoyé**, you sent; **vous avez apporté**, you brought
5 **ils ont acheté**, they bought; **ils ont vendu**, they sold
6 **elles ont donné**, they gave; **elles ont reçu**, they received

Locutions françaises

1 **se tirer d'affaire**, to get along
2 **pour lui faire savoir**, to let him know
3 **ce jour entre tous**, this day of days
4 **pour faire contrôler son billet**, to have his ticket checked
5 **pour faire peser ses bagages**, to have his baggage weighed
6 **s'occuper (de)**, to busy oneself with, to take care of, to look after
7 **être dans tous ses états**, to be extremely excited
8 **faire les valises**, to pack the suitcases
9 **monter en voiture**, to get in the car
10 **se mettre en route**, to set out
11 **faires ses adieux (à)**, to take leave of
12 **il est en route**, he is on his way

Exercise No. 161—Completion of Text

1 (It is five months) que M. Davis étudie le français.
2 (He has learned) les règles essentielles.

3 (He has really worked) **dur.**
4 (He has obtained) **son billet pour le trajet.**
5 (He has written) **une lettre à son représentant.**
6 **M. Parmentier** (has promised) **de le rencontrer.**
7 (He must be) **à l'aéroport à dix-sept heures.**
8 **La famille** (is not going with him).
9 **Les enfants** (must finish) **l'année scolaire.**
10 **M. Davis** (has packed) **les deux valises.**
11 (They all get) **en voiture.**
12 **M. Davis** (has his luggage weighed).
13 (He must pay) **trois livres de supplément.**
14 **M. Davis** (takes leave of) **sa femme et ses enfants.**
15 **Il est** (on his way).

Grammar Notes

1 More Irregular Past Participles

ouvrir, to open	**j'ai *ouvert*,** I have *opened* (I opened, did open)
couvrir, to cover	**il a *couvert*,** he has *covered* (he covered, did cover)
offrir, to offer	**elle a *offert*,** she has *offered* (she offered, did offer)
savoir, to know	**nous avons *su*,** we have *learned* (learned, did learn)[1]
vouloir, to want	**vous avez *voulu*,** you have *wanted* (you wanted, did want)
avoir, to have	**ils ont *eu*,** they have *had* (they had, they did have)
être, to be	**elles ont *été*,** they have *been* (they were)

NOTE 1. The conversational past of **savoir**—**j'ai su,** etc.—means I have learned (been informed), etc., *not* I have known, etc.

Exercise No. 162 Translate. Use the conversational past for these verbs.

Example: I have had (I had, I did have) = j'ai eu

1 he has wanted	7 I have not covered
2 you opened	8 have they learned?
3 I have learned	9 we did not open
4 did he open?	10 she was
5 we have had	11 did he want?
6 they have been	12 I offered

2 Past Participles Used as Adjectives

Past participles are often used as adjectives. Like all adjectives, they then agree with the noun they modify in number and gender.

le vase cassé, the broken vase	**le livre ouvert,** the open book
les vases cassés, the broken vases	**les livres ouverts,** the open books
la tasse cassée, the broken cup	**la porte ouverte,** the open door
les tasses cassées, the broken cups	**les portes ouvertes,** the open doors

Exercise No. 163 Complete each sentence with the correct form of the past participle in parenthesis.

Exemple: Il est assis près de la fenêtre ouverte.

1 **Il est assis près de la fenêtre** (ouvert)
2 **Au mur il y a des affiches** (*f*) (illustré)

3 Toutes les portes sont (fermé)
4 Le couturier Cardin est bien (connu)
5 Beaucoup de ces tasses (*f*) sont (cassé)
6 Tous les enfants sont (levé)
7 Jean n'est pas encore (habillé)
8 Voici des revues (*f*) (envoyé) par M. Picard.
9 Où est la chambre (réservé) pour M. Adams?
10 Nous avons trouvé les billets (perdu).

Exercise No. 164—Questionnaire

1 Combien de temps y a-t-il que M. Davis étudie le français?
2 Avec qui a-t-il passé beaucoup de temps à converser?
3 Qu'est-ce qu'il a appris?
4 Comment a-t-il travaillé?
5 Comment parle-t-il français maintenant?
6 Qu'est-ce que M. Davis a obtenu?
7 A qui M. Davis a-t-il écrit?
8 Qu'est-ce que son représentant lui a promis?
9 À quelle heure les enfants se sont-ils levés?
10 À quelle heure est-ce que l'avion quitte l'aéroport?
11 Qu'est-ce que chaque voyageur doit faire contrôler?
12 Est-ce que sa famille accompagne M. Davis en France?
13 Pourquoi est-ce que les enfants doivent rester à Londres?
14 Pourquoi est-ce que Mme Davis doit rester à Londres?

RÉVISION 7

CHAPITRES 28–31 PREMIÈRE PARTIE

Révision de mots

NOUNS

1 un aéroport	7 la familiarité	14 la règle
2 le bruit	8 la faute	15 le séjour
3 une arrivée	9 la formalité	16 la signification
4 la copie	10 un intérêt	17 la sortie
5 la difficulté	11 la main	18 le trajet
6 un espoir	12 le passeport	19 un homme d'affaires
	13 la politesse	20 le coffre

1 airport	7 familiarity	14 rule
2 noise	8 mistake, fault	15 stay, sojourn
3 arrival	9 formality	16 meaning
4 copy	10 interest	17 exit, departure
5 difficulty	11 hand	18 journey
6 hope	12 passport	19 businessman
	13 politeness	20 boot (of car)

VERBS

1 apprécier	7 s'occuper (de)	13 traiter
2 j'apprécie	8 elle s'occupe (de)	14 courir
3 avouer	9 pardonner	15 parcourir
4 contrôler	10 pardonnez-moi	16 permettre
5 dépasser	11 prier	17 souhaiter
6 s'habituer (à)	12 remarquer	18 surprendre

1 to appreciate	7 to be busy with	13 to treat
2 I appreciate	8 she takes care of	14 to run
3 to admit	9 to forgive	15 to glance through
4 to control, check	10 forgive me, excuse me	16 to permit
5 to exceed	11 to pray, to beg	17 to wish
6 to get used to	12 to notice	18 to surprise

ADJECTIVES

1 différent	4 distingué	7 sérieux (euse *f*)
2 dernier (ière *f*)	5 nerveux (euse *f*)	8 seul
3 digne	6 propre	9 las (lasse *f*)

1 different	4 distinguished	7 serious
2 last	5 highly-strung	8 alone
3 worthy	6 own	9 weary

ADVERBS

1 d'avance	2 malheureusement	3 heureusement
1 in advance	2 unfortunately	3 fortunately

FRENCH EXPRESSIONS

1 faire ses adieux (à)	4 faire peser les valises
2 faire ses amitiés (à)	5 faire venir
3 faire votre connaissance	6 faire savoir

7 descendre de voiture	13 quant à moi
8 monter en voiture	14 par conséquent
9 se mettre en route	15 deux fois par semaine
10 se tirer d'affaire	16 votre propre langue
11 voulez-vous bien	17 je vous prie
12 à la perfection	18 vers six heures

1 to bid goodbye to	10 to get along
2 to give one's regards to	11 will you kindly
3 to make your acquaintance	12 perfectly
4 to have bags weighed	13 as for me
5 to send for	14 consequently
6 to let know	15 twice a week
7 to get out of the car	16 your own language
8 to get into the car	17 please do
9 to set out	18 at about six o'clock

DEUXIÈME PARTIE

Exercise No. 165 Translate each past participle and give the infinitive of the verb from which it is derived. Thus: **vendu**, sold; **vendre**, to sell

1 obtenu	6 voulu	11 su	16 mangé	21 compris
2 laissé	7 reçu	12 rendu	17 fait	22 ouvert
3 été	8 écrit	13 mis	18 pris	23 eu
4 dit	9 lu	14 obéi	19 écouté	24 permis
5 fini	10 appris	15 vu	20 couvert	25 pu

Exercise No. 166 Select the group of words in Column II which best completes each sentence begun in Column I.

I

1 M. Davis a appris rapidement
2 Il parle bien le français, par conséquent
3 Il a un représentant à Paris
4 M. Picard n'a pas trouvé une seule faute
5 Il y a cinq mois qu'ils se rencontrent
6 Mme Davis s'occupera des enfants
7 Les Français croient que chaque homme
8 Avant le départ de M. Davis
9 Les deux guides que vous m'avez prêtés
10 Voulez-vous bien me faire savoir

II

(a) qui l'attendra à l'aéroport.
(b) me rendront grand service.
(c) deux fois par semaine chez M. Davis.
(d) est digne d'estime.
(e) il pourra se tirer d'affaire en France.
(f) l'heure de votre arrivée?
(g) parce qu'il a travaillé dur.
(h) dans la lettre que M. Davis a écrite.
(i) pendant l'absence de son mari.
(j) son professeur lui a donné de bons conseils.

Exercise No. 167 Complete each sentence in Column I by choosing the correct expression from Column II. Be sure to use the correct verb form.

I	II
1 (Have you packed) **les valises?**	(a) **monter en voiture**
2 (Give my regards) **à Mme Davis.**	(b) **descendre de la voiture**
3 **Embrassez les enfants** (for me).	(c) **faire ses adieux**
4 **Je parlerai avec vous** (in your own language).	(d) **me tirer d'affaire**
5 (Pardon me) **si je suis fier de mes compatriotes.**	(e) **faire les valises**
	(f) **pardonnez-moi**
6 **Je pourrai** (to get along) **en France.**	(g) **dans votre propre langue**
7 **J'aurai le plaisir** (of meeting you).	(h) **de faire votre**
8 (They get into the car) **et se mettent en route.**	**connaissance**
9 (They get out of the car) **à l'aéroport.**	(i) **faire mes amitiés**
10 **Là, M. Davis** (said goodbye) **à sa famille.**	(j) **de ma part**

Exercise No. 168 Read each question. Translate the English answers into French. In seven of the answers there is a direct object pronoun before the verb. Be sure that the past participle agrees with the direct object pronoun in number and gender.

Exemple 1. Oui, monsieur, je l'ai reçue.

1 **Avez-vous reçu ma lettre?**	1 Yes, sir, I have received it (*f*).
2 **À qui est-ce que M. Davis a écrit la lettre?**	2 He wrote it (*f*) to Mr. Parmentier.
3 **M. Davis a-t-il apprécié ses services?**	3 Yes, sir, he has appreciated them (*m*).
4 **Qui a fait la valise?**	4 Mr. Davis has packed it (*f*).
5 **Est-ce que les guides vous ont aidé?**	5 Yes, sir, they have helped me.
6 **Est-ce que la bonne a servi une tasse de thé au rhum?**	6 She served it.
7 **Avez-vous compris la question?**	7 No, sir, I did not understand it (*f*).
8 **Qui n'a pas appris les leçons?**	8 Philippe has not learnt them (*f*).
9 **Avez-vous vu le nouveau film?**	9 No, madame, we have not seen it (*m*).
10 **Qu'est-ce que le facteur a apporté?**	10 He has brought a parcel (**un colis postal**).

Dialogue—À l'aéroport

1 — **Bonjour, M. Parmentier. Est-ce que vous attendez quelqu'un?**

2 — **Oui, monsieur. J'attends M. Davis qui arrive de Londres. C'est le directeur de la maison que je représente à Paris.**

3 — **Est-ce que vous le connaissez?**

4 — **Je le connais seulement par correspondance. Mais j'ai sa photo et je crois que je le reconnaîtrai. C'est un homme d'environ quarante ans.**

5 — **À quelle heure doit-il arriver?**

6 — **L'avion est annoncé pour dix-neuf heures cinquante-cinq.**

7 — **Est-il en retard?**

8 — **Non, il est à l'heure. Ah! Le voilà. Il arrive. Il s'approche. Il atterrit. Excusez-moi, monsieur, je vais à la rencontre de M. Davis.**

1 Good day, Mr. Parmentier. Are you expecting someone?

2 Yes, I am waiting for Mr. Davis who is arriving from London. He is the head of the firm I represent in Paris.

3 Do you know him?

4 I know him only by correspondence. But I have his photo and I think I'll recognize him. He is a man of about forty.

5 At what time is he due?

6 The plane is due to arrive at 19.55.

7 Is it late?

8 No it's on time. Ah! There it is. It's coming. It's approaching. It is landing. Excuse me, I am going to greet Mr. Davis.

Dialogue 2—Bienvenu en France

1 — Soyez le bienvenu en France, M. Davis. Comment le trajet s'est-il passé?

2 — Merveilleusement bien! Je suis heureux d'être en France. J'ai tellement songé à ce moment.

3 — Et vous voilà! Je suis sûr que vous serez très heureux ici.

1 Welcome to France, Mr. Davis. How did the trip go?

2 Marvellously well. I am happy to be in France. I have thought about this moment so much.

3 And here you are! I am sure that you will be very happy here.

Exercise No. 169—Lecture

Un programme exceptionnel au cinéma

Ce soir M. et Mme Davis vont au cinéma. Ils n'aiment pas la plupart des films de Hollywood, surtout les 'Westerns' dans lesquels les 'cowboys' tirent des coups de feu[1] sur tout le monde et galopent sans cesse. Les films policiers ne les intéressent pas non plus.

Mais ce soir, il y a un programme exceptionnel dans un cinéma qui est tout près de chez eux.[2] Le film s'appelle *Un Voyage en France*. C'est un documentaire[3] sur le pays que notre ami Davis va visiter dans quelques mois. Il y a des scènes qui représentent l'histoire de la France, d'autres qui montrent ses paysages, ses rivières, ses montagnes, ses grandes villes, etc. C'est-à-dire que c'est un film très intéressant pour les touristes.

Les Davis arrivent au cinéma à vingt heures trente. Presque toutes les places sont prises, donc ils doivent s'asseoir[4] au troisième rang. Ceci ne plaît pas à M. Davis parce que les mouvements sur l'écran lui font mal aux yeux. Heureusement ils peuvent changer de place après un quart d'heure et ils se mettent[5] au treizième rang.

Les Davis aiment beaucoup ce film. Ils le trouvent absorbant.

En sortant du cinéma M. Davis dit à sa femme: — Sais-tu, Alice, je crois que je me tirerai bien d'affaire[6] en France. J'ai compris presque tout ce que les acteurs et les actrices ont dit.

NOTE 1. fire shots.

2. very near their home.

3. documentary film.

4. they have to sit.

5. take seats.

6. **se tirer d'affaire,** to get along. **Je me tirerai d'affaire,** I shall get along.

CHAPITRE 32 (TRENT-DEUX)

L'ARRIVÉE À PARIS

Mr. Davis is now in France and writes nine letters to Mr. Picard about some of the places he visits and about some of his experiences and impressions.

There are many references in his letters to things he has discussed with his teacher, so that much of the vocabulary of Chapter 3 to 31 is repeated here.

It is therefore very desirable that you re-read all the texts and dialogues of the previous chapters *before* proceeding with Chapter 32. You will be able to do this easily and rapidly, with little or no reference to the English translation. Thus, you will revise the vocabulary and important expressions in a pleasant manner.

You should continue your pronunciation practice by reading aloud as often as possible dialogues and parts of conversational texts from previous chapters.

Usage rend maître.   Practice makes perfect.

L'arrivée à Paris

La première lettre de Paris

Paris, le 4 juin, 1982.

Cher ami,

1 Quand l'avion est[1] arrivé à Orly, j'ai passé par la douane et je suis[1] allé à la salle d'attente.

2 Tout de suite un bel homme s'est[2] approché de moi et m'a demandé: — Pardon monsieur, êtes-vous M. Davis?

3 J'ai répondu: — Mais oui. Et vous, vous êtes M. Parmentier, n'est-ce pas? Je suis très content de faire votre connaissance.

Nous nous sommes[2] serré la main.

4 — Le plaisir est pour moi, a répondu M. Parmentier.

5 Vous vous rappelez, M. Picard, que M. Parmentier est le représentant de notre maison à Paris.

6 Nous sommes[1] sortis ensemble et nous avons pris un taxi pour l'Hôtel du Quai Voltaire.

7 Le taxi a pris le chemin de la ville à toute vitesse. Je me suis dit: — M. Picard se trompe au sujet de la vie tranquille en France.

8 En regardant autour de nous j'ai vu que tout: autos, camions, autobus, taxis, tout courait à une vitesse vertigineuse.

9 À la fin j'ai crié au chauffeur: — Pas si vite, s'il vous plaît! Je ne suis pas pressé!

10 — Ni moi non plus, monsieur, m'a-t-il répondu, en tournant le coin à toute vitesse.

11 Enfin nous sommes[1] arrivés à l'hôtel sains et saufs. Le taxi s'est[2] arrêté et nous sommes[1] descendus. M. Parmentier est[1] entré avec moi.

12 Je suis[1] allé au bureau de réception, et j'ai dit à l'employé: — Bonsoir, monsieur. Avez-vous une chambre réservée pour M. Davis?

13 — Soyez le bienvenu à Paris, M. Davis. Mais oui, nous vous avons réservé une belle chambre qui donne sur le quai, au troisième étage. C'est le numéro 35.

14 — Très bien, merci. Et quel est le prix s'il vous plaît?

15 — Deux cent trente francs par jour, service et taxe compris (S.T.C.).

16 — Bon. Voulez-vous faire monter mes bagages?

17 — Tout de suite, monsieur. Garçon! Mais vous parlez très bien le français, monsieur. Y a-t-il longtemps que vous êtes en France?

18 — Je viens d'arriver, ai-je dit, assez fier de moi-même.

19 — Est-ce que vous faites un voyage d'agrément?

20 — C'est à la fois un voyage d'agrément et un voyage d'affaires.

21 J'ai causé encore un peu avec M. Parmentier et ensuite nous nous sommes dit au revoir. M. Parmentier m'a promis en partant de me téléphoner pour prendre rendez-vous.

22 Je suis[1] monté par l'ascenseur à ma chambre, numéro 35. Elle est très commode. Je ne manque de rien. Je vous répète encore une fois, M. Picard, que je serai très heureux en France.

Cordialement, votre ami,
Jean Davis.

Paris, 4 June, 1980.

Dear Friend,

1 When the plane arrived at Orly I got through the customs and went to the waiting-room.

2 Immediately a fine-looking man approached me and asked: Excuse me, sir, are you Mr. Davis?

3 Yes, I answered. And you are Mr. Parmentier, aren't you? I am delighted to meet you.

We shook hands.

4 The pleasure is mine, answered Mr. Parmentier.

5 You remember, Mr. Picard, that Mr. Parmentier is the agent of our firm in Paris.

6 We went out together and took a taxi to the Hotel du Quai Voltaire.

7 The taxi took the road to the city going at full speed. I thought to myself: Mr. Picard is mistaken about the quiet life of France.

8 Looking around us, I saw that everything—cars, lorries, buses, taxis, everything—was rushing at a dizzy speed.

9 At last I shouted to the driver: Not so fast, please! I am not in a hurry!

10 Neither am I, he answered me, turning the corner at full speed.

11 At last we arrived safe and sound (*Lit.* sound and safe) at the hotel. The taxi stopped and we got out. Mr. Parmentier went in with me.

12 I went to the reception desk and said to the clerk: Good evening. Do you have a room reserved for Davis?

13 Welcome to Paris, Mr. Davis. Certainly, we have reserved for you a fine room on the third floor, which faces the quay. It is number 35.

14 Very good, thank you. And what is the charge, please?

15 Two hundred and thirty francs a day, including service and tax (S.T.C.).

16 Good. Would you please have my bags taken up?

17 Right away, sir. Porter! But you speak French very well. Have you been in France long?

18 I have just arrived, I said, quite proud of myself.
19 Are you on a pleasure trip?
20 This is a pleasure trip and a business trip combined.
21 I chatted a little more with Mr. Parmentier and then we said goodbye. On leaving, Mr. Parmentier promised to telephone me to make an appointment.
22 I went up in the lift to my room, number 35. It is very comfortable. I want for nothing. I repeat once more, Mr. Picard, that I shall be very happy in France.

Cordially your friend,
John Davis

NOTE 1. A certain number of French verbs form their conversational past by using the auxiliary **je suis, tu es, il est,** etc., instead of the auxiliary **j'ai, tu as, il a,** etc. These are called **être-**verbs, and are fully explained in the Grammar Notes of this chapter.

2. All reflexive verbs use **je suis, tu es, il est,** etc., to form their conversational past. This use is fully explained in the Grammar Notes of the next chapter.

Building Vocabulary

A. Antonyms

1 **il est allé,** he went; **il est venu,** he came
2 **il est arrivé,** he arrived; **il est parti,** he left
3 **il est entré,** he entered; **il est sorti,** he went out
4 **il est monté,** he went up; **il est descendu,** he went down
5 **il s'est rappelé,** he remembered; **il a oublié,** he forgot
6 **il a demandé,** he asked; **il a répondu,** he answered

B. Related Words

1 **appeler,** to call; **se rappeler,** to recall, remember; **s'appeler,** to be called, to be named
2 **entrer,** to enter; **rentrer,** to re-enter, return home
3 **tourner,** to turn; **retourner,** to return, go back
4 **venir,** to come; **revenir,** to come back; **devenir,** to become
5 **voir,** to see; **revoir,** to see again

Locutions françaises

Présentations (pre-zã-ta-sjɔ̃) Introductions

1 **permettez-moi de vous présenter M. Parmentier, un de mes amis**
2 **enchanté de faire votre connaissance**
3 **le plaisir est pour moi**
4 **veuillez (vø-je) me présenter à monsieur (madame) . . . ?**

1 allow me to introduce you to Mr. Parmentier, a friend of mine
2 (I am) glad to make your acquaintance; to know you
3 the pleasure is mine
4 would you kindly introduce me to Mr. (Mrs.) . . . ?

Salutations: Letters to Friends

1 **mon cher Louise,** dear Louise
2 **ma chère Colette,** dear Colette
3 **cher ami,** dear friend (*m*)
4 **chère amie,** dear friend (*f*)

Conclusions: Letters to Friends

1 **cordialement, votre ami,** cordially yours
2 **salutations amicales de votre ami,** kind greetings from your friend
3 **très affectueusement,** very affectionately yours
4 **une poignée de main amicale,** a friendly handshake
5 **embrasse tout le monde pour moi,** kiss everybody for me
6 **rappelle-moi au bon souvenir de ta famille,** remember me to your family

Exercise No. 170—Completion of Text

1 **Je suis allé** (to the waiting-room).
2 (Immediately) **un bel homme s'est approché.**
3 (He asked me): — **Êtes-vous M. Davis?**
4 (I answered): — **Mais oui.**
5 **Je suis content** (to make your acquaintance).
6 (The pleasure is mine), **a-t-il répondu.**
7 (We took) **un taxi.**
8 (I thought to myself): — **M. Parmentier se trompe.**
9 **Tout courait** (at a dizzy speed).
10 Not so fast!
11 **J'ai crié:** — (I am not in a hurry).
12 — (Neither am I), **m'a-t-il répondu.**
13 **Avez-vous une chambre** (reserved for Davis)?
14 (What is the charge), **s'il vous plaît?**
15 (Two hundred and thirty francs per day) **service et T.V.A. compris.**

Grammar Notes

1 Verbs with the Auxiliary **être** instead of **avoir.**

You have learned that the conversational past tense in French consists of some form of the auxiliary **avoir,** have, plus the past participle of the verb.

In French there is a certain number of verbs which take some form of the auxiliary **être,** to be, instead of **avoir,** to have. They are called **être**-verbs. The two most common of these are **aller,** to go, and **venir,** to come. Observe carefully the conversational past tense of **aller,** noting the auxiliary verb and the changes in the past participle.

I have gone, I went, I did go; you have gone, you went, you did go, etc.

je suis	allé allée	(ʒə sɥi za-le)	**nous sommes**	allés allées	(nu sɔm za-le)
tu es	allé allée	(ty ɛ za-le)	**vous êtes**	allé, allés allée, allées	(vu zɛt za-le)
il est	allé	(il ɛ ta-le)	**ils sont**	allés	(il sɔ̃ ta-le)
elle est	allée	(ɛl ɛ ta-le)	**elles sont**	allées	(ɛl sɔ̃ ta-le)

(*a*) The past participle of an **être**-verb agrees with the subject in number and gender.

(*b*) **je, tu** and **nous** may be masculine or feminine. If **je** or **tu** are feminine, add the feminine singular ending **-e** to the past participle. If **nous** is masculine, add **-s** to the past participle. If **nous** is feminine, add **-es** to the past participle.

Vous may be masculine or feminine and singular or plural. The agreeing past participle therefore has four possible forms.

(*masc. sing.*) **allé**, (*fem. sing.*) **allée**, (*masc. plur.*) **allés**, (*fem. plur.*) **allées**

2 List of être-Verbs.

Infinitive

aller	to go
venir	to come
revenir	to come back
devenir	to become
arriver	to arrive
partir	to leave, to depart
repartir	to leave again
retourner	to return
entrer	to come in
rentrer	to re-enter
sortir	to go out
ressortir	to go out again
monter	to go up
remonter	to go up again
descendre	to go down
redescendre	to go down again
naître	to be born
renaître	to be born again
mourir	to die
tomber	to fall
retomber	to fall again, to fall back
rester	to stay, to remain

Conversational Past

je suis allé(e)	I went
tu es venu(e)	you came
il est revenu	he came back
elle est devenue	she became
nous sommes arrivé(e)s	we arrived
vous êtes parti(s)(e)(es)	you departed
ils sont repartis	they left again
elles sont retournées, etc.	they came back

Note that all the être-verbs except **rester**, to remain, **mourir**, to die, and **naître**, to be born, are verbs of motion. They are all intransitive, that is, they cannot take direct objects.

Exercise No. 171 Translate each short dialogue. Note the agreement of the past participle. Read each dialogue aloud three times.

1 — Philippe est-il allé à la gare pour rencontrer son père?
  — Oui. Il est sorti de la maison il y a vingt minutes.
  — Est-ce que sa sœur Rosette est allée avec lui?
  — Oui. Sa sœur, Rosette, et aussi son frère, Henri, sont allés avec lui.

2 — Madame Davis est-elle revenue de la ville?
— Elle n'est pas encore revenue, mais elle reviendra bientôt.
— Pourquoi est-elle allée en ville?
— Elle y est allée pour faire ses achats.
3 — Pourquoi est-ce que M. Davis est rentré tard ce soir?
— Beaucoup de clients sont venus le voir l'après-midi.
— À quelle heure part-il de son bureau d'habitude?
— D'habitude il part à cinq heures précises, mais aujourd'hui il n'est pas parti avant six heures moins le quart.
4 — À quelle heure est-ce que M. Davis est parti pour l'aéroport?
— Il est parti à six heures du matin.
— À quelle heure est-il monté dans l'avion?
— Il est monté dans l'avion à sept heures quarante-cinq.

Exercise No. 172 Supply the correct form of the participle of the verb in parenthesis. Watch your endings. Read each completed sentence aloud three times.

  Exemple 1: Elle est est arrivée chez elle à six heures et demie.

1 Elle est (arriver) chez elle à six heures et demie.
2 Nous (*f*) sommes (aller) à la gare en voiture.
3 Abraham Lincoln est (naître) le 12 février 1809.
4 Il est (mourir) le 15 avril 1865.
5 Les enfants sont (devenir) très agités quand leur père est (monter) dans l'avion.
6 Mme Davis est (revenir) de la ville à trois heures et quart.
7 À quelle heure est-ce que la famille Davis est (partir) pour l'aéroport?
8 Ils sont (entrer) dans la salle d'attente à dix-sept heures précises.
9 Je (*m*) suis (rester) trois semaines à Paris.
10 Quand vous (*m plur.*) êtes (partir) nous (*m*) sommes (arriver).

Exercise No. 173—Questionnaire

1 Qu'est-ce que M. Davis a fait quand l'avion est arrivé?
2 Qui s'est approché de lui dans la salle d'attente?
3 Qu'est-ce que le monsieur a dit?
4 Qu'est-ce que M. Davis a répondu?
5 Comment le taxi est-il allé en ville?
6 Qu'est-ce qu'il a crié à la fin?
7 Qu'est-ce que le chauffeur a répondu?
8 Comment sont-ils arrivés à l'hôtel?
9 Qu'est-ce que M. Davis a dit à l'employé?
10 Qu'est-ce qu'il a répondu?

CHAPITRE 33 (TRENTE-TROIS)

M. DAVIS REND VISITE À LA FAMILLE PARMENTIER
DEUXIÈME LETTRE DE PARIS

Cher ami,

1 Lundi dernier M. Parmentier m'a appelé au téléphone pour m'inviter à prendre le thé chez lui le lendemain. Naturellement, j'ai saisi l'occasion de rendre visite à une famille française.

2 J'ai pris un taxi et à cinq heures de l'après-midi nous nous sommes arrêtés devant une maison charmante dans la rue de Vaugirard. Je suis monté au troisième étage par un escalier gracieux.

3 J'ai sonné et aussitôt j'ai entendu des pas rapides. Une petite bonne à l'air éveillé m'a ouvert la porte et elle m'a invité à entrer.

4 M. Parmentier s'est approché pour me saluer. — Bonjour, M. Davis, a-t-il dit, je suis content de vous voir.

5 Je lui ai dit: — Cette maison a l'air de dater du dix-huitième siècle. Elle est charmante.

6 — Il y a beaucoup de maisons de cette époque à Paris, et plusieurs qui datent d'encore beaucoup plus longtemps, comme vous le savez sans doute.

7 Nous sommes entrés dans un grand salon, meublé avec beaucoup de goût dans le style Louis XV (quinze). M. Parmentier m'a présenté à sa femme et à ses deux fils, des jeunes gens intelligents, travailleurs et très sérieux.

8 Les garçons font leurs études au Lycée Condorcet. L'aîné veut être médecin, le cadet veut être avocat.

9 Après avoir un peu bavardé,[1] ils se sont retirés pour aller faire leurs devoirs.

10 Nous nous sommes mis à table et Mme Parmentier m'a servi une tasse de thé et des petits gâteaux délicieux. Tout en prenant le thé, nous avons parlé de la vie en France, des coutumes du pays, et de l'art.

11 M. Parmentier m'a recommandé comme une des curiosités de Paris, le Marché aux Puces dont nous avons parlé il y a longtemps. Et Mme Parmentier m'a invité à l'accompagner au Marché aux Fleurs, dimanche matin.

12 J'ai répondu que les deux promenades m'intéressaient beaucoup, et j'ai accepté l'aimable invitation de Madame Parmentier.

13 Après avoir passé une heure agréable à parler de choses et d'autres, je suis parti, charmé de mes nouveaux amis.

14 Je suis revenu à l'hôtel à pied, en passant par les vieux quartiers de la rive gauche qui évoquent l'histoire de la France d'une manière si frappante.

Votre ami,
Jean Davis

Dear Friend

1 Last Monday Mr. Parmentier called me on the telephone to invite me to have tea at his house the next day. Naturally I jumped at the chance to visit a French family.

2 I took a taxi and at five o'clock in the afternoon we stopped in front of an attractive house in rue Vaugirard. I went up a graceful staircase to the third floor.

3 I rang and immediately I heard rapid steps. A bright-faced little maid opened the door (for me) and invited me to come in.

4 Mr. Parmentier approached to greet me. Good afternoon, Mr. Davis, he said. I'm glad to see you.

5 I said to him: This house has an eighteenth-century air. It is charming.

6 There are many houses of that period in Paris and several which date from even further back, as you no doubt know.

7 We went into a large living-room furnished with good taste in the style of Louis XV. Mr. Parmentier introduced me to his wife and to his two sons, very intelligent, hard working and serious young men.

8 The boys are being educated at the Condorcet Grammar School. The older one wants to be a doctor. The younger one wants to be a lawyer.

9 After chatting[1] a little they withdrew to go and do their homework.

10 We sat down at the table, and Madame Parmentier served me a cup of tea and some delicious little cakes. While taking tea we talked of life in France, of the customs of the country and of art.

11 Mr. Parmentier recommended (to me) as one of the sights of Paris the Flea Market, about which we talked a long time ago. And Madame Parmentier invited me to accompany her to the Flower Market on Sunday morning.

12 I answered that both outings interested me very much, and I accepted Madame Parmentier's kind invitation.

13 After spending a delightful hour in talking of one thing and another I left, delighted by my new friends.

14 I returned to the hotel on foot, passing through the old districts of the Left Bank which evoke the history of France in such a striking manner.

Your friend,
John Davis

NOTE 1. **après avoir bavardé** (*Lit.* after to have chatted)

Building Vocabulary

Quelques professions.   Some Professions

1 **un docteur,** doctor
2 **un médecin,** medical doctor
3 **un avocat,** lawyer, barrister
4 **un professeur,** professor, teacher in a secondary school (**lycée**), or in a university
5 **un maître d'école, un instituteur,** teacher in elementary school
6 **un ingénieur** (ɛ̃-ze-njœːr), engineer
7 **un acteur,** actor
8 **un écrivain,** writer
9 **une femme médecin, une doctoresse,** woman doctor
10 **une avocate,** woman lawyer
11 **une maîtresse, une institutrice,** elementary school teacher
12 **une actrice,** actress

Locutions françaises

1 **rendre visite (à)** *or* **faire visite (à)**, to visit (a person), to pay a visit to
2 **ils font leurs études,** they are studying (*Lit.* making their studies)
3 **ils font leurs devoirs,** they are doing their homework
4 **il veut être médecin (avocat),** he wants to be a doctor (a lawyer)
5 **beaucoup plus loin,** much longer ago, much farther away
6 **en parlant de choses et d'autres,** speaking of one thing and another
7 **il y a longtemps,** a long time ago

Exercise No. 174—Completion of Text

1 M. Parmentier (called me) **au téléphone.**
2 **Il m'a invité** (to have tea) **chez lui.**
3 (We stopped) **devant une maison charmante.**
4 (I went up) **au troisième étage.**
5 (I rang.) **La bonne** (invited me) **à entrer.**
6 M. Parmentier (approached to greet me).
7 **Il a dit: —** (I'm glad to see you).
8 (There are many houses) **de cette époque à Paris.**
9 (We entered) **dans un grand salon.**
10 M. Parmentier (presented me) **ses deux fils.**
11 **L'aîné** (wants to be) **médecin.**
12 **Ils** (withdrew) **pour aller faire** (their homework).
13 (We sat down) **à table.**
14 (We spoke) **de la vie en France.**
15 (I returned) **à l'hôtel à pied.**
16 **J'ai passé** (through the old districts).

Grammar Notes

1 The Conversational Past of Reflexive Verbs.

Observe carefully the *conversational past* of the reflexive verb **se laver,** to wash oneself. Note the auxiliary verb and the changes in the past participle.

I have washed (I washed, did wash) myself

je me suis lavé (lavée)	**nous nous sommes lavés (lavées)**
tu t'es lavé (lavée)	**vous vous êtes lavé(e), lavés (es)**
il s'est lavé	**ils se sont lavés**
elle s'est lavée	**elles se sont lavées**

s'est-il lavé?
est-ce qu'il s'est lavé? } did he wash himself?
il ne s'est pas lavé, he did not wash himself
est-ce qu'il ne s'est pas lavé? did he not wash himself?

(*a*) The auxiliary verb **être** is used to form the conversational past of reflexive verbs.
(*b*) The past participle agrees with the reflexive pronoun in number and gender when the reflexive pronoun is the direct object of the verb. The reflexive pronoun has the same gender and number as the subject.
(*c*) The reflexive pronoun is sometimes the indirect object of the verb. In that case the past participle does not agree with it.

Ils se sont donné des cadeaux. They gave gifts *to* each other.
Elle s'est lavé la figure. She washed her face. (*Lit.* She washed *to* herself the face.)

2 Present and Conversational Past of **s'asseoir** to seat oneself, to sit down, etc.

I sit down (I seat myself), I am sitting down, etc.

je m'assieds (ma-sjɛ)	**nous nous asseyons** (za-sɛ-jɔ̃)
tu t'assieds (ta-sjɛ)	**vous vous asseyez** (za-sɛ-je)
il, elle s'assied (sa-sjɛ)	**ils, elles s'asseyent** (sa-sɛj)

assieds-toi, sit down; **asseyons-nous,** let us sit down; **asseyez-vous,** sit down.

I have sat down (I sat down, I did sit down), etc.

je me suis assis (assise)	**nous nous sommes assis (assises)**
tu t'es assis (assise)	**vous vous êtes assis(e) (assises)**
il s'est assis	**ils se sont assis**
elle s'est assise	**elles se sont assises**

3 Some Reflexive Verbs You Have Met

Infinitive	*Conversational Past*
1 **se lever,** to get up	1 **je me suis levé(e)**
2 **se coucher,** to go to bed	2 **tu t'es couché(e)**
3 **s'habiller,** to dress	3 **il s'est habillé**
4 **s'amuser,** to enjoy oneself, have a good time	4 **elle s'est amusée**
5 **s'arrêter,** to stop	5 **nous nous sommes arrêtés**
6 **s'approcher,** to approach	6 **vous vous êtes approchés**
7 **se rencontrer,** to meet each other	7 **ils se sont rencontrés**
8 **se connaître,** to know each other	8 **elles se sont connues**
9 **se promener,** to go for a walk	9 **je ne suis pas promené(e)**
10 **se tromper,** to be mistaken	10 **il ne s'est pas trompé**
11 **se retirer,** to withdraw	11 **ne se sont-ils pas retirés?**
12 **s'asseoir,** to sit down	12 **est-ce qu'ils ne se sont pas assis?**

Exercise No. 175 Translate the conversational past tense of the 12 verbs listed above (Paragraph 3).

Exemple 1. je me suis levé(e) = I got up

Exercise No. 176 Translate each question and answer. Read each question and answer aloud three times.

1 **Est-ce que les enfants se sont couchés de bonne heure?**
   Oui. Ils se sont couchés de bonne heure.
2 **Est-ce que Jean s'est levé tard?**
   Non. Il ne s'est pas levé tard.
3 **Est-ce que Marie s'est habillée vite?**
   Oui. Elle s'est habillée vite.
4 **Est-ce que vous vous êtes trompé, Charles?**
   Non. Je ne me suis pas trompé.
5 **Est-ce que vous vous êtes amusée, Anne?**
   Non. Je ne me suis pas amusée.

6 Où est-ce que vous vous êtes rencontrés, messieurs?
   Nous nous sommes rencontrés au bureau.
7 Est-ce que les garçons se sont retirés?
   Oui. Ils se sont retirés.
8 Où est-ce que l'autobus s'est arrêté?
   Il s'est arrêté au coin là-bas.
9 Est-ce que Mme Davis s'est occupée des enfants?
   Oui. Elle s'est occupée des enfants.
10 Est-ce que le touriste s'est senti chez lui à Paris?
   Comme tous les touristes il s'est senti chez lui.

Exercise No. 177—Questionnaire

1 Qui a appelé M. Davis au téléphone?
2 À quelle heure est-ce que le taxi s'est arrêté chez M. Parmentier?
3 Qui a ouvert la porte?
4 Qui s'est approché pour saluer M. Davis?
5 Quel air cette maison a-t-elle?
6 Où les messieurs sont-ils entrés?
7 Qui sont les jeunes gens sérieux, travailleurs et intelligents?
8 Où font-ils leurs études?
9 Qu'est-ce que l'aîné veut faire?
10 Pourquoi se sont-ils retirés?
11 De quoi est-ce qu'on a parlé en prenant le thé?
12 Qu'est-ce que M. Parmentier a recommandé comme une des curiosités de Paris?
13 Où est-ce que Mme Parmentier l'a invité à l'accompagner?
14 Comment est-ce que M. Davis a passé une heure agréable?
15 ·Est-il revenu à son hôtel à pied ou en voiture?

CHAPITRE 34 (TRENTE-QUATRE)

UNE BELLE PROMENADE
TROISIÈME LETTRE

Cher ami,

1 Je vous écris attablé au café que vous m'avez fort recommandé, le Royale-Concorde. Il me reste peut-être des pieds,[1] mais certainement pas de jambes.

2 Ce matin M. Parmentier est venu me chercher à l'hôtel et nous avons commencé notre promenade en suivant le quai Malaquais, qui mène au pont des Arts.

3 Nous sommes restés très longtemps sur le pont, à regarder les pêcheurs qui restent des heures sans rien attraper, à regarder aussi les bateaux-mouches, et les enfants qui s'amusent à jeter des pierres dans l'eau.

4 Nous avons continué notre promenade sur le quai des Tuileries jusqu'à la place de la Concorde. Je pense que cela doit être la plus belle place du monde. Les jets d'eau, l'Obélisque, les jardins d'un côté, l'avenue des Champs-Élysées[2] de l'autre, tout est disposé en parfaite harmonie.

5 Nous avons pris l'avenue des Champs-Élysées. Quelle belle avenue avec ses grands arbres, son étendue royale!

6 Nous nous sommes attablés dans un de ces grands cafés pour prendre un café, mais surtout pour nous reposer. Ce qui m'a frappé tout de suite en France, c'est l'importance du café dans la vie quotidienne.

7 Le café est un club. On y rencontre ses amis, on y joue aux cartes, aux échecs, au billard, on y écrit des lettres comme me voici en train de le faire.

8 Le café est aussi un centre pour le commerce. Pour les hommes d'affaires c'est un autre bureau, c'est même peut-être le bureau le plus important.

9 Le café est un théâtre: les passants sont les acteurs et les actrices, parfois tragiques, plus souvent comiques, mais toujours intéressants.

10 Ensuite nous avons continué notre route sur l'avenue des Champs-Élysées jusqu'à la place de l'Étoile. Nous avons contemplé l'Arc de Triomphe qui se trouve au centre de la place de l'Étoile.[3]

11 Pour revenir au Café Royale-Concorde nous avons pris la belle avenue Marceau. À la place de l'Alma, M. Parmentier m'a quitté. J'ai suivi les quais en admirant la Tour Eiffel tout le long du chemin jusqu'à la place de la Concorde.

12 Ensuite j'ai pris la rue Royale et enfin je suis tombé sur la chaise la plus proche du Café Royale-Concorde, fatigué, épuisé et enchanté.

Votre ami, grand amoureux de Paris,
Jean Davis

Dear Friend,

1 I am writing to you seated at a table in the café which you have strongly recommended to me, the Royale-Concorde. I may have feet left, but certainly no legs.

2 This morning Mr. Parmentier came to call for me at the hotel and we

started our walk following the Quai Malaquais, which leads to the Ponts des Arts.

3 We stayed on the bridge for a long time watching the fishermen who stand for hours without catching anything; also watching the little pleasure boats, and the children amusing themselves by throwing stones in the water.

4 We continued our walk on the quay of the Tuileries up to the Place de la Concorde. I believe that this must be the most beautiful square in the world. The fountains, the Obelisk, the gardens on one side, the Avenue des Champs-Élysées on the other, everything is arranged in perfect harmony.

5 We took the Avenue des Champs-Élysées. What a lovely avenue with its large trees, its regal spaciousness!

6 We sat down at a table in one of those big cafés to have coffee, but especially to rest. What struck me at once in France is the importance of the café in daily life.

7 The café is a club. There one meets one's friends; there people play cards, chess, billiards; there one writes letters as I am doing now.

8 The café is also a business centre. For businessmen it is another office, perhaps even the main office.

9 The café is a theatre: the passers-by are the actors and actresses, sometimes tragic, more often comic, but always interesting.

10 Then we continued on our way along the Champs-Élysées up to the Place de l'Étoile. We observed the Arc de Triomphe which is in the centre of the Place de l'Étoile.

11 To return to the Cafe Royale-Concorde we took the beautiful Avenue Marceau. At the Place de l'Alma Mr. Parmentier left me. I followed the quays admiring the Eiffel Tower all along the way, up to the Place de la Concorde.

12 Then I went up Rue Royale, and finally I fell into the nearest chair of the Royale-Concorde Café, tired, worn out and delighted.

Your friend enamoured of Paris,
John Davis

Note 1. *Lit*. Feet perhaps remain to me.

  2. ʃɑ̃-ze-li-**ze**.

  3. *Lit*. Place of the star, because at this place a dozen avenues spread out like the points of a star.

Building Vocabulary

Related Words

1 **arrêter**, to stop (someone, something), to arrest (someone); **s'arrêter**, to stop (stand still); **un arrêt**, stop, halt

2 **approcher**, to bring nearer; **s'approcher (de)**, to come nearer; **une approche**, approach; **proche**, near

3 **écrire**, to write; **décrire**, to describe; **un écrivain**, the writer; **une écriture**, writing, handwriting

4 **la table**, table; **s'attabler**, to sit down at a table; **attablé**, seated at a table

5 **se reposer**, to rest; **le repos**, rest

6 **un amour**, love; **amoureux**, enamoured, in love; **un amoureux**, lover

7 **le pays**, country; **le paysan**, farmer, peasant; **le paysage**, landscape

8 **tirer**, to pull, to shoot; **retirer**, to pull back; **se retirer**, to retire, to withdraw

9 **vite**, quick, quickly; **la vitesse**, speed

10 **curieux**, curious; **la curiosité**, curiosity

Locutions françaises

1 **il vient me chercher,** he comes to call for (*Lit.* look for) me
2 **d'un côté,** on one side; **de l'autre côté,** on the other side
3 **jouer aux cartes (aux échecs, au billard),** to play cards (chess, billiards)
4 **tout le long du chemin,** all along the way
5 **combien de fois?** how many times? **une fois,** once; **deux fois,** twice; **quelquefois, parfois,** sometimes; **des fois,** at times; **à la fois,** at once, together; **encore une fois,** once more; **plusieurs fois,** several times

Exercise No. 178—Completion of Text

1 **M. Parmentier est venu** (to look for me).
2 (We stayed) **très longtemps sur le pont.**
3 **Les pêcheurs restent des heures** (without catching anything).
4 **Les enfants s'amusent** (throwing stones).
5 (We continued) **notre promenade sur le quai.**
6 **Cela doit être** (the most beautiful square) **du monde.**
7 What a beautiful avenue!
8 **Ce qui** (struck me) **c'est l'importance du café.**
9 (There people play) **aux cartes.**
10 (There one writes) **des lettres.**
11 (The passers-by) **sont les acteurs et les actrices.**
12 (Then) **nous avons continué** (our way).
13 **À la place de l'Alma M. Parmentier** (left me).
14 (I followed) **les quais.**
15 **Je suis tombé** (into the nearest chair).

Grammar Notes

1 Relative Pronouns

(*a*) **qui,** who, which, that, is used as a subject relative pronoun.

Connaissez-vous les acteurs *qui* sont assis à cette table? Do you know the actors *who* are seated at that table?

Où est le quai *qui* mène au pont des Arts? Where is the quay *that* leads to the Pont des Arts?

(*b*) **qui,** whom, is used as the object of a preposition.

Je ne connais pas la dame à *qui* vous avez parlé. I do not know the lady *to whom* you spoke.

(*c*) **que, qu',** whom, which, that, is used as a direct object relative pronoun.

Je suis attablé dans le café *que* vous m'avez recommandé. I am sitting at a table in the café *that* you recommended to me.

C'est un professeur *que* les étudiants admirent. He is a professor *whom* the students admire.

(*d*) **ce qui** (*subject*); and **ce que** or **ce qu'** (*object*); mean *what* (*that which*).

Savez-vous *ce qui* est dans cette grande caisse? Do you know *what* (*that which*) is in that large case?

Nous avons lu tout *ce que* vous avez écrit. We have read all *that* (*which*) you wrote.

Je n'ai pas entendu *ce qu'il* a dit. I did not hear *what* (*that which*) he said.

(*e*) **lequel (laquelle, lesquels, lesquelles)** *which, whom*—are used mainly for things after a preposition. They agree with the antecedent in number and gender.

J'ai reçu votre lettre *dans laquelle* vous décrivez 'Une Belle Promenade'.
I have received your letter *in which* you describe 'A Beautiful Walk'.

(*f*) **dont**, whose, of whom, of which, is used as a relative pronoun instead of **de** + **qui** and **de** + any form of **lequel**.

Nous allons rendre visite au professeur *dont* nous avons parlé hier. We are going to visit the teacher *of whom* we spoke yesterday.

Le Mont-Saint-Michel est un endroit *dont* les omelettes sont célèbres.
The Mont-Saint-Michel is a place *whose* omelettes are famous.

(*g*) A relative pronoun may sometimes be omitted in English. It is never omitted in French.

Les pêcheurs *que* vous voyez sur le quai sont bretons. The fishermen (*whom*) you see on the quay are Bretons.

Exercise No. 179 Translate each question and answer. Then read each one aloud three times.

1 **Avez-vous compris tout ce que le maître a dit?**
   Je n'ai pas tout compris.
2 **Avez-vous lu les deux guides que je vous ai prêtés?**
   Je les ai lus avec beaucoup d'intérêt.
3 **Quel est le premier secret de la bonne cuisine?**
   Tout ce qui entre dans un plat doit être de bonne qualité.
4 **Est-ce qu'on peut faire du ski en montagne?**
   Ceux qui sont jeunes et forts skient tout le temps.
5 **À quel café vous êtes-vous attablé aujourd'hui?**
   Je me suis attablé au Royale-Concorde dont nous avons souvent parlé.
6 **Où sont les valises dans lesquelles j'ai mis mes vêtements?**
   Elles sont dans votre chambre.

Exercise No. 180 Complete each sentence with the correct French relative pronoun:

1 **Montrez-moi le chapeau** (that) **vous venez d'acheter.**
2 **Vous rappelez-vous** (what) **il vous a dit?**
3 **Les touristes** (who) **visitent Paris se sentent chez eux.**
4 **Voyons** (what) **se trouve dans cette caisse.**
5 **Voilà le guide avec** (whom) **nous allons visiter la cathédrale.**
6 **Je cherche la boîte dans** (which) **j'ai mis ma montre.**
7 **Il y a trois élèves dans ma classe** (whose) **les parents sont français.**
8 **Tous les endroits** (which) **j'ai visités sont très intéressants.**
9 **Tout** (that) **se passe au café est intéressant.**
10 **Nous ne pouvons pas trouver les élèves** (whom) **nous cherchons.**

Exercise No. 181—Questionnaire

1 **Où est-ce que M. Davis écrit sa lettre?**
2 **Où est-ce que M. Parmentier est venu le chercher?**
3 **Où sont-ils restés très longtemps?**
4 **Qu'est-ce qu'ils ont vu?**
5 **Qu'est-ce que M. Davis pense au sujet de la place de la Concorde?**

6 Pourquoi les messieurs se sont-ils attablés?

7 Qu'est-ce qui a frappé M. Davis?

8 Qu'est-ce que c'est qu'un café pour les hommes d'affaires?

9 Que sont les passants?

10 Qu'est-ce qu'ils ont contemplé?

11 Où est-ce que M. Parmentier a quitté M. Davis?

12 Qu'est-ce que M. Davis a admiré tout le long du chemin?

13 Comment M. Davis est-il tombé sur la chaise du café?

CHAPITRE 35 (TRENTE-CINQ)

LE MONT-SAINT-MICHEL
QUATRIÈME LETTRE

Cher ami,

1 Devinez un peu d'où je vous écris. C'est ça! Vous avez raison. Je vous écris attablé dans un café. Vous allez croire que je ne fais que ça. C'est que le métier de touriste exige beaucoup de repos. Et où est-ce qu'on se repose mieux que dans un café?

2 Vous rappelez-vous notre conversation au sujet de mes voyages? Eh bien, j'ai commencé mon grand cercle en partant de Paris pour la Normandie. J'ai visité le Mont-Saint-Michel et me voilà à Perros-Guirec en Bretagne. En l'honneur de ma première visite en Bretagne, je prends un calvados.

3 Je veux vous décrire ma visite au Mont-Saint-Michel, pendant qu'elle est encore fraîche à ma mémoire.

4 Pendant que le train traversait les champs et les forêts, je regardais par la fenêtre. Il filait à toute vitesse et je voyais les paysans qui travaillaient dans les champs, et parfois, en passant par les villages, j'apercevais des femmes qui lavaient le linge au bord d'une rivière.[1]

5 A Pontorson, j'ai pris un taxi pour le Mont. Presque tout de suite j'ai vu ce rocher monumental isolé au milieu des sables.

6 Mais quand je suis arrivé au pittoresque village situé aux flancs du rocher, j'ai entendu un bruit terrifiant.

7 On criait, on hurlait: — Monsieur! Par ici! Souvenirs du Mont! Cartes postales! Monsieur! La véritable omelette de la Mère Poularde! Monsieur! Ici la vraie! Monsieur! Ici l'omelette Poularde! Cartes! Souvenirs! L'omelette! Ici! Ici! Monsieur! Monsieur! Monsieur!

8 La tête me tournait comme une toupie. J'avais envie de partir. Mais enfin je me suis dit: — En avant l'art et l'histoire. Courage! — J'ai fermé les oreilles mentalement et j'ai vite grimpé la pente raide jusqu'à l'escalier de l'Abbaye.

9 La visite de l'Abbaye a duré une heure environ. Ce bâtiment gothique avec ses grandes salles, ses escaliers, ses galeries, ses cloîtres, ses jardins en terrasses est un spectacle grandiose. Je voulais rester pour contempler les sculptures mais ce n'était pas possible.

10 Vous savez que le visiteur d'un monument historique n'a aucun[2] droit. On est poussé par-ci, on est tiré par-là et on doit suivre comme un mouton. Malgré tout, cet îlot rocheux m'a fait une forte impression.

11 Maintenant je me tourne vers la Bretagne: la mer, les marins, les poissons, les chapelles et le calvados dont les marins bretons sont fervents. Perros-Guirec me plaît beaucoup. Je finirai peut-être par aimer le calvados.

Très cordialement,
Votre ami
Jean Davis

Dear Friend,

1 Just guess where I'm writing from. That's it! You're right. I am writing to you, sitting at a table in a café. You're going to think that it's all I do. The thing is that the profession of tourist demands a great deal of rest. And where can you rest better than in a café?

2 Do you recall our conversation on the subject of my travels? Well, I started my round trip, leaving Paris for Normandy. I visited the Mont-Saint-Michel and here I am in Perros-Guirec in Brittany. In honour of my first visit to Brittany, I am drinking a calvados (brandy).

3 I want to describe to you my visit to the Mont-Saint-Michel while it is still fresh in my memory.

4 While the train was crossing fields and forests, I was looking out of the window. It was going along at top speed and I saw the country-people working in the fields, and sometimes in passing through the villages, I could see women washing clothes at the edge of a stream.

5 At Pontorson I took a taxi to the Mont. Almost at once I saw this monumental rock isolated in the middle of the sands.

6 But when I reached the picturesque village situated on the sides of the rocky hill I heard a terrifying din.

7 People were calling, yelling: Mister! This way. Souvenirs of the Mont! Postcards! Sir! Mother Poularde's genuine omelette! Sir! Here you get the real one! Sir! The Poularde omelette! Cards! Souvenirs! The omelette! Here! Here! Sir! Sir! Sir!

8 My head was spinning like a top. I wanted to go away. But at last I said to myself: Onward with art and history. Courage! I mentally closed my ears and I quickly climbed the steep slope up to the stairs of the Abbey.

9 The visit to the Abbey lasted about an hour. This Gothic structure with its ample halls, its staircases, its galleries, its cloisters, its terraced gardens is a grandiose spectacle. I wanted to stop to contemplate the sculpture but it wasn't possible.

10 You know that the visitor at a historic site has no rights. One is pushed this way, pulled that way, and one has to follow like a sheep. In spite of everything, this rocky islet made a strong impression on me.

11 Now I turn towards Brittany: the sea, the sailors, the fish, the chapels and the calvados to which the Breton sailors are addicted. I like Perros-Guirec very much. I shall end up perhaps by liking calvados.

Cordially,
Your friend
John Davis

NOTE 1. un fleuve is a larger river than une rivière.

     2. aucun, aucune, any.

Building Vocabulary

le corps (kɔːr), body
la tête (tɛːt), head
les cheveux (ʃvø), hair
la figure (fi-gyːr), face
un œil (œ̃-nœːj), eye

la langue (lãːg), tongue
la main (mɛ̃), hand
le doigt (dwa), finger
le pied (pje), foot
le bras (bra), arm

les yeux (lɛ zjø), eyes
le nez (ne), nose
la bouche (buʃ), mouth

la jambe (ʒãːb), leg
le cœur (kœːr), heart

Locutions françaises

me voici, here I am
te voici, here you are
le (la) voici, here he (she, it) is
le (la) voilà, there he (she, it) is

nous voici, here we are
vous voici, here you are
les voici, here they are
les voilà, there they are

Exercise No. 182—Completion of Text

1 (You are right.)
2 (Here I am) **dans un café.**
3 (I am drinking) **un calvados.**
4 **Le train traversait** (the fields and the forests).
5 **Je regardais** (out of the window).
6 (The farmers) **travaillaient dans** (the fields).
7 **Les femmes lavaient** (the linen).
8 (I took a taxi) **pour le Mont.**
9 (Almost at once) **j'ai vu ce rocher monumental.**
10 **On criait: — Monsieur,** (this way)!
11 **J'ai fermé** (my ears).
12 **La visite de l'Abbaye** (lasted) **une heure.**
13 **Je voulais** (to stop to contemplate) **la sculpture.**
14 **On** (is pushed) **par-ci, on** (is pulled) **par-là.**
15 (One must follow) **comme un mouton.**

Grammar Notes

1 The Imperfect Tense. What *was happening, used to happen.*

The conversational past, as you have seen, tells what *has happened, happened,* or *did happen.*

The imperfect tense tells what *was happening* or *used to happen.* For convenience we call the imperfect the *was, were, used to* tense.

Note carefully the endings of the imperfect tense of **parler, finir, vendre, prendre, avoir** and **être.**

I was speaking, you were speaking, etc.

je parlais	nous parlions
tu parlais	vous parliez
il parlait	ils parlaient
elle parlait	elles parlaient

I was finishing, you were finishing, etc.

je finissais	nous finissions
tu finissais	vous finissiez
il finissait	ils finissaient
elle finissait	elles finissaient

I was selling, you were selling, etc.

je vendais	nous vendions
tu vendais	vous vendiez
il vendait	ils vendaient
elle vendait	elles vendaient

I was taking, you were taking, etc.

je prenais	nous prenions
tu prenais	vous preniez
il prenait	ils prenaient
elle prenait	elles prenaient

I had, you had, etc.		I was, you were, etc.	
j'avais	nous avions	j'étais	nous étions
tu avais	vous aviez	tu étais	vous étiez
il avait	ils avaient	il était	ils étaient
elle avait	elles avaient	elle était	elles étaient

(*a*) The imperfect tense endings of all French verbs are: Singular: **-ais** (ε), **-ais** (ε), **-ait** (ε). Plural: **-ions** (jɔ̃), **iez** (je), **aient** (ε).

(*b*) To form the imperfect tense drop the ending **-ons** from the **nous-** form of the present tense and add the imperfect tense endings. This way of forming the imperfect tense applies to all verbs except **être**. Thus:

Infinitive	*Nous-form of Present*	*Imperfect* (was, were, used to)
parler	nous parl-ons	je parlais, tu parlais, etc.
vendre	nous vend-ons	je vendais, tu vendais, etc.
finir	nous finiss-ons	je finissais, tu finissais, etc.
dormir	nous dorm-ons	je dormais, tu dormais, etc.
prendre	nous pren-ons	je prenais, tu prenais, etc.
dire	nous dis-ons	je disais, tu disais, etc.
faire	nous fais-ons	je faisais, tu faisais, etc.
lire	nous lis-ons	je lisais, tu lisais, etc.
écrire	nous écriv-ons	j'écrivais, tu écrivais, etc.
vouloir	nous voul-ons	je voulais, tu voulais, etc.
avoir	nous av-ons	j'avais, tu avais, etc.
être	nous sommes	j'étais, tu étais, etc.

(*c*) Present and Imperfect of **il y a** and **venir de**

Present	*Imperfect*
il y a, there is (are)	**il y avait**, there was (were)
y a-t-il? *or* **est-ce qu'il y a?** is (are) there	**y avait-il?** *or* **est-ce qu'il y avait?** was (were) there?
qu'y a-t-il? *or* **qu'est-ce qu'il y a?** what is (are) there?	**qu'y avait-il?** *or* **qu'est-ce qu'il y avait?** what was (were) there?
il n'y a pas, there is (are) not	**il n'y avait pas**, there was (were) not
n'y a-t-il pas? *or* **est-ce qu'il n'y a pas?** is (are) there not?	**n'y avait-il pas?** *or* **est-ce qu'il n'y avait pas?** was (were) there not?
il vient de voir, he has just seen.	**il venait de voir**, he had just seen.

Exercise No. 183 Translate the following brief dialogues. Practise them aloud:

1 — Qu'est-ce M. Davis faisait quand vous êtes entré dans le salon?
— Il lisait à haute voix (aloud) une lettre qu'il venait de recevoir de son représentant à Paris.
— M. Picard, que faisait-il?
— Il l'écoutait.
2 — Que faisiez-vous pendant que le train traversait les champs et les forêts?
— Je regardais par la fenêtre.
— Qu'est-ce que vous voyiez?
— Je voyais les paysans qui travaillaient dans les champs.

3 — Y avait-il beaucoup de vendeurs au Mont-Saint-Michel?
— Il y en avait une armée.
— Qu'est-ce qu'ils vendaient?
— Ils vendaient des souvenirs du Mont.
4 — Jouez-vous souvent au tennis?
— Autrefois (formerly) je jouais presque tous les jours mais cette année je n'ai joué qu'une seule fois.

Exercise No. 184 Each of these sentences indicates an action that *was happening* (*imperfect*) and another action that interrupted it at a definite time (*conversational past*). Complete with the correct French verbs. Translate the completed sentences.

1 Les vendeurs (were calling and yelling) quand je suis arrivé au marché.
2 Pendant que (I was listening to) la radio, on m'a téléphoné.
3 Quand (we were doing) nos devoirs, ils sont entrés dans notre chambre.
4 Elle est tombée quand elle (was getting out) de l'auto.
5 Quand le taxi (was going) à toute vitesse, j'ai crié: — Pas si vite!
6 Nous lui avons rendu visite quand (he was) malade.
7 (There were) beaucoup de monde[1] à l'aéroport quand notre avion est arrivé.
8 Pendant que (we were waiting for) l'autobus, il a commencé à pleuvoir.
9 Nous les avons rencontrés quand (we were coming) du cinéma.
10 M. Davis est revenu pendant que les enfants (were sleeping).

NOTE 1. beaucoup de monde: a lot of people, crowded.

Exercise No. 185—Questionnaire

1 D'où M. Davis écrit-il?
2 Qu'est-ce que le métier de touriste exige?
3 Où est le café?
4 Qu'est-ce que M. Davis prend en l'honneur de sa première visite en Bretagne?
5 Qu'est-ce que M. Davis faisait pendant que le train traversait les champs et les forêts?
6 Qu'est-ce qu'il voyait?
7 Qu'est-ce qu'il apercevait dans les villages?
8 Qu'a-t-il entendu quand il est arrivé?
9 Pourquoi avait-il d'abord envie de partir?
10 Pourquoi est-ce que M. Davis voulait rester?
11 Vers où se tourne-t-il maintenant?
12 Combien de temps la visite de l'Abbaye a-t-elle duré?

CHAPITRE 36 (TRENTE-SIX)

GUIGNOL
CINQUIÈME LETTRE

Cher ami,

1 Je suis revenu à Paris de mon voyage en Bretagne de plus en plus amoureux de la France, mais sans avoir appris à aimer le calvados.

2 Ce matin je suis allé au Louvre pour le visiter à fond. Je l'ai visité tellement à fond que je ne peux rien vous dire.

3 Si la tête me tournait comme une toupie au Mont-Saint-Michel à cause du bruit, elle me tournait dix fois plus vite en quittant le silence du Louvre. Je me suis dit: — Imbécile! Pourquoi n'es-tu pas sorti il y a deux heures? Crois-tu que le Louvre va s'envoler?

4 Enfin, après un déjeuner délicieux arrosé d'un bon vin, j'étais délassé et avide de nouvelles aventures.

5 Je me suis donc dirigé vers le Jardin du Luxembourg attiré par le soleil et les fleurs. Je marchais tranquillement quand tout à coup j'ai entendu de grands éclats de rire. Je me suis approché, tout curieux.

6 J'ai vu un joli petit théâtre, dont la scène était encadrée d'un rideau de velours bleu ciel. Des enfants se serraient sur les bancs qui formaient la petite salle. Ils riaient à la folie.

7 Sur la scène il n'y avait que Guignol.[1] Il ne bougeait pas. Il ne disait rien. Mais ce n'était pas nécessaire. Il n'avait qu'à paraître, et les enfants éclataient de rire.

8 J'ai pris place à côté d'une toute petite fille qui m'a saisi par la main en criant: — Papa! Très flatté, j'ai répondu: — Bonjour, ma chérie.

9 Sa maman, toute rose, lui a dit: — Regarde, Cricri, voilà Gringalet, le fils de Guignol. Et à moi: — Christine pense que tous les messieurs s'appellent papa.

— Mais j'en suis ravi, madame, ai-je répondu en souriant.

10 Un fou rire nous a fait regarder la scène. Le petit Gringalet était en train de donner de grands coups de tête dans le ventre de Guignol. Les enfants n'étaient pas du tout fâchés. Au contraire, ils étaient ravis.

11 J'ai dit au revoir à Cricri et à sa mère, et l'enfant m'a répondu gentiment: — Au revoir, papa.

12 Je dois vous dire qu'à ce moment-là ma femme et mes enfants me manquaient beaucoup.[2]

Salutations amicales de votre ami,
Jean Davis

Dear Friend,

1 I returned to Paris from my trip to Brittany more and more in love with France, but still without having learned to love calvados.

2 This morning I went to the Louvre to visit it thoroughly. I visited it so thoroughly that I am not able to tell you anything.

3 If my head was spinning like a top at the Mont-Saint-Michel because of the noise, it was spinning ten times faster when I left the silence of the Louvre. I said to myself: Fool! Why didn't you leave two hours ago? Do you think the Louvre is going to fly away?

4 Well, after a delicious lunch washed down with a good wine, I was refreshed and eager for new adventures.

5 I therefore made my way towards the Luxembourg Gardens attracted by the sun and the flowers. I was strolling quietly along when all of a sudden I heard roars of laughter. I drew near, very curious.

6 I saw a pretty little theatre, the stage framed by a sky blue velvet curtain. Children were crowding on the benches which formed the tiny auditorium. They were laughing wildly.

7 On the stage there was only Guignol. He was not moving. He was not saying anything. But it wasn't necessary. He had only to appear and the children would burst out laughing.

8 I took a seat next to a very little girl who seized my hand and called out: Daddy! Very flattered, I answered: Hello, pet.

9 Her mother said to her, blushing: Look Cricri, here is Gringalet, Guignol's son. And to me: Christine thinks that all gentlemen are called daddy.

But I'm delighted, Madame, I answered, smiling.

10 A wild shout of laughter made us look at the stage. Little Gringalet was giving Guignol hard blows in the stomach with his head. The children were not at all annoyed. On the contrary, they were delighted.

11 I said goodbye to Cricri and her mother and the child answered sweetly: Goodbye, daddy.

12 I must tell you that at that moment I missed my wife and my children[2] very much.

Greetings from your friend,
John Davis

Note 1. **Guignol** (gi-ɲɔl), chief character in French puppet shows. His son, a puny fellow, is called **Gringalet** (grɛ̃-ga-lɛ).
 2. *Lit*, my wife and children were missing to me.

Building Vocabulary

Antonyms

1 **le bruit**, noise; **le silence**, silence
2 **fatigué**, tired; **délassé**, refreshed
3 **paraître**, to appear; **disparaître**, to disappear
4 **rire**, to laugh; **pleurer**, to weep
5 **fâché**, annoyed; **ravi**, delighted
6 **nouveau (nouvel)**[1] **nouvelle** (*f*), new; **vieux (vieil) vieille** (*f*), old
7 **mener**, to lead; **suivre**, to follow
8 **monter en voiture**, to get into a car; **descendre de la voiture**, to get out of the car

Note 1. **nouvel** and **vieil** are forms used before masculine nouns beginning with a vowel or **h** (usually), thus: **un nouvel article; un vieil homme**

Locutions françaises

1 **de plus en plus,** more and more
2 **à fond,** thoroughly
3 **tout à coup,** suddenly
4 **à la folie,** wildly, uproariously
5 **il n'y avait que Guignol,** there was only Guignol
6 **éclater de rire,** to burst out laughing
7 **un éclat de rire,** a roar of laughter

Exercise No. 186—Completion of Text

1 (I returned) **de mon voyage.**
2 **J'étais** (more and more) **amoureux de la France.**
3 **Ce matin** (I went) **au Louvre.**
4 (I am not able) **rien vous dire.**
5 (My head) **me tournait comme une toupie.**
6 (I said to myself): — **Imbécile.**
7 **Pourquoi n'es-tu pas sorti** (two hours ago)?
8 (I was) **délassé.**
9 (I was walking) **tranquillement.**
10 (I approached) **tout curieux.**
11 **Des enfants** (were crowding) **sur les bancs.**
12 (They were laughing) **à la folie.**
13 **Guignol** (was not moving).
14 He was saying nothing.
15 **Les enfants** (were not at all) **fâchés.**
16 (I said) **au revoir à Cricri et à sa mère.**

Grammar Notes

1 **rire,** to laugh; **vivre,** to live (Present, Imperfect, Conversational Past).

Present

I laugh, I am laughing, etc.

je ris (ri)	**nous rions**
tu ris (ri)	**vous riez**
il rit (ri)	**ils rient** (ri)
elle rit (ri)	**elles rient** (ri)

I live, I am living, etc.

je vis	**nous vivons**
tu vis	**vous vivez**
il vit	**ils vivent**
elle vit	**elles vivent**

Imperative: **ris,** laugh; **rions,** let us laugh; **riez,** laugh; **vis,** live; **vivons,** let us live; **vivez,** live.

Imperfect

I was laughing, etc.

je riais	**nous riions**
tu riais	**vous riiez**
il riait	**ils riaient**
elle riait	**elles riaient**

I was living, etc.

je vivais	**nous vivions**
tu vivais	**vous viviez**
il vivait	**ils vivaient**
elle vivait	**elles vivaient**

Conversational Past

I laughed, etc.

j'ai ri	**nous avons ri**
etc.	etc.

I lived, etc.

j'ai vécu	**nous avons vécu**
etc.	etc.

Like **rire,** to laugh, is **sourire,** to smile

2 vouloir, pouvoir, savoir, devoir and **avoir** generally use the imperfect instead of the conversational past.

Il nous devait cinq francs.	He owed us five francs.
Je ne pouvais pas lui écrire.	I was not able to write him.

3 The Past Infinitive

(*a*) The *past infinitive* is formed by the auxiliary **avoir** or **être** plus the *past participle* of the verb.

Present Infinitive	*Past Infinitive*
parler, to speak	**avoir parlé**, to have spoken
finir, to finish	**avoir fini**, to have finished
aller, to go	**être allé**, to have gone
sortir, to go out	**être sorti**, to have gone out

(*b*) You have learned that prepositions (except **en**) take the present infinitive in French instead of the present participle as in English.

sans apprendre, without learning	**en admirant**, (while) admiring
avant de partir, before leaving	**en sortant**, (on) leaving

Prepositions may also take past infinitives

après avoir appris,[1] after learning (*Lit.* after to have learned)
après être allé, after going (*Lit.* after to have gone)

NOTE 1. **après** always takes a past infinitive.

Exercise No. 187 Complete the following sentences in French with the imperfect tense of the verbs in parentheses:

Exemple: Les enfants riaient à la folie.

1 Les enfants (were laughing) **à la folie.**
2 M. Parmentier (was living) **à Paris.**
3 Les femmes (were washing) **le linge.**
4 (Were they) **fâchés?**
5 Jean (was coming out) **du cinéma.**
6 Nous (were paying a visit) **à M. Duval.**
7 M. Davis (was he thinking) **à sa famille?**
8 Marie (was getting out) **de la voiture.**
9 Je (was coming back) **à l'hôtel à pied.**
10 Nous (were going up) **au troisième étage.**
11 Toute la ville (was smiling).
12 (I was) **content de vous voir.**
13 Un bel homme (was approaching).
14 Ils (were beginning)[1] **à parler français.**
15 Elle (was eating)[1] **des gâteaux délicieux.**
16 Ils (used to meet) **tous les jeudis.**
17 Nous (did not have) **d'argent.**
18 Elles (did not want) **partir.**
19 (Were you able) **lui rendre visite?**
20 Personne ne (knew) **combien il (owed).**

NOTE 1. Verbs ending in -cer have a soft c (like *s*). Verbs ending in -ger have a soft g (ʒ). To keep the c and g soft before endings beginning with a or o, the c must have a cedilla, and the g must be followed by a silent e. See grammar Notes 2. p. 152. Thus:

commencer	manger
Present: nous commençons	*Present*: nous mangeons
Imperfect: je commençais, il commençait	*Imperfect*: je mangeais, ils mangeaient

But:

Imperfect: nous commencions	*Imperfect*: nous mangions

Exercise No. 188—Questionnaire

1 Pourquoi M. Davis est-il allé au Louvre?
2 Qu'est-ce que M. Davis s'est dit?
3 Où s'est-il tourné?
4 Qu'est-ce qu'il a entendu tout à coup?
5 Qu'est-ce qu'il a vu quand il s'est approché?
6 Qui ne bougeait pas?
7 Qu'est-ce que les enfants faisaient chaque fois que Guignol paraissait?
8 Où est-ce que M. Davis a pris place?
9 Qu'est-ce que la petite fille a crié?
10 Qu'est-ce que le petit Gringalet était en train de faire?
11 Est-ce que les enfants étaient fâchés?
12 Qu'est-ce que l'enfant a répondu quand M. Davis lui a dit au revoir?

RÉVISION 8

CHAPITRES 32–36 PREMIÈRE PARTIE
DEUXIÈME PARTIE

Révision de mots

NOUNS

1 un arbre	10 un écrivain	19 la manière
2 un avocat	11 un escalier	20 le paysan
3 un ascenseur	12 la figure	21 le pas
4 le banc	13 la fontaine	22 la pierre
5 le camion	14 la forêt	23 le repos
6 le champ	15 les gens	24 la rivière
7 le chemin	16 la jambe	25 le village
8 le docteur	17 le lycée	26 la vitesse
9 la douane	18 la mémoire	27 le ventre

1 tree	10 writer	19 manner
2 lawyer, barrister	11 staircase	20 peasant
3 lift	12 face	21 step
4 bench	13 fountain	22 stone
5 lorry	14 forest	23 rest
6 field	15 people, folk	24 stream, river
7 road	16 leg	25 village
8 doctor	17 grammar school	26 speed
9 customs	18 memory	27 stomach

VERBS

1 s'approcher (de)	9 essayer	16 se retirer
2 s'arrêter	10 jeter	17 retourner
3 bavarder	11 marcher	18 rentrer (dans)
4 crier	12 monter	19 rire
5 décrire	13 oublier	20 sauter
6 disparaître	14 pousser	21 se tromper
7 descendre	15 se rappeler	22 se serrer
8 durer		

1 to approach, come near	9 to try	16 to withdraw
2 to stop	10 to throw	17 to go back
3 to chat	11 to walk	18 to re-enter
4 to cry, to shout	12 to go up	19 to laugh
5 to describe	13 to forget	20 to leap, to jump
6 to disappear	14 to push	21 to be mistaken
7 to go down	15 to recall, to remember	22 to crowd
8 to last		

ADJECTIVES

1 amoureux (euse f)	5 fâché	9 frais (fraîche f)
2 chéri	6 fatigué	10 frappant
3 délassé	7 flatté	11 gracieux (ieuse f)
4 éveillé	8 fier (fière f)	12 meublé

214

13 neuf (neuve *f*)　　16 proche　　　　18 sauf
14 nouveau (elle *f*)　　17 sain　　　　　19 sincère
15 plusieurs

1 amorous, in love	8 proud	14 new, another
2 dear, beloved, darling	9 fresh	15 several
3 rested	10 striking	16 near
4 lively, perky	11 graceful	17 healthy
5 angry, vexed	12 furnished	18 safe
6 tired	13 brand new	19 sincere
7 flattered		

ADVERBS

1 aussitôt que　　　3 ensuite　　　　5 cordialement
2 enfin　　　　　　4 longtemps　　　6 tellement

1 as soon as　　　　3 then, afterwards　　5 cordially
2 finally　　　　　　4 long, a long while,　　6 so, in such manner
　　　　　　　　　　　for a long time

PREPOSITIONS

1 parmi　　　　　2 au bord (de)　　　3 au milieu (de)

1 among　　　　2 on the edge of　　3 in the middle of

FRENCH EXPRESSIONS

1 d'accord　　　　　　7 faire leurs devoirs
2 en avant　　　　　　8 rendre visite à
3 à la fois　　　　　　9 jouer aux cartes
4 de plus en plus　　　10 le plaisir est pour moi
5 tout à coup　　　　　11 le café me plaît
6 faire ses études　　　12 je ne manque de rien

1 agreed, in agreement　　7 to do their homework
2 forward, onward　　　　8 to pay a visit to
3 together, at the same time　9 to play cards
4 more and more　　　　　10 the pleasure is mine
5 suddenly　　　　　　　11 I like the café
6 to be educated　　　　　12 I want for nothing

DEUXIÈME PARTIE

Exercise No. 189 Translate each sentence. Then read it aloud three times.
 1 M. Davis est parti pour Paris.
 2 Sa femme est restée à la maison.
 3 Mme Picard est sortie il y a une heure.
 4 Elle n'est pas encore rentrée.
 5 Nous sommes montés par l'ascenseur.
 6 Ils sont descendus à pied.
 7 Pourquoi êtes-vous revenue si tard, Marie?
 8 Je suis allée au marché pour faire mes achats.
 9 Son grand-père est mort ce matin.
10 Ma grand-mère est née le cinq juin 1900.

Exercise No. 190 Fill in the correct form of the past participle of each verb in parenthesis.

Exemple 1. Un bel homme s'est approché.

1 Un bel homme s'est (approcher).
2 Ils se sont (rencontrer) à la gare.
3 J'ai (prendre) un taxi pour l'hôtel.
4 Nous sommes (sortir) ensemble.
5 Le taxi s'est (arrêter) devant le théâtre.
6 Elle est (arriver) saine et sauve.
7 M. Davis est (descendre) de la voiture.

8 On lui a (réserver) un belle chambre.
9 Ma sœur est (naître) le 5 janvier.
10 Il a (mettre) son pardessus.
11 Qu'est-ce que vous avez (dire)?
12 Je n'ai pas (faire) les valises.
13 Ont-ils (demander) des renseignements?
14 Les fenêtres sont (ouvrir). Qui les a (ouvrir)?

Exercise No. 191 Complete each sentence by selecting from the parenthesis the tense of the verb that fits best. Translate each sentence.

1 Demain nous ...... visite à la famille Davis. (rendrons, rendions, avons rendu)
2 Hier soir les enfants ...... au ciné. (iront, allaient, sont allés)
3 Les élèves n'écoutaient pas pendant que le professeur .... (parlera, parlait, a parlé)
4 Où ...... l'hiver dernier? (passerez-vous, passiez-vous, avez-vous passé)
5 Je ne les ...... avant demain. (verrai pas, voyais pas, ai pas vus)
6 Nous faisions nos devoirs pendant qu'ils ...... aux cartes. (joueront, jouaient, ont joué)
7 Elles sont restées à la maison parce qu'il ...... à verse. (pleuvra, pleuvait, a plu)
8 ...... un voyage en Europe l'été prochain? (ferez-vous, faisiez-vous, avez-vous fait)
9 Il nous ...... cinq francs hier. (prêtera, prêtait, a prêté)
10 À quelle heure est-ce que ...... hier matin? (vous vous lèverez, vous vous leviez, vous vous êtes levé)

Exercise No. 192 Complete each sentence in French. Then read it aloud three times.

1 (It was raining hard) quand M. Picard a frappé à la porte.
2 (I was very happy) lorsque (when) j'ai reçu sa lettre.
3 Ils prenaient du thé au rhum (when Mr. Davis received) un télégramme.
4 Nous dînions (when my agent telephoned me).
5 Autrefois (we used to go) souvent au théâtre.
6 (I did not know)[1] ce qu'ils disaient.
7 (We were not able)[1] trouver le stylo.
8 (Did they want[1]) voyager partout?
9 (She did not have[1] time) d'aller au ciné.
10 (She was to[2]) nous rendre visite hier.

Note 1. Use the imperfect.
      2. Use the imperfect of devoir.

Dialogue
À la station-service

M. Davis entre dans la station pour faire le plein d'essence.
Tout de suite un jeune homme s'approche pour le servir.
— Bonjour, monsieur, lui dit le jeune homme.
— Bonjour, jeune homme, répond M. Davis. Voulez-vous me faire le plein?
— Ordinaire, ou super?
— Ordinaire, s'il vous plaît. Voulez-vous vérifier l'huile, l'eau et les pneus?
— Avec plaisir, monsieur, répond l'employé.
Le jeune homme fait le plein, vérifie l'huile, l'eau et les pneus.
— Tout va bien, dit-il à notre touriste.
— Merci beaucoup. Combien est-ce que je vous dois?
— Ça fait cent soixante-quinze francs.
M. Davis lui donne deux billets de cent francs, et le jeune homme lui rend la monnaie, vingt-cinq francs.
M. Davis fait le compte et il voit que tout est en ordre.
— Très bien, dit-il à l'employé. Merci beaucoup et au revoir.
Le jeune homme répond: — Au revoir et bon voyage.

Mr. Davis goes to the petrol station to fill up the tank.
Immediately a young man approaches to serve him.
Good afternoon, sir, the young man greets him.
Good afternoon, young man, answers Mr. Davis, Will you fill it up, please?
Regular or Super?
Regular, please. Will you please check the oil, water and the tyres?
With pleasure, sir, the employee replies.
The young man fills the tank, checks the oil, the water and the tyres.
Everything is all right, he says to our tourist.
Many thanks. How much do I owe you?
It comes to hundred and seventy-five francs.
Mr. Davis gives him two hundred-franc notes and the young man gives him the change, twenty-five francs.
Mr. Davis works out the amount and sees that all is in order.
Very good, he says to the employee. Thank you very much and goodbye.
The young man answers: Goodbye and a pleasant trip.

Exercise No. 193—Lecture 1
Une excursion à Versailles

Un jour M. Davis a invité les fils de M. Parmentier à l'accompagner en excursion à Versailles. Ce n'est pas très loin de Paris et ils sont arrivés sans aucune difficulté. En route pour le palais, M. Davis a eu une idée lumineuse.

— Mangeons sur l'herbe[1] dans le grand parc au bord du lac. On m'a dit que c'est permis.

— Merveilleux! Allons-y.

Ils sont entrés dans une épicerie[2] pour acheter du jambon, un camembert et une bouteille de vin rouge. Dans une boulangerie à côté, ils ont acheté trois baguettes[3] et trois éclairs.

— Moi, j'ai un appétit de loup, a dit l'aîné en sortant de la boulangerie.

— Allons manger tout de suite, a dit M. Davis. Mais que faire pour les ustensiles?

— Voyons ce qu'il y a dans nos poches, a dit le cadet.[4] Les deux garçons ont trouvé quatre couteaux; un tout neuf, deux passables, et le dernier dans un état[5] lamentable.

— Voilà! Et nous boirons à la bouteille.[6]

Ils sont entrés dans le parc du palais par la grande grille, mais au lieu de faire la visite ils ont traversé l'immense jardin.

Le jardin avec ses statues, ses jets d'eau et ses bosquets[7] a fait une forte impression sur M. Davis. Les deux garçons étaient d'accord: — Je vous assure que le jardin est le bijou de Versailles, a dit le cadet. Mais le palais nous ennuie[8] à mourir.

M. Davis a répondu en riant: — Nous ne sommes pas forcés d'y aller.

Arrivés au lac ils se sont assis sur l'herbe pour manger. Ils ont causé de choses et d'autres en mangeant, et M. Davis a été frappé[9] encore une fois par leur intelligence. Les garçons ont mangé comme deux loups et ils se sont amusés énormément.

Tous les trois se souviendront[10] longtemps de cette excursion à Versailles.

NOTE 1. grass.
2. grocer's.
3. long loaf.
4. the younger one.
5. state.
6. from the bottle.
7. groves of trees.
8. **ennuyer,** to bore; **ça m'ennuie,** it bores me.
9. struck.
10. will remember; **se souvenir de,** to remember.

Exercise No. 194—Lecture 2
L'avenue de l'Opéra

Nous nous promenons[1] sur l'avenue de l'Opéra. C'est une belle avenue large qui mène du jardin des Tuileries à l'Opéra.

Il y a beaucoup de monde sur l'avenue. Tous les touristes s'y rencontrent.[2] Les trottoirs[3] sont bordés de boutiques de luxe[4] où on peut acheter toutes sortes de belles choses, si on a de l'argent: des bijoux,[5] de la lingerie fine, des gants, de la céramique, des blouses, des articles de cuir, et aussi des livres, car nous sommes en France où on aime lire. Il y a même une petite librairie à l'Opéra, au deuxième étage.

Il y a aussi un café-restaurant bien connu: La Brasserie Universelle. Allons-y prendre un bock,[6] voulez-vous? Avec plaisir.

NOTE 1. We are strolling. **se promener,** to go for a walk, to stroll.
2. meet there.
3. pavements.
4. luxury shops.
5. jewellery.
6. a beer.

CHAPITRE 37 (TRENTE-SEPT)

In Chapters 37–40 there is no parallel translation of the texts. However, the new words and expressions that appear are given in the vocabularies which follow each text. There is also the French–English vocabulary in the Appendix to which you can refer for words you may have forgotten.

You should therefore have no difficulty in reading and understanding the texts. As a means of testing your understanding, a series of English questions to be answered in English are given under the heading 'Test of Reading Comprehension', instead of the usual French Questionnaire. You can check your answers in the 'Answers' Section of the Appendix.

LA GRAND-RUE DU VILLAGE

Cher ami,

J'ai remarqué que, malgré la différence qui existe entre les villages français ils ont tous une grand-rue qui mène à une place entourée d'arbres.

Derrière les arbres, les boutiques du village sont rangées bien en ordre. La teinturerie est souvent peinte en violet. La vitrine de la boulangerie-pâtisserie à côté est remplie de gâteaux délicieux. Le boucher du coin a pendu ses gigots élégants en plein air. Quelques mouches s'y promènent tranquillement, mais personne n'y prête attention.

Dans la vitrine de l'épicerie on voit un tas de boîtes de sardines, et quand on passe on sent une forte odeur de café. La blanchisseuse est une artiste. Elle arrange sa vitrine avec des papiers bleus, roses et violets pour encadrer une blouse blanche. La laiterie est toujours comble.

Sur la place, à peu près au milieu du village, il y a la mairie d'un côté et l'église de l'autre. Au fond de la place se trouve l'école. Quelquefois on entend des rires, des chansons, mais en général le silence règne. Les enfants sont sages en France.

L'aspect de la rue change à toute heure. Pour ne rien manquer du spectacle je me lève de bonne heure. La matinée est grise. Toutes les fenêtres et tous les volets sont fermés. On dort. J'entends un coq. Puis un autre. Les chiens réveillés commencent à se saluer. Tout le monde se réveille. On ouvre les volets, on ouvre les fenêtres.

Voilà un garçon, le premier, qu'on envoie chercher du pain. Il se précipite dans la rue, court à une vitesse vertigineuse, et s'arrête soudain au coin pour examiner quelque chose qui attire son attention. Ensuite il reprend sa route au pas militaire. En voilà un autre. Et encore un. Ce que les Français mangent comme pain! Notre héros, le premier, revient avec un pain presque aussi long que lui, qu'il fait tourner comme une canne.

Il n'est que sept heures et demie. Je dois tout de même vous quitter, car j'ai rendez-vous avec les jeunes Parmentier pour faire une excursion à Chartres.

Je vous quitte en vous serrant la main, jusqu'à ma prochaine lettre dans laquelle je vous décrirai nos aventures de cet après-midi.

Votre ami,
Jean Davis

219

Vocabulaire

la canne, cane, walking-stick	**reprendre,** to take again
la chanson, song	**se réveiller,** to wake up
le coq (kɔk), cock	**comble,** crowded
une église, church	**entouré (de),** surrounded by
le gigot (ʒi-go), leg of lamb	**peint,** painted
la mairie, town hall	**rangé,** arranged
la mouche, fly	**réveillé,** awakened
le tableau, picture, painting	**sage,** well-behaved
le volet, shutter	**soudain,** suddenly
la vitrine, shop window	**en plein air,** in the open air
régner (rɛ-ɲe), to reign	**au milieu (de),** in the middle of
pendre, to hang	**pour ne rien manquer,** in order to miss
se précipiter, to hurl oneself, rush	nothing

Boutiques et marchands   Shops and Shopkeepers

la blanchisseuse, laundress	**la couturière,** dressmaker
la blanchisserie, laundry	**un épicier, une épicière,** grocer
le boucher, la bouchère, butcher	**une épicerie,** grocer's shop
la boucherie, butcher's shop	**la laiterie,** dairy
le boulanger, la boulangère, baker	**le laverie,** launderette
la boulangerie, baker's shop	**un marchand de nouveautés,** draper
le bureau de tabac, tobacco shop	**la papeterie,** stationer's
la confiserie, sweet shop	**la pâtisserie,** pastry shop, pastry
le cordonnier, la cordonnière	**la pharmacie,** chemist's shop
shoemaker	**le tailleur,** tailor
le couturier, dress designer	**la teinturerie,** cleaners and dyers

Exercise No. 195—Test of Reading Comprehension

Answer these questions fully in English:

1 What has Mr. Davis noticed?
2 Where does the street often lead to?
3 What is behind the trees?
4 What shop is often painted purple?
5 Where can one see delicious cakes? A heap of sardines? A white blouse which looks like a painting?
6 Where are the flies peacefully walking about?
7 What three buildings are on the square?
8 How do the children behave in France?
9 Why does Mr. Davis get up early?
10 What does he hear first?
11 Who rushes into the street?
12 Why does he suddenly stop?
13 With what does our hero return?
14 Why must Mr. Davis stop writing?
15 What will he describe in his next letter?

Exercise No. 196—Completion of Text

1 **La rue mène** (to a square surrounded by trees).
2 **Les boutiques du village sont** (well arranged).

3 **La teinturerie** (is painted) **en violet.**
4 **La vitrine de la pâtisserie** (is filled with delicious cakes).
5 **Le boucher** (has hung his legs of lamb) **en plein air.**
6 **Quelques mouches** (are walking on them) **tranquillement.**
7 (In the middle of the village) **il y a la mairie.**
8 **Parfois on entend** (laughter and songs).
9 (In order not to miss anything of the spectacle) **je me lève de bonne heure.**
10 People are sleeping.
11 **Les chiens réveillés commencent** (to greet each other).
12 **Tout le monde** (wakes up).
13 (What the French eat) **comme pain!**
14 **Notre héros** (returns with a loaf of bread).
15 (I must nevertheless) **vous quitter.**

Grammar Notes

1 Summary of Single Object Pronouns.

You have learned:

(*a*) The direct object and indirect object pronouns.

Direct Object		Indirect Object	
me, me	**nous,** us	**me,** (to) me	**nous,** (to) us
te, you (*fam.*)	**vous,** you	**te,** (to) you	**vous,** (to) you
le, him, it (*m*)	**les,** them	**lui** {(to) him (to) her	**leur,** (to) them
la, her, it (*f*)			

Reflexives (*Direct and Indirect Objects*)

me, myself	**nous,** ourselves
te, yourself	**vous,** yourself, yourselves
se {himself, herself itself, oneself	**se,** themselves

(*b*) The use of the partitive pronoun **en,** some, any, none, not any, of it, of them. Some, any, etc., are often omitted in English, but **en** is never omitted in French.

Avez-vous du beurre?   Have you any butter?
J'en ai une livre.   I have a pound (of it).
A-t-elle acheté des œufs?   Has she bought some eggs?
Elle en a acheté une douzaine.   She has bought a dozen (of them).

(*c*) The use of **y** to refer to a place already mentioned.

Combien de temps restera-t-il à Paris?   How long will he stay in Paris?
Il y restera trois semaines.   He will stay there three weeks.

(*d*) Object pronouns precede the verb except in the affirmative imperative.

Avez-vous acheté les tableaux?   Have you bought the paintings?
Je ne les ai pas achetés.   I have not bought them.
Achetez-les. Ne les achetez pas.   Buy them. Do not buy them.

2 Two Object Pronouns.

When a verb has two object pronouns their arrangement is as follows:

(*a*) If there are two pronoun objects of different persons—**me, te, nous, vous** (first and second persons) precede **le, la, l', les** (third person).

M'enverrez-vous les billets?　Will you send me the tickets?
Nous *vous les* enverrons demain.　We shall send *them to you* tomorrow.

(*b*) If there are two pronoun objects of the third person, the direct object (**le, la, l'**, or **les**) precedes the indirect object (**lui** or **leur**).

Avez-vous prêté votre crayon à Jean?　Did you lend your pencil to John?
Oui. Je *le lui* ai prêté.　Yes. I lent *it to him.*

(*c*) When **y** or **en** are used with another object pronoun, either one follows that object pronoun.

A-t-elle mis les tasses sur le buffet?　Has she put the cups on the buffet?
Elle *les y* a mises.　She has put *them there.*

(*d*) If **y** and **en** both appear, **y** precedes **en**.

This combination is rarely seen except with **il y a**, there is, are.
Combien de chaises y a-t-il dans le salon?　How many chairs are there in the parlour?
Il y *en a* six.　There are six (*of them*).

(*e*) In the affirmative imperative the order of two object pronouns is exactly as in English.

Donnez-*les-moi*.[1] Envoyez-*m'en*.　Give *them to me.* Send me *some* (*of it*).

NOTE 1. **moi** and **toi** are used for **me** and **te** in the affirmative imperative except before **en** when the contraction **m'en** and **t'en** are used.

Exercise No. 197 Translate the following sentences. Practise them aloud. They will give you a 'feeling' for the double object pronoun. Remember, however, that in ordinary conversation a simple *yes* or *no* answer will often serve, or an answer with only one pronoun object. Thus, in Question No. 1 the answer might be:

Oui, or, **Oui, nous l'avons envoyée.** **Non**, *or*, **Non, nous ne l'avons pas envoyée.**

1 **Est-ce que vous avez envoyé la poterie à M. Davis?**
　Oui, nous la lui avons envoyée.
2 **Est-ce que beaucoup de gens se rencontrent sur l'avenue de l'Opéra?**
　Tous les touristes s'y rencontrent.
3 **Envoyez-moi les journaux français s'il vous plaît.**
　Nous vous les enverrons demain.
4 **Est-ce que le garçon vous a donné l'addition?**
　Il ne me l'a pas encore donnée.
5 **Avez-vous demandé les billets à l'employé?**
　Je ne les lui ai pas encore demandés parce qu'il est très occupé.
6 **Combien de plats y a-t-il dans cette caisse?**
　Il y en a vingt-cinq douzaines.

7 Lui avez-vous rendu l'argent que vous lui avez emprunté (borrowed)?

Je le lui rendrai ce soir.

8 La bonne a-t-elle mis sur le bureau la porcelaine que M. Davis vient de recevoir de Limoges?

Elle l'y a mise.

9 Me prêterez-vous votre parapluie?

Je vous le prêterai; mais rendez-le-moi demain, s'il vous plaît.

Merci beaucoup. Je vous le rendrai demain.

10 Montrez-moi, s'il vous plaît, la nouvelle robe que vous avez achetée.

Je ne peux pas vous la montrer parce qu'elle n'est pas encore arrivée du magasin.

CHAPITRE 38 (TRENTE-HUIT)

UNE EXCURSION À CHARTRES

Cher ami,

Mes jeunes amis sont venus me chercher de bonne heure car j'ai voulu revenir à temps pour aller à l'Opéra le soir. Ils avaient préparé (*they had prepared*) un bon déjeuner qu'on avait l'intention de faire en route sur l'herbe, comme à Versailles. Mais cette fois-ci ils avaient apporté (*they had brought*) un beau panier rempli d'une nappe, de serviettes, de couteaux, de fourchettes, et aussi d'un poulet.

La voiture que j'avais louée (*I had hired*) nous attendait en bas. Nous y sommes montés tout en parlant et en riant, et nous voilà en route.

Je conduisais à mon aise, quand tout à coup j'ai entendu un bruit que j'ai reconnu tout de suite. — Qu'est-ce que c'est? ont demandé les garçons.

J'ai stoppé et nous sommes descendus. — Nous avons crevé un pneu, ai-je répondu.

J'ai voulu changer le pneu et les jeunes gens voulaient m'aider. Très heureux ils ont commencé à chercher le cric. Mais, malheur! Il n'y avait pas de cric dans l'outillage. Que faire?

De temps en temps une auto passait à toute vitesse. Malgré nos signaux désespérés personne ne s'est arrêté. Il était presque midi et le soleil donnait à plomb sur nos têtes. Nous nous sommes assis sous un arbre près de la route pour attendre notre destin.

Bientôt un gros camion s'est approché rapidement et il s'est arrêté court devant nous avec un grand bruit de freins. Le camionneur est descendu.

— Vous êtes à plat? Voulez-vous un coup de main? Ce grand gaillard avait une voix très douce. Il souriait.

— Nous n'avons pas de cric, lui ai-je dit.

— Mais c'est un désastre, m'a-t-il répondu, en cherchant le sien (*his*).

— En tout cas nous avons un pneu de rechange.

— C'est toujours ça! Tout le monde s'est mis à la besogne. En cinq secondes tout était prêt.

Je n'osais pas lui offrir un pourboire. Il avait tant de dignité naturelle. Mais les deux garçons ont eu une idée lumineuse: — Voulez-vous bien déjeuner avec nous? Nous avons un poulet énorme.

— Très volontiers, a répondu le camionneur. A condition que j'ajoute mon jambon et ma bouteille de vin. Nous nous sommes assis sous notre arbre et nous avons déjeuné gaiement de bon appétit.

— Le jambon est délicieux, avons-nous dit avec enthousiasme.

Il a souri: — Ma femme me soigne bien.[1]

Le déjeuner fini, nous avons tous fait nos adieux. Le gros camion est parti pour Paris et nous avons repris la route de Chartres.

Et voilà qu'encore une fois je n'ai pas le temps de vous décrire mes impressions, car ce soir je vais à l'Opéra et je dois m'habiller.

Bien cordialement à vous,
Jean Davis

NOTE 1. **soigner quelqu'un,** to look after, to nurse someone.

Vocabulaire

A. **le camion,** lorry
   le camionneur, lorry driver
   le désastre, disaster
   le coup de main, a helping hand
   le destin, fate
   le gaillard, jovial fellow
   le malheur, misfortune
   le panier, basket
   la nappe, table cloth
   la serviette, napkin
   le son, sound

B. **une automobile (la voiture),** car
   une autoroute, motorway
   le cric (krik), jack
   le dépôt d'essence, petrol station
   les freins, brakes
   le pneu, tyre
   le pneu de rechange, spare tyre
   le permis de conduire, driving
     licence
   un outillage, tool kit
   le volant, steering wheel

ajouter, to add, join
couper, to cut
louer, to rent, let, book, hire
oser, to dare
soigner, to look after
court, short
désespéré, desperate
gros (grosse *f*), big, fat
au-dessous (de), underneath
en bas, below, downstairs

changer l'huile, to change the oil
conduire, to drive, to conduct
être à plat, to have a puncture
crever un pneu, to burst (puncture) a
   tyre
faire le plein d'essence, to fill up the
   tank
stationner, to park
stopper, to stop
vérifier, to check

Locutions françaises

1 **qu'est-ce qui est arrivé?** what has happened?
2 **crever un pneu,** to get a puncture
3 **le soleil donnait à plomb,** the sun was shining directly
4 **être à plat,** to have a flat tyre
5 **c'est toujours ça,** that's all to the good
6 **se mettre à la besogne,** to set to work
7 **et voilà qu'encore une fois,** and so it is that once more

Exercise No. 198—Test of Reading Comprehension

1 Why did Mr. Davis' young friends call for him early?
2 What had they prepared?
3 Where was the car that Mr. Davis had rented?
4 What did he hear all of a sudden?
5 What had happened?
6 What did the young men want to do?
7 Why could they not change the tyre?
8 What did the lorry driver who came along soon offer to do?
9 Why didn't Mr. Davis dare to offer him a tip?
10 What brilliant idea did the boys have?

11 What did they eat and drink for lunch?
12 What did the boys say about the lorry driver's ham?
13 What did the lorry driver say about his wife?
14 What did they do after lunch?
15 Why, once again, doesn't Mr. Davis have time to describe his impressions of Chartres?

Exercise No. 199—Completion of Text

1 **Mes amis sont venus** (to get me).
2 (They had prepared) **un bon déjeuner.**
3 A tablecloth, some napkins, some knives, some forks
4 (And there we were) **en route.**
5 (All of a sudden) **j'ai entendu un bruit.**
6 We have a puncture.
7 (There was no jack) **dans l'outillage.**
8 (Nobody) **s'est arrêté.**
9 (We sat down) **sous un arbre.**
10 (Soon a large lorry) **s'est approché rapidement.**
11 **Voulez-vous** (a helping hand)?
12 (At any rate) **nous avons un pneu de rechange.**
13 **Tout le monde** (set to work).
14 **Je n'osais pas** (to offer him a tip).
15 **Voulez-vous bien** (to have lunch with us)?

Grammar Notes

1 The Past Perfect. What *had happened.* Model Verbs, **parler, finir, vendre.**

j'avais parlé (fini, vendu)	I had spoken (finished, sold)
tu avais parlé (fini, vendu)	you had spoken (finished, sold)
il avait parlé (fini, vendu)	he had spoken (finished, sold)
elle avait parlé (fini, vendu)	she had spoken (finished, sold)
nous avions parlé (fini, vendu)	we had spoken (finished, sold)
vous aviez parlé (fini, vendu)	you had spoken (finished, sold)
ils avaient parlé (fini, vendu)	they had spoken (finished, sold)
elles avaient parlé (fini, vendu)	they had spoken (finished, sold)
avait-il parlé (fini, vendu)?	had he spoken (finished, sold)?
il n'avait pas parlé (fini, vendu)	he had not spoken (finished, sold)
n'avait-il pas parlé (fini, vendu)?	had he not spoken (finished, sold)?

As in English the past perfect tense is usually formed by the auxiliary verb **j'avais**, etc. (*I had, etc.*) plus the past participle of the verb.

Exercise No. 200 Change these sentences from the conversational past to the past perfect. Translate each sentence in the past perfect.

Exemple 1. Il avait appris les règles essentielles.
He had learned the essential rules.

1 **Il a appris les règles essentielles.**
2 **Nous avons vraiment travaillé dur.**
3 **Ils n'ont pas encore obtenu leurs billets.**
4 **A-t-il écrit une lettre à son ami?**
5 **Qui a promis de le rencontrer à l'aéroport?**

6 J'ai oublié mon parapluie.
7 Ont-ils réservé une chambre pour M. Davis?
8 Avez-vous lu beaucoup de guides?
9 Ses jeunes amis ont préparé un bon déjeuner.
10 N'a-t-il pas loué une voiture?

2 The Past Perfect of être-verbs. Model verb **aller**.

I had gone, you had gone, etc.

j'étais allé (allée)	nous étions allés (allées)
tu étais allé (allée)—	vous étiez allé(s), allée(s)
il était allé	ils étaient allés
elle était allée	elles étaient allées

être-verbs in the past perfect take the auxiliary **j'étais**, etc., instead of **j'avais**, etc. **J'étais**, etc., is the imperfect of **être**, to be. As an auxiliary verb it is translated *I had*, etc., not *I was*, etc.

Reflexive verbs also take the auxiliary **j'étais**, etc., in the past perfect.

Conversational Past. **Un bel homme s'est approché.** A handsome man approached.

Past Perfect. **Un bel homme s'était approché.** A handsome man had approached.

Exercise No. 201 Change these sentences from the conversational past to the past perfect. Translate each sentence in the past perfect.

Exemple 1. Mes jeunes amis étaient venus me chercher.
My young friends had come to get me.

1 Mes jeunes amis sont venus me chercher.
2 Un gros camion s'est approché rapidement.
3 Nous nous sommes assis sous un grand arbre.
4 Je suis allé à la salle d'attente.
5 Nous ne sommes pas sortis ensemble.
6 Ils sont arrivés sains et saufs.
7 Le taxi s'est arrêté devant l'hôtel.
8 Êtes-vous allé à la douane?
9 Nous nous sommes dit au revoir.
10 Elles ne sont pas restées quinze jours à Paris.

3 The Possessive Pronouns **le mien**, mine, etc.

(a) In French, as in English, there are possessive adjectives and possessive pronouns. The possessive adjectives (**mon, ton, son,** etc.) are very important and useful words. You have learned and used them a great deal. The possessive pronouns are used rather less frequently. Study the following examples:

Possessive Adjectives	*Possessive Pronouns*
Son père (his or her father) est docteur.	Le mien (mine) est avocat.
Sa sœur (his or her sister) est petite.	La mienne (mine) est grande.
Ses livres (his or her books) sont neufs.	Les miens (mine) sont vieux.
Ses recettes (his or her recipes) sont bonnes.	Les miennes (mine) sont mauvaises.

The possessive pronoun agrees in number and gender with the noun for which it stands. The complete table of possessive pronouns follows:

Singular			Plural	
Masc.	**Fem.**		**Masc.**	**Fem.**
le mien	la mienne	(mine)	les miens	les miennes
le tien	la tienne	(yours)	les tiens	les tiennes
le sien	la sienne	(his, hers)	les siens	les siennes
le nôtre	la nôtre	(ours)	les nôtres (noːtr)	les nôtres
le vôtre	la vôtre	(yours)	les vôtres (voːtr)	les vôtres
le leur	la leur	(theirs)	les leurs	les leurs

(a) After the verb **être, à** + an independent pronoun is generally used instead of the possessive pronoun:

> **Cette montre est à moi (à toi, à lui, à elle).**   This watch is mine (yours, his, hers).
> **Ces places sont à nous (à vous, à eux, à elles).**   These seats are ours (yours, theirs (*m*), theirs (*f*).

Exercise No. 202 Translate these sentences. Practise them aloud.

1 Nous avons de bons professeurs. Comment trouvez-vous les vôtres?
2 Allons à la poste dans votre voiture. La nôtre a crevé un pneu.
3 Prêtez-moi votre stylo, s'il vous plaît. Le mien n'écrit pas.
4 J'ai oublié mon parapluie. Voulez-vous me prêter le vôtre?
5 Vous n'avez pas de cric. Voulez-vous emprunter (borrow) le mien?
6 La bicyclette de Louis coûte plus cher que la mienne, mais la mienne est meilleure que la sienne.
7 Jeanne et moi nous avons acheté des billets de théâtre hier. J'ai les miens, mais elle a perdu les siens malheureusement.
8 Voici nos chapeaux. Celui-ci est à moi. Celui-là est à vous.

CHAPITRE 39 (TRENTE-NEUF)

M. DAVIS ACHÈTE UN BILLET DE LOTERIE

Cher ami,

Je ne suis pas joueur, M. Picard. C'est-à-dire que jusqu'à la semaine dernière je n'avais jamais été joueur.

Ce qui est arrivé? Je vais tout vous raconter.

Comme vous le savez il y a des kiosques où l'on vend des billets de loterie partout à Paris.

Quand je suis arrivé à Paris j'ai remarqué tout de suite qu'on s'occupait beaucoup de la Loterie Nationale. Je voyais des affiches illustrées dans le métro, dans les autobus, dans les rues, enfin un peu partout. Quand (*Whenever*) je voyais une de ces affiches je commençais à rêver: — Si je gagnais le premier prix, le gros lot, j'aurais (*would have*) assez d'argent pour voyager partout en Europe l'année prochaine. Ma femme m'accompagnerait (*would accompany me*) et les enfants iraient (*would go*) à l'école quelque part en France pour apprendre le français. Ma femme pourrait (*would be able*) faire la connaissance des Parmentier et nous pourrions (*could*) peut-être faire un voyage ensemble tous les quatre.

Je pourrais (*would be able*) acheter beaucoup de belles choses. J'achèterais (*would buy*) des objets d'art, non pas pour les vendre, mais pour les garder chez moi. Je serais (*would be*) l'homme le plus heureux du monde.

C'est ainsi que je rêvais.

Mercredi dernier je descendais la rue de Rivoli. Au coin de la rue Cambon j'ai vu un de ces petits kiosques. La jeune fille qui était de service m'a vu regarder l'annonce 'Loterie Nationale'. Elle m'a dit:

— Monsieur, achetez ce billet. C'est le bon. Il vous portera bonheur.

— Comment savez-vous que celui-là est le bon?

— Parce qu'il a trois zéros. Regardez.

J'ai regardé et en effet le numéro finissait par trois zéros. Je me suis dit: — Celui-là, il sort de l'ordinaire. Allons-y!

Et voilà comment je suis devenu joueur!

Le lendemain, je me suis levé de bonne heure, j'ai sonné tout de suite pour demander mon café, mes croissants et mon journal. Ils sont arrivés tous à la fois, mais à ce moment-là je ne m'intéressais qu'au journal. Je l'ai vite ouvert, le cœur battant. Mais où est-ce qu'on les a cachés, ces numéros? Ah, les voilà! Qu'est-ce que je vois? Le numéro qui a gagné le gros lot finit par trois zéros: 26 000. Je ne respire plus. Je cherche mon billet, en faisant des voyages dans la lune. Enfin je le trouve. Je peux à peine le tenir. Voilà les trois zéros. Voilà le deux. Mais, malheur! C'est un cinq, pas un six. Tant pis! Et j'ai pris mon petit déjeuner en riant de moi-même.

J'ai décidé que les émotions d'un joueur ne sont pas pour moi. J'aime la vie tranquille comme je vous l'ai dit à Londres.

—Très cordialement, votre ami,

Jean Davis

Vocabulaire

une **affiche**, poster
une **annonce**, advertisement
le **bonheur**, happiness
le **cœur**, heart
le **croissant**, roll (crescent shaped)
le **gros lot**, first prize
la **lune**, moon
le **joueur**, gambler
le **métro**, underground, tube

le **kiosque**, stall
battre, to beat
cacher, to hide, conceal
gagner, to win, gain, earn
s'occuper (de), to be busy with
respirer, to breathe
rêver, to dream
rire (de), to laugh at

Locutions françaises

1 **être de service**, to be on duty
2 **il sort de l'ordinaire**, it is something out of the ordinary
3 **allons-y**, let's go, let's take it
4 **tant pis**, so much the worse
5 **à peine**, scarcely
6 **quelque part**, somewhere

Exercise No. 203—Test of Reading Comprehension

1 What kind of man had Mr. Davis never been?
2 What had he noticed right away when he came to France?
3 When he saw one of the illustrated posters what did he dream of doing?
4 If he won the first prize for what would he have sufficient money?
5 What would his wife do?
6 What would the children do?
7 From whom did Mr. Davis buy a lottery ticket, whose number ended in three zeros?
8 What did he ring for the next morning?
9 What was the only thing that interested him at the moment?
10 What happened when he saw that the winning number had three zeros?
11 What was he doing mentally while he looked for his ticket?
12 What number did Mr. Davis have?
13 What number won the prize?
14 What did Mr. Davis decide?
15 What sort of life does he like?

Exercise No. 204—Completion of Text

1 (I had never been) **joueur**.
2 **Il y a** (lottery ticket stalls) **partout à Paris**.
3 **J'ai remarqué tout de suite** (that people were very much taken up with) **la Loterie Nationale**.
4 (I saw illustrated posters) **dans le métro**.
5 (If I won the first prize) **j'aurais assez d'argent pour voyager partout en Europe**.
6 (I would be able to buy) **beaucoup de belles choses**.
7 **Je serais** (the happiest man in the world).
8 (And that is how) **je suis devenu joueur**.
9 **Je me suis levé** (early).
10 **À ce moment** (I was interested only in the newspaper).

11 (I look for) **mon billet.**
12 **Je peux** (scarcely hold it).
13 **Mais malheur!** (It's a five, not a six).
14 **J'ai pris mon petit déjeuner** (laughing at myself).

Grammar Notes

1 The Present Conditional. What *would happen.* Model Verbs **parler, finir, vendre.**

The present conditional may be called the *would* tense. Its use in French is much the same as in English.

je parlerais (finirais, vendrais)	I should, would speak (finish, sell)
tu parlerais (finirais, vendrais)	you would speak (finish, sell)
il parlerait (finirait, vendrait)	he would speak (finish, sell)
elle parlerait (finirait, vendrait)	she would speak (finish, sell)
nous parlerions (finirions, vendrions)	we should, would speak (finish, sell)
vous parleriez (finiriez, vendriez)	you would speak (finish, sell)
ils parleraient (finiraient, vendraient)	they (*m*) would speak (finish, sell)
elles parleraient (finiraient, vendraient)	they (*f*) would speak (finish, sell)

(*a*) The personal endings of the present conditional of all verbs are **-ais, -ais, -ait; -ions, -iez, -aient.** They are exactly like the endings of the imperfect tense. (See Chapter 35, p. 206, Grammar Notes No. 1.)

(*b*) To form the present conditional, add the conditional endings to the *infinitive* as a base. If the *infinitive* ends in **-re**, as in **vendre**, drop the final **e** before adding the conditional endings.

Thus the base for the present conditional is the same as the base for the future.

Infinitive to	*Future* I shall, will, you will, etc.	*Present Conditional* I should, would, you would, etc.
parler	**je parlerai, tu parleras, etc.**	**je parlerais, tu parlerais, etc.**
finir	**je finirai, tu finiras, etc.**	**je finirais, tu finirais, etc.**
vendre	**je vendrai, tu vendras, etc.**	**je vendrais, tu vendrais, etc.**

2 The Irregular Present Conditional

Those verbs that have an irregular base for the future have the same irregular base for the conditional.

Infinitive to	*Future* shall, will	*Pres. Cond.* should would	*Infinitive* to	*Future* shall, will	*Pres. Cond.* should, would
avoir	**j'aurai**	**j'aurais**	**pouvoir**	**je pourrai**	**je pourrais**
être	**je serai**	**je serais**	**devoir**	**je devrai**	**je devrais**
aller	**j'irai**	**j'irais**	**recevoir**	**je recevrai**	**je recevrais**
envoyer	**j'enverrai**	**j'enverrais**	**vouloir**	**je voudrai**	**je voudrais**
venir	**je viendrai**	**je viendrais**	**valoir**	**je vaudrai**	**je vaudrais**
tenir	**je tiendrai**	**je tiendrais**	**voir**	**je verrai**	**je verrais**
courir	**je courrai**	**je courrais**	**savoir**	**je saurai**	**je saurais**
faire	**je ferai**	**je ferais**	**falloir**	**il faudra**	**il faudrait**

Exercise No. 205 Change these sentences from the future to the present conditional. Translate each sentence in the present conditional.

Exemple 1. Je voyagerais partout en Europe.
I would travel everywhere in Europe.

1 Je voyagerai partout en Europe.
2 Il visitera la France et l'Italie.
3 Nous apprendrons le français.
4 Ma famille ne m'accompagnera pas.
5 Elle pourra acheter beaucoup de belles choses.
6 Aura-t-il assez d'argent?
7 Ils achèteront des objets d'art.
8 Serez-vous content de rester ici?
9 Elle ne vous connaîtra pas.
10 Ils ne feront pas leurs devoirs.
11 Je vous enverrai les revues.
12 Ils ne viendront pas la semaine prochaine.

CHAPITRE 40 (QUARANTE)

M. DAVIS S'EN VA

Cher ami,

Quand je suis parti de Londres j'étais assez bien renseigné sur la France. J'avais lu quelques livres sur son histoire et sur les coutumes du pays. Je savais parler français passablement.

Maintenant que je suis sur le point de partir de France il me semble que je parle avec beaucoup plus de facilité. J'ai visité beaucoup de ces endroits dont nous avons parlé dans nos conversations. Dans mes lettres je ne pouvais décrire que très peu de chose de tout ce que j'ai vu et appris. Le reste, je dois le laisser pour notre prochaine rencontre.

J'aime tant de choses en France: Paris, les monuments historiques, les paysages, la peinture, et la cuisine. Mais j'aime surtout les Français. J'aime leur sentiment marqué de la dignité de l'homme, leur sens vif du comique, leur politesse et leur passion pour la discussion.

La vie à Paris ressemble à celle de Londres, malgré mes premières impressions dans le taxi qui me conduisait à une vitesse vertigineuse de l'aéroport à l'hôtel.

Comme vous le savez, c'était un voyage d'agrément aussi bien qu'un voyage d'affaires. Heureusement, j'ai bientôt terminé mes affaires et j'ai pu me consacrer entièrement aux distractions.

Je n'ai pas eu le temps d'aller au Maroc ni en Corse. Dommage! Mais j'ai préféré passer mon temps à mieux connaître la France. Il y a tant à voir, à faire et à apprendre. Tout m'a enchanté.

J'aurai beaucoup à vous dire au sujet des personnes que j'ai rencontrées, des endroits que j'ai visités, et de tout ce que j'ai appris sur les coutumes, la vie, la langue, et les arts de la France.

Je reviendrai certainement en France. Je voudrais revenir l'année prochaine. Mais cette fois-ci toute la famille m'accompagnerait. Je suis sûr que je pourrais faire le guide sans difficulté. Je n'ai pas gagné le gros lot à la Loterie, mais je reviendrai tout de même.

Ceci est la dernière lettre que je vous écris avant de partir pour Londres le premier août. Je me ferai le plaisir de vous téléphoner dès mon arrivée pour vous inviter à dîner en famille.

Nous passerons sans doute des heures à parler de la France et de notre Paris bien-aimé.

À bientôt,
Votre ami,
Jean Davis

Vocabulaire

le comique, comic(al)	le sens, sense
la facilité, facility	s'en aller, to go away
la marque, mark, symbol, brand	conduire, to drive

le reste, remainder, rest
la rencontre, meeting

renseigné, informed
dès, as early as, from

Locutions françaises

1 je m'en vais, I go away, I am
going away, etc.
tu t'en vas, you go away
il, elle s'en va, he, she goes away
nous nous en allons, we go away
vous vous en allez, you go away
ils, elles s'en vont, they go away
2 être sur le point de partir, to be
about to leave

3 tant à voir, so much to see
4 faire le guide, to act as guide
5 dès mon arrivée, immediately on my
arrival
6 combien de choses, how many things
7 beaucoup de choses, many things
8 tant de choses, so many things

Exercise No. 206—Test of Reading Comprehension

1 Before leaving for France, how had Mr. Davis obtained knowledge of that
country?
2 How much was he able to describe in his letters?
3 What does he like best in France?
4 What does he like about the French people?
5 How does he compare life in Paris with life in London?
6 When did he get a different impression?
7 Why did he not go to Morocco or Corsica?
8 Who would accompany him on his next trip to France?
9 What is he sure of?
10 When is he leaving for London?
11 What will he be glad to do immediately on his arrival home?
12 What does he think he and Mr. Picard will do when they are together
again?

Grammar Notes

1 The Past Conditional. What *would have happened*, parler, aller

I should, would have spoken
you would have spoken, etc.

I should, would have gone
you would have gone, etc.

j'aurais parlé	nous aurions parlé	je serais allé(e)	nous serions allés(es)
tu aurais parlé	vous auriez parlé	tu serais allé(e)	vous seriez allé(e, s, es)
il aurait parlé	ils auraient parlé	il serait allé	ils seraient allés
elle aurait parlé	elles auraient parlé	elle serait allée	elles seraient allées

The past conditional is formed by the auxiliary j'aurais, etc., plus the past
participle, for all avoir-verbs; and by the auxiliary je serais, etc., plus the past
participle, for all être-verbs (including reflexive verbs).

2 Conditional Sentences. si (*if*)-clauses

A conditional sentence is one that includes a si (*if*)-clause. Compare the
tenses of the verbs used in the following French conditional sentences with
those used in the corresponding English sentences:

1 Si je le vois, je lui parlerai.

1 If I see (shall see) him I shall speak
to him.

2 **S'il gagne le prix, il ira en Europe.**

3 **Si je le voyais, je lui parlerais.**

4 **S'il gagnait le prix, il irait en Europe.**

5 **Si je l'avais vu, je lui aurais parlé.**

6 **S'il avait gagné le prix, il serait allé en Europe.**

2 If he wins (will win) the prize he will go to Europe.

3 If I saw (should see, were to see) him I would speak to him.

4 If he won (should win, were to win) the prize he would go to Europe.

5 If I had seen him I would have spoken to him.

6 If he had won the prize he would have gone to Europe.

In general, the tenses of conditional sentences in French are the same as the tenses in the corresponding English conditional sentences. Note, however, these differences:

French never uses a future tense in the si-clause. See sentences 1, 2.

French uses the imperfect tense in the si-clause where English uses the past or *should* or *were to*. See sentences 3, 4.

3 Si (*whether*)

When si means *whether*, it is followed by the same tenses as in English.

Je ne sais pas s'il fera un voyage en Europe l'été prochain. I don't know whether he will take a trip to Europe next summer.

Exercise No. 207 Practise the French sentences aloud:

1 Si j'ai le temps, je vous accompagnerai jusqu'à la gare.
2 Si vous la voyez, faites-lui mes amitiés.
3 Si vous revenez à Paris, j'espère avoir le plaisir de vous revoir.
4 Si nous pouvons vous aider, nous le ferons.
5 Si les affaires ne retiennent pas M. Davis à Paris, il visitera la Côte d'Azur.
6 Si nous vivions en France, les enfants iraient à l'école pour apprendre le français.
7 Si vous parliez plus lentement, je vous comprendrais mieux.
8 Seriez-vous surpris, si je vous disais que j'étudie le français?
9 Si j'allais à Paris, je rendrais visite à la famille de M. Parmentier.
10 Si j'avais assez d'argent, je ferais un voyage autour du monde.
11 Ils auraient réussi à l'examen, s'ils avaient travaillé dur.
12 Si elle avait cherché un peu plus longtemps, elle l'aurait trouvé.
13 Nous serions allés au cinéma, si nous avions fini nos devoirs plus tôt.
14 Si M. Davis n'avait pas lu les guides, il n'aurait pas su se tirer d'affaire en France.

1 If I have (shall have) time I shall accompany you as far as the station.
2 If you see her give her my regards.
3 If you return to Paris I hope to meet you again.
4 If we are able to help you we shall do so.
5 If business does not detain Mr. Davis in Paris he will visit the Côte d'Azur.
6 If we were living in France the children would go to school to learn French.
7 If you spoke (were to speak) more slowly, I would understand you better.
8 Would you be surprised if I told you (should tell) that I am studying French?
9 If I were going to Paris I would pay a visit to the family of Mr. Parmentier.

10 If I had enough money I would take a trip around the world.
11 They would have passed (succeeded in) the examination if they had worked hard.
12 If she had looked a little longer she would have found it.
13 We would have gone to the cinema if we had finished our homework sooner.
14 If Mr. Davis had not read the guide book, he would not have known how to get along in France.

RÉVISION 9

CHAPITRES 37–40 PREMIÈRE PARTIE

Révision de mots

NOUNS

1 une annonce	8 une herbe	15 le panier
2 le bijou (Les bijoux *p.*)	9 une huile	16 le reste
3 le bonheur	10 le jambon	17 le sentiment
4 la boutique	11 la lune	18 la serviette
5 le coq	12 le lendemain	19 le son
6 une essence	13 le métro	20 le trottoir
7 une église	14 la nappe	21 la vitrine

1 advertisement	8 grass	15 basket
2 jewel	9 oil	16 remainder
3 happiness	10 ham	17 feeling
4 shop	11 moon	18 napkin, towel
5 cock	12 next day	19 sound
6 petrol	13 underground, tube	20 pavement
7 church	14 tablecloth	21 shop-window

VERBS

1 ajouter	7 il nous ennuie	13 respirer
2 battre	8 gagner	14 réveiller
3 cacher	9 louer	15 rire (de)
4 conduire	10 négliger	16 rêver
5 couper	11 oser	17 se souvenir (de)
6 ennuyer	12 reprendre	18 je me souviens (de)

1 to add	7 he bores us	13 to breathe
2 to beat	8 to earn, win, gain	14 to awake
3 to hide	9 to rent, let	15 to laugh at
4 to lead, drive	10 to neglect	16 to dream
5 to cut	11 to dare	17 to remember
6 to bore	12 to take again	18 I remember

ADJECTIVES

1 ne ... aucun (aucune)	3 gros (grosse *f*)	5 entouré (de)
2 délicieux (euse *f*)	4 sage	6 renseigné

1 no, no one, none	3 big, large, stout	5 surrounded by
2 delicious	4 well-behaved	6 informed

NOTE 1. aucun may be used as a pronoun or as an adjective. Thus:

aucun de ses amis n'était à la gare, none of his friends was at the station.

il n'avait aucune intention de l'acheter, he had no intention of buying it.

ADVERBS

1 soudain	2 tant (de)	3 vraiment
1 suddenly	2 so much so many	3 truly, really

237

FRENCH EXPRESSIONS

1 être de service	6 se mettre à la besogne
2 être à plat	7 il sort de l'ordinaire
3 faire le compte	8 tant pis
4 faire le plein d'essence	9 c'est toujours ça
5 faire le guide	
1 to be on duty	6 to set to work
2 to have a flat tyre	7 it's out of the ordinary
3 to add up the bill	8 so much the worse
4 to fill up the tank	9 that's all to the good
5 to act as guide	

DEUXIÈME PARTIE

Exercise No. 208 Translate the following sentences accurately. All the tenses you have learned are here illustrated.

1 Elles sont allées au marché pour faire des achats.
2 Les Français ont fait une forte impression sur M. Davis.
3 Il est allé à la gare pour demander des renseignements.
4 Je pourrai me tirer d'affaire en France parce que je parle bien le français.
5 Après-demain nous rendrons visite à M. Duval.
6 Le jeune homme avait déjà fait le plein d'essence et vérifié l'huile.
7 L'été prochain M. Davis pourra faire le guide pour toute la famille.
8 Si M. Davis avait eu plus de temps, il aurait fait un voyage au Maroc.
9 À l'Hôtel du Quai Voltaire nous n'avons manqué de rien.
10 Après avoir terminé ses affaires, M. Davis s'est consacré complètement aux distractions.
11 Je vais écrire une lettre à mon représentant pour lui faire savoir la date de mon arrivée.
12 Après avoir fait nos adieux, nous sommes montés dans l'avion.
13 Je pensais aux conseils de mon professeur pendant que le taxi filait à toute vitesse dans les rues de Paris.
14 Autrefois M. Davis faisait traduire sa correspondance française, mais à l'avenir (in future) il la traduira lui-même.
15 Les enfants s'amusaient à jeter des pierres dans l'eau.
16 Si vous trouvez les paquets que j'ai laissés chez vous, rendez-les-moi s'il vous plaît.
17 Je n'oublierai pas de vous les rendre.
18 Je n'avais jamais vu un spectacle pareil.
19 Lorsque M. Davis voyageait en Europe, Mme Davis s'occupait des enfants.
20 Je n'ai jamais été en France mais je compte y aller l'été prochain.

Exercise No. 209 Complete the following sentences in French:

1 M. Davis (is a businessman of London).
2 Il a fait (a trip to Paris in order to visit his agent).
3 Il voulait (to get acquainted with him).
4 Avant de partir pour la France (he had learned to speak French well).
5 (He had also read many books) sur la France.
6 Il a écrit (many letters to his friend and teacher).
7 Il a décrit (the interesting places they had spoken of in their conversations).

8 **Malgré ses premières impressions** (he had found life in Paris similar to that in London).
9 **Il pensait au taxi** (which had taken him to his hotel).
10 (The dizzy speed of the taxi) **ne lui avait pas fait plaisir.**
11 **Heureusement** (he soon finished his business).
12 **Il aime surtout les Français** (their politeness and their marked feeling for the dignity of man).
13 **Tout de même** (he did not have time to go to Morocco or Corsica).
14 **Il y avait** (so much to see, so much to do, so much to learn).
15 **Il avait beaucoup appris** (about the customs, the life, the language and the arts of France).
16 **L'année prochaine** (he will return to France).
17 **Toute la famille** (would accompany him).
18 (He has not won the first prize in the lottery) **mais il aura** (enough money).
19 **Ceci est la dernière lettre** (which Mr. Davis will write before leaving France).
20 **Sans aucun doute** (he will invite Mr. Picard to dinner with his family) **quand il sera de retour**[1] **à Londres.**

NOTE 1. **être de retour** = to be back

Exercise No. 210—Lecture
Nice, capitale de la Côte d'Azur

Il y a vraiment deux villes à Nice: la ville italienne et la ville française, la vieille ville et la ville moderne. On peut se promener dans les vieux quartiers où on n'entend rien que de l'italien, et pourtant, il y a longtemps que Nice est devenue française. Dans ce quartier, on vend des macaronis, des raviolis, des olives et des saucisses.[1] L'air est parfumé d'ail[2] et de sauce tomate. On crie, on chante, on marchande.[3] C'est une ville tout à fait italienne.

Mais à deux pas,[4] en traversant la Place Masséna, on se trouve dans la ville française. On monte l'Avenue de la Victoire sous une allée d'arbres superbes et on admire les boutiques magnifiques. On voit des voitures longues comme des trains. On voit des fourrures[5] sur les dames, des perruques[6] sur les messieurs, et des brillants[7] sur les chiens! C'est la ville de luxe.

Nice est aussi un centre sportif. Il y a un club de tennis magnifique; il y a le terrain de golf de Cagnes, tout près; les célèbres sports d'hiver à Beuil, dans les montagnes; le yachting et les bains de mer. Il est vrai que la plage est pierreuse,[8] mais cela ne fait rien;[9] on y va tout de même pour adorer le soleil.

Mais la ville où on est né, où on va à l'école, où on gagne son pain, cette ville-là existe aussi. Cette ville a son commerce: le tourisme, les fleurs, les parfums, les olives, la pêche.[10] Elle a sa vie culturelle: la musique, qu'elle prend très au sérieux, l'opéra, le théâtre, les conférences, les librairies et surtout son université dont elle est très fière. Comme dans les villes typiques de la France on y possède[11] le goût de[12] la science, et le goût de l'art.

Mais la vraie gloire de Nice est sa situation. Entourée de collines ornées de villas fleuries,[13] elle s'étend de la mer bleue jusqu'au pied des montagnes neigeuses. Le ciel est d'un bleu intense comme la mer. L'air est doux, embaumé.

Tout y est pour rendre les gens heureux.

Note 1. sausage.
2. garlic.
3. people bargain.
4. close by.
5. furs.
6. wigs.
7. diamonds.
8. **pierreux (pierreuse *f*)**, rocky.
9. that does not matter.
10. fishing.
11. **posséder**, to possess.
12. **le goût de**, an interest in *or* taste for.
13. flower covered.

VOCABULARY—ENGLISH–FRENCH

A

a (an), un, une
able, capable
able (to be), pouvoir
aboard: all aboard! en voiture!
about, de; sur; autour de (*around*)
    What's it about? De quoi s'agit-il?
above, au-dessus (de); en haut
absolutely, absolument
accept (to), accepter
accident, un accident
accompany (to), accompagner
accomplish (to), accomplir
according to, selon
accurate, juste; exact
accuse (to), accuser
accustomed: to get accustomed to,
    s'habituer (à)
acquaintance, la connaissance; to make
    the acquaintance of, faire la connais-
    sance (de)
acquainted with (to be), connaître
across, en travers, à travers
active, actif (active *f*)
actor, un acteur; une actrice
actually, réellement
add (to), ajouter, additionner
address, une adresse
address (to), (s') adresser (à)
admire (to), admirer
admission, une entrée
admit (to), admettre
adore (to), adorer
adorned, orné
advance (to), avancer
advantage, un avantage
advertise (to), annoncer
advertisement, une annonce
advice, le conseil
advise (to), conseiller
affair, une affaire
afraid (to be), avoir peur (de)
after, ensuite, après
afternoon, un *or* une après-midi; in the
    afternoon (p.m.), de l'après-midi
afterwards, après
again, encore

against, contre
age, un âge
agent, un agent; le représentant
ago, il y a; ten years ago, il y a dix ans
agree (to), consentir (à); être d'accord
agreeable, agréable
agreed, entendu, d'accord
aid (to), aider
air, un air; in the open air, en plein air
airmail, par avion
airport, un aéroport
alike, pareil (pareille *f*); semblable
all, tout, toute, tous, toutes; not at all,
    pas du tout; all right, parfait, entendu
allow (to), permettre
allowed, permis
almost, presque
alone, seul
along, le long (de)
already, déjà
also, aussi; I also, moi aussi
although, bien que; quoique
always, toujours
ambassador, un ambassadeur
ambitious, ambitieux (ambitieuse *f*)
American, américain; un Américain
among, parmi
amount, la somme
amuse (to), (s') amuser
and, et
angry, fâché; to get angry, se fâcher
animal, un animal
anniversary, un anniversaire
announce (to), annoncer
annoy (to), ennuyer
another, un autre, une autre; one more,
    encore un (une) autre
answer, la réponse
answer (to), répondre (à)
any, quelque; de (*partitive*); anybody,
    anyone, quelqu'un
anything, quelque chose
appear (to), apparaître; paraître (*to
    seem*)
appetite, un appétit
apple, la pomme
appointment, le rendez-vous
appreciate (to), apprécier

approach (to), s'approcher (de)
April, avril *m*
argue (to), discuter
arise (to), se lever
arm, le bras
around, autour (de)
arrange (to), arranger
arrival, une arrivée
arrive (to), arriver
art, un art
article, un article
artist, un *or* une artiste
artistic, artistique
as . . . as, aussi . . . que; **as well as,** aussi
   bien que; **as little as,** aussi peu que;
   as much as, autant que; **as long as,** tant
   que; **as if,** comme si
ashtray, le cendrier
ask for (to), demander
ask (to ask questions), poser des questions
asleep, endormi
assist (to), aider (à)
assortment, un assortiment
assure (to), assurer
astonish (to), étonner
at, à; **at first,** d'abord; **at last,** enfin; **at
   once,** tout de suite; **at home,** chez moi
attention, une attention; **to pay attention
   to,** faire attention (à)
August, août *m*
aunt, la tante
author, un auteur
autumn, un automne; **in the autumn,**
   en automne
avenue, une avenue
awake, éveillé
awaken (to), réveiller
away, absent; **to go away,** s'en aller
awhile, un peu; un instant

B

baby, le bébé
back, le dos (*body*); **to be back,** être de
   retour
backwards, en arrière
bad, mauvais; **badly,** mal
baker, le boulanger, la boulangère
bakery, la boulangerie
ball, la balle
banana, la banane
bank, la banque; la rive (*river*)
bank-note, le billet de banque
bar, la buvette; le bar (*drinking*)
barber, le coiffeur
bargain (to), marchander

basket, le panier; la corbeille
bath, le bain; **bathroom,** la salle de bain
bathe (to), se baigner
be (to), être; **to be hungry,** avoir faim;
   to be right, avoir raison; **to be wrong,**
   avoir tort; **to be sleepy,** avoir sommeil;
   to be thirsty, avoir soif; **to be in the act
   of,** être en train (de)
beach, la plage
beautiful, beau, bel (belle *f*)
because, parce que
become (to), devenir
bed, le lit; **bedspread,** le dessus de lit
bedroom, la chambre à coucher
beef, le bœuf; **steak,** le bifteck
beer, la bière
before, avant (*time*) devant (*place*)
begin (to), commencer (à) *or* (de); se
   mettre (à)
beginning, le commencement
behind, derrière
believe (to), croire
bell, la cloche; la sonnette
below, en bas
belt, la ceinture
bench, le banc
besides, d'ailleurs
best, le meilleur (*adj.*); le mieux (*adv.*)
better, meilleur (*adj.*); mieux (*adv.*);
   so much the better, tant mieux
between, entre
bicycle, la bicyclette
big, grand
bill, la note (*at hotels, etc.*); le compte,
   une addition (*at restaurants*)
birthday, un anniversaire
biscuit, le biscuit; la gaufrette
bit (a), un peu
black, noir
blanket, la couverture
block of offices or flats, un immeuble
blouse, la blouse, le chemisier
blow, le coup
blue, bleu
boat, le bateau
body, le corps
book, le livre
bookshop, la librairie
born (to be), naître
born, né(e)
borrow (to), emprunter
both, les deux
bottle, la bouteille
bottom, le bas; le fond
box, la boîte
boy, le garçon

bracelet, le bracelet
brake, le frein
brandy, le cognac
brave, courageux
bread, le pain
break (to), casser; rompre
breakfast, le petit déjeuner; **to have breakfast**, prendre le petit déjeuner
breathe (to), respirer
Breton, breton (onne *f*)
brief, bref (brève *f*)
bright, clair; **bright faced**, à l'air éveillé
bring (to), apporter; **to bring back**, rapporter
Brittany, la Bretagne
broad, large
broken, cassé
brother, le frère
brown, brun
brush, la brosse
brush (to), brosser
buffet (dresser), le buffet
build, construire; bâtir
building, un édifice
burn (to), brûler
bus, un autobus
business, une affaire; **in business**, dans les affaires; **to do business in**, faire le commerce (de)
businessman, un homme d'affaires
busy, occupé
but, mais
butcher, le boucher, la bouchère
butcher's shop, la boucherie
butter, le beurre
buy (to), acheter
buyer, un acheteur, une acheteuse
by, par

C

cab, le taxi
cake, le gâteau
calendar, le calendrier
call (to), appeler; **to be called**, s'appeler
calm, calme
camera, un appareil photographique
can (to be able), pouvoir
capital (city), la capitale
car, la voiture (*see* motor car); **by car**, en voiture; **car boot**, le coffre
card, la carte; **postcard**, la carte postale
care: **to take care of**, s'occuper (de)
carry (to), porter; **to carry away**, emporter

case, le cas; la caisse (*box*); **in any case**, en tout cas
cashier, le caissier
castle, le château
cat, le chat
catch (to), attraper; **to catch a cold**, attraper un rhume
cause, la cause; la raison
cease (to), cesser (de)
ceiling, le plafond
celebrate (to), célébrer
centre, le centre
ceramics, la céramique
certain, certain; sûr
certificate, le certificat
chair, la chaise
chance, la chance; **Good luck!** Bonne chance!
change (to), changer; **to change money**, changer de l'argent
charm (to), enchanter; charmer
charming, charmant; ravissant
chat (to), causer
cheap, bon marché
cheaper, meilleur marché
check (to), vérifier; contrôler
cheerful, gai
cheese, le fromage
chemist's shop, la pharmacie
cheque, le chèque
chicken, le poulet
child, un *or* une enfant
chocolate, le chocolat
choose (to), choisir
Christmas, Noël
church, une église
cigar, le cigare
cinema, le cinéma; le ciné *fam.*
circle, le cercle
city, la ville; **to the city**, en ville
class, la classe; la sorte
clean, propre
clear, clair
clerk, un employé de bureau
climate, le climat
cloak, le manteau
clock, une horloge
close (to), fermer; **closed**, fermé
cloth, une étoffe; le drap; le tissu
clothe (to), habiller
clothes, les habits *m*; les vêtements *m*
club, le cercle; le club
coach, un autocar; le car
coast, la côte
coat, le manteau; le veston (*of suit*)
coffee, le café

coin, la pièce,

cold, froid; **it (weather) is cold,** il fait froid; **I am cold,** j'ai froid; **I have a cold,** je suis enrhumé

colour, la couleur; **What is the colour of . . .?** De quelle couleur est . . .?

comb, le peigne

comb (to), peigner

come (to), venir; **to come back,** revenir; **to come in,** entrer

comfortable, confortable; commode

commerce, le commerce

common, courant; ordinaire

Common Market, le Marché commun

companion, le (la) camarade

compare (to), comparer

complete, complet (complète *f*)

compliment, le compliment

concern, la maison (*business*); **that does not concern me,** cela ne me regarde pas

concert, le concert

conduct (to), conduire

conductor, le receveur (*on train, bus, etc.*)

confess (to), avouer

confidentially, entre nous

congratulate (to), féliciter

congratulation, la félicitation

consent (to), consentir

consequently, par conséquent

considerable, considérable

consist of (to), consister (en)

contain (to), contenir

content (to be), être content; être satisfait

continue (to), continuer (à) *or* (de)

contrary, le contraire; **on the contrary,** au contraire

contribute (to), contribuer

conversation, la conversation

cook, la cuisinière

cook (to), cuire; faire la cuisine

cool, frais; **it (weather) is cool,** il fait frais

corner, le coin

correct, correct; exact; **that's right,** c'est correct

correspondence, la correspondance

cost, le prix

cost (to), coûter

costume, le costume; **tailor-made costume,** le costume tailleur

cotton, le coton

count (to), compter

country, la campagne (*opposite of city*); le pays (*nation*)

course, le cours; le plat (*of meal*); **Of course!** Bien entendu! Mais oui!

cousin, le cousin; la cousine

cover (to), couvrir

covered, couvert

cream, la crème

cross (to), traverser

crowd, la foule

cry (to), crier (*shout*); s'écrier (*exclaim*); pleurer (*weep*)

cup, la tasse

curiosity, la curiosité

custom, un usage; la coutume

customary, habituel

customer, le client

custom-house, la douane

customs official, le douanier

cut (to), couper

D

daily, quotidien (ienne *f*)

dairy, la laiterie

damp, une humidité

dance, la danse

dance (to), danser

dangerous, dangereux (euse *f*)

darling (my), mon chéri; ma chérie

date, la date

daughter, la fille

day, le jour, la journée; **day after tomorrow,** après-demain; **day before yesterday,** avant-hier

dead, mort

dear, cher (chère *f*)

death, la mort

December, décembre *m*

decide (to), décider (de)

declare (to), déclarer

deed, le fait; une action

delay (to), tarder

delicious, délicieux (euse *f*)

delighted, ravi

delightful, ravissant

deliver (to), livrer

demand (to), exiger

dentist, le dentiste

department, le département; le rayon (*of a store*)

departure, le départ

descend (to), descendre

describe (to), décrire

description, la description

design, le dessin

desire, le désir; une envie; **to have a desire (a mind) to,** avoir envie (de)

desk, le bureau

dessert, le dessert

detain (to), retenir

develop (to), développer
devote (to), se consacrer (à)
devoted, dévoué, fervent
dictionary, le dictionnaire
die (to), mourir
difference, la différence
different, différent
difficult, difficile
difficulty, la difficulté
diligent, assidu; travailleur
diligently, assidûment
dinner, le dîner
dine (to), dîner
dining-room, la salle à manger
direction, la direction
dirty, sale
disagreeable, désagréable
disappear (to), disparaître
discontented with, mécontent (de)
discover (to), découvrir
discuss (to), discuter
dish, le plat
distance, la distance
distribute (to), distribuer
district, le quartier
divide (to), diviser
do (to), faire
doctor, le médecin; le docteur
dog, le chien, la chienne
door, la porte
doubt, le doute
downstairs, en bas
dozen, la douzaine
drama, le drame
dream (to), rêver; to dream of, songer (à)
dress, la robe
dress (to), habiller; s'habiller
dressmaking, la couture
dress designer, le couturier
dressmaker, la couturière
drink (to), boire
drive (to), conduire (*a car*)
driver, le chauffeur
driving licence, le permis de conduire
drop (to), laisser tomber (*to let fall*)
dry, sec (sèche *f*)
duck, le canard
during, pendant; durant
duty, le devoir
dwell (to), demeurer
dye (to), teindre

E

each, chaque (*adj.*); chacun (*pron.*)
ear, une oreille
early, de bonne heure; tôt

earn (to), gagner
earth, la terre
easily, facilement
east, l'est *m*
Easter, Pâques *m*
easy, facile
eat (to), manger
edge, le bord; at the edge of, au bord de
to be educated at, faire ses études (à)
effect, un effet
effort, un effort
egg, un œuf
either, l'un ou l'autre
electric(al), électrique
elegant, élégant
else: somebody else, quelqu'un d'autre
embassy, une ambassade
embroidered, brodé
employee, un employé; une employée
empty, vide
end, la fin
end (to), terminer
England, l'Angleterre *f*
English, anglais; l'anglais (*language*);
    an Englishman, un Anglais
enjoy (to), jouir (de); to enjoy oneself,
    s'amuser
enough, assez
enter (to), entrer (dans)
entirely, tout à fait
envelope, une enveloppe
equal, égal
erase (to), effacer
especially, surtout
essential, essentiel (ielle *f*)
estimate (to), estimer
etc., ainsi de suite; etc.
Europe, l'Europe *f*; European, européen
    (éenne *f*); European Community, la
    Communauté européenne; a Euro-
    pean, un Européen
even, même; even though, quand même
evening, le soir; Good evening! Bonsoir!
    yesterday evening, hier soir; tomorrow
    evening, demain soir; this evening, ce
    soir
ever, jamais; toujours
every, chaque; every day, tous les jours;
    chaque jour
everybody, tout le monde
everything, tout
everywhere, partout
exact, précis; exact
examine (to), examiner
exceed (to), dépasser
excellent, excellent

except, sauf; excepté
excite (to), (s') exciter; (s') agiter
exclaim (to), s'écrier
excursion, une excursion
excuse (to), (s') excuser; **excuse me!** excusez-moi!
exit, la sortie
expect (to), espérer; attendre
explain (to), expliquer
express, un express; le rapide (*train*)
exquisite, exquis
extra, en plus, supplémentaire
eye, un œil; des yeux

F

face, la figure; le visage
face (to), donner (sur)
fact, le fait; **in fact,** en fait
factory, la fabrique; une usine
fail: without fail, sans faute
fail (to), manquer; **do not fail to write to me,** ne manquez pas de m'écrire
fall (to), tomber
false, faux (fausse *f*)
family, la famille
famous, célèbre; fameux (euse *f*)
far, loin (de); **as far as,** jusqu'à
fare, le prix de la place; le prix du voyage; le prix du trajet
farther, plus loin
farthest, le plus éloigné
fashion, la mode
fashionable, à la mode
fast, vite
fasten (to), attacher
fat, gros (grosse *f*); gras (grasse *f*)
father, le père
fault, la faute
favour, le service; **Would you do me a favour?** Voulez-vous me rendre un service?
fear, la peur
fear (to), avoir peur (de); craindre
feather, la plume
February, février *m*
feel (to), (se) sentir; **he feels at home,** il se sent chez lui; **How do you feel?** (health) Comment vous portez-vous?
feeling, le sentiment
fetch (to), apporter; aller chercher
few, peu; **few people,** peu de gens
field, le champ
fill (to), remplir; **fill the tank with petrol,** faites le plein d'essence
film, le film

finally, enfin; finalement
find (to), trouver
fine, fin (*not coarse*)
finger, le doigt
finish (to), finir; terminer
fire, le feu
firm (business), la maison; la compagnie
first (the), le premier; la première
first, d'abord; **at first,** d'abord
fish, le poisson
fit (to), aller (à); **this dress fits me well,** cette robe me va bien
fitting (suitable), convenable
flat, plat; **I have a flat tyre,** je suis à plat
flat, un appartement
flatter (to), flatter
flavour, le goût; la saveur, le parfum
flight, le vol (*in air*)
floor, le plancher; un étage (*storey*)
flower, la fleur
fly (to), voler
fog, le brouillard
follow (to), suivre
following, suivant
fond of (to be), aimer; être friand (de)
food, une alimentation; la nourriture; les vivres
foot, le pied; **on foot,** à pied
for, pour; **for me,** pour moi; car (*since, because*)
force (to), forcer
foreigner, un étranger, une étrangère
forest, la forêt
forget (to), oublier
forgive (to), pardonner
fork, la fourchette
form, la forme
form (to), former
formality, la formalité
former (the), celui-là, celle-là; ceux-là, celles-là
formerly, autrefois
fortunate, heureux (euse *f*)
fortunately, heureusement
forward, en avant
found, trouvé
fountain-pen, le stylo
fragrant, parfumé
frame, le cadre
frame (to), encadrer
franc, le franc
France, la France
free, libre; gratis
French, français, le français (*lang.*); **the Frenchman,** le Français; **the French-woman,** la Française

frequently, fréquemment
fresh, frais (fraîche *f*)
Friday, vendredi *m*
friend, un ami, une amie
friendly, aimable
frighten (to), effrayer
from, de
front: in front of, devant
fruit, le fruit
full, plein
fun, un amusement; **to have fun,** s'amuser
funny, drôle
fur, la fourrure
furious, furieux (ieuse *f*)
furnish (to), meubler (*a room*)
furnished, meublé
furniture, les meubles *m*
further, plus loin
future, un avenir; **in the future,** à
  l'avenir

G

gaiety, la gaieté
gain (to), gagner
gamble (to), jouer
gambler, le joueur
game, le jeu; la partie
garage, le garage; la station-service
garden, le jardin
garish, voyant
gate, la porte
gay, gai
gem, la pierre précieuse
general, général; **in general,** en général
generous, généreux (euse *f*)
gentle, doux (douce *f*)
gentleman, le monsieur; **gentlemen,** les
  messieurs; **Ladies and gentlemen,**
  Mesdames et messieurs
genuine, authentique; véritable
geography, la géographie
German, allemand; **a German,** un Allemand (ande *f*)
Germany, l'Allemagne *f*
get (to), obtenir; recevoir
get up (to), se lever
get into (to), monter en voiture (*car*)
gift, le cadeau
girl, la fille; la jeune fille
give (to), donner
give back (to), rendre
glad, content; heureux
gladly, volontiers
glass, le verre; **drinking glass,** le verre;
  fine glass, le cristal

glitter (to), briller
glove, le gant
go (to), aller
go away (to), s'en aller
go back (to), retourner; rentrer; revenir
go down (to), descendre
go out (to), sortir (de)
go to bed (to), se coucher
go to sleep (to), s'endormir
go up (to), monter
God, Dieu *m*
gold, l'or *m*
good, bon (bonne *f*) (*adj.*); bien (*adv.*);
  **Good morning! Bonjour! Good after-
  noon! Bonjour! Good evening! Bonsoir! Good night! Bonne nuit! Bonsoir!**
goodbye, au revoir; adieu; **to bid goodbye to,** faire ses adieux (à)
goodness, la bonté
goods, la marchandise
grand, magnifique
grand-daughter, la petite-fille
grandfather, le grand-père
grandmother, la grand-mère
grandson, le petit-fils
grant (to), accorder; **Granted, D'accord!**
grape, le raisin
grasp (to), saisir
grateful, reconnaissant
great, grand
green, vert
greet (to), saluer
greeting, la salutation
grey, gris
grocer, un épicier, une épicière
grocer's shop, une épicerie
ground, la terre
group, le groupe
guard, le garde
guard (to), garder
guess (to), deviner
guide, le guide
guide (to), guider

H

hair, les cheveux *m*
hair-do, la coiffure
hairdresser, le coiffeur
half, demi; la moitié
ham, le jambon
hand, la main; **to shake hands,** se donner
  la main
handbag, le sac à main
handkerchief, le mouchoir
handsome, beau, bel (belle *f*)

happen, arriver; se passer; **What is happening?** Qu'est-ce qui se passe?

happy, heureux (euse *f*)

hard, difficile (*difficult*); dur (*not soft*)

hat, le chapeau

have (to), avoir; **to have to** (*must*) devoir; **I have the trunk weighed,** je fais peser la malle

he, il

head, la tête

headache: **I have a headache,** j'ai mal à la tête

health: **Here's to your health!** A votre santé!

hear (to), entendre

heart, le cœur

heaven, le ciel; **Good Heavens!** Mon Dieu!

heavy, lourd

help (to), aider

her, la; lui (*pron.*); son, sa, ses (*adj.*)

here, ici; **here is (are),** voici

herself, se; elle-même

high, haut

him, le; lui

himself, se; lui-même

hire (to), louer

his, son, sa, ses (*adj.*); à lui; le sien, la sienne, les siens, les siennes (*pron.*)

history, une histoire

hold (to), tenir

holiday, le jour de fête; **vacation, holidays,** les vacances *f*

home, la maison; **at home,** à la maison; chez moi, chez lui, etc.

hope (to), espérer

horse, le cheval (chevaux *pl.*)

horseback (on), à cheval

hospital, un hôpital

hot, chaud; **it (weather) is hot,** il fait chaud; **I am hot,** j'ai chaud

hotel, un hôtel

hour, une heure

house, la maison

how, comment; **How much does that cost?** Combien cela coûte-t-il? **How much money?** Combien d'argent? **How many books?** Combien de livres? **How often?** Combien de fois? **How pretty!** Que c'est joli! **How are you?** Comment allez-vous?

however, cependant; pourtant

hundred, cent

hunger, la faim

hungry (to be): **Are you hungry?** Avez-vous faim?

hurry (to), se dépêcher, se hâter; **I am in a hurry,** je suis pressé

hurt (to), faire mal (à)

husband, le mari

I

I, je; moi

ice-cream, la glace

if, si; **if not,** sinon

ill, malade

illustration, une illustration

imagine (to), s'imaginer

immediately, tout de suite; immédiatement

imperfect, défectueux

import (to), importer

important, important

importer, un importateur

impossible, impossible

in, dans; en

inch, le pouce

included, compris

incorrect, inexact

increase (to), augmenter

incredible, incroyable

indeed, en effet; vraiment; **Yes, indeed!** Mais oui!

indicate (to), indiquer

indispensable, indispensable

industrious, assidu

industry, une industrie

infant, le petit enfant; le bébé

influence, une influence

inform (to), informer; faire savoir

information: **he asks for information,** il demande des renseignements

inhabit (to), habiter

ink, une encre

inn, une auberge

inquire (to), prendre des renseignements

inside, dedans

insist (to), insister

instantly, à l'instant

instead of, au lieu (de)

instruct (to), enseigner

instrument, un instrument

intelligent, intelligent

intend (to), avoir l'intention (de); compter

interest, un intérêt; **to be interested in,** s'intéresser (à)

interesting, intéressant

into, dans; en

introduce (to), présenter

invitation, une invitation

invite (to), inviter

irritate (to), irriter

it, il, elle, ce; **it's late,** il est tard; **it's five o'clock,** il est cinq heures; **it's true,** c'est vrai

Italian, italien; l'italien (*lang.*); **an Italian,** un Italien, une Italienne

Italy, l'Italie *f*

its, son, sa, ses

itself, se; lui-même; elle-même

J

jacket, la veste; le veston

January, janvier *m*

jewel, le bijou (bijoux *pl.*)

joke, la plaisanterie

joke (to), plaisanter

journey, le voyage; le trajet

joyous, joyeux (euse *f*)

judge, le juge

juice, le jus; **orange juice,** les jus d'orange

July, juillet *m*

jump (to), sauter

June, juin *m*

just, juste; **I have just eaten,** je viens de manger

keep (to), garder

key, la clef

kill (to), tuer

kind, la sorte

kindly: **Will you kindly take it?** Voulez-vous avoir la bonté de le prendre?

kindness, la bonté

kiss, le baiser

kiss (to), embrasser

kitchen, la cuisine

knife, le couteau

knock (to), frapper

know (to), savoir (*to have knowledge of, to know how*); connaître (*to be acquainted with*)

L

lack (to), manquer; **I lack nothing,** je ne manque de rien

lady, la dame; **Ladies and gentlemen,** Mesdames et messieurs

lamb, un agneau; **leg of lamb,** le gigot

lamp, la lampe

land (to), atterrir (*plane*); débarquer (*ship*)

landscape, le paysage

language, la langue; le langage

large, grand; gros (grosse *f*)

last, le dernier, la dernière; **last night,** hier soir

late, tard; en retard

laugh (to), rire; **they laugh at him,** ils se rient de lui

launderette, la laverie

laundry, la blanchisserie

lavatory, les toilettes *f*; les lavabos *m*

lay (to), poser

lazy, paresseux (euse *f*)

lead (to), conduire

leap (to), sauter

learn (to), apprendre

least, le moins; **at least,** au moins

leather, le cuir

leave (to), partir (*depart*); quitter (*quit*)

left, gauche; **to the left,** à gauche

leg, la jambe

lemon, le citron

lemonade, la limonade; la citronnade

lend (to), prêter

length, la longueur

less, moins (de); **less than one,** moins d'un

lesson, la leçon

let (to), permettre (*permit*)

letter, la lettre

library, la bibliothèque

lie (to), mentir (*to tell a lie*)

lie down (to), se coucher

life, la vie

lift, un ascenseur

lift (to), lever; soulever

light, la lumière

like, comme; pareil (pareille *f*)

like (to), aimer; vouloir; **I should like,** je voudrais

likewise, également; aussi

linen, le linge

liner, le paquebot

lip, la lèvre

list, la liste

listen (to), écouter

little, petit; peu de; **little money,** peu d'argent

live (to), vivre; habiter; demeurer (*to dwell*)

lively, gai; vif (vive *f*)

living-room, le salon

long, long (longue *f*); **he left a long time ago,** il est parti il y a longtemps; depuis longtemps

look (to), regarder; chercher (*to look for*); **Look out! Attention!**

lose (to), perdre

lost, perdu

lot (a), beaucoup; **a lot of people,** beaucoup de monde (de gens)

loud, haut, fort; in a loud voice, à haute voix
love, un amour; in love, amoureux (euse *f*)
love (to), aimer
lovely, charmant
low, bas (basse *f*)
luck, la chance
lucky, heureux (euse *f*)
luggage, les bagages *m*
lunch, le déjeuner; I have lunch, je déjeune

M

madam, madame
magazine, la revue
magnificent, magnifique
maid, la bonne (*servant*)
mail, le courrier
majority, la majorité
make (to), faire
man, un homme
manner, la manière
manufacture (to), fabriquer
many, beaucoup; many others, beaucoup d'autres
map, la carte
March, mars *m*
market, le marché
marvellous, merveilleux (euse *f*)
master, le maître
match, une allumette
matter, une affaire; la chose; in the matter of, au sujet (de); it does not matter, n'importe
mattress, le matelas
May, mai *m*
may, pouvoir (*to be able*)
me, me; moi
meal, le repas
mean (to), vouloir dire
meaning, la signification
meanwhile (in the), en attendant
measure, la mesure
measure (to), mesurer
meat, la viande
mechanic, le mécanicien
medicine, la médecine (*the art*); le médicament (*the remedy*)
meet (to), rencontrer
meeting, la recontre; la réunion
memory, la mémoire; le souvenir
mend (to), réparer
merchandise, la marchandise
merchant, le marchant; le négociant; le commerçant

message, le message
metal, le métal
middle, le milieu; in the middle of, au milieu (de)
midnight, minuit
mild, doux (douce *f*)
milk, le lait
million, le million
mind, un esprit; I have a mind to, j'ai envie (de)
mine, à moi; le mien, la mienne, les miens, les miennes
minute, la minute; Wait a minute! Attendez un instant!
mirror, le miroir
miscellaneous, divers
misfortune, le malheur
Miss, mademoiselle
miss (to), manquer; I shall miss you, vous me manquerez
mistake, la faute
mistaken (to be), se tromper
Mister, monsieur
mistress, la maîtresse
mode, la mode
model, le modèle
modern, moderne
moment, le moment; Just a moment! Un instant!
Monday, lundi *m*
money, un argent; la monnaie (*change*)
money-order, le mandat
month, le mois
moon, la lune
more, plus; more than, plus que; plus de (*before a number*); not any more, ne . . . plus
morning, le matin; la matinée; in the morning (*a.m.*), du matin
most, le (la) plus; most of the people, la plupart des gens; for the most part, pour la plupart
mother, la mère; la maman
motor, le moteur
motor (to), aller en auto
motor car, une automobile; une auto; la voiture
motorway, une autoroute
mountain, la montagne
mouth, la bouche
move (to), bouger; déménager (*to new home*)
much, beaucoup (de); much more, beaucoup plus
museum, le musée
music, la musique

musician, le musicien; la musicienne
must, devoir; falloir; **I** must (*ought to*) do
  it, je dois le faire; **I** must (*have to*) go,
  il me faut partir
my, mon, ma, mes
myself, me; moi-même

N

name, le nom; **What is your name?**
  Comment vous appelez-vous?
namely, c'est-à-dire
napkin, la serviette
narrow, étroit
nation, la nation
naturally, naturellement
nature, la nature
near, près (de); proche (*adj.*)
nearly, presque; à peu près
neat, propre
necessary, nécessaire; **it is necessary,** il
  faut
neck, le cou
necklace, le collier
need, avoir besoin (de); **I need a pen,** j'ai
  besoin d'un stylo
neglect (to), négliger
neighbour, le voisin
neither, non plus; **neither** . . . **nor,** ne . . .
  ni . . . ni
never, ne . . . jamais
nevertheless, tout de même
new, nouveau, nouvel (nouvelle *f*); neuf
  (neuve *f*)
news, les nouvelles; **What's the news?**
  Quelles sont les nouvelles?
nice, gentil (gentille *f*)
night, la nuit; le soir
no, non; **No parking!** Défense de stationner! **No smoking!** Défense de
  fumer!
nobody, personne; ne . . . personne
noise, le bruit
none, ne . . . aucun
noon, midi
nor, neither . . . nor, ne . . . ni . . . ni
Norman, normand
Normandy, la Normandie
north, le nord
nose, le nez
not, ne . . . pas; ne . . . point
notebook, le carnet
nothing, rien; ne . . . rien
notice (to), remarquer
notify (to), avertir
November, novembre *m*

now, maintenant; **now and then,** de
  temps en temps
nowhere, nulle part
number, le nombre; le numéro

O

obey (to), obéir (à)
object, un objet
oblige (to), obliger
observe (to), observer
obtain (to), obtenir
occupation, le métier; une occupation
October, octobre *m*
of, de; **of it, of them,** en; **I have some** (*of
  it, of them*), j'en ai
offer (to), offrir
office, le bureau
officer, un officier
often, souvent; **quite often,** assez souvent
oil, une huile
old, vieux, vieil (vieille *f*); **How old are
  you?** Quel âge avez-vous?
once, une fois; **at once,** tout de suite; **all
  at once,** tout à coup; **once more,**
  encore une fois
one, un, une; on (*people, you*) **How does
  one say?** Comment dit-on?
only, seul; seulement; ne . . . que
open, ouvert
open (to), ouvrir
opera, un opéra
opposite, en face (de)
or, ou; **either** . . . **or,** ou . . . ou
order, un ordre; **in order to,** afin de
order (to), commander
ordinary, ordinaire
other, autre
otherwise, sinon
our, notre, nos
out, dehors
outside, dehors; hors de
over, au-dessus (de)
overcoat, le pardessus
owe (to), devoir
own propre; **his own language,** sa propre
  langue
own (to), posséder

P

pack (to), emballer; **he packs his bags,**
  il fait ses valises
pain (to), faire mal (à), faire souffrir
painting, la peinture
pair, la paire

pale, pâle
pancake, la crêpe
pants, le pantalon; la culotte
paper, le papier
parcel, le paquet
parcel post, le colis postal
park, le parc
park (to), stationner (a car)
part, la partie
pass (to), passer
passenger, le voyageur
passport, le passeport
past, passé; last week, la semaine dernière
pastry shop, la pâtisserie
pause, la pause
pause (to), faire une pause
pavement, le trottoir
pay (to), payer
pea, le pois
pear, la poire
pearl, la perle
pedestrian, le piéton
pen, la plume
pencil, le crayon
people, le peuple; les gens; on
perceive (to), apercevoir
per cent, pour cent
perfect, parfait; Perfect! Parfait! Très bien!
performance, la représentation; la séance
perfume, le parfum
perhaps, peut-être
permit (to), permettre
permitted, permis
person, la personne
petrol, une essence
petrol station, la station-service
pharmacy, la pharmacie
photograph, la photographie; to take a photograph, prendre une photographie
physician, le médecin
pick up (to), ramasser
picture, le tableau; une image
piece, le morceau; la pièce
pillow, un oreiller
pin, une épingle
pitcher (milk), le pot au lait
pity: What a pity! Quel dommage!
place, un endroit; le lieu; to take place, avoir lieu; in place of, au lieu de
plane (air), un avion
plate, une assiette
play, la pièce de théâtre
play (to), jouer
pleasant, agréable

please (to), plaire (à); (if you) please, s'il vous plaît; that pleases me, cela me plaît
pleasure, le plaisir
pocket, la poche
point, le point; on the point of departure, sur le point de partir
police, la police
policeman, un agent de police
politely, poliment
poor, pauvre
porter, le porteur
portrait, le portrait
possess (to), posséder
possible, possible
poster, une affiche
postman, le facteur
post-office, la poste; le bureau de poste
potato, la pomme de terre
pottery, la poterie; le céramique
pound, la livre
power, la poudre
practise (to), pratiquer
praise (to), louer
pray (to), prier
precede (to), précéder
precious, précieux (euse f)
prefer, préférer; aimer mieux
prepare (to), préparer
present, présent; at present, actuellement; to be present at, assister (à)
present, le cadeau
present (to), offrir, présenter
press (to), presser; to press clothes, repasser des vêtements
pretty, joli
price, le prix
prize, le prix
probably, probablement; sans doute
produce (to), produire
profession, la profession
professor, le professeur
profit, le profit; le bénéfice
programme, le programme, une émission
prohibit (to), défendre
promise (to), promettre
pronounce (to), prononcer
propose (to), proposer
protect (to), protéger
provided that, pourvu que
publish (to), éditer
publisher, un éditeur
pull (to), tirer
punish (to), punir
pupil, un or une élève
purchase, un achat; une emplette

purchase (to), acheter
purchaser, un acheteur (euse *f*)
purse, le porte-monnaie
push (to), pousser
put (to), mettre; poser; **to put on,** mettre

Q

quality, la qualité
quantity, la quantité
quarter, le quart; le quartier
question, la question
question (to), poser des questions
quick, rapide
quickly, rapidement; vite
quiet, tranquille; calme; **Keep quiet!**
  Restez tranquille!
quieten (to), calmer
quit (to), quitter
quite, tout à fait; **quite often,** assez
  souvent
quote (to), citer

R

radio, la radio
railway, le chemin de fer
rain, la pluie
rain (to), pleuvoir; **it is raining,** il pleut
raincoat, un imperméable
raise (to), lever, élever
rapid, rapide
rapidly, rapidement
rate, le tarif
rather, plutôt; **rather than,** plutôt que;
  I would rather, j'aimerais mieux
razor (safety), le rasoir de sûreté;
  (electric), le rasoir électrique
reach (to), arriver (à)
read (to), lire
ready, prêt
realize (to), comprendre; se rendre
  compte (de)
really, vraiment! en vérité
rear (in the), au fond
reason, la raison
recall (to), se rappeler (*to remember*)
receipt, la quittance
recipe, la recette
receive (to), recevoir
reckon (to), calculer
recognize (to), reconnaître
recommend (to), recommander
recommendation, la recommandation
record, le disque (*sound recording*)
recover (to), se remettre (*health*)
red, rouge

reference, la référence; **in reference to,**
  à propos (de)
reflect (to), réfléchir
refreshment, le rafraîchissement
refund (to), rembourser
refuse (to), refuser
regards: **give my regards to,** faites mes
  amitiés (à)
regret (to), regretter
reign (to), régner
relate (to), raconter
relative, le parent
rely upon (to), compter (sur)
remainder, le reste
remark (to), remarquer
remarkable, remarquable
remember (to), se rappeler; se souvenir (de)
remembrance, le souvenir
remove (to), enlever
rent (to), louer
repair (to), réparer
repeat (to), répéter
reply, la réponse
reply (to), répondre
represent (to), représenter
representative, le représentant
request (to), demander
require (to), avoir besoin (de)
resemble (to), ressembler (à)
reserve (to), retenir; réserver
reside (to), demeurer
residence, la résidence; la maison
respect, le respect
respect (to), respecter
responsible, responsable
rest, le reste (*remainder*); le repos (*repose*)
rest (to), se reposer
rested, délassé
restless, agité
result, le résultat
retail: **to retail,** vendre au détail
retain (to), retenir
retire (to), se retirer
return, le retour
return (to), revenir (*to come back*);
  rendre (*to give back*); retourner (*to go
  back*)
rum, le rhum
rice, le riz
rich, riche
ride (to), se promener; **in a car, on a
  bicycle, on horseback,** en voiture, à
  bicyclette, à cheval
right, droit; **to the right,** à droite
right, juste, exact; **that's right,** c'est exact
  (juste); **you are right,** vous avez raison

ring, un anneau, une bague; un coup de sonnette (*bell*)
ring (to), sonner
river, le fleuve (*large*); la rivière
road, le chemin; la route
room, la chambre
rough, rude
round, rond
route, la route
row, le rang
ruler, la règle (*measuring*)
run (to), courir

S

sad, triste; sadly, tristement
safe, sauf; safe and sound, sain et sauf
sailor, le marin
sake: for the sake of, pour l'amour de
salad, la salade
sale, la vente
salesgirl, la vendeuse
salesman, le vendeur
salt, le sel
same, même; all the same, tout de même
sample, un échantillon
satisfactory, satisfaisant
satisfy (to), contenter, satisfaire
Saturday, samedi *m*
sauce, la sauce
saucer, la soucoupe
sausage, la saucisse
say (to), dire
scarcely, à peine
scarf, une écharpe; un foulard
scene, la scène
schedule, un horaire
school, une école; to school, à l'école
scissors, les ciseaux *m*
sea, la mer; at sea, en mer
seaport, le port de mer
seashore, la côte
season, la saison
seat, la place
seated, assis
second, le (la) deuxième
see (to), voir
seek (to), chercher
seem (to), sembler; paraître
seize (to), saisir
seldom, rarement
sell (to), vendre
send (to), envoyer
sense, le sens; common sense, le sens commun
sentiment, le sentiment
separate (to), séparer

September, septembre *m*
serious, sérieux (euse *f*)
servant, la bonne; le (la) domestique
serve (to), servir
set (to), mettre; placer; to set out, se mettre en route
several, plusieurs
sew (to), coudre; sewing, la couture
shake (to), secouer; they shake hands, ils se serrent (se donnent) la main
shape, la forme
shave (to), se raser
shawl, le châle
shine (to), briller
ship (to), expédier
shipment, un envoi
shirt, la chemise
shoe, le soulier; la chaussure
shoemaker, le cordonnier
shop, la boutique; le magasin; shop-window, la vitrine
shopping (to go), faire des achats, des courses
short, court
shorthand typist, la sténo-dactylo
shoulder, une épaule
shout (to), crier
show (to), montrer
shut, fermé
shut (to), fermer
sick, malade
sickness, la maladie
side, le côté; at the side of, à côté (de)
signify (to), signifier
silence, le silence
silk, la soie; a silk dress, une robe de soie
silver, un argent
similar, semblable
simple, simple
since, depuis (*time*); puisque (*because*)
sincerely, sincèrement; Yours sincerely, Votre tout dévoué
sing (to), chanter
singer, le chanteur; la chanteuse
single, seul; célibataire (*unmarried*)
sir, monsieur
sister, la sœur
sit (to), être assis; to sit down, s'asseoir; sit down, asseyez-vous
sitting, assis
size, la taille; la grandeur; la pointure (*shoes, gloves*)
skin, la peau
skirt, la jupe
sky, le ciel
sleep, le sommeil

sleep (to), dormir; **to fall asleep,** s'endormir

sleeping-car, le wagon-lit

sleepy: **I am sleepy,** j'ai sommeil

slowly, lentement

small, petit

smell, une odeur

smell (to), sentir

smile, le sourire

smile (to), sourire

smoke (to), fumer; **No smoking!** Défense de fumer!

snapshot, un instantané

snow, la neige

snow (to), neiger

so (thus), ainsi; donc; **and so forth,** ainsi de suite

soap, le savon

sock, la chaussette

soft, doux (douce *f*)

soldier, le soldat

solid, solide

some, quelque, quelques; des

somebody, quelqu'un

someone, quelqu'un

something, quelque chose

sometimes, parfois; quelquefois

somewhere, quelque part

son, le fils

song, la chanson

soon, bientôt; **sooner,** plus tôt; **as soon as possible,** le plus tôt possible

sorry: **I am sorry,** je le regrette

sort, la sorte

sound, le son; le bruit

soup, la soupe

south, le sud; le midi

southern, du sud

Spain, l'Espagne *f*

Spanish, espagnol; l'espagnol (*language*); **a Spaniard,** un Espagnol (ole *f*)

speak (to), parler

spend (to), dépenser (*money*); passer (*time*)

spectacle, le spectacle

spectacles, les lunettes *f*

spectator, le spectateur

speed, la vitesse; **at full speed,** à toute vitesse

spinach, les épinards *m*

spirit, un esprit

spit (to), cracher

splendid, splendide

spoil (to), gâter

spoon, la cuiller *or* la cuillère

sport, le sport

spring, le printemps; **in spring,** au printemps

stairs, un escalier

stamp, le timbre (*postage*)

stand (to), être debout; **Stand up!** Levez-vous!

start (to), commencer

station, la gare (*railway*)

stay, le séjour (*visit*)

stay (to), rester

steak, le biftteck; **small steak,** une entrecôte

steamer, le paquebot

steel, un acier

step, le pas

stick, le bâton

still, calme; tranquille

still, encore; toujours; **it is still raining,** il pleut toujours

stocking, le bas

stop (to), s'arrêter; cesser; **bus stop,** un arrêt d'autobus

store, le grand magasin

story, une histoire; **storey,** un étage

straight, droit

strange, curieux (euse *f*)

stranger, un étranger (ère *f*)

strawberry, la fraise

street, la rue

strike, la grève

strike (to), battre; frapper

stroll (to), faire une promenade (un tour)

strong, fort

student, un étudiant, une étudiante

studious, assidu; travailleur

study, une étude

study (to), étudier

stuff, une étoffe

stupid, stupide, bête

style, le style; **in the latest style,** à la dernière mode

subject, le sujet; **to change the subject,** parler d'autre chose

suburbs, la banlieue

succeed (to), réussir (à)

success, le succès; la réussite

such, tel, telle, tels, telles; **such a man,** un tel homme

suddenly, tout à coup

suffer (to), souffrir

sufficient: **that's sufficient,** cela suffit

sugar, le sucre

suggest (to), proposer

suit, le costume; le complet; un ensemble

suitable, convenable

sum, la somme

summary, le résumé

summer, un été; **in summer**, en été
sun, le soleil
Sunday, dimanche *m*
supper, le souper
suppose (to), supposer
sure, sûr
surname, le nom de famille
surprise (to), surprendre
surprised, surpris; étonné
surroundings, les environs *m*
sweater, le chandail
sweet, doux (douce *f*)
sweet shop, la confiserie
swift, rapide
swim (to), nager
sympathetic, sympathique

T

table, la table; **to set the table**, mettre la
    table, le couvert
tablecloth, la nappe
tailor, le tailleur
take (to), prendre; **to take away**, em-
    porter
talk (to), parler; causer
tall, grand
tank, le réservoir; **to fill the tank with
    petrol**, faire le plein d'essence
taste, le goût
taste (to), goûter
tax, un impôt
taxi, le taxi
tea, le thé
teacher, le professeur (*secondary*); un
    instituteur, une institutrice (*ele-
    mentary*)
telegram, le télégramme
telegraph (to), télégraphier
telephone, le téléphone
telephone (to), téléphoner
television, la télévision
tell (to), dire; raconter
temperature, la température
text, le texte
than, que
thank (to), remercier
thanks, merci; les remerciements *m*
that, ce, cet, cette (*adj.*); celui, celle; cela
    (*pron.*); qui, que
the, le, la, les
theatre, le théâtre
their, leur, leurs
theirs, le leur, la leur, les leurs; à eux, à elles
them, les, leur; eux, elles
then, alors; puis; ensuite

there, là; y; voilà; **There he is! Le voilà!**
    there is (are), il y a; **over there**, là-bas
therefore, donc
these, ces (*adj.*); ceux, celles (*pron.*)
they, ils, elles
thick, épais, (épaisse *f*)
thing, la chose; un objet
think (to), penser; croire; **I think so**, je
    crois que oui; **I think not**, je crois que
    non
thirst, la soif; **I'm thirsty**, j'ai soif
this, ce, cet, cette; **this one**, celui-ci, celle-
    ci; ceci
thoroughly, à fond
these, ces (*adj.*); ceux, celles (*pron.*)
though, quoique
thought, la pensée; une idée
thousand, mil (*dates*), mille
throat, la gorge
throw (to), jeter
thumb, le pouce
Thursday, jeudi *m*
thus, ainsi
ticket, le billet; **single ticket**, le billet
    simple, le billet d'aller; **return ticket**,
    le billet d'aller et retour
ticket (booking office), le guichet
tie, la cravate
tights, les collants *m*
time, le temps; une heure (*hour*); **from
    time to time**, de temps en temps;
    **What time is it? Quelle heure est-il?
    to have a good time**, s'amuser
time: **one time**, une fois; **How many
    times? Combien de fois? At times**,
    parfois; **sometimes**, quelquefois
timetable, un horaire
tin, la boîte de conserve
tip, le pourboire (*gratuity*)
tip (to), donner un pourboire
tired, fatigué
tiresome, ennuyeux
to, à, en, vers, pour
tobacco, le tabac
today, aujourd'hui
together, ensemble
tomato, la tomate
tomorrow, demain; **till tomorrow**, à
    demain
tone, le ton
tongue, la langue
tonight, ce soir
too, aussi (*also*); trop (de) (*too much*)
tooth, la dent
toothache: **I have a toothache**, j'ai mal
    aux dents

toothbrush, la brosse à dents
toothpaste, la pâte dentifrice
total, le total; le montant
touch (to), toucher
tour, le tour; le voyage; une excursion
tourist, le (la) touriste
towards, vers; envers
towel, la serviette; **bath-towel**, la serviette de toilette
town, la ville; **town hall**, l'hôtel de ville; la mairie
toy, le jouet; le joujou (*fam.*)
traffic, la circulation
train, le train
translate (to), traduire
travel (to), voyager
traveller, le voyageur
tray, le plateau
treat (to), traiter
tree, un arbre
tremendous, énorme
trip, le voyage; **to take a trip**, faire un voyage
trouble, la difficulté
trouble (to), déranger; inquiéter; **Don't trouble yourself!** Ne vous dérangez pas!
trousers, le pantalon
true, vrai
truly, vraiment; **Yours truly**, Agréez, Monsieur, l'assurance de ma considération distinguée
trunk, la malle
truth, la vérité
truthful, sincère
try (to), essayer; tâcher
turn (to), tourner; **Turn left!** Prenez la première à gauche!
twice, deux fois
typewriter, la machine à écrire
tyre, le pneu (*car*); **spare tyre**, le pneu de rechange

U

ultimately, à la fin
umbrella, le parapluie
unbelievable, incroyable
uncle, un oncle
uncover (to), découvrir
under, sous, au-dessous (de)
undergo (to), subir
understand (to), comprendre
undertake (to), entreprendre
undertaking, une entreprise
undress (to), se déshabiller

unequal, inégal
unexpected, inattendu
unfair, injuste
unfamiliar, peu connu
unfortunately, malheureusement
unheard of, inouï
unite (to), unir
united, uni
United States, les États-Unis *m*
university, une université
unknown, inconnu
unless, à moins que
unoccupied, inoccupé; libre
unpack (to), déballer
unpleasant, désagréable
unsatisfied, mécontent
until, jusqu'à; **until now**, jusqu'à présent
up to, jusqu'à
upon, sur
upstairs, en haut
us, nous
use (to), se servir (de)
useful, utile
useless, inutile
usherette, une ouvreuse
usual, ordinaire; **usually**, d'ordinaire
utensil, un ustensile

V

vacation, les vacances *f*
vain: in vain, en vain
valise, la valise
valley, la vallée
valuable, de valeur
varied, varié
variety, la variété
various, divers
vase, le vase
veal, le veau; **veal fricassee**, la blanquette de veau
vegetable, le légume
verify (to), vérifier
very, très
vicinity, les environs *m*
view, la vue
view (to), voir
village, le village
vinegar, le vinaigre
visit, la visite
visit (to), visiter; rendre visite (à)
visitor, le visiteur
visa, le visa
voice, la voix; **in a loud voice**, à haute voix; **in a low voice**, à mi-voix
voyage, le voyage

W

wafer, la gaufrette
wages, le salaire
wait (to), attendre
waiter, le garçon
wake (to), réveiller; se réveiller
walk, la promenade; **to go for a walk,** se promener
walk (to), aller à pied
wallet, le portefeuille
wardrobe, la garde-robe; une armoire
warm, chaud; **it (weather) is warm,** il fait chaud; **I am warm,** j'ai chaud
wash (to), (se) laver; **I wash (myself),** je me lave
washroom, les toilettes *f*; les lavabos *m*
watch, la montre
water, une eau
way, la manière; **by the way,** à propos
we, nous
weak, faible
wear (to), porter
weather, le temps; **What's the weather?** Quel temps fait-il? **The weather is fine (bad),** il fait beau (mauvais)
week, la semaine; **twice a week,** deux fois par semaine
weep (to), pleurer
weigh (to), peser
welcome, bienvenu; **Welcome!** Soyez le bienvenu (la bienvenue)! **You're welcome (Don't mention it),** il n'y a pas de quoi
well, bien; **Well!** Eh bien!
west, l'ouest *m*
what (*adj.*), quel, quelle, quels, quelles
what? (*subj. of verb*), qu'est-ce qui?
what? (*obj. of verb*), que? qu'est-ce que?
what? (*obj. of prep.*), quoi?
when, quand; lorsque
where, où
whether, si
which (*adj.*), quel, quelle, quels, quelles
which (*rel. pron.*), qui, que
which (*that which*), ce qui, ce que
which one, lequel, laquelle
which ones, lesquels, lesquelles
while, pendant que
who? qui? qui est-ce qui?
whom? qui? qui est-ce que?
who (*rel. pron.*), qui
whom (*rel. pron.*), que
width, la largeur
wife, la femme
willingly, volontiers

win (to), gagner
windy: **it's windy,** il fait du vent
window, la fenêtre
wine, le vin
winter, un hiver; **in winter;** en hiver
wipe (to), essuyer
wise, sage
wish (to), désirer, vouloir
with, avec
withdraw (to), se retirer
without, sans; **to do without,** se passer (de)
woman, la femme
wonder, la merveille
wonderful, merveilleux; **wonderfully,** à merveille
wood, le bois
wool, la laine; **a woollen dress,** une robe de laine
word, le mot; la parole
work, le travail; une œuvre
work (to), travailler
worker, un ouvrier; une ouvrière
work of art, une œuvre d'art
world, le monde
worried, inquiet (inquiète *f*)
worry (to), s'inquiéter; **Don't worry!** Ne vous inquiétez pas!
worst, le plus mauvais; le pire
worth, la valeur
worthy, digne
wrap (to), emballer
wrist-watch, la montre-bracelet
writer, un écrivain
written, écrit
wrong, faux (fausse *f*)
wrong (to be), avoir tort; **he is wrong,** il a tort

Y

year, un an, une année
yellow, jaune
yes, oui; si; **yes, indeed!** mais oui!
yesterday, hier; **day before yesterday,** avant-hier
yet, encore; **not yet,** pas encore
you, vous; tu, te, toi
young, jeune
your, votre, vos; ton, ta, tes
yours, à vous, à toi
yourself, vous-même; toi-même

Z

zero, le zéro
zoo, le jardin zoologique

VOCABULARY—FRENCH–ENGLISH

A

à, to; at; on; in; until

un abord, access; d'abord, at first

un accord, harmony; d'accord, agreed; granted

un achat, purchase; aller faire des achats, to go shopping

acheter, to buy

les actualités, f, news

actuellement, now; at present

une addition, bill

une affaire, business; affair; M. Davis est dans les affaires, Mr. Davis is in business

une affiche, poster

un âge, age; Quel âge avez-vous? How old are you?

un agent, agent; l'agent de police, policeman

aider, to help

ailleurs, elsewhere; d'ailleurs, besides

aimer, to like; love; aimer mieux, to prefer

un aîné (une aînée), eldest or elder son or daughter

ainsi, thus; so; ainsi de suite, and so forth, etc.

un air, air; look; expression; en plein air, in the open air

ajouter, to add; join

aller, to go; s'en aller, to go away; Comment allez-vous? How are you? Ça va bien, I am well; cette robe me va bien, this dress fits me; suits me

une allumette, match

alors, well; then; in that case; and so

un amateur, lover; fancier; devotee

une ambassade, embassy

un ami (une amie), friend

un amour, love

amoureux (euse f), in love; lover

s'amuser, to enjoy oneself; have fun; amusons-nous, let's have some fun

un an, year

ancien (ienne f), old; ancient

anglais, English; l'anglais, English (language); un Anglais, Englishman

l' Angleterre f, England; en Angleterre, in England

une année, year; l'année scolaire, school year

un anniversaire, birthday; anniversary

announcer, to announce

apercevoir, to perceive; observe; notice

un appartement, flat

apparaître, to appear

appeler, to call; s'appeler, to be called (named); Comment vous appelez-vous? What is your name? Je m'appelle . . . My name is . . .

un appétit, appetite

apporter, to bring

apprécier, to appreciate

apprendre, to learn; teach

s'approcher (de), to approach; get near, go up to; je me suis approché de la voiture, I approached the car

après, after; afterwards; après-demain, the day after tomorrow

un or une après-midi, afternoon; de l'après-midi, in the afternoon, p.m.

un arbre, tree

un argent, money; silver

un arrêt, stop; halt

s'arrêter, to stop; l'autobus s'arrête là-bas, the bus stops over there

une arrivée, arrival

arriver (à), to arrive (at); reach; happen; Qu'est-ce qui est arrivé? What has happened?

un art, art

un ascenseur, lift

un aspect, appearance; look

s'asseoir, to sit down; asseyez-vous, sit down

une assiette, dish; plate

assez, enough; c'est assez, that's enough; assez souvent, quite often

assidu, diligent

assidûment, diligently

assis, seated

un assortiment, assortment

s'attabler, to sit down at table; attablé, seated at table

259

attendre, to wait (for); await; **en attendant,** in the meantime

atterrir, to land; **l'avion atterrit,** the plane is landing; **nous atterrissons,** we are landing

attraper, to catch; **attraper un rhume,** to catch a cold

un auberge, inn

aucun (aucune), none; no one; not any

au-dessous (de), below; under

au-dessus (de), above; over

aujourd'hui, today

aussi, also; as; **moi aussi,** I too; **aussi bien que,** as well as

aussitôt, soon; immediately; **aussitôt que possible,** as soon as possible

autant que, as much (many) as; **je travaille autant que jamais,** I am working as much as ever

une automobile; une auto, motor car

une autoroute, motorway

autour (de), around

autre, other; another; different; **autrefois,** formerly; **quelque chose d'autre,** something else

une avance, advance; **d'avance,** beforehand; in advance

avancer, to advance; progress

avant, before; **avant-hier,** day before yesterday

avec, with

avide, eager

un avion, plane; **en (par) avion,** by plane

un avocat, lawyer; barrister

avoir, to have; **Quel âge avez-vous? j'ai dix ans,** How old are you? I am ten years old; **avoir peur (de),** to be afraid of; **avoir raison (tort),** to be right (wrong); **avoir envie (de),** to have a mind to; **avoir besoin (de),** to have need of; **avoir l'intention (de),** to intend to; **avoir mal à la tête (mal aux dents),** to have a headache (toothache)

avouer, to confess

une annonce, advertisement; announcement

un annonceur, advertiser

B

les bagages *m,* luggage

la baguette, long loaf (of bread); wand

le bain, bath; **la salle de bain,** bath-room

la banc, bench

la banlieue, suburbs

la barbe, beard

la bas, stocking

bas (basse *f*), low, **en bas,** downstairs; **tout bas,** in a low voice; **là-bas,** over there

le bateau, boat

le bâtiment, building

bâtir, to build; **nous bâtissons,** we build

battre, to beat

bavard, talkative

bavarder, to chat

beau, bel (*before vowel or h mute*), **belle** *f,* beautiful

beaucoup (de), much; very much; many; **beaucoup d'autres,** many others; **beaucoup plus,** much more; **merci beaucoup,** many thanks

la besogne, work; job; **se mettre à la besogne,** to set to work

besoin, avoir besoin (de), to need; **nous en avons besoin tout de suite,** we need it (have need of it) at once

le beurre, butter

la bibliothèque, library; bookcase

bien, well; fine; very; **bien sûr,** surely; **assez bien,** quite well; **bien des fois,** many times

bientôt, soon; **à bientôt,** goodbye for now

bienvenu, welcome; **soyez le bienvenu,** (be) welcome!

le bijou (les bijoux), jewel(s)

le billet, note; ticket; **le billet d'aller et retour,** return ticket; **le billet d'aller (le billet simple),** single ticket

blanc (blanche *f*), white

la blanchisserie, laundry

bleu, blue

la blouse, blouse

un bock, a glass of beer

le bœuf, beef; **le bœuf bourguignon,** Burgundy beef

boire, to drink; **boire à la bouteille,** to drink from the bottle

le bois, wood

la boisson, beverage; drink

la boîte, box; tin (of food); **la boîte aux lettres,** letter-box

bon (bonne *f*), good; **bon marché,** cheap; **c'est bon,** that's fine

le bonheur, happiness

le bord, edge; **au bord de la mer,** at the seaside

le bosquet, grove

la bouche, mouth

le boucher, la bouchère, butcher

la boucherie, butcher's shop

bouger, to move; budge

la boulangerie, baker's shop; le boulanger,
la boulangère, baker
bousculé, pushed around; jostled
le bout, bit; tip; end; faire un bout de
toilette, to have a wash
la bouteille, bottle
la boutique, shop
le bras, arm
la Bretagne, Brittany
breton (onne *f*), breton
briller, to shine
la brise, breeze
le brouillard, fog
le bruit, noise; sound
brun, brown
le bureau, office; le bureau de poste, post
office
la buvette, bar

C

ça (cela), that; it (see Chapter 22, p. 130,
Grammar Notes 2)
cacher, to conceal; hide
le cadeau, gift
le cadet, the younger; young brother;
younger son
le cahier, exercise book; le cahier de
musique, music book
la caisse, case; box; cashier's desk
calculer, to reckon
le calvados, brandy of Normandy
le, la camarade, comrade; friend
le camion, lorry
le camionneur, lorry driver
la campagne, the country; countryside;
à la campagne, in the country
car, for; because; since
le carnet, notebook
la carte, menu; map; card; la carte
postale, postcard
le cas, case; en tout cas, in any case
casser, to break
la cause, cause; case; à cause de, because
of
causer, to chat; to talk
ce, cet, cette, ces, *demonstrative adj.*, this;
that; these; those (see Chapter 10, p.
61, Grammar Notes 2)
ceci, *demonstrative pron.*, this (see p.
130, Grammar Notes 2)
la ceinture, belt
cela (ça), *demonstrative pron.*, that (see
p. 130, Grammar Notes 2)
célèbre, famous
célébrer, to celebrate

celui (celle *f*), *demonstrative pron.*, this
one; that one (see p. 130)
le cendrier, ashtray
une centaine, a hundred; a hundred or so
cependant, however
certain, certain, sure
cesser, to cease; stop
ceux (celles *f*), *demonstrative pron.*,
these; those (see p. 130)
chacun (chacune *f*), each; each one
la chaise, chair; la chaise-longue, couch
le châle, shawl
la chaleur, heat
la chambre, room; la chambre à coucher,
bedroom
le champ, field
changer, to change; changer de l'argent,
to change money; changer de place, to
change one's seat
la chanson, song
chanter, to sing
le chapeau, hat
chaque, each; every
le château, castle; manor
chaud, hot; warm; le chaud, heat,
warmth; il fait chaud, it (weather) is
warm (hot); j'ai chaud, I am (feel) warm
la chausette, sock
la chaussure, shoe; footwear; une pair de
chaussures, a pair of shoes
le chemin, road; le chemin de fer, railway
le chemise, shirt
le chemisier, woman's shirt
cher (chère *f*), dear; plus cher, dearer
chercher, to look for; to seek
chéri (chérie *f*), dear; darling; mon chéri
ma chérie, my dear
le cheval, les chevaux, horse(s)
les cheveux *m*, hair
chez, at the house (home) of; chez moi,
at my house; chez M. Davis, at Mr.
Davis' house
le chien, la chienne, dog
choisir, to choose; nous choisssions, we
choose
la chose, thing; quelque chose, something; pas grand-chose, not much
le ciel, sky
le cinéma, cinema
citer, to cite; to mention
clair, clear
la classe, class; en classe, in school
la clef, key
le cœur, heart; par cœur, by heart
le coffre, car boot
le coin, corner

le colis postal (les colis postaux), parcel
le collant, tights
la colline, hill
combien (de), how much, how many; Combien cela coûte-t-il? How much does this cost?
comique, comic; funny
comme, like; as; for; how; comme ci comme ça, so so; Comme il est tard! How late it is!
commencer, to begin
comment, how; Comment ça va? How are you?
le commerçant, businessman; tradesman
commode, comfortable; convenient
la Communauté européenne, European Community
la compagnie, company
complet (ète *f*), complete; le complet, suit of clothes
comprendre, to understand
le compte, the bill; faire le compte, to add up the bill
compter, to intend; to count
compris, understood; included
conduire, to drive; to conduct; lead
la conférence, lecture
la connaissance, knowledge; acquaintance; faire la connaissance (de), to make the acquaintance of; to meet
connaître, to know; to be acquainted with
connu, known
le conseil, advice
conséquent: par conséquent, consequently
construire, to construct; to build
content, happy
continuer (à) *or* (de), to continue; keep on
contre, against; par contre, on the other hand
contrôler, to control; to check
le coq, cock
la corbeille, basket
le corps, body; group of people acting together
corriger, to correct
le costume, costume; le costume tailleur, suit (woman's)
la côte, seashore
le côté, side; à côté (de), at the side of
se coucher, to lie down; go to bed
la couleur, colour; De quelle couleur est ... ? What is the colour of ... ?
le coup, blow; stroke; tout à coup, all of a sudden; un coup de main, a helping hand

couper, to cut
courant, common; current; au courant, well informed
courir, to run
le courrier, mail
le cours, course
court, short
le couteau, knife
coûter, to cost
la coutume, custom; habit
la couture, dress designing; dressmaking; sewing
le couturier (la couturière), dress designer; dressmaker
couvert, covered
la couverture, cover; la couverture de lit, blanket
couvrir, to cover
la cravate, tie
le crayon, pencil
la crème, cream
crever, to break; to puncture; crever un pneu, to have a puncture
crier, to cry out; to shout
croire, to believe; to think; je crois que oui (non), I think so (not)
la croix, cross
la cuisine, kitchen; cooking
le croissant, crescent shaped bun
la cuiller *or* la cuillère, spoon
curieux (ieuse *f*), curious

D

la dame, lady
dans, in, into
la date, date
de, of; from; by; with
debout, standing; il est (reste) debout, he is standing
débrouillard, resourceful
découvrir, to discover; uncover
décrire, to describe
la défense, prohibition; defense; Défense de fumer! No smoking! Défense de stationner! No parking!
dehors, outside; out of doors
déjà, already
le déjeuner, lunch; le petit déjeuner, breakfast
délassé, refreshed; rested
demain, tomorrow; à demain, until tomorrow; demain matin, tomorrow morning
demander, ask for; se demander, to wonder

déménager, to move

demeurer, to reside; to live

le demi-kilo, 500 grams

la demi-livre, 250 grams

la dent, tooth; avoir mal aux dents, to have a toothache

le départ, departure

dépasser, to exceed; le poids des bagages dépasse cinquante kilos, the weight of the luggage exceeds 50 kilos

se dépêcher, to hurry

depuis, since; for (duration)

dernier (dernière *f*), last; final

derrière, behind

dès, since; from; as early as; dès mon arrivée, immediately on my arrival

descendre, to descend; go down

désespérer, to despair; to be without hope

désirer, to desire; want; wish

le dessert, dessert

le dessin, design; drawing

dessous, under; underneath; au-dessous (de) (*prep.*), under; underneath; below

dessus, over; above; au-dessus (de) (*prep.*), on; upon; above

le dessus de lit, bedspread

la dette, debt

devant, in front of; before

deviner, to guess

devenir, to become

le devoir, duty, les devoirs, homework; faire ses devoirs, to do his (her) homework

devoir, to owe; to be obliged to; to have to; to be supposed to

difficile, difficult

la difficulté, difficulty

digne, worthy

dîner, to dine; le dîner, dinner

le diplôme, diploma

dire, to say; tell; c'est-à-dire, that is to say; dites-moi, tell me

distingué, distinguished

la distraction, recreation

divers, various; several; sundry

le doigt, finger

dominer, to reign; to dominate

le dommage, injury; Quel dommage! What a pity!

donc, therefore; so

donner, to give

dont, of which; of whom; whose

dormir, to sleep

la douane, the customs; custom-house

le doute, doubt; sans doute, of course, without doubt

doux (douce *f*), gentle; sweet; balmy

le drap, cloth; sheet

le droit, law; right; duty; droit, right, straight; à droite, to the right; tout droit, straight ahead; la main droite, the right hand

durant, during

E

une eau, water; l'eau-de-vie, brandy

un échantillon, sample

une écharpe, a scarf

un éclat, brightness; glitter; de tout son éclat, in all its brilliance

éclater, to burst out; to resound

une école, school

écouter, to listen to; nous écoutons le professeur, we listen to the teacher

un écran, screen

écrire, to write

un écrivain, writer

un effet, effect; en effet, as a matter of fact; indeed

égaler, to equal

égayer, to cheer up; brighten up

une église, church

un *or* une élève, pupil

elle, she; it; her; elle-même, herself; elles, they; them

une embouchure, mouth (of river)

embrasser, to kiss

une émission, broadcast; programme

une emplette, purchase; faire des emplettes, to go shopping

un employé, employee; clerk

employer, to employ

emporter, to carry away; to take away

emprunter, to borrow

en, in; into; while; on; to; of it; of them; en attendant, in the meantime

en arrière, behind; backwards

encadré, framed

enchanté, enchanted; charmed; delighted

encore, still; yet; again; encore une fois, once more; encore un (une), one more; another; pas encore, not yet

une encre, ink

un endroit, place

un *or* une enfant, child

enfin, finally

ennuyer, to bore; annoy

enrhumé: je suis enrhumé, I have a cold

ensemble, together; whole

enseigner, to teach

ensuite, then; afterwards

entendre, to hear; understand; **entendu,** agreed; all right; **bien entendu,** of course

entouré, surrounded

entre, between; **entre nous,** confidentially

une entrecôte, steak

une entrée, entrance; first dish

entreprendre, to undertake

entrer (dans), to enter; come in

une envie, wish; desire; longing; **j'ai envie de dormir,** I feel like sleeping

environ, about; nearly

les environs *m,* vicinity; neighbourhood; outskirts

s'envoler, to fly away

envoyer, to send

un épicier, une épicière, grocer

une épicerie, grocery shop

épuisé, worn out

équivaloir, to equal

un escalier, staircase

l'Espagne, *f* Spain

espagnol, Spanish; **l'espagnol,** Spanish language; **un Espagnol, une Espagnole,** a Spaniard

espérer, to hope; hope for; expect

essayer, to try; to try on

une essence, petrol; **faire le plein d'essence,** to fill the tank with petrol

l'est *m,* east

un estomac, stomach; **avoir mal l'estomac,** to have a stomach-ache

et, and

un étage, storey or floor (of house)

un étalage, display

un état, state; **dans tous ses états,** terribly excited

un été, summer; **en été,** in summer

une étoffe, cloth; stuff

une étoile, star

étonner, to astonish

être, to be; **être en train de,** to be in an act of

les étrennes *f,* New Year's presents

une étude, study; **ils font leurs études,** they are being educated

un étudiant, student

étudier, to study

l'Europe *f,* Europe; **européen (éenne** *f);* **un Européen,** a European

éveillé, awake; **à l'air éveillé,** bright faced

évoquer, to evoke

excepté, except

excuser, to excuse; **excusez-moi,** excuse me

un exemple, example; **par exemple,** for example

exiger, to demand

expliquer, to explain

exprimer, to express

extra, extra; **c'est de l'extra,** *fam.* it is especially good

la fabrique, factory

fâché, annoyed, cross; **j'en suis fâché,** I am sorry

facile, easy

la facilité, facility

le facteur, postman

la faim, hunger; **j'ai faim,** I am hungry

faire, to make; to do;

    il fait ses adieux à son ami, he is saying goodbye to his friend;

    faites mes amitiés à Mme Picard, give my regards to Mrs. Picard;

    il fait beau (mauvais), the weather is nice (bad);

    il fait le compte, he adds up the bill;

    je veux faire sa connaissance, I want to meet him;

    ils font leurs devoirs, they are doing their homework;

    elle fait ses courses, she is shopping;

    ils font des progrès, they are making progress;

    il fait peser ses valises, he is having his bags weighed;

    il fait le plein d'essence, he is filling up the tank with petrol;

    cela nous fait plaisir, that pleases us;

    ça ne fait rien, that doesn't matter;

    nous allons faire un voyage, we are going to take a trip;

    nous allons faire *or* **rendre visite à mon oncle,** we are going to visit my uncle

faire la grève, to go on strike

le fait, act; deed; fact; **tout à fait,** entirely; quite

fait, done (*past participle of faire*)

falloir, to be necessary; **il faut,** it is necessary

la famille, family; **en famille,** together with the family

fatigué, tired

faut: il faut, it is necessary

la faute, mistake

faux (fausse *f),* false

féliciter, to congratulate

la femme, woman; wife

la fenêtre, window
fermer, to close
le fermier, la fermière, farmer
le fête, holiday; festival
le feu, fire; traffic light; le feu d'artifice, fireworks
fier (fière f), proud
la figure, face
filer, to spin; run off; en filant à toute vitesse, running at full speed
la fille, daughter; la jeune fille, girl
le film, film; le film policier, detective film; le documentaire, documentary film
le fils, son
la fin, end; à la fin (de), at the end of
finir, to finish; nous finissons, we finish
flatté, flattered
la fleur, flower; le Marché aux Fleurs, Flower Market
le fleuve, large river
la fois, time; deux fois, twice; combien de fois, how many times; encore une fois, once more; quelquefois, sometimes
la folie, madness; à la folie, madly
le fond, bottom; au fond, at the bottom, at the back; à fond, thoroughly
forcer, to force
la forêt, forest
le foulard, scarf
fort, strong; loud; loudly
fournir, to furnish; to supply
la fourrure, fur
la fraîcheur, coolness; freshness; frais (fraîche f), cool; fresh; il fait frais, it is cool
la fraise, strawberry
français, French; le français, French (language); le Français, Frenchman; la Française, Frenchwoman
la France, France
frapper, to knock; strike
le frein, brake
le frère, brother
friand de, fond of
froid, cold; le froid, the cold; coldness; il fait froid, it (the weather) is cold; j'ai froid, I am cold
fumer, to smoke; Défense de fumer! No smoking!

G

gagner, to gain; win; earn
gai, gay; merry

le garçon, boy; waiter; le garçon de bureau, office boy
garder, to guard; to keep; il garde la chambre, he keeps to his room
la gare, railway station
le gâteau, cake
gauche, left; awkward; la main gauche, the left hand
les gens m, people; persons; folk
gentil (ille f), nice; kind
le gigot, leg of lamb
la glace, ice-cream
le goût, taste; flavour
grâce: grâce à vous, thanks to you
grand, big; large; great; tall
la grand-mère, grandmother
le grand-père, grandfather
gras (grasse f), fat
le or les gratte-ciel, skyscraper(s)
gris, grey
gros (grosse f), big; large; stout; thick; en gros, wholesale
le guichet, ticket window; booking office
Guignol, Punch and Judy; puppet show

H

s'habiller, to dress oneself; get dressed
habiter, to live in; to inhabit
une habitude, habit; custom; d'habitude, usually
s'habituer (à), to get accustomed to
haut, high; loud; à haute voix, in a loud voice
la hauteur, height
une herbe, grass
une heure, hour; de bonne heure, early; Quelle heure est-il? What time is it?
heureux (euse f), happy
hier, yesterday; hier soir, last night; hier matin, yesterday morning
un hiver, winter; en hiver, in winter
un homme, man; l'homme d'affaires, businessman
les hors-d'œuvre m appetizers
une huile, oil; salad oil
une humidité, damp

I

ici, here
une idée, idea; Quelle bonne idée! What a good idea!
un immeuble, block of flats or offices

un imperméable, raincoat
un importateur, importer
importer, to import; to matter; n'importe, it doesn't matter; never mind
un ingénieur, engineer
intéresser, to interest; s'intéresser (à), to be interested in
un intérêt, interest
isolé, isolated
un itinéraire, itinerary; route

J

jamais, ever; ne . . . jamais, never; mieux vaut tard que jamais, better late than never
la jambe, leg
le jambon, ham
le jardin, garden
jaune, yellow
jeter, to throw
le jeu, game
jeune, young; la jeune fille, girl
la joie, joy
joli, pretty
joliment, jolly
jouer, to play; jouer (à), to play (a game); jouer (de), to play (an instrument)
le jouet, toy
le joueur, gambler
jouir de, to enjoy
le joujou (*fam.*), toy
le jour, day; tous les jours, everyday; le jour de l'an, New Year's Day; de jour en jour, from day to day
le journal, les journaux, newspaper(s)
la journée, the day; toute la journée, all day
la jupe, skirt
le jus, juice; le jus d'orange, orange juice
jusque, up to; until; as far as; jusqu'à présent, up to now; jusqu'ici, as far as here; till now

K

le kilogramme, kilogram
le kilomètre, kilometre (*about ⅝ mile or 0.624 mile*)

L

la *f*, *definite article*, the (see Chapter 3, p. 12, Grammar Notes 1)
la *f*, *direct obj. pron.*, her; it (see Chapter 15, p. 90, Grammar Notes 2)

là, there; là-bas, over there
la laine, wool; un châle de laine, a woollen shawl
laisser, to let; leave
le lait, milk
la langue, language; tongue
large, wide
la largeur, width
le lavabo, wash-basin; toilet
laver, to wash; se laver, to wash oneself
la laverie, launderette
la leçon, lesson
le légume, vegetable
le lendemain, the next day
lent, slow
le *m*, *definite article*, the (see Chapter 3, p. 12, Grammar Notes 1)
le *m*, *direct obj. pron.*, him; it (see Chapter 15, p. 90, Grammar Notes 2)
lequel (laquelle, lesquels, lesquelles), who; whom; which (see Chapter 34, p. 201, Grammar Notes 1); which one? which ones?
les, *definite article*, the pl. (see Chapter 3, p. 12, Grammar Notes 1)
les, *direct obj. pron.*, them (see Chapter 15, p. 90, Grammar Notes 2)
la lettre, letter; les belles-lettres, literature
leur (leurs), *poss. adj.*, their (see Chapter 13, p. 74, Grammar Notes 2)
leur, *indir. obj. pron.*, (to) them (see Chapter 20, p. 120, Grammar Notes 2)
lever, to raise, lift; se lever, to get up; rise; levez-vous, stand up
libre, free
le lieu, place; au lieu (de), instead of; avoir lieu, to take place
la librairie, bookshop
le linge, linen
lire, to read
le lit, bed; au lit., in bed
le livre, book
la livre, pound
la loi, law
loin, far; loin d'ici, far from here
long (longue *f*), long; le long du chemin, along the way
la longueur, length
longtemps, a long time; plus longtemps, longer
lorsque, when; lorsqu'il est arrivé, when he arrived
louer, to rent; to let

le loup, wolf

lourd, heavy

lui, *indir. obj. pron.*, (to) him; (to) her (see Chapter 20, p. 120, Grammar Notes 2)

lui, *independent pron.*, him (see Chapter 23, p. 134, Grammar Notes 2, 3)

la lumière, the light

la lune, moon

le luxe, luxury; les articles de luxe, luxury articles

le lycée, French secondary school

M

ma *f*, my (see Chapter 13, p. 74, Grammar Notes 2)

madame, lady; madam; Mrs.

mademoiselle, young lady; Miss

le grand magasin, store; le magasin, shop

la main, hand; la main gauche, left hand; la main droite, right hand; à main gauche (droite), on the left (right); ils se donnent la main, they shake hands

maintenant, now

mais, but; mais oui, of course; yes indeed

la maison, house; home; à la maison, at home; chez moi (vous, etc.), at my (your, etc.) home

le maître, master; teacher

la maîtresse, teacher; mistress

mal, badly; le mal, pain; j'ai mal à la tête, (mal aux dents, à l'estomac), I have a headache (toothache, stomach-ache); ça fait mal aux yeux, it hurts the eyes

malade, sick; le (la) malade, sick person

malgré, in spite of

le malheur, misfortune

malheureux (euse *f*), unhappy; unfortunate

malheureusement, unfortunately

manger, to eat

la manière, manner

manquer, to lack; need; je ne manque de rien, I lack nothing; manquer, to fail, to miss; ne manquez pas de faire vos devoirs; don't fail to do your homework; vous me manquerez, I shall miss you (Lit. you will be missing to me)

le manteau, coat

le marchand, merchant; shopkeeper, le marchand de nouveautés, draper

marchander, to bargain

la marchandise, merchandise

le marché, the market; faire son marché, to do one's shopping; le Marché Commun, Common Market

marcher, to walk; to march

le mari, husband

marier, to marry; se marier, to get married

le marin, sailor; seaman

le matin, morning; du matin, in the morning, a.m.

matinal, early rising

la matinée, morning

le médecin, medical doctor; physician

meilleur, better; le meilleur, best; meilleur marché, cheaper

même, same; even; self; la même chose, the same thing; tout de même, all the same; moi-même, myself; même les plus riches, even the wealthiest

mener, to lead

la mer, sea; en mer, at sea

merci, thanks; merci beaucoup, many thanks

la mère, mother

la merveille, marvel; à merveille, wonderfully

merveilleux (euse *f*), wonderful

mes, my (see Chapter 13, p. 74, Grammar Notes 2)

le métier, trade; business; c'est mon métier, that's my trade

mettre, to put; put on; se mettre à table, to sit down at table; se mettre en route, to set out; se mettre (à), *infinitive*, to begin to; il se met à écrire, he is beginning to write

les meubles *m*, furniture

midi *m*, noon; le midi de la France, south of France

mieux, *adv.*, better; tant mieux, so much the better; ça va mieux, I feel better; mieux vaut tard que jamais, better late than never

le milieu, middle; au milieu (de), in the middle of

le miroir, mirror

la mode, fashion; à la mode, fashionable

moi, me; to me; I (see Chapter 23, pp. 134–5, Grammar Notes 2)

le mois, month

moins, less; minus; moins de cinq, fewer than five

mon (ma, mes), *poss. adj.*, my (see Chapter 13, p. 74, Grammar Notes 2)

le monde, world; tout le monde, everybody

la **monnaie,** coin; money; change; currency; **en monnaie,** in change

le **monsieur,** gentleman; sir; Mr.; **les messieurs,** gentlemen

la **montagne,** mountain

le **montant,** total

monter, to go up; ascend; carry up; **monter en voiture,** to get into the car

la **montre,** watch; **le bracelet-montre,** wrist-watch

montrer, to show

le **morceau,** piece; morsel

mort, dead; **la mort,** death

le **mot,** word

le **mouchoir,** handkerchief

mourir, to die; **ennuyer à mourir,** to bore to death

les **moyens** *m,* means

le **mur,** wall; **au mur,** on the wall

N

naître, to be born; **né,** born; **je suis né,** I was born

nager, to swim

la **nappe,** tablecloth

ne: ne ... pas, not; **ne ... jamais,** never; **ne ... rien,** nothing; **ne ... plus,** no longer; **ne ... que,** only; **ne ... ni ... ni** ... neither, nor; **je n'ai qu'un professeur,** I have only one teacher

nécessaire, necessary

la **neige,** snow

neiger, to snow

neuf (neuve *f***),** brand new

le **nez,** nose

ni ... ni, neither ... nor; **ni moi non plus,** neither do I

noir, black

le **nom,** name

le **nombre,** number

non, no; **non plus,** neither

le **nord,** north

la **Normandie,** Normandy

normand, Norman

la **note,** bill; mark; **la note d'hôtel,** hotel bill

notre (nos), our, *poss. adj.* (see Chapter 13, p. 74, Grammar Notes 2)

nouveau, nouvel (*before vowel or h mute*), **(nouvelle** *f***),** new

les **nouvelles,** news; **point de nouvelles, bonnes nouvelles,** no news is good news; **Quelles sont les nouvelles?** What is the news?

la **nuit,** night

O

obéir (à), to obey

un objet d'art, art object

obtenir, to obtain

une occasion, opportunity; occasion

s'occuper (de), to busy oneself with; to take care of; **Mme. Davis s'occupe des enfants,** Mrs. Davis looks after the children

un œuf, egg

un œil, eye; **des yeux,** eyes

une œuvre, work; **le chef-d'œuvre,** masterpiece

offrir, to offer

on, one; people; you; we; they; **on dit,** one says; people (they; you; we) say; it is said

un or, gold; **la montre d'or,** the gold watch

une oreille, ear

oser, to dare

ou, or; **où,** where

oublier, to forget

un outillage, tool kit

ouvert, open

une ouvreuse, usherette

un ouvrier, une ouvrière, worker

ouvrir, to open

P

le **pain,** bread; loaf of bread; **les petits pains,** rolls

pâle, pale

le **panier,** the basket

le **pantalon,** trousers

le **paquebot,** steamer; liner

Pâques, Easter

le **paquet,** parcel

par, by; through; **par ici,** this way; **par-ci par-là,** here and there

la **parapluie,** umbrella

paraître, to seem; to appear

parce que, because

parcourir, to glance through

le **pardessus,** overcoat

pardon, pardon me

pardonner, to forgive; **pardonnez-moi,** excuse me

pareil (pareille *f***),** like; equal; similar; such

parfait, perfect

parfois, at times

parler, to speak; **pour parler d'autre chose,** speaking of something else; changing the subject parmi, among

la parole, spoken word

la part, share; part; de ma part, from me; quelque part, somewhere; nulle part, nowhere

la partie, the part (first, second, etc); the game

partir (pour), to leave for; partir (de), to leave from; partir en voyage, to leave on a trip

partout, everywhere

pas, ne . . . pas, not; pas du tout, not at all; pas encore, not yet

le pas, step; un faux pas, slip; social error

le passeport, passport

passer, to spend; pass; se passer (de), to do without; Qu'est-ce qui se passe? What is happening

pauvre, poor

payer, to pay; payer ses repas, to pay for one's meals

le pays, country

le paysage, landscape; scenery

le paysan, peasant; farmer

la pêche, peach; fishing

le pêcheur, fisherman

la peinture, painting (the art)

pendant, during; pendant que, while

penser (à), to think (of); je pense que oui, I think so; il pense à son ami, he is thinking of his friend

perdre, to lose

le père, father; tel père, tel fils, like father like son

permettre, to permit

la personne, person; personne, nobody

peser, to weigh; faire peser, to have weighed

petit, small; little; petit à petit, little by little

peu, little, few; un peu plus, a little while longer; peu de choses, few things; beaucoup de choses, many things

peut-être, perhaps

la phrase, sentence

la pièce, room; piece; play; coin; patch

le pied, foot; à pied, on foot

la pierre, stone

pire, *adj.*, worse

pis, *adv.*, worse

la place, place; seat; square

la plage, beach

plaire, to please; il plaît, it pleases; s'il vous plaît, please (if it pleases you)

le plaisir, pleasure; le plaisir est pour moi, the pleasure is mine

le plat, dish; course

plat, flat; être à plat, to have a flat tyre

le plateau, tray

plein, full; faire le plein d'essence, to fill the tank

pleurer, to weep

pleuvoir, to rain; il pleut à verse, it's raining buckets

la pluie, rain

la plupart (de), most (of); the majority; la plupart de places, most of the seats; pour la plupart, for the most part

plus, more; plus de cinq, more than five; non plus, (not) either; en plus, in addition; plus tôt, sooner, de plus en plus, more and more; plus ou moins, more or less

plusieurs, several

plutôt, rather

la poche, pocket

le point, point; ne . . . point, not at all; il est sur le point de partir, he is about to leave, il ne parle point, he doesn't speak at all

le poids, weight

le pois, pea

le poisson, fish

politique, political

la pomme, apple; la pomme cuite, baked apple; la pomme de terre, potato

le pont, bridge; deck

le port de mer, seaport

la porte, door

la porte-parapluies, umbrella stand

porter, to bear; carry; wear; se porter, to feel (health); Comment vous portez-vous? How do you feel? How are you?

le porteur, porter

poser, to pose; to put; poser des questions, to ask questions

posséder, to possess

la poste, post-office; le mandat-poste, money order

le poste, station; le poste de radio, radio set; le poste de télévision, television set; le poste d'essence, petrol station

le pot au lait, milk jug

la poterie, pottery

le poulet, chicken

pour, for; to; in order to; for the sake of

le pourboire, tip

le pourcentage, percentage

pourquoi, why

pourtant, however; yet

pouvoir, to be able; can; may

précis, precise; sharp; **à cinq heures précises**, at five sharp

préférer, to prefer

premier (première *f*), first

prendre, to take; **prendre des renseignements**, to get information; **prendre le petit déjeuner**, to have breakfast; **prendre l'avion, le bateau**, to travel by plane, by boat; **prendre un billet**, to buy a ticket

près (de), near; close to; **à peu près**, pretty near; more or less

presque, almost; nearly

prêt, ready

prêter, to lend

prier, to pray; to beg

le prix, price; prize; **à prix fixe**, at a set price

le problème, problem

prochain, next

proche, near

produire, to produce

le produit, product

le professeur, teacher; professor

profond, profound

le programme, programme

le progrès, progress; **faire des progrès**, to make progress

le projet, project; plan

la promenade, walk; stroll; **faire une promenade**, to take a walk; **une promenade à bicyclette**, a bicycle ride

se promener, to go for a walk; **se promener en voiture**, to go for a drive

promettre, to promise

la propagande, propaganda

propos: **à propos**, by the way; **à propos du film**, with reference to the film

propre, own; clean; neat; **leur propre langue**, their own language

la puce, flea; **le Marché aux Puces**, the Flea Market

puis, then

puisque, since

punir, to punish

Q

la qualité, quality

quand, when

quant à, as for; as to; **quant à moi**, as for me

la quantité, quantity

le quart, quarter; 125 grams

que, qu'est-ce que, *interrog. pron. object*, what? Que voulez-vous? Qu'est-ce que vous voulez? What do you want?

que, *rel. pron. object*, whom; that; which (see Chapter 34, p. 201, Grammar Notes 1); **voilà le garçon que vous cherchiez**, there is the boy you were looking for

que, *conjunction*, that; than; **je sais qu'il a raison**, I know that he is right; **il est plus grand que moi**, he is taller than I

quel (quelle *f*), *adj.*, what; which; **Quelle cravate avez-vous choisie?** Which tie have you chosen? **Quel est le prix?** What's the price?

quelconque, any; whatsoever; **un dessert quelconque**, some sort of dessert

quelque, some; any; **quelque chose d'autre**, something else; **quelques films**, some films; **quelque part**, somewhere; **quelque peu**, somewhat; **quelquefois**, sometimes

quelqu'un, someone; somebody; **quelques-uns**, several

qu'est-ce qui, *interrog. pron. subject*, what? Qu'est-ce qui est arrivé? What has happened?

qui, *interrog. pron. subject or object*, who? whom? Qui est-ce? Who is it? Qui cherchez-vous? Whom are you looking for? De qui parlez-vous? Of whom are you speaking?

qui, *rel. pron. subject*, who (see Chapter 34, p. 201, Grammar Notes 1); **Connaissez-vous l'homme qui demeure ici?** Do you know the man who lives here?

la question, question; **poser des questions**, to ask questions

une quinzaine, two weeks; **dans une quinzaine**, in two weeks (fifteen days)

quitter, to leave; take off (*clothes*); **il quitte la chambre**, he leaves the bedroom

quoi, what, *interrog. pron. with prepositions*; À quoi pensez-vous? What are you thinking of? **il n'y a pas de quoi**, don't mention it; you're welcome

quoique, although

R

raconter, to tell; to recount

la radio, radio

la raison, reason; il a raison, he is right

le rang, row

ramasser, to pick up

se rappeler, to recall; remember; Je ne me rappelle pas son adresse, I don't recall his address

rapprocher, to bring nearer

rapporter, to bring back

le rasoir, razor; le rasoir de sûreté, safety razor; le rasoir électrique, electric razor

la recette, recipe

recevoir, to receive

réchauffer, to warm up

recommander, to recommend

recommencer, to begin again

regarder, to look at; en tout ce qui regarde les en-têtes, in everything that concerns the headings

la règle, ruler

régner, to reign

regretter, to regret; be sorry; je le regrette beaucoup, I'm very sorry

remarquer, to remark; to notice

remercier, to thank

remplir, to fill; rempli de, filled with

remporter, to carry back

la rencontre, meeting; je vais à la rencontre de Mme D, I am going to meet Mrs. D.

se rencontrer, to meet each other

rendre, to give back; render; rendre visite (à), to pay a visit to (somebody); rendre service (à), to do a service to; to aid; se rendre compte (de), to realize

le renseignement, information; prendre des renseignements, to ask for information; make inquiries

rentrer, to re-enter; come home

renvoyer, to send back

répéter, to repeat

répondre, to answer; reply

la réponse, answer

le repas, meal; repast

le repos, rest; repose

se reposer, to rest

réserver, to reserve

respirer, to breathe

ressembler (à), to resemble; be alike; ils se ressemblent, they resemble each other

le reste, remainder; rest

rester, to remain; rester (être) debout, to stand

retard, en retard, late; nous sommes en retard, we are late

retenir, to hold back; retain; reserve; retenir une place, to reserve a seat

se retirer, to withdraw

le retour, return; M. Davis est de retour, Mr. Davis is back

retourner, to return; go back

réussir (à), to succeed in

réveiller, to awaken; se réveiller, to wake up

revenir, to come back; return

rêver, to dream

revoir, to see again; au revoir, goodbye

la revue, magazine

le rhum, rum

riche, rich

le rideau, curtain

rien, ne ... rien, nothing; rien de plus facile, nothing easier; de rien or il n'y a pas de quoi, you're welcome

rire, to laugh; rire (de), to laugh at

la rive, bank (of river)

la rivière, stream; river

la robe, dress

le rôle, role; part

le roman, novel

rond, round; plump

la roue, wheel

rouge, red

la rue, street

S

sage, good; well-behaved; wise

sain, healthy

la saison, season

saisir, to seize

sale, dirty; nasty

la salle, room; la salle de classe, classroom; la salle à manger, dining-room; la salle d'attente, waiting-room

sans, without

sans cesse, unceasingly

la santé, health; À votre santé! Here's to you! Your health!

le salon, living-room

saluer, to greet

la saucisse, sausage

sauf, except; sauf (sauve *f*), safe; sain et sauf, safe and sound

sauter, to jump

savoir, to know; le savoir-faire, tact, know-how; le savoir-vivre, good manners

le savon, soap

la séance, performance

le séjour, sojourn

selon, according to

la semaine, week; **deux fois par semaine,** twice a week

sembler, to seem; appear

le sens, sense; opinion; meaning; direction; **le bons sens,** common sense; **sens unique,** one way

le sentiment, feeling; sentiment

sentir, to feel; perceive; smell; **il se sent chez lui,** he feels at home

la serviette, napkin; **la serviette de toilette,** bath towel

se serrer, to crowd

servir, to serve

seul, alone

seulement, only; **non seulement . . . mais aussi,** not only . . . but also

si, if; whether; **sinon,** otherwise

le siècle, century

la sœur, sister

la soie, silk; **une robe de soie,** a silk dress

la soif, thirst; **il a soif,** he is thirsty

le soir, evening; **ce soir,** this evening; tonight

le soleil, sun

la somme, sum

le sommeil, sleep; **j'ai sommeil,** I am sleepy

le son, sound

son (sa, ses), *poss. adj.,* his; hers; its (see Chapter 13, p. 75, Grammar Notes 2)

songer (à), to dream (of)

sonner, to sound; to ring

la sorte, sort; kind

la sortie, departure; exit

sortir, to go out; leave; **cela sort de l'ordinaire,** it's unusual

la soucoupe, saucer

soudain, suddenly

souffrir, to suffer

souhaiter, to wish for; to desire

le soulier, shoe

le souper, supper

sourire, to smile

sous, under

se souvenir de, to remember; **nous ne nous souvenons pas de toutes les circonstances,** we do not remember all the circumstances

souvent, often; **assez souvent,** quite often; **plus souvent,** more often

S.T.C., service et tax compris, including service and tax

la station-service, petrol station

stationner, to park; **Défense de stationner!** No parking!

la sténo-dactylo, shorthand typist

le style, style

le stylo, fountain-pen

le sucre, sugar

le sucrier, sugar bowl

le sud, south

suffire, to be sufficient; **cela suffit,** that's enough

la suite, sequence; result; continuation; **tout de suite,** immediately; **et ainsi de suite,** and so forth, etc.

suivre, to follow

le sujet, subject; **au sujet (de),** about; in the matter of

le supplément, supplement; extra; **en supplément,** in addition; extra

sur, on; upon; over; above, about

sûr, sure; **bien sûr,** certainly; indeed

surprendre, to surprise

surtout, above all; especially

sympathique, nice; pleasant

T

le tabac, tobacco

le tableau, painting (picture)

tacher, to try

tant, so much; so many; so; **tant mieux!** good! so much the better! **tant pis!** so much the worse! **tant d'exercices!** so many exercises!

tantôt, soon; **à tantôt,** see you soon

tard, late

la tarte, tart; pie

la tasse, cup

tel (telle *f,* **tels, telles),** such; like; **tel père, tel fils,** like father like son; **un tel homme,** such a man

téléphoner, to telephone

le temps, time; weather; **de temps en temps,** from time to time; **Quel temps fait-il?** How is the weather? **à temps,** in time

tenir, to hold; keep; **tiens! well! tenir table ouverte,** to keep open house

terminer, to finish

la tête, head; **le mal de tête,** headache; **avoir mal à la tête,** to have a headache

le timbre, stamp; **le timbre-poste,** postage stamp

tirer, to draw; pull; shoot; **se tirer d'affaire,** to get along

les toilettes *f,* lavatory; washroom

le toit, roof

tomber, to fall

le ton, tone

ton, ta, tes, *poss. adj.*, your (see Chapter 13, p. 74, Grammar Notes 2)

tort, wrong; **vous avez tort**, you are wrong

tôt, soon; early; **plus tôt**, sooner; earlier; **le plus tôt possible**, as soon as possible

toucher, to touch

toujours, always; still; **c'est toujours ça**, so much to the good; **il pleut toujours**, it is still raining

tourner, to turn

tout (toute *f*, tous, toutes), all; whole; every; **tout le monde**, everybody; **en tout cas**, in any case; **pas du tout**, not at all; **tout à fait**, quite; entirely; **tout à coup**, all of a sudden

traduire, to translate

le trajet, journey; flight; trip

le travail, work

travailler, to work

très, very

tremper, to soak

triste, sad

se tromper, to be mistaken

trop, too; too much; too many; **trop tard**, too late; **trop de livres**, too many books; **trop d'argent**, too much money

le trottoir, pavement

trouver, to find; **se trouver**, to be (somewhere); **Où se trouve mon chapeau?** Where is my hat?

la T.S.F. (**télégraphie sans fil**), radio (wireless)

U

une unité, unity

unir, to unite; **uni**, united; **les États-Unis**, the United States

un usage, custom; usage; **usage rend maître**, practice makes perfect

une usine, factory

un ustensile, utensil

utile, useful

V

la valeur, value

valoir, to be worth; **cela ne vaut rien**, that isn't worth anything

varier, to vary; to change

le veau, veal; **la blanquette de veau**, veal fricassee

la vedette, star (cinema)

le velours, valvet

le vendeur, la vendeuse, seller; salesman; salesgirl

vendre, to sell

venir, to come; **venir de**, to have just; **la caisse vient d'arriver**, the case has just arrived

le vent, wind; **il fait du vent**, it is windy,

la vente, sale; **en vente**, on sale

le ventre, stomach

la vérité, truth

le verre, glass (for drinking)

vers, about; towards

verser, to pour

vert, green

les vêtements *m*, clothes

la viande, meat

vide, empty

la vie, life; **l'eau-de-vie**, brandy

vieux, vieil (*before a vowel or h mute*), (vieille *f*), old; **le vieux portrait**, the old portrait; **le vieil arbre**, the old tree; **les vieux quartiers**, the old districts

vif (vive *f*), alive; living; lively

la ville, city; town; **en ville**, in town; **Mme Davis va en ville pour faire ses achats**, Mrs. Davis goes to town to shop

le vin, wine

le visage, face

la visite, visit; **nous allons lui rendre visite**, we are going to pay him a visit

visiter, to visit; **nous visiterons tous les musées**, we shall visit all the museums

vite, rapidly; quickly; fast

la vitesse, speed; **à toute vitesse**, at full speed

la vitrine, shop window

vivre, to live

voici, here is; here are; **le voici**, here he is; **me voici**, here I am; **les voici**, here they are

la voie, way; thoroughfare; **la voie publique**, public thoroughfare

voilà, there is, are (*pointing*); there now! behold! that's that! **la voilà**, there she is

voir, to see

la voiture, car; carriage; **en voiture**, by car; **En voiture!** All aboard!

la voix, voice; **à haute voix**, in a loud voice

le vol, flight; **l'avion prend son vol** *ou* **décolle**, the aeroplane takes off

volontiers, gladly; with pleasure

votre, vos, your, *poss. adj.* (see Chapter 13, p. 74, Grammar Notes 2)

vouloir, to want; wish; **Que veut dire ce mot?** What does this word mean? **Voulez-vous bien me dire ...?** Will you kindly tell me ...? **je voudrais l'acheter,** I should like to buy it

le voyage, voyage; trip; **Bon voyage!** Pleasant journey! **M. Davis est en voyage,** Mr. Davis is on a trip; **le voyage d'affaires,** the business trip; **le voyage d'agrément,** pleasure trip.

voyager, to travel

le voyageur (euse *f*), traveller; passenger

voyant, garish

vrai, true; **c'est vrai,** it's true

vraiment, really; truly; **Vraiment! Really!**

la vue, sight; view; **je le connais de vue,** I know him by sight

W

le wagon-lit, sleeper; pullman; **le wagon-restaurant,** dining car

Y

y, there

Z

le zéro, zero: nought

ANSWERS

Exercise No. 1

1 Qui	6 mère	11 bureau
2 commerçant	7 fils; et	12 Il est
3 dans	8 s'appellent; et	13 dernier
4 Il y a	9 cinq pièces	14 toute la journée
5 père	10 cuisine; salle de bain	

Exercise No. 2

1 La	4 Le	7 un	10 L'; le
2 une	5 La	8 La	11 L'; le
3 L'	6 une	9 La; une	12 une; un

Exercise No. 3

1 les chambres	5 les hommes	9 les bureaux	13 les commerçants
2 les mères	6 les salons	10 les personnes	14 les rues
3 les pièces	7 les Anglais	11 les oncles	15 les avenues
4 les fils	8 les étages	12 les enfants	

Exercise No. 4

1 M. Davis est un commerçant anglais.
2 Il habite à Londres.
3 Il y a six personnes dans la famille.
4 Il habite dans une villa.
5 Il y a cinq pièces dans la maison.
6 M. Davis est le père.
7 Mme Davis est la mère.
8 Le bureau est dans Oxford Street.
9 M. Davis prend le train.
10 Il travaille au bureau.

Exercise No. 6

1 Qui	7 aussi	13 Ils parlent
2 importateur	8 Mais	14 rapidement
3 objets d'art	9 C'est pourquoi	15 très intelligent
4 Au printemps	10 le professeur	16 un bon professeur
5 Il désire	11 un ami de M. Davis	
6 parler	12 rendez-vous	

Exercise No. 7

1 est	4 Parle-t-il	7 Il n'étudie pas	10 Il compte
2 Est-il	5 Il apprend	8 Il sait	11 faire
3 Il ne parle pas	6 Il désire	9 Ont-ils	12 parler

Exercise No. 8

1 (d)	3 (g)	5 (c)	7 (a)	9 (h)
2 (f)	4 (b)	6 (e)	8 (j)	10 (i)

Exercise No. 9

1 le français	9 très bien	17 où
2 le Français	10 rapidement	18 bon
3 merci	11 un peu	19 mauvais
4 aussi	12 là	20 avec
5 peut-être	13 de	21 des articles
6 le bureau	14 ici	22 des endroits
7 presque	15 grand	23 c'est pourquoi
8 toujours	16 mais	24 Comment allez-vous ?

Exercise No. 11

1 est assis	6 au-dessus du piano
2 beaucoup de choses	7 entre
3 Il faut savoir	8 des lettres
4 qu'est-ce que c'est que ça ?	9 C'est assez
5 joue; chante	10 À mardi

Exercise No. 12

2 au   3 des   4 du   5 à l'   6 à la   7 aux   8 au   9 à l'   10 de la

Exercise No. 13

2 près de la	5 entre les	7 derrière la	9 dans la
3 Sur le	6 autour de la	8 devant le	10 avec; dans le
4 au-dessus du bureau			

Exercise No. 14

1 M. Davis est assis dans le salon.
2 M. Picard est assis près de lui.
3 Il y a beaucoup de choses autour de nous.
4 Oui, elle chante bien.
5 Mme Davis joue bien du piano.
6 Il est sur le piano.
7 Il est au mur au-dessus du piano.
8 La bibliothèque est devant une fenêtre.
9 Le miroir est entre les fenêtres.
10 Le bureau est près de la porte.
11 Une chaise est près du bureau.
12 Il y a des livres sur la petite table.

Exercise No. 15

1 (g)   2 (e)   3 (i)   4 (h)   5 (j)   6 (k)   7 (l)   8 (a)   9 (d)   10 (c)   11 (b)   12 (f)

Exercise No. 16

1 toute la journée	7 Comment allez-vous ?
2 s'il vous plaît	8 Où
3 peut-être	9 Qu'est-ce que c'est que ça ?
4 Bonsoir	10 Qui
5 en ville	11 Qu'est-ce qui
6 C'est pourquoi	12 Quand

Exercise No. 17

1 (d)   2 (f)   3 (i)   4 (k)   5 (h)   6 (g)   7 (c)   8 (a)   9 (j)   10 (b)   11 (e)

Exercise No. 18

1 devant la maison	6 Les livres du garçon
2 autour de la table	7 La mère de la jeune fille
3 près de la porte	8 Le maître des enfants
4 derrière le bureau	9 au mur
5 sur le piano	10 À qui

Exercise No. 19

1 Qui est M. Davis?
2 C'est un commerçant anglais.
3 Où habite-t-il?
4 Il habite dans les environs de Londres.
5 Pourquoi apprend-il le français?
6 Il désire faire un voyage en France.
7 Qui est son professeur?
8 Son professeur est M. Picard.
9 Pourquoi apprend-il vite?
10 Il apprend vite parce qu'il est intelligent.
11 Combien d'enfants y a-t-il dans la famille Davis (*or* dans la famille de M. Davis)?
12 Il y a quatre enfants.
13 Combien de pièces y a-t-il dans la maison de M. Davis?
14 Il y a cinq pièces, une salle de bain et une cuisine.

Exercise No. 20

Mr. Davis Is Learning French

Mr. Davis is an English businessman who imports art objects from France. That is why he wants to make a trip to France in the spring. He wants to talk with his agent. He also wants to visit some interesting places in France. But he does not know how to speak French.

Mr. Davis has a good teacher. He is a Frenchman who lives in London and who is called Mr. Picard. Every Tuesday and Thursday the teacher takes the train to go to the home of his pupil. There the two gentlemen talk a little in French. Mr. Davis is very intelligent and he learns quickly. During the first lesson, for example, he learns by heart the greetings and farewells. He knows already how to say: — Hello. How are you? See you soon, and till tomorrow. He knows already how to say in French the names of many things which are in his living-room, and he knows how to answer correctly to the questions: — What is that? and — Where is . . . ? Mr. Picard is well satisfied with the progress of his pupil and he says: — Very good. That's enough for today. Goodbye.

Exercise No. 21

1 sont importants
2 des verbes
3 Pourquoi
4 Parce que
5 avec lui
6 d'autres pays
7 le bateau ou l'avion
8 Combien
9 très rapidement
10 Ça suffit (*or* c'est assez) pour aujourd'hui

Exercise No. 22

2 ils ne parlent pas	4 elles désirent	6 demeurez-vous?
3 nous comptons	5 je travaille	7 il écoute

8 il ne coûte pas	11 elles habitent	14 importe-t-il
9 nous causons	12 elle ne visite pas	15 Qui parle?
10 vous étudiez	13 vous commencez	16 Les enfants jouent

Exercise No. 23

2 Paul n'étudie pas . . .	7 Qui n'étudie pas . . . ?
3 Nous ne parlons pas . . .	8 Nous ne travaillons pas . . .
4 Ils n'écoutent pas . . .	9 Elle ne compte pas . . .
5 ne jouez pas . . .	10 Vous ne travaillez pas . . .
6 Elle ne désire pas . . .	

Exercise No. 25

1 Les messieurs sont assis dans le salon chez M. Davis.
2 M. Picard commence à parler.
3 M. Davis écoute avec attention.
4 M. Picard pose les questions.
5 M. Davis répond aux questions.
6 Oui monsieur, les verbes sont importants.
7 Oui, il importe des objets d'art.
8 Non monsieur, il ne parle pas français.
9 Il désire faire un voyage en France.
10 Il compte visiter la France, le Maroc, et peut-être la Corse.
11 Il va prendre l'avion.
12 M. Davis apprend rapidement.

Exercise No. 26

1 ouvre	7 Nous sommes
2 Entrez, monsieur	8 l'aîné
3 Passez au salon s'il vous plaît	9 dix ans
4 Ma fille	10 la plus jeune
5 Avez-vous	11 ils causent
6 j'ai	12 accepte

Exercise No. 27

1 avez-vous	7 as-tu	12 a
2 J'ai	8 Je n'ai pas	13 avez-vous
3 a-t-elle	9 ont-elles	14 J'ai
4 Elle a	10 Elles n'ont pas	15 ont-elles
5 Avez-vous	11 a	16 ont
6 Nous n'avons pas		

Exercise No. 28

1 va-t-il?
2 Il va
3 Allez-vous
4 nous allons
5 vont-ils
6 va
7 vas-tu
8 va
9 Allez-vous
10 Nous n'allons pas
11 allez-vous
12 Nous allons
13 Comment allez-vous? (*or* Comment ça va?)
14 Je vais bien (*or* ça va bien) (*Lit.* It goes well)

Exercise No. 29

1 est	7 Êtes-vous	12 Ils sont
2 est	8 je suis	13 Êtes-vous
3 est	9 sont	14 nous ne sommes pas
4 est	10 Ils sont	15 Nous sommes
5 est-il	11 sont-ils	16 N'est-il pas
6 il n'est pas		

Exercise No. 30

1 M. Picard sonne à la porte.
2 La bonne ouvre la porte.
3 M. Davis attend M. Picard dans le salon.
4 Annette est malade.
5 Oui, elle est enrhumée.
6 Il a quatre enfants.
7 Il y a six personnes dans sa famille.
8 Ils s'appellent Phillipe, Henri, Rosette et Annette.
9 Philippe a dix ans.
10 Oui, ils vont à l'école.
11 Il invite M. Picard à visiter son bureau.
12 Oui, il accepte l'invitation.

Exercise No. 31

1 grandes	5 de vous voir	9 bleu
2 On peut	6 J'aime beaucoup	10 Mon Dieu!
3 journaux	7 Je vois	11 Pas loin d'ici
4 est assis	8 De quelle couleur	12 Tant mieux! Allons-y!

Exercise No. 32

1 assise	5 commode	9 bon	13 grande
2 petits	6 haute	10 jolies	14 rouge; bleu
3 intelligente	7 gris	11 grands	15 noires
4 jolies	8 assidus	12 illustrées	16 vieux

Exercise No. 33

1 belle	4 bonnes	7 Quel	10 Quels
2 bonne	5 blanches	8 Quelles	11 toute
3 belles	6 longue	9 quelle	12 tous

Exercise No. 34

1 Le bureau de M. Davis est très commode.
2 Les fenêtres du bureau sont grandes.
3 Il y a des affiches illustrées aux murs.
4 Il y a des journaux français sur la table.
5 Le ciel sur l'affiche est bleu.
6 Le soleil est jaune.
7 Comment allez-vous, M. Davis?
8 Très bien, merci.
9 J'ai faim.
10 Moi aussi j'ai faim.

Exercise No. 35

1 Il est au dernier étage d'un grand immeuble.
2 Il n'est pas grand.
3 Oui, il est commode.
4 Il y a des affiches illustrées aux murs.
5 Il y a beaucoup de papiers sur le bureau de M. Davis.

6 Il y a un petit bureau près de la porte.
7 Il y a une longue table entre les fenêtres.
8 M. Davis est assis.
9 Le soleil est jaune.
10 Les cheminées sont noires.
11 La colline est verte.
12 Oui, madame, le ciel est bleu.
13 Le château est blanc.
14 Le toit est rouge.
15 Oui, il a faim.

Exercise No. 36

1 Ses parents	7 Je l'étudie
2 Son ami	8 Le français me plaît
3 Voici	9 à merveille
4 n'est-ce pas	10 Je comprends M. Picard.
5 J'apprends	11 Vous êtes
6 n'est pas trop difficile	12 Pas du tout; la vérité

Exercise No. 37

1 Are you learning French? Yes, I am learning French. Is Charles learning French? No, he is not learning French.
2 Are you writing a letter? I am not writing a letter. What are you writing? I am writing the French lesson.
3 What are you reading? I am reading a French newspaper. What is Anna reading? She is reading a French magazine.
4 Do you understand your teacher when he speaks fast? No, but we understand him well when he speaks slowly.
5 What does Mr. Davis sell? He sells art objects. Does he sell wholesale or retail? He only sells wholesale.
6 Whom is Mr. Davis waiting for? He is waiting for Mr. Picard. Where is he waiting for him? He is waiting for him in the living-room.

Exercise No. 38

2 Nous apprenons	8 Ils ne prennent pas	14 Écrivons
3 Je comprends	9 Nous répondons	15 vendent-ils
4 Ils lisent	10 Qui apprend	16 Lisez
5 Écrivez-vous	11 Lit-il	17 Nous attendons
6 lisez-vous	12 Ils ne comprennent pas	18 Entendez-vous
7 Je prends	13 nous n'écrivons pas	

Exercise No. 39

1 M. Dupont demeure à Londres.
2 Oui, il parle bien le français.
3 Non, monsieur, ses parents ne sont pas américains. Ils sont canadiens.
4 Il sait que M. Davis apprend le français.
5 Il entre un jour dans le bureau de M. Davis.
6 Il salue M. Davis en français.
7 M. Davis apprend à parler, à lire et à écrire le français.
8 Il étudie assidûment.
9 M. Picard est son professeur de français.
10 C'est un bon professeur.
11 Il comprend bien quand M. Picard parle français.
12 Il apprend les mots et les expressions de la vie quotidienne.
13 M. Davis va faire un voyage en France.
14 Il espère partir au printemps.
15 M. Dupont dit: Bon voyage, et bonne chance!

Exercise No. 40

1 (c) 2 (e) 3 (a) 4 (g) 5 (i) 6 (b) 7 (j) 8 (d) 9 (h) 10 (f)

Exercise No. 41

1 Je parle français.
2 Ils demeurent en Angleterre.
3 Nous avons faim.
4 La revue est blanche et noire.
5 Les maisons sont rouges.
6 J'ai quinze ans.
7 Les professeurs posent des questions
8 Nous répondons aux questions.
9 Il attend son ami.
10 J'écris des lettres.

Exercise No. 42

1 travaillons
2 apprennent
3 ne savez pas
4 écris
5 lisent
6 ne comprends pas
7 étudie
8 prenez
9 attendent
10 ne répondez pas
11 lisez
12 n'attendez pas

Exercise No. 43

1 J'ai faim; je n'ai pas faim.
2 Je suis enrhumé; je ne suis pas . . .
3 J'étudie la leçon; je n'étudie pas . . .
4 J'attends le professeur; je n'attends pas . . .
5 Je compte voyager; je ne compte pas . . .
6 J'apprends à écrire le français; je n'apprends pas . . .
7 Je lis la revue; je ne lis pas . . .
8 J'écris la lettre; je n'écris pas . . .
9 Je comprends les questions; je ne comprends pas . . .
10 J'accepte l'invitation; je n'accepte pas . . .
11 Je commence à lire; je ne commence pas . . .
12 Je réponds à la question; je ne réponds pas . . .

Exercise No. 44

1 Qui
2 Qui
3 Qui
4 qui
5 qui
6 Qu'est-ce que
7 Qu'
8 Qui
9 Qu'est-ce qui
10 Que
11 Qu'est-ce que
12 Qu'est-ce qui

Exercise No. 45

Mr. Davis already knows the names of all the objects in his house. Now he is beginning to study the verbs because he wants to learn to read, write and speak in French. He also wants to learn the numbers in French. As he wants to visit his agent in Paris who does not speak English, he wants to learn to speak French as soon as possible. Therefore he needs much practice with people who speak French well. Luckily he has two French friends who are in business near his office in Oxford Street.

One day Mr. Davis goes to visit these French gentlemen. The two gentlemen listen with attention while Mr. Davis talks with them in French. After ten minutes of conversation the gentlemen ask their friend many questions, and they are well satisfied with his progress.

Exercise No. 46

Thursday, April twenty-six at nine o'clock in the evening Mr. Picard arrives at the house of his pupil, Mr. Davis. The eldest son, a boy of ten, opens the door, and greets the teacher politely. They go into the living-room, where Mr. Davis usually awaits his teacher.

But this evening he is not there. Mrs. Davis is not there either. Mr. Picard is very much surprised, and he asks the boy: — Where is your daddy? The son answers sadly: — Daddy is ill. He is in bed because he has a bad cold.

The teacher becomes sad and says: — What a pity! Well, next week we shall study for two hours. Till next Tuesday, then. Goodbye son. The boy answers: — Goodbye, sir.

Exercise No. 47

1 Ils prennent	6 très jolie	11 Comme vous dites
2 ces tasses	7 presque aussi jolie	12 C'est un plat simple
3 fleurs bleues	8 Vous connaissez	13 encore une tasse
4 célèbre	9 C'est vrai	14 Tout
5 Chaque région	10 beaucoup de	

Exercise No. 49

1 nous disons	6 Que dites-vous?	11 ils disent
2 je vois	7 Que voyez-vous?	12 Que disent-ils?
3 il ne dit pas	8 ils voient	13 elle ne voit pas
4 il dit	9 Vois-tu?	14 voyons
5 Dit-il?	10 je ne vois pas	15 dites-moi

Exercise No. 50

1 ce	3 ce	5 cette	7 ce	9 ces	11 ces
2 ces	4 ces	6 cet	8 cette	10 cet	12 cet

Exercise No. 52

1 Ils sont assis dans la salle à manger.
2 Ils prennent du café avec des gâteaux.
3 M. Davis dit: — Comment trouvez-vous ces tasses et ces soucoupes? —
4 La tasse blanche est de Limoges.
5 La porcelaine de Limoges est célèbre.
6 Il est de Vallauris.
7 Elle est célèbre pour sa poterie.
8 Elle est en Provence.
9 Elle est très jolie.
10 M. Davis connaît bien son métier.
11 Il a des échantillons de poterie ordinaire.
12 Elle est simple.
13 Il accepte encore une tasse de café.
14 Il dit: — Merci bien. Tout est délicieux.

Exercise No. 53

1 Vous savez
2 aussi importante que
3 à quoi
4 Je crois que oui; voulez dire
5 Vous avez raison; sont indispensables
6 Nous avons besoin
7 Sans argent; grand-chose
8 En attendant; vous avancez rapidement
9 C'est
10 À jeudi prochain

Exercise No. 54

1 Je veux	5 Nous voulons	8 Pouvez-vous
2 Je peux (puis)	6 Nous ne pouvons pas	9 Veut-il
3 Voulez-vous	7 Ils ne veulent pas	10 Peut-elle
4 Pouvez-vous		

Exercise No. 55

(a) trente	(d) quarante-neuf	(g) dix-sept	(j) soixante-huit
(b) dix	(e) seize	(h) quinze	(k) vingt-quatre
(c) cinquante	(f) trente-huit	(i) soixante-deux	(l) treize

Exercise No. 56

(a) deux et six font huit
(b) dix et sept font dix-sept
(c) sept fois huit font cinquante-six
(d) neuf fois sept font soixante-trois
(e) dix-neuf moins huit fait onze
(f) dix-huit moins six fait douze
(g) soixante divisé par dix fait six
(h) soixante-neuf divisé par trois fait vingt-trois

Exercise No. 57

2 Il y a douze mois dans une année.
3 Il y a vingt-quatre heures dans une journée.
4 Il y a soixante minutes dans une heure.
5 Il y a soixante secondes dans une minute.
6 Il y a trente jours dans le mois de septembre.
7 Il y a trente-six étudiants dans la classe.
8 J'ai dix-sept ans.
9 Il a dix-neuf ans.
10 Il y a quinze autos dans le garage.

Exercise No. 58

1 Il sait déjà que le nom des choses et des personnes est important.
2 Les nombres sont aussi importants que les noms et les verbes.
3 Nous avons besoin des nombres pour le commerce.
4 Il pense tout de suite au commerce.
5 Nous avons besoin des nombres pour téléphoner.
6 M. Davis veut comprendre et employer les nombres correctement.
7 Il avance rapidement.
8 dix, vingt, trente, quarante, cinquante, soixante.

Exercise No. 59

1 Combien de fois; en voyage	6 vaut	
2 On; pour prendre des billets	7 à peu près	
3 dans les grands magasins	8 Vous voulez acheter	
4 Connaissez-vous	9 Vous donnez	
5 Je le connais	10 Il me rend	

Exercise No. 60

1 What are you doing? I am writing a letter.
2 What is John doing? He is playing the piano.
3 What is Mary doing? She is studying the French lesson.
4 What are the girls doing? They are shopping.
5 What are you doing, child? I am playing ball.
6 What is Mr. Martin doing? He is having the luggage weighed.
7 Do you believe this story? I do not believe it.
8 Does your friend believe it? He doesn't believe it either.

Exercise No. 61

(a) quatre cents
(b) mille
(c) sept cent cinquante-trois
(d) mille neuf cent soixante-quatorze
(e) quatre-vingt-quinze

(f) soixante-dix-sept
(g) quatre-vingt-six
(h) soixante et onze
(i) six cent soixante-dix
(j) quatorze mille cinq cent quatre-vingt-six

Exercise No. 63

1 Je reçois 60 (soixante) francs.
2 Je paie 150 (cent cinquante) francs.
3 Je paie 34 (trente-quatre) francs.
4 Je reçois 6,50 (six francs cinquante).
5 J'ai en poche 175 (cent soixante-quinze) francs.
6 Oui, monsieur, il est millionnaire.
7 Un billet de cinq livres a plus de valeur qu'un (*than a*) billet de dix francs.
8 Je ne sais pas, monsieur.

Exercise No. 64

1 Savez-vous
2 Nous connaissons
3 Nous ne savons pas
4 Il sait (comment)

5 Je sais
6 Ils ne connaissent pas
7 Je connais

8 Savez-vous (comment)
9 Connaissent-ils
10 savoir

Exercise No. 65

1 Nos	5 ses	9 Sa	13 ton; mon
2 ma	6 vos	10 Leurs	14 son
3 notre	7 votre	11 notre	15 leur
4 Leurs	8 Son	12 son	

Exercise No. 66

16 seize
32 trente-deux
48 quarante-huit
64 soixante-quatre
80 quatre-vingts
160 cent soixante

Exercise No. 67

1 Nous dînons au restaurant.
2 L'addition pour tout le monde se monte à 371,45 F (trois cent soixante et onze francs quarante-cinq).
3 Nous ne laissons pas de pourboire.
4 Je porte une valise très lourde à la gare.
5 Elle pèse 30 (trente) kilos.
6 En France on compte les distances en kilomètres.
7 M. Davis sait changer les kilomètres en milles.
8 M. Davis achète trois paires de gants.
9 Le sujet de la prochaine conversation est: les heures de la journée.
10 M. Davis dit: — Mieux vaut tard que jamais.

Exercise No. 68

1 À quelle heure
2 La première séance; seize heures trente
3 d'autres questions
4 la gare

5 demande des renseignements
6 un billet d'aller et retour
7 est-ce que le train part
8 Arrive-t-il
9 de bonne heure
10 Les voici
11 Merci bien (*or* Merci beaucoup)
12 À votre service

Exercise No. 69

1 part	4 ne dort pas	7 Je ne sens pas	9 Je sors
2 partez-vous	5 sert	8 sortent-ils	10 Ne dormez pas
3 Nous dormons	6 Sentez-vous		

Exercise No. 70

2 vingt-deux heures quinze
3 six heures trente
4 douze heures
5 seize heures trente
6 dix-huit heures quarante
7 à vingt et une heures
8 seize heures dix
9 sept heures quarante-cinq
10 neuf heures moins vingt du matin (*or* huit heures quarante)

Exercise No. 71

1 Tout le monde veut savoir l'heure.
2 M. Davis joue le rôle du voyageur.
3 M. Picard joue le rôle de l'employé du guichet.
4 Il désire un billet de deuxième classe.
5 Un billet d'aller et retour coûte 74 F (soixante-quatorze francs).
6 M. Picard joue le rôle de l'employée du cinéma.
7 M. Davis demande des renseignements.
8 Il y a trois séances à ce ciné.
9 Il prend deux billets pour la troisième séance.
10 Il paie ces deux billets cinquante-deux francs.

Exercise No. 72

1 (*f*)   2 (*h*)   3 (*a*)   4 (*j*)   5 (*b*)   6 (*i*)   7 (*c*)   8 (*d*)   9 (*e*)   10 (*g*)

Exercise No. 73

2 Nous avons besoin d'	6 Aimez-vous	10 Vous avez raison
3 connaît son métier	7 j'ai faim	11 vous avez tort
4 changer de l'argent	8 voulez-vous dire	12 avez-vous besoin
5 pensez-vous	9 Nous payons nos repas	

Exercise No. 74

1 (*c*) 2 (*h*) 3 (*a*) 4 (*d*) 5 (*g*) 6 (*k*) 7 (*b*) 8 (*e*) 9 (*l*) 10 (*f*) 11 (*i*) 12 (*j*)

Exercise No. 75

2 je veux faire . . .	5 je pars . . .	8 je connais . . .
3 je peux acheter . . .	6 je compte . . .	9 je donne . . .
4 je porte . . .	7 je dis . . .	10 je sais . . .

Exercise No. 76

2 nous ne calculons pas . . .
3 nous ne trouvons pas . . .
4 nous ne lisons pas . . .
5 nous n'écrivons pas . . .
6 nous ne dînons pas . . .

7 nous ne connaissons pas . . .
8 nous n'achetons pas . . .
9 nous n'avons pas . . .
10 nous ne savons pas . . .

Exercise No. 77
The Davis Family Drops In On Daddy
(Lit. Makes A Little Visit To Daddy)

It is the first time that the Davis family is coming to see Mr. Davis at his office. Mrs. Davis and her four children enter a block of offices and go up to the top floor in the lift. Annette, the youngest, who is only five years old is very inquisitive. She asks her mother many questions about the office.

When they arrive at the office the father gets up and says: — What a pleasant surprise! How glad I am to see you!

The children admire all the objects they see in the office: the typewriter, the articles from Paris, the samples of French ceramics, the French magazines, and especially the coloured posters on the walls. Everybody is very happy.

Philip the eldest, looks out of the large window and sees the blue sky and the sun which is shining. Below he sees the cars which are passing through the street. From the top floor they seem very small.

The visit over, the whole family goes into a restaurant which is not far from the office. They all eat heartily, especially the boys, because they are very hungry.

Exercise No. 78
The Draught Horse and the Car
A Modern Fable

Annette, the youngest of Mr. Davis' children, is very fond of Aesop's old fables. She also like this modern fable which Mr. Picard has written for her. Here is the fable: 'The Percheron and the Car'.

A car is passing along the road and sees a Percheron. The Percheron is a French horse, big and strong. However, this Percheron seems very tired. He is harnessed to a heavy cart.

The car stops and says to the Percheron: — Good morning. You are going along very slowly. Don't you want to go fast like me?

— Oh, yes, madam. But tell me how it is possible?

— It is not difficult, says the car. — My petrol tank is full. Drink some and you'll see something!

Then the Percheron drinks some petrol. Now he does not go along slowly any more. He does not go fast either. In fact, he does not go at all. He has a stomach-ache.

Poor horse! He is not very intelligent, is he? He does not know that petrol is good for cars but that it is no good at all for horses.

Exercise No. 79

1 J'aime beaucoup voir
2 ne m'intéressent pas
3 Ils adorent
4 toutes les vedettes de l'écran
5 Ils les connaissent

6 près de chez vous
7 à pied
8 Nous préférons
9 rester (*or* être) debout
10 Donc; de bonne heure

Exercise No. 80

1 Je viens
2 Ils ne viennent pas
3 vient
4 viennent

5 Venez
6 Venez-vous
7 Nous revenons
8 revient-il

9 Elle ne vient pas
10 Venez-vous
11 devenir
12 Je veux devenir

Exercise No. 81

1 les	5 le	9 nous	13 vous
2 la	6 la	10 nous	14 m'
3 l'	7 le	11 y	15 t'
4 les	8 vous	12 y	

Exercise No. 82

1 M. Davis sait demander des renseignements.
2 Ils préfèrent le théâtre.
3 Ils préfèrent le ciné.
4 Oui, monsieur, ils les connaissent bien.
5 La famille Davis habite une petite ville dans les environs de Londres.
6 Il est près de la maison de M. Davis.
7 Ils préfèrent les places au quatorzième ou au quinzième rang.
8 De là, il est possible de bien voir et bien entendre.
9 L'ouvreuse vient les aider au cinéma.
10 Ils arrivent de bonne heure.

Exercise No. 83

1 Vous savez (comment)	5 une date triste	9 D'ailleurs
2 un événement important	6 une date victorieuse	10 Il m'apprend
3 Commençons	7 Finissons	11 C'est vous
4 Comme	8 aussi bien que	12 Pas du tout

Exercise No. 84

1 finissez-vous	5 punit	9 Ils ne finissent pas
2 Nous finissons	6 il n'obéit pas	10 remplit
3 choisissez-vous	7 bâtissent	11 Choisissons
4 Je choisis	8 Remplissez	12 saisir

Exercise No. 85

1 première	4 cinquième	6 premier	8 neuvième
2 troisième	5 douzième	7 dernière	9 derniers
3 quatorzième			

Exercise No. 86

1 le dix-huit avril dix-sept cent (*or* mil sept cent) soixante-quinze.
2 le douze octobre quatorze cent (*or* mil quatre cent) quatre-vingt-douze.
3 le vingt-deux février dix-huit cent (*or* mil huit cent) neuf.
4 le premier mai dix-neuf cent (*or* mil neuf cent) cinquante-six.

Exercise No. 87

1 Il apprend vite parce qu'il aime les questionnaires en français.
2 M. Picard va citer quelques dates de l'histoire de France.
3 M. Davis va citer un événement important pour chacune.
4 Il cite la prise de la Bastille.
5 Il cite la bataille de Waterloo.
6 C'est une date triste.
7 Il cite la victoire des Alliés à la fin de la première guerre mondiale.
8 C'est une date glorieuse pour les Parisiens.
9 Il la connaît bien.
10 Son professeur M. Picard lui apprend à aimer la France.

Exercise No. 88

1 Voyons; la géographie de la France.
2 que je vous pose
3 recevoir de prix
4 est situé
5 de café, de coton, et de sucre
6 le fleuve le plus long
7 beaucoup plus longue que
8 plus petite que
9 la montagne la plus haute
10 plus haut que
11 que vous avez raison
12 est terminé

Exercise No. 89

1 je mets
2 Qui met?
3 Pourquoi mettez-vous?
4 Que mets-tu? *or* Qu'est-ce que tu mets?
5 nous mettons
6 ils ne mettent pas
7 je ne permets pas
8 permet-il?
9 Pourquoi permettez-vous?
10 nous permettons
11 Ne permet-il pas?
12 permettez-moi

Exercise No. 90

1 Are French films better than American films?
2 Some are better, some are worse. In France and in the United States one can see the best and also the worst films. In general, I like French films better.
3 George sings badly. Henry sings worse than George. But William sings worst of all.
4 Philip writes well. But you write better than he. Jane writes best of all.
5 Where do they make the best porcelain? They make it at Limoges.
6 Better late than never.

Exercise No. 91

2 plus aimable que
3 le meilleur stylo
4 si bonne que
5 plus grande que
6 le plus assidu
7 la plus jeune
8 plus intéressant que
9 le plus long
10 une des plus grandes villes
11 plus long et plus large que
12 si mal
13 les meilleurs films
14 le pire (le plus mauvais)
15 plus de

Exercise No. 92

1 La question est: sur quel grand fleuve est-ce que la ville de Paris est située?
2 Il est situé à l'embouchure de la Seine.
3 C'est un grand marché de café, de coton et de sucre.
4 La Volga est plus longue et plus large que la Loire.
5 Le Mont Blanc est plus haut que le Ben Nevis.
6 (*a*) M. Dupont est le plus jeune des trois.
  (*b*) M. Arnaud est le plus âgé des trois.
  (*c*) M. Millet est plus âgé que M. Dupont.
  (*d*) M. Dupont est le plus riche.
  (*e*) M. Arnaud est le moins riche.
  (*f*) M. Millet n'est pas si riche que M. Dupont (*or* Il est moins riche que M. Dupont).

Exercise No. 93

1 une journée typique
2 à six heures et demie
3 matinal
4 de bonne heure
5 Que mangez-vous
6 du café, des petits pains et des œufs
7 Parfois
8 au bureau
9 mon courrier; les réponses
10 Que faites-vous
11 me voir
12 finissez-vous
13 Je quitte
14 Nous nous mettons

Exercise No. 94

2 se	6 se	10 s'	13 vous
3 se, s'	7 se	11 m'	14 me
4 vous	8 nous	12 toi	15 se
5 vous	9 vous		

Exercise No. 95

1 What is your name? My name is John Martin.
2 At what time do you get up? I get up at 7 a.m.
3 At what time do you go to bed? I go to bed at 11 p.m.
4 Do you dress quickly? Yes, I dress very quickly.
5 How are you? I'm well, thank you.
6 How is your father? He is not well. He has a cold.
7 At what time does Mr. Davis sit down at table? He sits down at table at 7 p.m.
8 Are the boys having a good time playing football? Yes, they are having a very good time.

Exercise No. 96

1 Il se lève à six heures et demie.
2 Il se lave et il s'habille.
3 Il s'habille en une demi-heure environ.
4 Vers sept heures, il se met à table dans la salle à manger.
5 Elle se lève de bonne heure.
6 Ils déjeunent ensemble.
7 Il prend du jus d'orange, du café, des petits pains, et des œufs.
8 Parfois il mange des céréales au lieu d'œufs.
9 Il est prêt à partir à sept heures et demie.
10 Il arrive à son bureau à neuf heures.
11 Il déjeune à une heure.
12 Il prend un sandwich, un café et un dessert quelconque.
13 Des clients viennent le voir l'après-midi.
14 Il finit sa journée à cinq heures.

Exercise No. 97

1 bien renseigné
2 Tout de même
3 Nous restons
4 son marché
5 des fruits, des légumes, du lait, du beurre, du fromage, et du café
6 des collants et des casseroles
7 stationner
8 à son aise
9 de bons camarades
10 J'ai envie de déménager

Exercise No. 98

1 du, du	5 des	8 de
2 du; du; des	6 d'	9 de l'
3 de	7 de la; de la; des	10 de
4 des		

Exercise No. 99

2 Oui, elle en achète.	5 N'en mangez pas.	7 Merci. Je n'en veux pas.
3 Non, je n'en ai pas.	6 Il en a trente.	8 Oui, ils en ont assez
4 Prenez-en.		

Exercise No. 100

1 M. Picard est toujours curieux.
2 Il sait déjà que M. Davis rentre assez tard.
3 La famille Davis ne finit pas de dîner beaucoup avant huit heures et demie.
4 Parce que les enfants ne veulent pas se coucher.
5 Il s'appelle 'supermarché'.
6 On y achète des fruits, des légumes, du lait, du café, des conserves, toutes sortes de viande, et ainsi de suite (etc.)
7 On n'y trouve pas de pardessus.
8 Plusieurs grands magasins y ont des succursales.
9 Ils aiment leurs maîtres d'école.
10 M. Picard a envie de déménager en banlieue.

Exercise No. 101

1 (*i*)   2 (*e*)   3 (*f*)   4 (*h*)   5 (*g*)   6 (*a*)   7 (*c*)   8 (*j*)   9 (*b*)   10 (*d*)

Exercise No. 102

1 le fleuve le plus long
2 plus grand que
3 plus fatigué que
4 si grand que
5 plus haut que
6 la plus haute montagne
7 le premier jour
8 le 30 janvier 1956 (dix-neuf cent cinquante-six)
9 de la famille
10 mon meilleur ami

Exercise No. 103

1 Do you have coffee or chocolate for your breakfast? I have neither. I drink a glass of water.
2 Do you want cream and sugar in your coffee? I would like some cream, but I do not want any sugar.
3 What do they have for breakfast in France? They have very little; generally rolls and coffee.
4 What do they have for breakfast in Britain? Sometimes they begin with orange juice. Then they eat cereals, eggs or bacon, often both. English people are also very fond of toast. Of course there is also tea, coffee, milk, bread, or rolls.

Exercise No. 104

2 Non, je ne le préfère pas.
3 Oui, ils les connaissent bien.
4 Oui, nous vous attendons.
5 Non, je me lève tard.
6 Nous nous couchons à onze heures.
7 Oui, ils s'habillent très vite.
8 Je m'appelle Jean Martin.
9 Nous les finissons à quatre heures de l'après-midi.
10 Oui, ils le finissent maintenant.

Exercise No. 105

1 fatiguée; pareille
2 Ils se mettent à table
3 Ils sont (*or* restent) debout
4 sont assis
5 De temps en temps; au lieu de
6 attraper un rhume
7 la plupart de
8 à l'heure
9 Nous sommes; les bienvenus
10 de bonne heure; tard

Exercise No. 106
A Visit to the Liner *Île de France*

It is Saturday. Mr. Davis gets up at eight o'clock, and he looks out the window. The sky is blue. The sun is shining. He says to his wife: — Today let's visit the liner *Île de France*, which arrived this morning. I have some goods on board. We'll have a good opportunity to visit the ship.

— Fine, says Mrs. Davis.

At nine o'clock they leave by car and a few hours later they arrive at the pier. At the entrance they see a group of boys eating ice-cream and talking French.

Mr. Davis greets the boys and chats a little with the nearest one. Here is the conversation:

— Good morning, young man. Are you French?

— No, sir, I am English.

— But you speak French very well.

— Well, these boys who work on the liner *Île de France* are my friends, and they teach me how to speak correctly. They are my teachers. Besides, I study French at the grammar school, and every day I read a few pages of French. By the way, are you French?

— Thank you for the compliment. No, young man, I am English, and like you I am studying French. But I have only one teacher.

— I see. But you speak very well.

— Thanks again. Goodbye and good luck.

— Goodbye, sir. Hope to see you again.

Mr. Davis goes back to his wife, who is waiting for him smiling, and they continue on their way for the visit to the steamer.

— Il est sympathique, ce garçon, says Mr. Davis to his wife, and then he translates the sentence because she doesn't understand French.

Exercise No. 107

1 Quel sale temps!	5 ça va mieux	9 leur apporte
2 Entrez, entrez; trempé	6 attraper un rhume	10 Prenez
3 votre imperméable	7 on ne doit pas sortir	11 Permettez-moi
4 Mettez	8 Venez	12 il pleut toujours

Exercise No. 108

2 nous	6 lui	10 nous	13 leur
3 lui	7 m'	11 nous	14 lui
4 leur	8 lui	12 moi	15 lui
5 leur	9 lui		

Exercise No. 109

1 Il pleut à verse.
2 La bonne ouvre la porte.
3 Il le met dans le porte-parapluies.
4 Il les laisse dans l'entrée
5 Ils entrent dans la salle à manger.
6 Ils prennent du thé au rhum.
7 Elle met sur la table des tasses, des soucoupes, une théière pleine de thé, un sucrier, des cuillers à thé et une bouteille de rhum.
8 Après, elle sort de la salle à manger.
9 M. Davis sert M. Picard.
10 Il y verse du thé avec une portion libérale de rhum.

Exercise No. 110

1 en buvant
2 à pleuvoir
3 il fait chaud
4 il fait très froid
5 il pleut souvent
6 Je préfère (*or* j'aime mieux)
7 préférez-vous (*or* aimez-vous mieux)
8 parlons plutôt
9 d'humidité et de brouillard
10 doit
11 il fait beau
12 bleu; doux; sourit

Exercise No. 112

2 n' . . . pas encore
3 ne . . . jamais
4 n' . . . pas . . . non plus
5 ne . . . rien; ne . . . rien
6 ne . . . pas
7 n' . . . plus
8 ne . . . pas non plus
9 n' . . . rien
10 n' . . . qu'
11 rien
12 pas encore
13 jamais
14 ne . . . jamais
15 ne . . . ni . . . ni

Exercise No. 113

1 Ils parlent du climat.
2 Le climat de la France est un peu différent du climat de l'Angleterre.
3 Il fait chaud. Parfois il fait très chaud.
4 Il préfère l'automne.
5 Il préfère le printemps.
6 Il y a une différence assez marquée entre les saisons en France.
7 Il pleut beaucoup, il fait du vent, le ciel est gris.
8 Le ciel est bleu clair et l'air est doux et embaumé.
9 Il est content parce qu'il va être à Paris au printemps.
10 Il compte partir au mois de mai.

Exercise No. 114

1 nous allons continuer
2 très désagréable
3 qui ont les moyens
4 Est-ce qu'il n'y a pas d'hiver
5 Il ne fait jamais froid
6 Il faut mettre
7 nager le matin
8 On peut voir
9 doit être
10 Si vous avez le temps

Exercise No. 115

1 Which pottery do you prefer, that of Vallauris or that of Biot? I prefer that of Biot.
2 Which hat do you like better? This one or that one? I prefer that one.
3 Which climate is milder, that of France or that of Canada? That of France is milder.
4 How do you like these dresses? I like this one, but I find the colours of that one too garish.
5 Which seats do you prefer, those in the front rows or those in the rear? We prefer those in the front rows.
6 What kind of handkerchiefs are you going to buy? I am going to buy those which are the cheapest.

Exercise No. 116

2 ceux
3 celui-là
4 celles-là
5 celles-là
6 ceux-là
7 celui-ci; celui-là
8 celle-ci; celle-là
9 celui
10 cela

Exercise No. 117

1 Ils quittent Paris en hiver parce que le climat est désagréable.
2 Ils vont en Suisse ou sur la Côte d'Azur.
3 L'hiver est doux. Le soleil brille presque tous les jours.

4 En été il fait plus chaud, mais il y a toujours une jolie brise de mer.
5 Sur la Côte d'Azur on peut nager le matin et faire du ski l'après-midi.
6 On peut voir les montagnes couvertes de neige.
7 Il fait frais pendant la nuit.
8 Il fait très froid dans les montagnes.
9 Les montagnes sont à une distance d'environ quatre-vingts kilomètres.
10 M. Davis va tâcher de faire ce petit voyage au mois de juin.

Exercise No. 118

1 la bonne cuisine française
2 un des plus grands plaisirs
3 à déjeuner
4 Cela arrive
5 nous fait cadeau
6 Envoyez à votre femme
7 Je vais vous dire
8 Tout ce qui; de bonne qualité
9 Il faut avoir
10 du beurre, du beurre et encore du beurre

Exercise No. 119

1 avec moi
2 pour toi
3 chez moi
4 chez nous
5 chez elle
6 sans eux
7 près d'elle
8 autour de nous
9 à nous
10 à elles

Exercise No. 120

1 Lui. Elle
2 Moi
3 moi; nous; eux
4 toi
5 moi
6 lui
7 Elle et moi
8 Moi
9 à vous
10 à lui

Exercise No. 121

1 La bonne cuisine française est un des plus grands plaisirs du touriste en France.
2 Oui. Il connaît un peu la cuisine française.
3 Elle nous fait cadeau de beaucoup d'expressions d'usage courant.
4 Il doit faire une liste de ses plats préférés.
5 Non, pas vraiment. La cuisine française n'est pas compliquée.
6 Le troisième secret est: du beurre, du beurre et encore du beurre.
7 Oui. Il va tout de suite le dire à sa femme.
8 M. Davis est un mari modèle.
9 M. Davis a un appétit de loup.
10 M. Picard va casser la croûte avec lui.

Exercise No. 122

1 (c) 2 (f) 3 (a) 4 (e) 5 (g) 6 (i) 7 (k) 8 (b) 9 (d) 10 (l) 11 (h) 12 (j)

Exercise No. 123

1 j'ai froid
2 j'ai chaud
3 il fait chaud
4 il pleut beaucoup
5 il fait frais
6 il fait froid
7 un imperméable
8 un pardessus
9 tombe
10 toutes les saisons

Exercise No. 124

1 (d) 2 (f) 3 (a) 4 (g) 5 (i) 6 (h) 7 (e) 8 (b) 9 (j) 10 (c)

Exercise No. 125

1 lui 2 lui 3 l' 4 le 5 la; se 6 moi; vous 7 les 8 la 9 m' 10 leur

Exercise No. 126

1 Je ne connais personne.
2 Nous ne mangeons jamais de viande.
3 Je n'ai qu'un professeur.
4 Elle ne veut plus de ce chapeau-là.
5 Jeanne ne va pas encore à l'école.
6 Je ne suis pas fatigué non plus.
7 Nous n'avons plus le temps.
8 Pourquoi ne dites-vous rien?
9 Nous n'avons ni temps ni argent.

Exercise No. 127

Phillip Does not Like to Study Arithmetic

One day on returning from school Philip says to his mother: — I don't like studying arithmetic. It's so difficult. Why do we need so many exercises and so many problems? We have calculating machines, haven't we? Well, then!

Mrs. Davis looks at her son and says: — You are wrong, dear (my little one). We cannot do without numbers. For example, one always needs to change money, go shopping, estimate distances and then, and then. . . . The mother stops speaking on seeing that Philip is not paying attention to what she says.

— By the way, dear, she continues, smiling, — football doesn't interest you either?

— What an idea! You're joking.

— Well then, if the Spurs have won eighty games and they have lost thirty do you know what percentage of games they have won?

On hearing this Philip exclaims: — You're right, mum. Numbers, arithmetic and mathematics are very important. I think that now I'm going to study much more.

Exercise No. 128

1 quelques	8 Les pêcheurs et les marins
2 les allumettes; le cendrier	9 Les fermiers
3 très à mon aise	10 Les mineurs
4 Ils se ressemblent	11 Nous n'avons pas besoin
5 partout	12 ne ressemble pas
6 comme vous dites	13 discuter
7 quelques-unes de ces	14 un roman d'amour

Exercise No. 129

1 étudions, étudiant	10 connaissons, connaissant
2 venons, venant	11 apprenons, apprenant
3 lisons, lisant	12 appelons, appelant
4 achetons, achetant	13 comptons, comptant
5 voulons, voulant	14 dormons, dormant
6 disons, disant	15 mettons, mettant
7 choisissons, choisissant	16 faisons, faisant
8 finissons, finissant	17 avons, ayant
9 bâtissons, bâtissant	18 sommes, étant

Exercise No. 130

1 quelqu'un	4 Quelques-unes	7 quelque chose	9 quelques-unes
2 quelques	5 quelques-unes	8 quelques	10 quelqu'un
3 Quelques-uns	6 quelques		

Exercise No. 131

1 Il va poser quelques questions à M. Picard sur les Français.

2 Il demande si les Français se ressemblent plus ou moins.

3 Oui. Il est vrai qu'il y a de très grandes différences entre tous les Français.

4 Il y des différences entre les Français à cause de la géographie et aussi à cause de leurs métiers.

5 Les pêcheurs de la Bretagne sont très dévots et très fervents du calvados.

6 L'homme du Midi est bavard et blagueur.

7 Non. Il ne ressemble pas trop au montagnard de l'Auvergne.

8 Oui. Les Français aiment beaucoup discuter.

9 Ils sont fiers de leur tradition de démocratie, de philosophie, de belles-lettres et de science.

10 Ils aiment tous la bonne cuisine et le bon vin.

Exercise No. 132

1 vient de recevoir	6 les beaux-arts
2 est en train d'admirer	7 La peinture, la sculpture, l'architecture
3 non seulement . . . mais aussi	8 Je compte sur le plaisir
4 que vous n'aimez pas	9 tout à fait exceptionnel
5 n'est-ce pas?	10 Je vous admire

Exercise No. 133

1 Elle achète	4 Répétons	7 Je me lève	10 jettent
2 Préférez-vous	5 J'espère	8 on célèbre	11 appelle
3 je préfère	6 vous levez-vous	9 s'appelle	12 Je lève

Exercise No. 134

1 Il vient de recevoir une grande caisse de marchandises.
2 M. Picard est en train de regarder et d'admirer.
3 Il y a des échantillons de riches étoffes de soie.
4 La belle étoffe de laine est de la maison Cardin.
5 M. Picard croit que M. Davis n'aime pas la mode.
6 M. Davis est amateur des arts.
7 Il va étudier l'art des grands maîtres.
8 Il espère visiter aussi les musées d'art moderne.
9 M. Davis s'intéresse à l'art, à l'histoire et aux belles-lettres.
10 Ils vont former une société d'estime mutuelle.

Exercise No. 135

1 la grande fête nationale	8 en dormant
2 On célèbre	9 Le jour de l'an
3 Tout le monde	10 les étrennes
4 toute la journée; toute la nuit	11 table ouverte
5 Guignol	12 doit être
6 J'espère	13 tout le monde quitte Paris
7 célébrée	

Exercise No. 136

1 Il tient	7 prononcez-vous
2 Nous obtenons	8 Nous le prononçons
3 Je ne retiens pas	9 Nous ne mangeons pas
4 tient table ouverte	10 nous nageons
5 Nous commençons à travailler	11 Nous corrigeons
6 changeons-nous	12 Recommençons

Exercise No. 137

1 on	4 rien	7 Rien	9 personne
2 personne ne	5 personne	8 Personne	10 Personne ne
3 On	6 rien		

Exercise No. 138

1 Ils vont parler des jours de fêtes en France.
2 On célèbre le quatorze juillet dans les rues.
3 On danse dans les rues.
4 On vend des beignets chauds, des gaufrettes, des glaces et toutes sortes de friandises.
5 Il y a des petits chevaux de bois et Guignol pour les enfants.
6 Il faut dire *la Noël*.
7 On dort parce qu'on a réveillonné toute la nuit.
8 Les enfants reçoivent leurs cadeaux à Noël et au jour de l'an.
9 On les appelle les étrennes.
10 La ville est morte.

Exercise No. 139

1 Je prendrai	8 Je reviendrai
2 Je visiterai	9 mieux que moi
3 Il vous faudra	10 sera
4 Je ferai	11 qui arrive à tout le monde
5 J'irai	12 chez soi
6 Je passerai	13 Laissons
7 je prendrai	14 J'ai grande envie

Exercise No. 140

1 Where will you go next summer? I shall go to France. When will you leave London? I shall leave May 31st.

2 How long will you stay in France? I shall spend three months there. Will you travel by plane or by boat? I shall travel by plane.

3 Will you take a trip to Morocco? I shall take a trip to Morocco and perhaps to Corsica also. Will Mr. Picard be able to accompany you? Alas, he will not be able to accompany me.

4 Will you see your agent in Paris? Yes indeed. He will wait for me at the airport. How long will you stay in Paris? I shall stay there two weeks.

5 Will you visit the famous Riviera? Of course I shall visit it. When will you return to Britain? I shall return on September 1st.

Exercise No. 141

1 il visitera	7 ils ne partiront pas	13 j'aurai
2 je voyagerai	8 nous vendrons	14 tu n'écouteras pas
3 nous irons	9 ne finira-t-il pas?	15 nous étudierons
4 ils n'écriront pas	10 elle n'apprendra pas	16 je ne ferai pas
5 il faudra	11 il sera	17 pourrez-vous?
6 verrez-vous?	12 viendrez-vous?	18 irez-vous?

Exercise No. 142

1 Il prendra l'avion.

2 Il verra la Vénus de Milo, la Joconde et la salle de céramique grecque.

3 Il passera par le jardin des Tuileries.

4 Il prendra un taxi à la place de l'Étoile.

5 Il visitera la Tour Eiffel.

6 Il se promènera au Bois de Boulogne.

7 M. Davis connaît le Paris des guides.

8 On se sent chez soi à Paris.

9 Le soir du quatorze juillet, on voit jouer les grands jets d'eau à Versailles.

10 M. Davis mangera trois omelettes au Mont-Saint-Michel.

11 Il prendra des bains de mer et de soleil sur la Côte d'Azur.

12 Il reviendra à Paris par la route des Alpes.

Exercise No. 143

1 (e)	3 (l)	5 (b)	7 (i)	9 (m)	11 (h)	13 (d)	15 (f)
2 (g)	4 (n)	6 (c)	8 (o)	10 (j)	12 (k)	14 (a)	

Exercise No. 144

1 la ceinture de cuir, leather belt	7 le voyage d'affaires, business trip
2 la robe de soie, silk dress	8 le cahier de musique, music book
3 la montre d'or, gold watch	9 le tissu de coton, cotton cloth
4 la salle de bain, bathroom	10 le bracelet d'argent, silver bracelet
5 la chemise de nylon, nylon shirt	11 l'objet d'art, art object
6 le bureau de poste, post office	12 le chapeau de paille, straw hat

Exercise No. 145

2 Elle coûtera cinquante francs.
3 J'irai en France.
4 Je reviendrai en Angleterre le 31 décembre.
5 Je me coucherai à minuit.
6 Je me lèverai à six heures du matin.
7 Je ne lui dirai rien.
8 Personne n'ira avec moi.
9 Je travaillerai toute la journée.
10 Nous nous rencontrerons à l'entrée du théâtre.

Exercise No. 146

2 Nous n'avons pas besoin de continuer.
3 Elle a l'intention de porter son manteau neuf.
4 Avez-vous envie de m'accompagner?
5 Il fera tout son possible pour vous aider.
6 Allez-vous faire des achats au Marché aux Puces?
7 M. Davis est en train d'ouvrir la caisse.
8 Avez-vous peur de dire la vérité?
9 Allez-vous vous promener au Bois de Boulogne?
10 Vous savez que M. Davis ne s'intéresse pas à la mode.

Exercise No. 147

1 mon chapeau	5 notre ceinture de cuir	9 Cette robe
2 ton manteau	6 vos gants rouges	10 Cette cravate
3 sa chemise de nylon	7 leur imperméable	11 Ces gants
4 sa robe de soie	8 leur écharpe	12 Cette jupe

Exercise No. 148

Mrs. Davis' Birthday

It is March 22nd, the birthday of Mrs. Davis. She is thirty-five years old today. To celebrate this festive day, the Davis family is going to dine in an elegant restaurant in Soho, London.

When they enter the restaurant they see on the table reserved for the Davises a beautiful basket full of white roses. Naturally, Mrs. Davis is very surprised. She thanks and kisses her dear husband warmly.

At the end of a delicious dinner Annie, the youngest, says in a low voice to the other children: — Now! And each of the four children takes out from under the table a pretty little box. These are presents for their mother.

Annie gives her a silk handkerchief; Rosie, a nylon blouse; Henry, a pair of gloves; and Philip, a polyester scarf.

The following week, Mr. Davis works out the bill for that day, which follows:

Dinner (including service)	£120.00
Tip	5.00
Flowers.................................	30.00
Gifts	23.00
Total	£178.00

Exercise No. 149

1 à la main
2 vient d'arriver
3 qui suit

4 Je partirai
5 J'ai l'intention
6 très occupé
7 Par conséquent
8 Depuis quelque temps; deux fois par semaine
9 une seule faute
10 Voulez-vous bien

Exercise No. 150

2 recevra
3 Ils sauront
4 Il ne voudra pas
5 courront

6 ne vaudront pas
7 Ils nous devront
8 Ils tiendront
9 Traduirez-vous

10 Nous ne suivrons pas
11 Je ferai
12 Nous pourrons

Exercise No. 151

2 pendant les mois
3 Depuis quand
4 depuis dix ans
5 depuis deux ans
6 depuis trois heures

7 Combien de temps
8 Il y a trois jours
9 Depuis quand habitez-vous
10 Nous y habitons

Exercise No. 152

1 Ils sont assis dans le salon chez M. Davis.
2 Il tient deux lettres à la main.
3 Il va lire sa lettre à M. Parmentier.
4 Il partira de Londres le 31 mai.
5 Il passera deux mois en France (*or* Il y passera deux mois).
6 Il restera trois semaines à Paris.
7 En partant de Paris, il fera quelques excursions.
8 Il espère aller par avion au Maroc, et peut-être en Corse.
9 M. Parmentier est très occupé.
10 Il veut faire la connaissance de M. Parmentier.
11 Il écrit d'avance dans l'espoir de pouvoir arranger un rendez-vous.
12 Il y a cinq mois que M. Davis prend des leçons de français.

Exercise No. 153

1 Il est en train de lire
2 J'ai reçu
3 pendant les mois
4 Je compte sur le plaisir
5 que je causerai en français

6 vous féliciter
7 Vous avez connu
8 si je suis fier
9 Vous verrez
10 Je pourrai

Exercise No. 154

1 Did Mr. Picard ask Mr. Davis some difficult questions? Yes, he asked some difficult questions. Did Mr. Davis answer well? Yes, he answered all the questions well.

2 When did Mr. Davis write the letter to his agent? He wrote the letter two weeks ago today. To whom did he read a copy of the letter? He read the copy to Mr. Picard.

3 Did Mr. Picard find many mistakes in the letter? He did not find a single mistake. What book helped Mr. Davis a great deal? The book, *Commercial Correspondence,* helped him a great deal.

4 Did Mr. Davis appreciate the services of Mr. Parmentier? Yes, he always appreciated his loyal services. What did Mr. Picard say when Mr. Davis finished reading the letter? He said: — It is a nice letter.

Exercise No. 155

2 décidé	5 vendu	8 rendu	11 fini
3 apprécié	6 écrit	9 fait	12 servi
4 contribué	7 lu	10 entendu; dit	

Exercise No. 156

1 M. Davis a écrit une lettre à son représentant.
2 Il a lu la copie de cette lettre à son professeur.
3 Il n'a pas trouvé une seule faute.
4 M. Parmentier sera à Paris pendant les mois de juin et juillet.
5 Il va rencontrer M. Davis (*or* Il va le rencontrer) à l'aéroport d'Orly.
6 Il va causer en français avec lui.
7 M. Parmentier veut féliciter M. Davis aussi bien que son professeur.
8 Il l'a connu en tant que représentant sérieux.
9 M. Davis est certain qu'il sera heureux parmi les Français.
10 Les deux messieurs auront leur dernier rendez-vous mardi prochain.
11 Ils se rencontreront au bureau de M. Davis.
12 M. Picard lui donnera quelques derniers conseils.

Exercise No. 157

1 Par la fenêtre ouverte
2 J'ai envie
3 Voulez-vous me donner
4 avec plus de formalité
5 Chaque homme est digne
6 se connaître
7 est plus tranquille
8 Avez-vous lu
9 J'ai parcouru
10 Je passerai
11 Vous allez me manquer *or* Vous me manquerez
12 Je serai content

Exercise No. 158

1 parcouru	4 promis	7 couru	9 pris
2 compris; dit	5 entendu; compris	8 appris	10 pris
3 mis	6 vu		

Exercise No. 159

1 Have you recommended these guides? I have recommended them.
2 Did he write the answer? He wrote it.
3 Where did he find the money? He found it on the desk.
4 Did you understand the question? I did not understand it.
5 Has she learned the proverb? She hasn't learned it.
6 Who reserved the two seats? My father reserved them yesterday.
7 When did you see your friend? I saw her yesterday evening.
8 When did they finish the examination? They finished it at two o'clock.
9 When did the postman bring the letters? He brought them this morning.
10 Did you hear the bell? I did not hear it.
11 Has Mr. Davis been through all the guide-books? He has been through them all.
12 What letter did he read to Mr. Picard? He read the letter which he received from Mr. Parmentier.

Exercise No. 160

1 Ils se trouvent dans le bureau de M. Davis.
2 Il fait chaud.
3 On entend les bruits de la rue.
4 M. Davis est content de quitter la ville.
5 M. Picard a envie d'accompagner M. Davis (*or* de l'accompagner).
6 Il répond: — Malheureusement, ce n'est pas possible.
7 On fait les choses avec plus de formalité en France.
8 Chaque homme est digne d'estime.
9 Il a remarqué que les affaires se traitent en France avec plus de formalité qu'ici.
10 M. Davis est las d'être bousculé.
11 M. Davis a lu des livres sur la France.
12 M. Picard les a recommandés.
13 M. Picard passera l'été à Londres.
14 M. Davis pensera souvent à M. Picard.
15 Il lui écrira des lettres de temps en temps.

Exercise No. 161

1 Il y a cinq mois	6 a promis	11 Ils montent tous
2 Il a appris	7 il doit être	12 a fait peser ses bagages
3 Il a vraiment travaillé	8 ne l'accompagne pas	13 Il doit payer
4 Il a obtenu	9 doivent finir	14 fait ses adieux à
5 Il a écrit	10 a fait	15 en route

Exercise No. 162

1 il a voulu	7 je n'ai pas couvert
2 vous avez ouvert	8 ont-ils su?
3 j'ai su	9 nous n'avons pas ouvert
4 a-t-il ouvert?	10 elle a été
5 nous avons eu	11 a-t-il voulu?
6 ils ont été	12 j'ai offert

Exercise No. 163

2 illustrées	5 cassées	7 habillé	9 reservée
3 fermées	6 levés	8 envoyées	10 perdus
4 connu			

Exercise No. 164

1 Il y a cinq mois qu'il étudie le français.
2 Il a passé beaucoup de temps à converser avec son professeur M. Picard.
3 Il a appris les règles essentielles de la grammaire.
4 Il a vraiment travaillé dur.
5 Il parle bien le français maintenant.
6 M. Davis a obtenu son billet et son passeport.
7 Il a écrit à son représentant.
8 Son représentant lui a promis de le rencontrer à l'aéroport.
9 Ils se sont levés à sept heures du matin.
10 Il quitte l'aéroport à dix-huit heures précises.
11 Chaque voyageur doit faire contrôler son billet et son passeport.
12 Sa famille n'accompagne pas M. Davis en France (*or* ne l'accompagne pas).
13 Ils doivent finir l'année scolaire.
14 Elle doit rester à Londres pour s'occuper des enfants.

Exercise No. 165

1 obtained, **obtenir**
2 left, **laisser**
3 been, **être**
4 said, **dire**
5 finished, **finir**
6 wanted, **vouloir**
7 received, **recevoir**
8 written, **écrire**
9 read, **lire**
10 learned, **apprendre**
11 known, **savoir**
12 given back, **rendre**
13 put, **mettre**
14 obeyed, **obéir**
15 seen, **voir**
16 eaten, **manger**
17 done, made, **faire**
18 taken, **prendre**
19 listened, **écouter**
20 covered, **couvrir**
21 understood, **comprendre**
22 opened, **ouvrir**
23 had, **avoir**
24 permitted, **permettre**
25 been able, **pouvoir**

Exercise No. 166

1 (*g*)   2 (*e*)   3 (*a*)   4 (*h*)   5 (*c*)   6 (*i*)   7 (*d*)   8 (*j*)   9 (*b*)   10 (*f*)

Exercise No. 167

1 Avez-vous fait
2 Faites mes amitiés
3 de ma part
4 dans votre propre langue
5 Pardonnez-moi
6 me tirer d'affaire
7 de faire votre connaissance
8 Ils montent en voiture
9 Ils descendent de la voiture
10 a fait ses adieux

Exercise No. 168

2 Il l'a écrite.
3 Il les a appréciés.
4 M. Davis l'a faite.
5 Ils m'ont aidé
6 Elle l'a servie.
7 Je ne l'ai pas comprise.
8 Philippe ne les a pas apprises.
9 Nous ne l'avons pas vu.
10 Il a apporté un colis postal.

Exercise No. 169

An Unusual Programme at the Cinema

This evening Mr. and Mrs. Davis are going to the cinema. They don't like the majority of Hollywood films, especially the Westerns in which cowboys fire shots at everybody and are always galloping. Thrillers don't interest them either.

But this evening there is an unusual programme in a cinema very near their home. The picture is called *A Journey in France*. This is a documentary film on the country which our friend Davis is going to visit in a few months. There are scenes representing the history of France, others which show its countryside, its rivers, its mountains, its large cities, etc. That is to say it is a most interesting film for tourists.

The Davises arrive at the cinema at 20.30. Almost all the seats are taken, and so they have to sit in the third row. Mr. Davis does not like this because the movements on the screen hurt his eyes. Fortunately they are able to change their seats after a quarter of an hour, and they take seats in the thirteenth row.

The Davises enjoy this picture very much. They find it absorbing.

On leaving the cinema, Mr. Davis says to his wife: — Do you know Alice, I think that I'll get along well in France. I understood almost all that the actors and actresses said.

Exercise No. 170

1 à la salle d'attente
2 Tout de suite
3 Il m'a demandé
4 J'ai répondu
5 de faire votre connaissance
6 Le plaisir est pour moi

7 Nous avons pris un taxi
8 Je me suis dit
9 à une vitesse vertigineuse
10 Pas si vite!
11 je ne suis pas pressé

12 Ni moi non plus
13 reservée pour M. Davis
14 Quel est le prix
15 Deux cent trente francs par jour

Exercise No. 171

1 Did Philip go to the station to meet his father? Yes, he left the house twenty minutes ago. Did his sister Rosette go with him? His sister Rosette and also his brother Henry went with him.

2 Has Mrs. Davis returned from town? She has not returned, but she will return soon. Why did she go to town? She went there to do her shopping.

3 Why did Mr. Davis return late this evening? Many customers came to see him in the afternoon. At what time does he usually leave his office? Usually he leaves at five o'clock sharp, but today he did not leave until a quarter to six.

4 At what time did Mr. Davis leave for the airport? He left at six o'clock in the morning. At what time did he get into the plane? He got into the plane at seven forty-five.

Exercise No. 172

2 allées	5 devenus; monté	7 partie	9 resté
3 né	6 revenue	8 entrés	10 partis; arrivés
4 mort			

Exercise No. 173

1 Il a passé par la douane et il est allé à la salle d'attente.
2 Un bel homme s'est approché.
3 Il a dit: — Pardon monsieur, êtes-vous M. Davis?
4 Il a répondu: — Mais oui.
5 Le taxi est allé en ville à toute vitesse.
6 À la fin il a crié: — Je ne suis pas pressé!
7 Le chauffeur a répondu: — Ni moi non plus.
8 Ils sont arrivés à l'hôtel sains et saufs.
9 Il a dit: — Bonjour monsieur. Avez-vous une chambre réservée pour M. Davis?
10 Il a répondu: — Soyez le bienvenu à Paris, Monsieur Davis.

Exercise No. 174

1 m'a appelé
2 à prendre le thé
3 Nous nous sommes arrêtés
4 Je suis monté
5 J'ai sonné; m'a invité
6 s'est approché pour me saluer
7 je suis content de vous voir
8 Il y a beaucoup de maisons

9 Nous sommes entrés
10 m'a présenté
11 veut être
12 se sont retirés; leurs devoirs
13 Nous nous sommes mis
14 Nous avons parlé
15 Je suis revenu
16 par les vieux quartiers

Exercise No. 175

2 you went to bed, you lay down
3 he dressed (himself)
4 she enjoyed herself
5 we stopped
6 you approached
7 they met each other

8 they knew each other
9 I did not take a walk
10 he was not mistaken
11 did they not withdraw?
12 did they not sit down?

Exercise No. 176

1 Did the children go to bed early? They went to bed early.
2 Did John get up late? He did not get up late.
3 Did Mary dress quickly? She dressed quickly.
4 Were you mistaken, Charles? I was not mistaken.
5 Did you have a good time, Anne? I did not have a good time.
6 Where did you meet, gentlemen? We met at the office.
7 Did the boys withdraw? Yes, they withdrew.
8 Where did the bus stop? It stopped on the corner over there.
9 Did Mrs. Davis look after the children? She looked after the children.
10 Did the tourist feel at home in Paris? Like all tourists he felt at home.

Exercise No. 177

1 M. Parmentier a appelé M. Davis au téléphone.
2 Il s'est arrêté à cinq heures.
3 Une petite bonne à l'air éveillé a ouvert la porte.
4 M. Parmentier s'est approché pour le saluer.
5 Elle a l'air de dater du dix-huitième siècle.
6 Les messieurs sont entrés dans un grand salon.
7 Ce sont les fils de M. Parmentier.
8 Ils font leurs études au Lycée Condorcet.
9 L'aîné veut être médecin.
10 Ils se sont retirés pour aller faire leurs devoirs.
11 On a parlé de la vie en France.
12 M. Parmentier a recommandé le Marché aux Puces.
13 Mme Parmentier l'a invité à l'accompagner au Marché aux Fleurs.
14 Il a passé une heure agréable à parler de choses et d'autres.
15 Il est revenu à pied.

Exercise No. 178

1 me chercher	9 On y joue
2 Nous sommes restés	10 On y écrit
3 sans rien attraper	11 Les passants
4 à jeter des pierres	12 Ensuite; notre route
5 Nous avons continué	13 m'a quitté
6 la plus belle place	14 J'ai suivi
7 Quelle belle avenue!	15 sur la chaise la plus proche
8 m'a frappé	

Exercise No. 179

1 Did you understand all that the teacher said? I did not understand all (of it).
2 Did you read the guide-books that I lent you? I read them with much interest.
3 What is the first secret of good cooking? All that goes into a dish must be of good quality.
4 Can one ski in the mountains? Those who are young and strong ski all the time.
5 At what café did you sit today? I sat at the Royale-Concorde of which we have spoken often.
6 Where are the suitcases in which I have put my clothes? They are in your room.

Exercise No. 180

1 que	4 ce qui	7 dont	9 tout ce qui
2 ce qu'	5 qui	8 que	10 que
3 qui	6 laquelle		

Exercise No. 181

1 Il écrit sa lettre (*or* il l'écrit) attablé au café Royale-Concorde.
2 Il est venu le chercher à l'hôtel.
3 Ils sont restés très longtemps sur le pont des Arts.
4 Ils ont vu des pêcheurs, des bateaux-mouches, et des enfants.
5 Il pense que cela doit être la plus belle place du monde.
6 Ils se sont attablés pour prendre un café, mais surtout pour se reposer.
7 L'importance du café dans la vie quotidienne l'a frappé.
8 Le café est un autre bureau pour les hommes d'affaires.
9 Les passants sont les acteurs et les actrices.
10 Ils ont contemplé l'Arc de Triomphe.
11 Il a quitté M. Davis à la place de l'Alma.
12 Il a admiré la Tour Eiffel.
13 Il est tombé, fatigué, épuisé et enchanté sur la chaise du café.

Exercise No. 182

1 Vous avez raison
2 Me voilà
3 Je prends (je bois)
4 les champs et les forêts
5 par la fenêtre
6 Les fermiers; les champs
7 le linge
8 J'ai pris un taxi
9 Presque tout de suite
10 Par ici
11 les oreilles
12 a duré
13 rester pour contempler
14 est poussé; on est tiré
15 On doit suivre

Exercise No. 183

1 What was Mr. Davis doing when you entered the living-room? He was reading aloud a letter which he had just received from his agent in Paris. What was Mr. Picard doing? He was listening to him.
2 What were you doing while the train was crossing the fields and the forests? I was looking out of the window. What did you see (were you seeing)? I saw the peasants who were working in the fields.
3 Were there many vendors at Mont-Saint-Michel? There was an army of them. What were they selling? They were selling souvenirs of the Mount.
4 Do you often play tennis? Formerly I played (used to play) almost every day, but this year I have played only once.

Exercise No. 184

1 (criaient et hurlaient) The vendors were calling and yelling when I arrived at the market.
2 (J'écoutais) While I was listening to the radio, somebody telephoned me.
3 (nous faisions) When we were doing our homework, they entered our room.
4 (elle descendait) She fell when she was getting out of the car.
5 (allait) When the taxi was going at full speed, I cried: 'Not so fast.'
6 (il était) We visited him when he was ill.
7 (Il y avait) There were many people at the airport when our plane arrived.
8 (attendions) While we were waiting for the bus it began to rain.
9 (sortions) We met them when we were coming out of the cinema.
10 (dormaient) Mr. Davis returned while the children were sleeping.

Exercise No. 185

1 Il écrit attablé à un café.
2 Le métier de touriste exige beaucoup de repos.
3 Le café est dans la ville de Perros-Guirec.
4 Il prend un calvados.

5 Il regardait par la fenêtre.
6 Il voyait les paysans qui travaillaient dans les champs.
7 Il apercevait des femmes qui lavaient le linge.
8 Il a entendu un bruit terrifiant.
9 La tête lui tournait comme une toupie.
10 Il voulait rester pour contempler les sculptures.
11 Il se tourne vers la Bretagne.
12 La visite de l'Abbaye a duré une heure.

Exercise No. 186

1 Je suis revenu	7 il y a deux heures	12 Ils riaient
2 de plus en plus	8 J'étais	13 ne bougeait pas
3 je suis allé	9 Je marchais	14 Il ne disait rien
4 Je ne peux	10 Je me suis approché	15 n'étaient pas du tout
5 La tête	11 se pressaient	16 J'ai dit
6 Je me suis dit		

Exercise No. 187

2 vivait	7 pensait-il	12 J'étais	17 n'avions pas
3 lavaient	8 descendait	13 s'approchait	18 ne voulaient pas
4 Étaient-ils	9 revenais	14 commençaient	19 Pouviez-vous
5 sortait	10 montions	15 mangeait	20 savait; devait
6 rendions visite à	11 souriait	16 se rencontraient	

Exercise No. 188

1 M. Davis est allé au Louvre pour le visiter à fond.
2 Il s'est dit: — Imbécile.
3 Il s'est tourné vers le Jardin du Luxembourg.
4 Il a entendu de grands éclats de rire.
5 Il a vu un joli petit théâtre.
6 Guignol ne bougeait pas.
7 Les enfants éclataient de rire.
8 Il a pris place à côté d'une toute petite fille.
9 Elle a crié: — Papa.
10 La petit Gringalet était en train de donner de grands coups de tête dans le ventre de Guignol.
11 Non, monsieur, les enfants n'étaient pas fâchés.
12 L'enfant a répondu gentiment: — Au revoir, papa.

Exercise No. 189

1 Mr. Davis has left for Paris.
2 His wife remained at home.
3 Mrs. Picard went out one hour ago.
4 She hasn't returned yet.
5 We went up in the lift.
6 They went down on foot.
7 Why did you return so late, Mary?
8 I went to the market to do my shopping.
9 His grandfather died this morning.
10 My grandmother was born on 5 June 1900.

Exercise No. 190

2 rencontrés	7 descendu	11 dit
3 pris	8 réservé	12 fait
4 sortis	9 née	13 demandé
5 arrêté	10 mis	14 ouvertes; ouvertes
6 arrivée		

Exercise No. 191

1 **(rendrons)** Tomorrow we shall pay a visit to the Davis family.
2 **(sont allés)** Yesterday evening the children went to the cinema.
3 **(parlait)** The pupils were not listening while the teacher was talking.
4 **(avez-vous passé)** Where did you spend last winter?
5 **(verrai)** I shall not see them until tomorrow.
6 **(jouaient)** We were doing our homework while they were playing cards.
7 **(pleuvait)** They remained at home, because it was raining hard.
8 **(ferez-vous)** Will you take a trip to Europe next summer?
9 **(a prêté)** He lent us five francs yesterday.
10 **(vous vous êtes levé)** At what time did you get up this morning?

Exercise No. 192

1 Il pleuvait à verse
2 J'étais très content
3 quand M. Davis a reçu
4 quand mon représentant m'a téléphoné
5 nous allions
6 Je ne savais pas
7 Nous ne pouvions pas
8 Voulaient-ils voyager *or* Est-ce qu'il voulaient voyager
9 Elle n'avait pas le temps
10 Elle devait

Exercise No. 193

One day Mr. Davis invited Mr. Parmentier's sons to accompany him on an excursion to Versailles.

It is not very far from Paris, and they arrived without any difficulty. On the way to the Palace Mr. Davis had a brilliant idea:

— Let's have lunch on the grass in the big park at the edge of the lake. I'm told that it's allowed.

— Wonderful! Let's go.

They entered a grocer's shop to buy some ham, a Camembert cheese, and a bottle of red wine. In a bakery next door, they bought three long loaves of bread and three éclairs.

— I'm as hungry as a wolf, said the elder one as they left the bakery.

— Let's eat right away, said Mr. Davis. — But what to do about utensils?

— Let's see what there is in our pockets, said the younger one. The two boys unearthed four knives: one brand new, two fairly good, and one in a bad state.

— There! And we'll drink out of the bottle.

They entered the Palace grounds through the great iron gate, but instead of visiting the Palace they crossed the immense garden. The garden with its statues, fountains, and groves of trees made a strong impression on Mr. Davis. The two boys were in agreement. The younger one said: — I assure you that the garden is the jewel of Versailles. But the Palace bores us to death.

Mr. Davis answered laughing: — We're not obliged to go there.

When they arrived at the lake they sat down on the grass to eat. They talked of one thing and another while eating, and Mr. Davis was struck once more by their intelligence. The boys ate like two wolves, and they had a wonderful time. All three will remember this excursion to Versailles for a long time.

Exercise No. 194

The Avenue of the Opera

We are strolling along the Avenue of the Opera. It is a beautiful avenue which leads from the Tuileries Gardens to the Opera.

There are many people on the avenue. All tourists meet there. The pavements are lined with luxury shops where one can buy all sorts of beautiful things, if one has money: jewellery, fine lingerie, gloves, china, blouses, leather goods, and also books, for we are in France, where people like to read. There is even a small bookshop inside the Opera house, on the second floor.

There is also a well-known café-restaurant, the Brasserie Universelle. Let's go and have a beer, shall we? With pleasure.

Exercise No. 195

1 Mr. Davis has noticed that, although French villages differ they all have a High Street.

2 The street often leads to a square surrounded by trees.

3 Behind the trees are the well arranged shops of the village.

4 The cleaners' and dyers' shop is painted purple.

5 One can see delicious cakes in the window of the bakery. In the grocery window. In the laundry window.

6 The flies are walking peacefully on the legs of lamb hanging up in the butcher's shop.

7 The town hall, the church and the school are all on the square.

8 The children are well-behaved in France.

9 Mr. Davis gets up early so as not to miss anything of the street scene.

10 First he hears a cock crowing.

11 A small boy rushes into the street.

12 He suddenly stops to examine something which catches his eye.

13 Our hero returns with a loaf of bread almost as long as he is.

14 It is seven-thirty and Mr. Davis has an appointment with the Parmentier boys to go to Chartres.

15 He will describe the adventures of that afternoon.

Exercise No. 196

1 à une place entourée d'arbres	9 Pour ne rien manquer du spectacle
2 bien rangées	10 On dort
3 est peinte	11 à se saluer
4 est remplie de gâteaux délicieux	12 se réveille
5 a pendu ses gigots	13 Ce que les Français mangent
6 s'y promènent	14 revient avec un pain
7 Au milieu du village	15 Je dois tout de même
8 des rires et des chansons	

Exercise No. 197

1 Did you send the pottery to Mr. Davis? We sent it to him.

2 Do many people meet on the Avenue de l'Opéra? All tourists meet there.

3 Please send me the French newspapers. We shall send them to you tomorrow.

4 Has the waiter given you the bill? He hasn't given it to me yet.

5 Did you ask the employee for the tickets? I haven't asked him for them yet because he is very busy.

6 How many dishes are there in this case? There are twenty-five dozen (of them).

7 Did you return the money (to him), which you borrowed from him? I shall return it to him this evening.

8 Has the maid put on the desk the porcelain which Mr. Davis has just received from Limoges? Yes, she has put it there.

9 Will you lend me your umbrella? I shall lend it to you; but please return it to me tomorrow. Many thanks. I shall return it to you tomorrow.

10 Show me, please, the new dress you have bought? I cannot show it to you, because it has not yet arrived from the shop.

Exercise No. 198

1 Mr. Davis wanted to be back in time to go to the opera.
2 They had prepared a good lunch.
3 The car was waiting downstairs.
4 He heard a sound that he recognized immediately.
5 They had a flat tyre.
6 The young men wanted to help change the tyre.
7 There was no jack in the tool kit of the car.
8 The lorry driver offered to give them a hand.
9 The lorry driver had so much natural dignity.
10 The boys invited him to share their lunch.
11 They ate their chicken and the lorry driver's ham, and drank the bottle of wine.
12 They said:— This ham is delicious.
13 He said: — My wife looks after me well.
14 They all said goodbye after lunch.
15 Mr. Davis has to dress to go to the opera.

Exercise No. 199

1 me chercher
2 Ils avaient préparé
3 Une nappe, des serviettes, des couteaux, des fourchettes
4 Et nous voilà
5 Tout à coup
6 Nous avons crevé un pneu
7 Il n'y avait pas de cric
8 Personne ne
9 Nous nous sommes assis
10 Bientôt un gros camion
11 un coup de main
12 En tout cas
13 s'est mis à la besogne
14 lui offrir un pourboire
15 déjeuner avec nous

Exercise No. 200

2 **Nous avions vraiment travaillé** . . . We had really worked hard.
3 **Ils n'avaient pas encore obtenu** . . . They had not yet obtained their tickets.
4 **Avait-il écrit . . . ?** Had he written a letter to his friend?
5 **Qui avait promis . . . ?** Who had promised to meet him at the airport?
6 **J'avais oublié** . . . I had forgotten my umbrella.
7 **Avaient-ils réservé . . . ?** Had they reserved a room for Mr. Davis?
8 **Aviez-vous lu . . . ?** Had you read many guide books?
9 **Ses jeunes amis avaient préparé** . . . His young friends had prepared a good lunch.
10 **N'avait-il pas loué . . . ?** Had he not rented a car?

Exercise No. 201

2 **Un gros camion s'était approché** . . . A large lorry had approached rapidly.
3 **Nous nous étions assis** . . . We had sat down under a large tree.
4 **J'étais allé** . . . I had gone to the waiting room.
5 **Nous n'étions pas sortis** . . . We had not gone out together.
6 **Ils étaient arrivés** . . . They had arrived safe and sound.
7 **Le taxi s'était arrêté** . . . The taxi had stopped before the hotel.
8 **Étiez-vous allé . . . ?** Had you gone to the customs office?
9 **Nous nous étions dit** . . . We had said goodbye to each other.
10 **Elles n'étaient pas restées** . . . They had not stayed in Paris two weeks.

Exercise No. 202

1 We have good teachers. What are yours like?
2 Let's go to the post-office in your car. Ours has a flat tyre.
3 Please lend me your pen. Mine does not write.
4 I have forgotten my umbrella. Will you lend me yours?
5 You have no jack. Would you like to borrow mine?
6 Louis' bicycle costs more than mine, but mine is better than his.
7 Jane and I bought theatre tickets yesterday. I have mine, but she has lost hers unfortunately.
8 Here are our hats. This one is mine and that one is yours.

Exercise No. 203

1 He had never been a gambler.
2 He had noticed that people were greatly taken up with the National Lottery.
3 He dreamt of winning the first prize.
4 He would have sufficient money to travel all over Europe.
5 His wife would go with him.
6 The children would go to school somewhere in France.
7 Mr. Davis bought a lottery ticket from a young girl at a kiosk.
8 The next morning he rang for coffee, rolls and the newspaper.
9 Only the newspaper interested him.
10 He stopped breathing and began to look for his ticket.
11 He was making trips to the moon.
12 Mr. Davis had the number 25,000.
13 The prize-winning number was 26,000.
14 Mr. Davis decided that the emotions of the gambler were not for him.
15 He likes a quiet life.

Exercise No. 204

1 Je n'avais jamais été
2 des kiosques de la Loterie Nationale
3 qu'on s'occupait beaucoup de
4 Je voyais des affiches illustrées
5 Si je gagnais le premier prix
6 Je pourrais acheter
7 l'homme le plus heureux du monde
8 Et voilà comment
9 de bonne heure
10 je ne m'intéressais qu'au journal
11 Je cherche
12 à peine le tenir
13 c'est un cinq, pas un six
14 en riant de moi-même

Exercise No. 205

2 Il visiterait . . . He would visit France and Italy.
3 Nous apprendrions . . . We would learn French.
4 Ma famille ne m'accompagnerait pas. My family would not accompany me.
5 Elle pourrait acheter . . . She would be able to buy many beautiful things.
6 Aurait-il . . . ? Would he have enough money?
7 Ils achèteraient . . . They would buy some art objects.
8 Seriez-vous . . . ? Would you be satisfied to remain here?
9 Elle ne vous connaîtrait pas . . . She would not know you.
10 Ils ne feraient pas . . . They would not do their homework.
11 Je vous enverrais . . . I would send you the magazines.
12 Ils ne viendraient pas . . . They would not come next week.

Exercise No. 206

1 Mr. Davis had read a few books on the history of France and on its customs.
2 He was able to describe only a little of what he had seen and learnt.
3 He particularly likes the French people.
4 He likes their politeness, their marked feeling for the dignity of man, and their keen sense of humour.

5 He thinks life in Paris resembles that in London.
6 He got a different impression in the taxi when he first arrived.
7 He did not have the time to go to Morocco or Corsica.
8 His whole family would accompany him.
9 He is sure he could act as a guide without any trouble.
10 He is leaving on August 1.
11 He will be glad to telephone Mr. Picard when he returns.
12 He thinks they will spend hours in talking about France and the Paris they love.

Exercise No. 208

1 They went to the market to shop.
2 French people made a strong impression on Mr. Davis.
3 He went to the railway station to ask for information.
4 I shall be able to get along in France because I speak French well.
5 The day after tomorrow we shall visit Mr. Duval.
6 The young man had already filled the tank and checked the oil.
7 Next summer Mr. Davis will be able to act as guide for his whole family.
8 If Mr. Davis had had more time, he would have taken a trip to Morocco.
9 At the Hotel du Quai Voltaire we lacked nothing.
10 Having finished his business matters, Mr. Davis devoted himself completely to entertainment.
11 I'm going to write a letter to my agent to let him know the date of my arrival.
12 After saying goodbye we boarded the plane.
13 I was thinking of my teacher's advice while the taxi was going at full speed through the streets.
14 Formerly Mr. Davis had his French correspondence translated, but in future he will translate it himself.
15 The children were amusing themselves by throwing stones into the water.
16 If you find the parcels which I left at your house, return them to me please.
17 I shall not forget to return them to you.
18 I had never seen such a sight.
19 When Mr. Davis was travelling in Europe, Mrs. Davis was looking after the children.
20 I have never been in France, but I intend to go there next summer.

Exercise No. 209

1 est un commerçant de Londres.
2 un voyage à Paris pour rendre visite à son représentant.
3 faire sa connaissance.
4 il avait appris à bien parler le français.
5 Il avait aussi lu beaucoup de livres.
6 beaucoup de lettres à son ami, le professeur.
7 Les endroits intéressants dont ils avaient parlé dans leurs conversations.
8 il avait trouvé la vie à Paris semblable à la vie à Londres.
9 qui l'avait conduit à son hôtel.
10 La vitesse vertigineuse du taxi.
11 il a bientôt terminé ses affaires.
12 leur politesse et leur sentiment marqué de la dignité de l'homme.
13 il n'a pas eu le temps d'aller au Maroc ni en Corse.
14 tant à voir, à faire et à apprendre.
15 au sujet des coutumes, de la vie, de la langue et des arts de la France.
16 il reviendra en France.
17 l'accompagnerait.
18 Il n'a pas gagné le gros lot à la loterie mais il aura assez d'argent.
19 que M. Davis écrira avant de quitter la France.
20 il invitera M. Picard à dîner en famille.

Exercise No. 210
Nice, Capital of the Riviera

There are really two towns in Nice: the Italian town and the French town; the old town and the modern town. One can walk in the old districts where one hears nothing but Italian, and yet Nice became French a long time ago. In this district they sell macaroni, ravioli, olives, and sausage. The air is perfumed with garlic and tomato sauce. People shout, sing, bargain. This town is entirely Italian.

But close by, crossing the Place Massena, you are in the French town. You walk up Avenue de la Victoire under a row of lofty trees and you admire the magnificent shops. You see cars as long as trains. You see furs on the ladies, wigs on the gentlemen, and diamonds on the dogs! It is the city of luxury.

Nice is also a sports centre. There is a magnificent tennis club; there is the golf course at Cagnes, near-by; the famous winter sports at Beuil in the mountains: yachting, and sea bathing. It is true that the beach is stony, but that does not matter. You go there anyway to worship the sun.

But the town where one is born, where one goes to school, where one earns a living, this town exists too. This town has its commerce: tourism, flowers, perfume, olives, fishing. It has its cultural life: music, which it takes very seriously, the opera, theatres, lectures, and bookshops and above all its university of which it is very proud. As in the typical towns of France, there is an interest in science, and an interest in art.

But the real glory of Nice is its position. Surrounded by hills adorned with flower-covered villas, it stretches from the blue sea to the foothills of the snowy mountains. The sky is intensely blue like the sea. The air is mild and balmy.

Everything is there to make people happy.

SUMMARY OF VERBS

REGULAR VERBS

Infinitive Present Participle	Present Tense			Future Conditional	Imperfect Convers. Past
parler, to speak parlant	je parle nous parlons	tu parles vous parlez	il parle ils parlent	je parlerai je parlerais	je parlais j'ai parlé
finir, to finish finissant	je finis nous finissons	tu finis vous finissez	il finit ils finissent	je finirai je finirais	je finissais j'ai fini
vendre, to sell vendant	je vends nous vendons	tu vends vous vendez	il vend ils vendent	je vendrai je vendrais	je vendais j'ai vendu

AUXILIARY VERBS

Infinitive Present Participle	Present Tense			Future Conditional	Imperfect Convers. Past
avoir, to have ayant	j'ai nous avons	tu as vous avez	il a ils ont	j'aurai j'aurais	j'avais j'ai eu
être, to be étant	je suis nous sommes	tu es vous êtes	il est ils sont	je serai je serais	j'étais j'ai été

COMMON IRREGULAR VERBS

Infinitive Present Participle	Present Tense		Future Conditional	Imperfect Convers. Past
aller, to go	je vais	il va	j'irai	j'allais
allant	nous allons	ils vont	j'irais	je suis allé
s'asseoir, to sit down	je m'assieds (m'assois)	il s'assied (s'assoit)	je m'assiérai (m'assoirai)	je m'asseyais
s'asseyant	nous nous asseyons (nous assoyons)	ils s'asseyent (s'assoient)	je m'assiérais (m'assoirais)	je me suis assis
	tu t'assieds (t'assois)			
	vous vous asseyez (vous assoyez)			
battre, to beat	je bats	il bat	je battrai	je battais
battant	nous battons	ils battent	je battrais	j'ai battu
	tu bats			
	vous battez			
boire, to drink	je bois	il boit	je boirai	je buvais
buvant	nous buvons	ils boivent	je boirais	j'ai bu
	tu bois			
	vous buvez			
conduire, to conduct, drive	je conduis	il conduit	je conduirai	je conduisais
conduisant	nous conduisons	ils conduisent	je conduirais	j'ai conduit
	tu conduis			
	vous conduisez			
connaître, to know	je connais	il connaît	je connaîtrai	je connaissais
connaissant	nous connaissons	ils connaissent	je connaîtrais	j'ai connu
	tu connais			
	vous connaissez			
courir, to run	je cours	il court	je courrai	je courais
courant	nous courons	ils courent	je courrais	j'ai couru
	tu cours			
	vous courez			
couvrir, to cover	je couvre	il couvre	je couvrirai	je couvrais
couvrant	nous couvrons	ils couvrent	je couvrirais	j'ai couvert
	tu couvres			
	vous couvrez			
croire, to believe	je crois	il croit	je croirai	je croyais
croyant	nous croyons	ils croient	je croirais	j'ai cru
	tu crois			
	vous croyez			
devoir, to owe, must, have to	je dois	il doit	je devrai	je devais
devant	nous devons	ils doivent	je devrais	j'ai dû
	tu dois			
	vous devez			

Infinitive / Participle	Present (je)	Present (nous)	Present (tu)	Present (vous)	Present (il)	Present (ils)	Future	Conditional	Imperfect	Passé composé
dire, to say / disant	je dis	nous disons	tu dis	vous dites	il dit	ils disent	je dirai	je dirais	je disais	j'ai dit
dormir, to sleep / dormant	je dors	nous dormons	tu dors	vous dormez	il dort	ils dorment	je dormirai	je dormirais	je dormais	j'ai dormi
écrire, to write / écrivant	j'écris	nous écrivons	tu écris	vous écrivez	il écrit	ils écrivent	j'écrirai	j'écrirais	j'écrivais	j'ai écrit
envoyer, to send / envoyant	j'envoie	nous envoyons	tu envoies	vous envoyez	il envoie	ils envoient	j'enverrai	j'enverrais	j'envoyais	j'ai envoyé
faire, to do, make / faisant	je fais	nous faisons	tu fais	vous faites	il fait	ils font	je ferai	je ferais	je faisais	j'ai fait
falloir, to be necessary					il faut		il faudra	il faudrait	il fallait	il a fallu
lire, to read / lisant	je lis	nous lisons	tu lis	vous lisez	il lit	ils lisent	je lirai	je lirais	je lisais	j'ai lu
mentir, to lie / mentant	je mens	nous mentons	tu mens	vous mentez	il ment	ils mentent	je mentirai	je mentirais	je mentais	j'ai menti
mettre, to put / mettant	je mets	nous mettons	tu mets	vous mettez	il met	ils mettent	je mettrai	je mettrais	je mettais	j'ai mis
mourir, to die / mourant	je meurs	nous mourons	tu meurs	vous mourez	il meurt	ils meurent	je mourrai	je mourrais	je mourais	je suis mort
naître, to be born / naissant	je nais	nous naissons	tu nais	vous naissez	il naît	ils naissent	je naîtrai	je naîtrais	je naissais	je suis né
offrir, to offer / offrant	j'offre	nous offrons	tu offres	vous offrez	il offre	ils offrent	j'offrirai	j'offrirais	j'offrais	j'ai offert

COMMON IRREGULAR VERBS—*continued*

Infinitive / Present Participle	Present Tense			Future / Conditional	Imperfect / Convers. Past
ouvrir, to open / ouvrant	j'ouvre / nous ouvrons	tu ouvres / vous ouvrez	il ouvre / ils ouvrent	j'ouvrirai / j'ouvrirais	j'ouvrais / j'ai ouvert
paraître, to appear / paraissant	je parais / nous paraissons	tu parais / vous paraissez	il paraît / ils paraissent	je paraîtrai / je paraîtrais	je paraissais / j'ai paru
partir, to set out, leave, depart / partant	je pars / nous partons	tu pars / vous partez	il part / ils partent	je partirai / je partirais	je partais / je suis parti
plaire, to please / plaisant	je plais / nous plaisons	tu plais / vous plaisez	il plaît / ils plaisent	je plairai / je plairais	je plaisais / j'ai plu
pleuvoir, to rain / pleuvant			il pleut	il pleuvra / il pleuvrait	il pleuvait / il a plu
pouvoir, to be able, can / pouvant	je peux (puis) / nous pouvons	tu peux / vous pouvez	il peut / ils peuvent	je pourrai / je pourrais	je pouvais / j'ai pu
prendre, to take / prenant	je prends / nous prenons	tu prends / vous prenez	il prend / ils prennent	je prendrai / je prendrais	je prenais / j'ai pris
recevoir, to receive / recevant	je reçois / nous recevons	tu reçois / vous recevez	il reçoit / ils reçoivent	je recevrai / je recevrais	je recevais / j'ai reçu
rire, to laugh / riant	je ris / nous rions	tu ris / vous riez	il rit / ils rient	je rirai / je rirais	je riais / j'ai ri
savoir, to know / sachant	je sais / nous savons	tu sais / vous savez	il sait / ils savent	je saurai / je saurais	je savais / j'ai su

sentir, to feel	je sens	tu sens	il sent	je sentirai	je sentais
sentant	nous sentons	vous sentez	ils sentent	je sentirais	j'ai senti
servir, to serve	je sers	tu sers	il sert	je servirai	je servais
servant	nous servons	vous servez	ils servent	je servirais	j'ai servi
sortir, to go out	je sors	tu sors	il sort	je sortirai	je sortais
sortant	nous sortons	vous sortez	ils sortent	je sortirais	je suis sorti
suivre, to follow	je suis	tu suis	il suit	je suivrai	je suivais
suivant	nous suivons	vous suivez	ils suivent	je suivrais	j'ai suivi
tenir, to hold	je tiens	tu tiens	il tient	je tiendrai	je tenais
tenant	nous tenons	vous tenez	ils tiennent	je tiendrais	j'ai tenu
valoir, to be worth	je vaux	tu vaux	il vaut	je vaudrai	je valais
valant	nous valons	vous valez	ils valent	je vaudrais	j'ai valu
venir, to come	je viens	tu viens	il vient	je viendrai	je venais
venant	nous venons	vous venez	ils viennent	je viendrais	je suis venu
vivre, to live	je vis	tu vis	il vit	je vivrai	je vivais
vivant	nous vivons	vous vivez	ils vivent	je vivrais	j'ai vécu
voir, to see	je vois	tu vois	il voit	je verrai	je voyais
voyant	nous voyons	vous voyez	ils voient	je verrais	j'ai vu
vouloir, to want	je veux	tu veux	il veut	je voudrai	je voulais
voulant	nous voulons	vous voulez	ils veulent	je voudrais	j'ai voulu

Index